The Key to Chinese Civilization

Thank you for choosing a SAGE product!
If you have any comment, observation or feedback,
I would like to personally hear from you.

Please write to me at **contactceo@sagepub.in**

Vivek Mehra, Managing Director and CEO, SAGE India.

Bulk Sales

SAGE India offers special discounts
for purchase of books in bulk.
We also make available special imprints
and excerpts from our books on demand.

For orders and enquiries, write to us at

Marketing Department
SAGE Publications India Pvt Ltd
B1/I-1, Mohan Cooperative Industrial Area
Mathura Road, Post Bag 7
New Delhi 110044, India

E-mail us at **marketing@sagepub.in**

Get to know more about SAGE
Be invited to SAGE events, get on our mailing list.
Write today to **marketing@sagepub.in**

This book is also available as an e-book.

The Key to Chinese Civilization
The Explication and Exploration of Chinese Characters

Dekuan Huang

Translated by Zhu Yuan

Los Angeles | London | New Delhi
Singapore | Washington DC | Melbourne

Copyright © Beijing Normal University Press, 2018

Not for sale in People's Republic of China

All rights reserved. No part of this book may be reproduced or utilised in any form or by any means, electronic or mechanical, including photocopying, recording, or by any information storage or retrieval system, without permission in writing from the publisher.

First published in 2018 by

SAGE Publications India Pvt Ltd
B1/I-1 Mohan Cooperative Industrial Area
Mathura Road, New Delhi 110 044, India
www.sagepub.in

SAGE Publications Inc
2455 Teller Road
Thousand Oaks, California 91320, USA

SAGE Publications Ltd
1 Oliver's Yard, 55 City Road
London EC1Y 1SP, United Kingdom

SAGE Publications Asia-Pacific Pte Ltd
3 Church Street
#10-04 Samsung Hub
Singapore 049483

Published by Vivek Mehra for SAGE Publications India Pvt Ltd, typeset in 10.5/13 pt Times New Roman by AG Infographics, Delhi and printed at Chaman Enterpieses, New Delhi.

Library of Congress Cataloging-in-Publication Data

Name: Huang, Dekuan, author.
Title: The key to Chinese civilization: the explication and exploration of Chinese characters / Dekuan Huang.
Description: Thousand Oaks, California : SAGE Publications, 2018. | Includes bibliographical references and index.
Identifiers: LCCN 2018002751| ISBN 9789352806744 (print (hb)) | ISBN 9789352806751 (e-pub) | ISBN 9789352806768 (e-book)
Subjects: LCSH: Chinese characters—History. | Chinese language—Writing.
Classification: LCC PL1171 .H7525 2018 | DDC 495.11/1—dc23 LC record available at https://lccn.loc.gov/2018002751

ISBN: 978-93-528-0674-4 (HB)

SAGE Team: Amrtia Dutta, Alekha Chandra Jena and Ritu Chopra

SAGE was founded in 1965 by Sara Miller McCune to support the dissemination of usable knowledge by publishing innovative and high-quality research and teaching content. Today, we publish over 900 journals, including those of more than 400 learned societies, more than 800 new books per year, and a growing range of library products including archives, data, case studies, reports, and video. SAGE remains majority-owned by our founder, and after Sara's lifetime will become owned by a charitable trust that secures our continued independence.

Los Angeles | London | New Delhi | Singapore | Washington DC | Melbourne

Contents

Preface	vii
Acknowledgements	xiii

Part I: Formation and Evolution

1	The Formation and Evolution of Chinese Characters	3
2	The Main Body of Chinese Characters: The Pictophonetic Structure	92

Part II: Textual Analysis and Interpretation

3	Method and Practice: The Explication of Ancient Chinese Characters	197
4	The Cultural Interpretation of Chinese Characters	241

Part III: Norm and Research

5	The Normalization of Chinese Characters and Philological Life	319
6	The Research of Chinese Characters: Past and Future	355

About the Author	410

Preface

The main objects of research in Chinese philology are Chinese characters, including their origins, structure, rules of evolution, application, related language policies and so on. China is an ancient civilization with a long history, and Chinese characters are the only writing system with the ancient origin and continuous use. Chinese civilization has been recorded and inherited in Chinese characters which are considered to be the most important medium of communication in China. Without an in-depth study of Chinese characters, Chinese civilization cannot be truly understood and appreciated, directly affecting many people today in terms of verbal communications. In addition, Chinese characters are also the means by which both mainland Chinese and overseas Chinese conduct their daily communications. Therefore, Chinese philology, old as it is, is definitely not outdated learning. With rich and profound signification, it does not only concern our understanding of the history of Chinese civilization but also the future development of our civilization. Meanwhile, it is closely related to our present-day life and to each one who uses Chinese characters.

People learn and use Chinese characters, but most of them are not quite aware as to how these characters came into being, what each character means and why they are not like the Western words that are spelt simply by means of letters. We take all these for granted or ignore them. I chose Chinese philology as my academic pursuit, thanks to my teacher for introducing it to me and recommending it. In the process of my study and research, I have become aware of the importance of this discipline and realized that it is of much theoretical value and practical significance to conduct an in-depth research of Chinese characters.

In 1977, in a significant move in the interest of the young people of China and Chinese society, the country resumed the national university entrance examination. Luckily, I too took part in it. When taking part in the examination, I did not hesitate to apply for the Chinese department because I liked the literature. In my sophomore year, as my horizon widened, I extended my reading from the literature to linguistics, history, philosophy and so on. I started reading Guo Moruo's historical works. That was the time when the country was still recovering from the catastrophe of the 'Great Cultural Revolution' and the academic enterprise was under reconstruction, so academic works were scarce in university libraries; nonetheless, Guo Moruo's works were available. Guo Moruo is a representative and influential figure in both historical and paleographical studies. By reading his historical and paleographical works, I encountered the oracle bone script (甲骨文) and bronze script (金文), and started to realize that palaeography was a profound and interesting academic discipline. By the time I graduated from college, I had read all the major works in this field available in the library and decided on my future academic pursuit in the direction of the ancient philological studies. From then on, I have been conducting research and teaching philology and palaeography till today.

I did my graduation from the Department of Chinese History, Nanjing University, Jiangsu Province, China. It has a long academic tradition and prestigious faculty. I received teachings from Professor Xu Jiating (徐家婷) and Professor Hou Jingchang (候镜昶) from Nanjing University as well as instructions from Professor Xu Fu (徐复) from Nanjing Normal University. They had the academic background of modern philology as well as the influence from Zhang Taiyan (章太炎) and Huang Kan (黄侃), emphasizing academic inheritance and development and forming a very pure academic atmosphere. Under such circumstances, I started to familiarize myself with the Chinese traditional learning and philology. In 1983, I was most fortunate to be sent by Nanjing University to attend a seminar on the studies of ancient Chinese characters organized by Professor Yu Xingwu (于省吾) at Jilin University. At that time, there was a shortage of succeeding researchers in the studies of ancient characters. This discipline was then called 'extinct learning', so the State Administration of Cultural Heritage and the Ministry of Education invited Professor Yu to organize a seminar to speed up the training of the professionals in this field. All of the more than 10 students in the seminar who were leading researchers and teachers in the related field were mostly from the units of relics and archaeology and higher institutions nationwide. This seminar was not only attended and guided by Professor Yu but also systematically taught by other teachers such as Yao Xiaosui (姚孝遂), Lin Yun (林沄), Chen Shihui (陈世辉) and He Linyi (何琳仪). Professor Yu was a master in the studies of palaeography, and all the other teachers were his influential disciples in the same field. The experience of this seminar had a great impact on my academic orientation. Later, I followed Professor Yao Xiaosui for my doctorate degree and received further systematic and strict training in the studies of palaeography.

I am truly fortunate to be instructed by so many top scholars during my school years. In comparison with the expectation and scholarship of the older generation, I still feel a huge gap. My research work has been strongly influenced by the education I received, and I have come to realize that to achieve some breakthroughs in the studies of philology, I must fulfil the 'three combinations' on the basis of inheriting the previous research achievements, that is, the combination of the advancement of traditional learning with the innovation of modern learning, the combination of the ancient characters from the archaeological excavation with the existent ancient characters and literature, and the combination of the individual character textual research and explication with the theoretical exploration of the Chinese character system.

By 'the combination of the advancement of traditional learning with the innovation of modern learning', I primarily mean the inheritance and development of learning. Philology is the traditional learning rooted in Chinese soil, which was established as early as the Han dynasty. As the foundation of the 'Chinese classical learning', traditional studies of the Chinese language and philology belong to the studies of Chinese classics, forming their own research objects, methodology and tradition. Generations of scholars throughout centuries have accumulated fruitful achievements, so we cannot ignore the existing rich tradition in this field of philology. Since the introduction of modern Western learning and especially modern linguistics, Chinese scholars have broadened their academic perspectives and have been much influenced by the modern Western research paradigms and theories. For a period of time, some scholars preferred Western learning to the academic tradition of philology. We believe that it is not likely to achieve much for contemporary scholars of Chinese philology just to stay on the level of inheriting the traditional learning; meanwhile, if they are obsessed with the Western learning, they will separate themselves from the reality of the Chinese language and characters and then they can hardly achieve true innovation. Only by valuing academic tradition, inheriting and promoting the essence of traditional learning as well as absorbing the nutrients from Western learning can we bring about the continuous innovation in the ancient learning of philology.

By 'the combination of the ancient characters from the archaeological excavation with the existent ancient characters and literature', I mainly refer to the application of the material in the research of philology. The previous research laid most stress on the material preserved in the *Origin of Chinese Characters* (说文解字》) such as the small seal script (小篆), a small number of ancient scripts (古文) and large seal script (籀文), but not much stress on the clerical script (隶书) and regular script (楷书) after the Han dynasty. However, the seal script in the *Origin of Chinese Characters* mainly belongs to the system of the characters of the Qin dynasty as the collated and standardized forms throughout a long period of historical development and as the final forms of the ancient Chinese characters. Although the large seal script and the ancient script originated from the Spring and Autumn and Warring States periods (春秋战国), most of them were copied numerous times and therefore resulted in many errors. If we use such material to study the system of Chinese characters of the ancient origin, then there will be obvious limitations. As the oracle bone script from the Shang dynasty was brought to light in the 25th year of the Guangxu Reign of the Qing dynasty (1899) and the modern Western scientific archaeology was introduced into China, over a hundred years, the original characters from the pre-Qin period and the succeeding Qin, Han, Wei and Jin periods have been discovered in large numbers. They demonstrate the basic clues of the evolution of Chinese characters in different historical periods, enabling people today to recover the actual changes of the forms and uses of the characters in different periods since the Shang dynasty. By combining the existent character material in different periods with the newly excavated material in the research, we can clarify many problems unsolved in the studies of characters, reveal the basic rules in the formation and evolution of the characters, and more accurately and scientifically understand Chinese characters. This is the inevitable progress to be achieved by the second combination in the studies of philology.

As for 'the combination of the individual character textual research and explication with the theoretical exploration of the Chinese character system', I consider it as an adjustment of the orientations of both traditional philology and the present studies of Chinese characters. Traditional philology mainly serves the purpose of explicating Confucious's classics, 'explicating classics by characters' and 'explicating characters by classics', developing the individual-character-explication-centred research tradition. There have been abundant achievements in this area. Nonetheless, this research tradition is what is called 'to see only the trees but not the forest', affecting the studies of both the contemporary philology and ancient philology. For a long time, the tradition of studying Chinese characters has been focused on specific textual research rather than on theoretical generalization and revelation of rules, resulting in the present feebleness of the theoretical research of Chinese characters, consequently limiting the development of this old and important discipline, directly affecting the advancement of philological research and restricting its full contribution to the studies of world languages and written texts.

The so-called three combinations are not only certain understanding that we have come to realize in the studies of philology but also certain positive illumination in the studies of philology over a 100 years.

I have said that among the variety of Chinese traditional learning, philology is one of the most successful disciplines in their modern transformation. The 'three combinations' are the main causes leading to the successful transformation of Chinese philology from traditional learning to modern learning. Without the inheritance and innovation of the academic tradition, the nutrients of Western learning and the large number of archaeological finds, this discipline, which enjoys a long historical tradition, could hardly be as prosperous as today.

There are many issues to explore in Chinese philology and the basic conditions have been well established, so I always believe that there is a promising prospect for the research of the 21st century philology. For example, there has not been a book of *General History of Chinese Characters* published in China, so we need to conduct a series of related research to complete such work. For the past few years, we have been making lots of necessary preparations for the work, but this is a huge and challenging research project. For a considerable period of time in the future, we will be continuing to try our best to complete this research task, and provide readers with a true general history of Chinese characters development.

And finally, I would like to take this opportunity to thank all the people who worked hard for the book's editing, translation and publishing abroad.

Acknowledgements

I must make the following acknowledgments upon the completion of the collation and compilation of this book.

First of all, I want to express my heartfelt respect and gratitude to Professor Yang Geng of Beijing Normal University Press and his staff! To promote the prosperity of research in the fields of philosophy and social sciences in our country, they publish this library of books by these philosophers and social scientists and in such a considerable size, which reflects their academic dedication and responsibility of the first-class university press and the deep humanistic feelings towards scholars in the humanities. I feel both trepidation and honour that this corpus of mine has the opportunity of being included in this library.

Second, I would like to express my thanks to Ms Zhao Yuehua for her arduous efforts on this corpus from the confirmation of the manuscripts to the compilation work. This book has involved many forms of ancient characters and complicated and unfamiliar characters, which has brought lots of challenges to the editing work, and it is her outstanding professionalism, rigorous and meticulous work attitude that have ensured the success of publishing this book.

Also, I am deeply appreciative of the support extended by the Chinese Fund for the Humanities and Social Sciences. I am very grateful for their contribution to social science research in China.

Finally, what I want to explain is that the time span of the papers collected in this corpus is comparatively long and the requirements of the journals where they were published are different. So, the annotations of the papers collected here have been compiled in accordance with the requirements of the style of this library and the titles of some papers have been slightly changed. Meanwhile, I have taken this opportunity and corrected some technical errors and replaced several forms of ancient characters in the original published versions by checking the related quotations and materials. However, all the basic contents and opinions of the papers collected here remain the same, although there may be some deficiencies judged by today's standard. I beg you, my dear fellows, to spare no effort to instruct me.

Part I

Formation and Evolution

CHAPTER 1

The Formation and Evolution of Chinese Characters

The Chinese Character Formation Modes: A System of Diachronic Evolution[1]

Analysing the formation of Chinese characters involves two concepts which are both closely related and somewhat different: the modes of formation and the types of structure. The modes of formation are the modes by which the formal signs of Chinese characters originate, whereas the types of structure are the results of the synchronic and static analyses and the generalization of the characters formed by various modes of formation.

For a long time, the focus of philology has been more on the analysis of the individual structure of Chinese characters, placing the Chinese characters of different historical periods within the same historical phase and making typological generalizations, but less on the exploration of the formation modes and their diachronic development. As a result, many elusive conclusions have been reached on the study of the theory of character formation. These conclusions do

---
[1] Originally published in *Anhui University Journal* 3 (1994).

not only concern the construction of the theory of philology but also directly affect the assessment of the development of Chinese characters, language policymaking and the teaching of Chinese characters. The present chapter attempts to reveal the reality of the diachronic evolution of the system of the Chinese character formation modes by means of studying their basic formation modes and their changes.

The Chinese character formation modes are a system of dynamic evolution that develops together with the changes of the whole system of Chinese characters. Since the different historical phases of Chinese characters, the system of their formation modes has been developing and adjusting itself accordingly. Such developments are reflected in the system of Chinese characters in the form of the changing distributions of different structural character types.

We take the statistical approach to investigate and reveal the distribution of structural types of Chinese characters. It is very complicated to do the statistical work of Chinese characters by their structural types. First of all, the material for statistical analysis must be representative enough to reflect the actual development of the formation of Chinese characters. Second, it requires much meticulous work to do the structural analysis of all the Chinese characters in the same period. In addition, it is inevitably inaccurate to do the exhaustive analysis of the Chinese characters in different periods due to the abundant simplification and confusion of their forms during their long period of development and the lack of evidence to explain the formation principles of some Chinese characters. Third, views differ greatly in explaining the Chinese characters of the same structure, and different scholars may not have the same criteria for their analysis. Therefore, this statistical approach only reflects the general tendency of the development of the formation modes, and the data we reached are by no means absolutely accurate. On this account, we take the representative Chinese characters after their systematic establishment as the objects for our statistics, including the oracle bone script (inscriptions on bones or tortoise shells 甲骨文) during the Yin-Shang period (until 1027 BC),[2] the small seal script (小篆) recorded in the *Origin of Chinese Characters* (the

---

[2] Chen Mengjia (陈梦家), *A Review of Yinxu Oracle Inscriptions* (Beijing: Zhonghua Book Company, 1988), 34, 80.

Origin;《说文解字》) during the terminating period of ancient Chinese characters (until 100 AD)[3] and the established regular script (楷书) represented in the *Six Categories of Chinese Characters* (《六书略》) by Zheng Qiao (郑樵) (until 1160). These three periods represent the three developmental stages of Chinese characters, which have certain significance of typicality. In addition, the structural analyses conducted by Li Xiaoding (李孝定), Zhu Junsheng (朱骏声) and Zheng Qiao can serve as a valuable reference.[4] However, they all classify the Chinese characters according to the traditional 'six categories', and they differ considerably in terms of the classification of the actual characters. To reflect the changes in the distribution of different structural types of Chinese characters, on the basis of the three scholars' classifications, we readjust and reclassify the actual characters by the unified standard according to our understanding of the basic structural types of the Chinese characters, deleting the repeated structural types. As a result, the statistical results have become quite different.[5] See Table 1.1 for the statistical results.

---

[3] Huang Dekuan (黄德宽), *A History of Chinese Philology* (Hefei: Anhui Education Press, 1990), 24–25.

[4] Li Xiaoding (李孝定), 'A Look at the Bone and Tortoise Shell Inscriptions from the Perspective of Six Categories', *Nanyang University Journal* 2 (1968); Zhu Junsheng (朱骏声), 'Trigrams in the Six Categories of the Origin of Chinese Characters', in *Explanations of the Origin of Chinese Characters*, vol. 1, comp. Ding Fubao (丁福保); Zheng Qiao (郑樵), 'An Outline of the Six Script Categories', *General Journals* 31.

[5] For example, the 129 phonetic loan characters in Mr Li's statistics belong to four basic structures, and they should not be repeated; 61 of the 70 'unknown' characters can be reclassified, so the actually classified characters should be 1,087, which are far short of the number of the individual bone and tortoise shell inscriptions. The mutually explanatory characters and phonetic loan characters in 'Trigrams in the Six Categories of the Origin of Chinese Characters' should not be included in the total number, and most of the associative characters with pictophonetic features should be included in the category of pictophonetic characters, thus amounting to 9,353 individual characters, which correspond with the number in *The Origin of Chinese Characters*. 'An Outline of the Six Script Categories' originally includes 24,235 characters; however, the mutually explanatory characters and phonetic loan characters are, in fact, repeated character forms, and together with other repeated characters, the actual number after deletion is 23,266 characters.

Table 1.1

Character Type	Category Distribution	Simple Indicatives	Pictographs	Associative Compounds	Pictophonetic Characters	Total
Oracle bone script	Number	47	310	411	319	1,087
	Percentage	4.32	28.52	37.81	29.35	100
Small seal script	Number	117	347	819	8,070	9,353
	Percentage	1.25	3.71	8.75	86.29	100
Regular script	Number	123	481	821	21,841	23,266
	Percentage	0.53	2.07	3.53	93.87	100

As seen from Table 1.1, in the early Chinese characters represented by the oracle bone script, the structural types of simple indicatives, pictographs and associative compounds take up more than 70 per cent, and the structural types of the pictophonetic characters take up less than 30 per cent. In fact, most of the unrecognized characters belong to the structural types of the simple indicatives, pictographs and associative compounds, only a small percentage of which belongs to the pictophonetic characters. In addition, the differences in the treatment of and statistical approaches to the actual material can also result in different conclusions. We have compared the number of the recognized pictophonetic characters with the total number of individual oracle bone script characters and reached the result that the pictophonetic characters take up about 18 per cent[6] of the oracle bone script. Nonetheless, the statistical figures in Table 1.1 are sufficient to demonstrate that the pictophonetic structure was not the main formation mode in the oracle bone script period, while the formation modes of the simple indicatives, pictographs and associative compounds took up the dominating advantage. The oracle bone script of the Yin-Shang period is the result of the accumulation and development of the primitive Chinese characters over a long period of time, whose dominating advantage reflects the position of the

---

[6] Cf. the two papers included in this book: 'The Dynamic Analysis of the Pictophonetic Structure' and 'The Phonetic Radicals of the Pictophonetic Structure'.

structural mode of the pictographs in the process of the Chinese character formation. If we carry on the investigation further into the development of the oracle bone script over 200 years or so, we realize that 'from the reign of Wu Ding to the reigns of Di Yi and Di Xin, the major development was the gradual increase of the pictophonetic characters'.[7] Although the pictophonetic structure was not the major formation mode in the period of the oracle bone script, it had already shown its developmental trend. The *Origin* reflects the system of the small seal script as a natural result of the development of the ancient characters over thousands of years. The small seal script ended in the Qin Dynasty, and yet there was an overlapping period between the beginning of the clerical script and the ending of the small seal script. When Xu Shen was compiling the *Origin* (ca 83–100 AD), the small seal script characters had already retreated from the daily usage, but they were still used under certain circumstances. Therefore, in terms of the analysis of the character structural types, the small seal script in the *Origin* basically reflects the system of the Chinese characters of that time. The structural types of simple indicatives, pictographs and associative compounds in the *Origin* only take up less than 14 per cent, while those of the pictophonetic structural types take up more than 86 per cent. This reflects the fundamental changes in the character formation function of different types of formation modes. The character formation function of the formation modes of the simple indicatives, pictographs and associative compounds declined, while the pictophonetic formation mode vigorously developed and occupied the dominating position. Until Song Dynasty when the regular script had been established, the ratio of the characters of the simple indicatives, pictographs and associative compounds declined to about 6 per cent while those of the pictophonetic structural type reached to 94 per cent. This fact demonstrates that the character formation mode practically stopped in its function of structural formation and the pictophonetic characters became the only formation mode.

If we further carry out the statistical analysis of the various formation modes for new characters and the growth and decline ratio of

---

[7] Chen Mengjia (陈梦家), *A Review of Yinxu Oracle Inscriptions*, 34, 80.

Table 1.2

Character Type	Category / Change	Simple Indicatives	Pictographs	Associative Compounds	Pictophonetic Characters
Oracle bone script	Number	47	310	411	319
	Percentage	4.32	28.52	37.81	29.35
Small seal script	Number	+70	+37	+408	+7,751
	Percentage	−3.07	−24.81	−29.06	+56.94
Regular script	Number	+6	+134	+2	+13,771
	Percentage	−0.72	−1.64	−5.22	+7.58

different types of Chinese characters in the whole system, the point becomes more obvious (see Table 1.2).

The simple indicatives increased by 117 per cent and 123 per cent, respectively, in the small seal script and the regular script. However, in the whole system of Chinese characters, the ratio declined from 4.32 per cent to 1.25 per cent and then to 0.53 per cent; the pictographs increased by 347 and 481, respectively, but the ratio declined from 28.52 per cent to 3.71 per cent and then to 2.07 per cent; the associative compounds increased by 819 and 821, respectively, but the ratio declined from 37.81 per cent to 8.75 per cent and then to 3.53 per cent. Therefore, as can be seen from Table 1.2, on the one hand, their absolute number gradually increased, and on the other hand, their ratio in the whole system of Chinese characters drastically declined. The increase and decline are in sharp contrast, but only the absolute number of the pictophonetic characters drastically increased (more than 24 times and 2.7 times, respectively), with the percentage also quickly rising. Obviously, the number of each character type is not extremely accurate in Table 1.2, but the growth and decline of the distribution of the four structural types of characters primarily correspond to the reality. The nature of the changes reflects the major adjustments that took place in the basic formation modes of Chinese characters. The earlier formation modes of the simple indicatives, pictographs and associative compounds gradually lost their power and the formation modes of Chinese characters tended to be singularized.

Due to these statistics concerning the whole system of Chinese characters over a long time span, the reliability of the statistical results naturally calls in question. Now let us again randomly take, for example, the Chinese characters with the three radicals of '口, 日, 鱼' according to dictionaries, recording Chinese characters from different historical periods—*A Compilation of the Oracle Bone Script* (《甲骨文编》) (1965), *A Compilation of the Bronze Script* (《金文编》) (1985), the *Origin* (Xu Xuan's edition 大徐本) and *Yu Pian* (《玉篇》) (edition from the Song Dynasty)—to conduct the exhaustive statistical analysis for the verification. In the statistical analysis, the repeated ancient scripts are not included, and the characters with the radical 他 in the *Origin* when listed with the three radicals above in *Yu Pian* are deleted. To ensure the accuracy of the analysis, all the characters of uncertain structural types are categorized as 'uncertain'. See the statistical results in Table 1.3.

The statistics in Table 1.3 compared with the previous two tables seem more revealing. In the case of the statistical analysis of the characters with the three radicals based on *A Compilation of the Oracle Bone Script*, due to the increasing ratio of 57.75 per cent of the 'uncertain' category, the structural types of simple indicatives, pictographs and associative compounds only take up 29.57 per cent, and the type of pictophonetic characters take up 12.68 per cent. Thus, the whole ratio obviously declines compared with the statistics in Table 1.1. However, if we use the statistical method in Table 1.1 and delete the 'uncertain' characters from the total, the computing result shows that the simple indicatives, pictographs and associative compounds take up 70 per cent, and the pictophonetic characters take up 30 per cent, and then the results of the two tables become quite unanimous. To the small seal script represented in the *Origin*, we add the characters of the Zhou Dynasties reflected in *A Compilation of the Bronze Script*, the distribution of which then indicates that in the Zhou Dynasties, the simple indicatives, pictographs and associative compounds declined by 37.29 per cent and the pictophonetic characters rose by 45.76 per cent, and thus the associative type of characters losing its former absolute advantage and the pictophonetic type of characters starting to take advantage. This addition makes the statistical analysis more comprehensible of the small seal script represented in the *Origin*. The

Table 1.3

Character Type	Category / Distribution	Simple Indicatives	Pictographs	Associative Compounds	Pictophonetic Characters	Uncertain	Total
Oracle bone script	Number	1	5	15	9	41	71
	Percentage	1.41	7.04	21.12	12.68	57.75	100
Bronze script	Number	1	3	18	27	10	59
	Percentage	1.69	5.09	30.51	45.76	16.95	100
Origin of Chinese characters	Number	1	3	32	320	0	356
	Percentage	0.28	0.84	8.99	89.89	0	100
Yu Pian	Number	1	3	39	999	14	1,056
	Percentage	0.10	0.28	3.69	94.60	1.33	100

ratio of the pictophonetic characters and associative compounds in the *Origin* and *Yu Pian* shown in Table 1.3 is primarily the same as in Table 1.1, while the ratio of the simple indicatives and pictographs declines more. Thus, the statistics in Table 1.3 can fully testify the reliability of the statistical results of Tables 1.1 and 1.2.

By investigating the increase of the actual characters with the three radicals of '口, 日, 鱼', we discover that not a single new simple indicative has been added since the time of the oracle bone script. The characters '晕' and '周' from the period of the oracle bone script, which used to be of the simple indicative structure, later developed into the pictophonetic structure. As a result, the pictographs with the three radicals, in fact, decreased by two characters and the associative compounds only increased by limited numbers. Compared with the number of characters included in *A Compilation of the Oracle Bone Script*, *A Compilation of the Bronze Script* includes 7 new simple indicatives, the *Origin* includes 12 and *Yu Pian* includes 10, only amounting to the total of less than 30. In comparison, the pictophonetic characters rapidly increased by dozens of times. This fact completely coincides with the aforementioned results.

To sum up, the system of the structural mode of Chinese characters had started to adjust itself internally since the Yin-Shang period. It gradually lost the formation function for the basic structural modes of simple indicatives and pictographs after the Yin-Shang period, and it only retained the weak formation function for the associative compounds, while since the Western Zhou Dynasty, the formation mode of the pictophonetic characters had rapidly developed into the most important one. Inducing the basic structural types of Chinese characters by the synchronic and static approaches only reveals the distribution of the structural types of Chinese characters in the system which has been accumulating for thousands of years, but it does not reflect the actual situation of the system of the Chinese character formation modes. In fact, the Chinese character formation modes are a dynamic system in which different formation modes are only temporary and ostensible in their coexisting and overlapping relationship in certain historical periods, and in different developmental periods of Chinese characters exists the substituting relationship of development and evolution between different formation modes.

The development of the formation mode system is closely related to the profound internal changes of various formation modes. As regards the changes of the quantity of Chinese characters of various structural types, the subsequent changes of the formation functions of various formation modes and the adjustments of the structural formation mode system reflected in the aforementioned statistical results, we need to seek forceful evidence from the internal development of various formation modes. Is the situation the same as we expect? By the general investigation of the development of the four basic kinds of formation modes, we can obtain definite answers.

The capability of generating written signs by a simple indicative formation mode is relatively weak in the Chinese character formation system. The so-called simple indicatives formed by the combinations of marks (or abstract signs), in origin, inherited more from the primitive carved signs for recording events. After the Chinese characters developed until the Yin-Shang period, there were no more new simple indicatives coming into being, formed by abstract signs; however, the capability is still relatively strong in forming new simple indicatives by adding indicating signs on the basis of pictographs, such as '白', '百'; '舌', '言'; '又', '尤, 厷, 肘'; '口', '曰, 甘'; '矢', '寅, 黃'; '夕', '月'; '弓', '弘'; '止', '之'; '矢' and '至'. There are numerous cases which show the relationship between the original pictographs (the former) and the simple indicatives (the latter) generated by adding the indicating signs on the basis of the former. These characteristics have already been revealed by the oracle bone script scholars. After the Yin-Shang period, the signifying enhancement of Chinese characters had an important impact on the simple indicative structural formation mode in two aspects. On the one hand, the pictographs gradually lost their pictographic features, leading to the loss of the basis for the simple indicative structural formation; on the other hand, the high degree of signification of the Chinese character system overwhelmed the simple indicative adding signs, thus leading to the extinction of the unique features of the indicating formation by signs. As a result, after the Western Zhou Dynasty, the simple indicative formation quickly dwindled, and only under the circumstances where there were fewer changes in the forms of pictographs and the contrasts and distinctions were clear appeared some few derivative characters, such as

'木' and '本, 末', '衣' and '卒', '言' and '音', '不' and '丕', '止' and '世', and so on. Now we can make the tentative inference that after the Zhou Dynasties, the simple indicative formation mode primarily did not have the function of forming new characters.

The pictographic formation mode is the most essential in forming Chinese characters. Without the pictographs, there would be no sign system of Chinese characters with their unique features. The definition of pictograph in the 'Preface' of the *Origin* goes as follows: The written sign is made by 'drawing the thing and following its outline in twists and turns'. This definition is succinct and accurate. It is a commonly accepted view that pictograph as a formation mode is derived from primitive drawing and recording by pictures. Pictographs were made either by unconsciously inheriting from the primitive recording by pictures and the signs of primitive drawings or by imitating the outlines of the things to be expressed verbally. These two means represent the two different stages of the development of the pictographic formation. Up to the Yin-Shang period, the pictographic formation mode had obviously entered its self-conscious stage through a long period of development. Although some pictographs are vivid and lively, most of them are succinct in their formation signs, only resembling their meanings. Some signs have no distinctive features for what they describe, whose writing of the character forms has become mostly linear. Some characters resembling animal forms adapt themselves to the requirement of stroke patterns and take up the vertical forms. More importantly, most pictographs can be used as signs for character formation or become phonetic loan characters. This shows that most of the pictographs in the Yin-Shang oracle bone script originated very early and the pictographic formation mode had already fully developed before the Yin-Shang period. If we examine and compare the pictographs in the *Origin*, we find that almost all the pictographs have their presence either as separate entities or as character formation components in the oracle bone script. This indicates that after the period of the oracle bone script, the pictographic formation mode primarily stopped generating new pictographs. (The pictographs such as '伞, 凸, 凹' are rare exceptions.) Such formation mode may have undergone its golden phase and lost its character formation function as early as the Yin-Shang period.

The associative formation mode originated as early as the pictographic mode. In the pottery signs that reflect the primitive state of Chinese characters, excavated on the Dawenkou ancient cultural relic site in Shandong, we witness the coexistence of pictographic signs and the associative pictorial signs formed by the pictographic signs. In the bronze inscriptions, the pictorial characters with the more primitive forms are also mostly of the associative structure. The early associative compounds, in the compound relationship with the pictographs, directly signify the meanings, in obvious and close inheriting association with the recording means by pictures. In the Yin-Shang period, the associative compounds still retained their primitive features of the combinations of character components. For example, the directions and differences in positions of the character components are used to form different associative compounds (e.g., '出' and '各', '立' and '替', '伐' and '戍', '陟' and '降', and so on). The character components that indicate different human postures and the combinations with related character components are used to directly and graphically represent the formation connotations (e.g., '望, 监, 既, 飨'). These kinds of associative compounds made up of the combinations of character components take up considerable proportion of the oracle bone script. Even after the Western Zhou Dynasty until the end of the ancient script, the associative formation mode still retained certain power of generating new characters. Due to the complexity of the characters generated by the formation mode of the combinations of character components and the overreliance on the pictographic features of the character components and their combinations, such character forms are rather limited. As a result, in the development of Chinese character system, there gradually appeared the transformation from the combinations of character components to the combinations of character meanings, such as the formation modes of '止 plus 戈 makes up 武' ('止戈为武': how to stop the dagger-axe means the art of war) and '人 plus 言 makes up 信' ('人言为信': human words mean trust).[8] The exact time of the

---

[8] The form of the character '武' can be seen in the bone and tortoise shell inscriptions, which should also be an associative compound made by the association of the form; '信' may be considered as a pictophonetic character. Here, we only quote the commonly accepted view, but it does not necessarily represent our own view on the forms of the two characters.

transformation is still uncertain for the time being. However, by examining the associative compounds from the Yin-Shang period to the Zhou Dynasties, we see that they are primarily of the formation mode of the combinations of character components. In regard to the new characters formed by the relationship between character components in the formation mode of the combinations of character meanings, there are characters such as '美' and '武' in the oracle bone script, and the character '昶' in the Spring-Autumn bronze inscriptions if we follow the explanations in the *Origin*. Mr Yu Xingwu (于省吾) has already had definitive comment on the formation of the character '美'.⁹ As for the character '昶' according to the newly added explanation in the *Origin*, it means 'a long day' (日长也), which is a typical combination of the characters' meanings. We estimate that the associative formation mode based on the combination of character meanings may have actually appeared after the Spring-Autumn period. However, as the associative formation mode was taking place, the pictophonetic formation mode had already developed into somewhat mature stage, exhibiting great advantage. Naturally, people would not shirk the easy path and take the difficult one. They would not run counter to the mainstream of the formation modes and take the combination of character meanings as the main formation mode. Examining the state of the newly added associative compounds, we can clearly see that characters formed by this mode are very rare, such as '劣, 昊, 尘, 嵩, 岩, 凭'. In the Wei–Jin and Southern–Northern Dynasties, some popular forms of Chinese characters were coined by this formation mode, but most of them did not actually enter the Chinese character system in the end. Therefore, from the perspective of the reality of the formation modes, due to the termination of the development of ancient script, despite the possible internal adjustments of the associative formation mode, its formation mode was still very weak, which however existed only as a languish formation mode.

The development of the pictophonetic formation mode represents the mainstream of the Chinese character formation system. We have conducted full discussions on the pictophonetic structure as an

---

⁹ Yu Xingwu (于省吾), 'An Interpretation of 羌, 苟, 敬, 美', *Jilin University Journal of Social Science* 1 (1963).

important structural type.¹⁰ We will here focus on the development of the pictophonetic formation mode. Up to the Yin-Shang period, the pictophonetic structure had developed to its conscious stage. There appeared three types of characters: picto-added pictophonetic characters (注形形声字), such as 祝, 祖, 唯, phono-added pictophonetic characters (注声形声字), such as 风, 星, 卢, and picto-phono-added pictophonetic characters (形声同取形声字), such as 洹, 狈, 杞. However, if we look at the combining forms of character components (the matching of pictographic components and phonetic components) and the distributive proportions of pictophonetic characters, in the Yin-Shang period, the pictophonetic formation mode was still on its initiative stage of development. After the Yin-Shang period, the pictophonetic characters emerged in large numbers and gradually became the only generative formation mode. This is closely related to the internal optimization and adjustment of the pictophonetic formation mode.

The phonetic components of the pictophonetic structures remain relatively stable and uniform, playing a leading and central role in the pictophonetic structures.¹¹ The selection of the phonetic components as the signs for recording pronunciations is somewhat restricted. In addition, the derivation of new pictophonetic characters is often centred on phonetic components. Thus, they gradually form the basic pictophonetic system.

The basic pictophonetic system includes certain numbers of phonetic components. According to statistics from the *Origin* conducted by the scholars in the Qing Dynasty, such numbers vary greatly, ranging from 1543 to 651.¹² Shen Jianshi's (沈兼士) statistical result of

---

¹⁰ Cf. the chapters in this book: 'The Exploration of the Origin of the Pictophonetic Characters', 'The Phonetic Radicals of the Pictophonetic Structure', 'The Pictographic Radicals of the Pictophonetic Structure' and 'The Dynamic Analysis of the Pictophonetic Structure'.

¹¹ Cf. 'The Phonetic Radicals of the Pictophonetic Structure' and 'The Dynamic Analysis of the Pictophonetic Structure' in this book.

¹² The collation of the phonetic radical system started by the scholars in the Qing dynasty. Dai Dongyuan (戴东原) proposed the concept of the pictophonetic pedigree of the pictophonetic characters in 'A Reply to Duan Ruoying on Phonology'. Duan Yucai (段玉裁) included 1,543 phonetic radicals of the

phonetic components is 947[13] from the *General Rhyming Dictionary* (《广韵》). By the method of extracting the most essential phonetic components, we get to know that there are approximately 500 phonetic components in the period of ancient script, and the total number of phonetic components in the Chinese character system will perhaps not exceed 1,000. The fact that the phonetic components, as one of the two main elements of the pictophonetic formation mode, can form the system shows that in forming the pictophonetic characters, the selection of phonetic components is limited in scope and restricted by certain set tendency; the emergence of the phonetic component system restricts the number of the basic components and forms the functional roles for some components, helping further regulate the pictophonetic formation mode.

The optimization and adjustment of pictographic components are the main aspects of the internal development of the pictophonetic formation mode. In the Yin-Shang and Zhou Dynasties, the pictophonetic formation mode was on the rapidly developing stage. The pictographic components are very active formation elements in the pictophonetic structure, demonstrating obvious characteristics. First of all, they are dynamic—the pictographic components can be added or reduced and their positions are unfixed; second, the same pictophonetic character may vary with its multiple pictophonetic components, resulting in

---

pictophonetic characters from the *Origin of Chinese Characters* in 'A Diagram of Pictophonetic Characters in 17 Categories'. Jiang Yuan (江沅) included 1,291 in 'A Phonological Diagram of the *Origin of Chinese Characters*'. Zhang Huiyan (张惠言) included 1,263 in 'A Chart of Pictophonetic Characters in the *Origin of Chinese Characters*'. Chen Li (陈立) included 1,211 in 'An Extended Account of Pictophonetic Characters in the *Origin of Chinese Characters*'. Zhu Junsheng (朱骏声) included 1,137 in 'A Phonetic Interpretation of the *Origin of Chinese Characters*'. Long Qirui (龙启瑞) included 1,121 in 'A General Comment on Ancient Phonology'. Yao Wentian (姚文田) included 1,112 in 'A Phonological Chart of the *Origin of Chinese Characters*'. Yan Kejun (严可均) included 938 in 'A Phonological Classification of the *Origin of Chinese Characters*'. Miao Kui (苗夔) included 651 in 'A Phonetic Diagram of the *Origin of Chinese Characters*', etc. The numbers vary greatly due to the different divisions of the pictophonetic characters by different scholars.

[13] Shen Jianshi (沈兼士), *The Phonetic System of the General Rhymes* (Beijing: Fu Jen University, 1945).

many variants; third, the pictographic components with similar meanings can be interchangeable.[14] These are the unique phenomena on the developmental stage of the pictophonetic structure.

The optimization of pictographic components has undergone the following three stages.

First, the roles of the pictographic components to indicate meanings are generalized, and differentiating and marking become the main functions of the pictographic components. The early pictophonetic characters, whether they are picto-added, phono-added or picto-phono-added, are relatively clear in indicating meanings for their pictographic components. In the process of their development, some early pictographic components with more concrete indication of meanings gradually became abstract in their indication of meanings. For example, the character '邑' in the Western Zhou period was mainly used to mean capital (都邑), whose meanings were very concrete in the combinations with '邦', '都', etc. Then in the late Western Zhou and Spring–Autumn periods, its meanings were expanded to include all vassal states and further to refer to all kinds of villages, towns, counties and places. This is certainly a typical example. However, the semantic scope of some frequently used pictographic components such as '水, 心, 止, 又, 示, 金' is also expanded to various degrees, which is what we call 'generalization'. The generalization of the semantic function of pictographic components shows that it no longer matters whether their semantic functions are strong or weak. The generalization of the semantic function leads to the adjustment of the pictographic components with concrete semantic indication but complex formation. For example, the pictographic components of the characters '城, 坏, 垣, 堵, 堝' were originally not '土' but the pictograph of city wall '章'. With the semantic function of the pictographic components being generalized, all these characters replaced their pictographic components with '土' accordingly. Although the ancient cities were built with rammed earth and had something to do with '土', in terms of the degree of the semantic function, the component of '土' was far from the original

---

[14] Cf. 'The Dynamic Analysis of the Pictophonetic Structure' and 'The Pictographic Components of the Pictophonetic Structure' in this book.

pictographic component. The generalization of the semantic function also leads to the assimilation of different pictographic components. For example, the pictographic components of some pictographic characters for utensils were assimilated and changed from '匚', '皿' and '缶' to '金', '木' and '竹', respectively. The names of animals were mostly assimilated with the pictographic component '犬', and the names of insects and reptiles mostly followed the pictographic component '虫', etc. The generalization of the semantic function of the pictographic components and the increasing flexibility of selecting the pictographic components are the important manifestations of the change of the features of pictographic components from the semantic function to marking. This change greatly strengthens the character formation function of the pictographic formation mode.

Second, the system of pictographic components gradually came into being. In the Yin-Shang period, there were fewer pictographic characters, and the pictographic components were not complete. With the development of the pictophonetic structure, there appeared new pictographic components after the Zhou Dynasties. These components gradually became distinct in their functions and roles in the formation process. For example, the most common pictographic components '水, 木, 心, 人, 大, 女, 又, 手, 口, 目, 耳, 页, 示, 力, 牛, 羊, 马, 犬, 虫, 鱼, 糸, 衣, 巾, 食, 米, 禾, 木, 竹, 缶, 皿, 车, 舟, 刀, 戈, 弓, 矢, 斤, 广, 土, 雨, 山, 日, 月, 石, 火, 金' are usually not used as phonetic components in the character formation process. Except for their separate usage, their main function is to serve as semantic components (pictographic components). Thanks to the gradual formation of this function division, we may assume that along with the system of phonetic components, there is also a system of pictographic components. The summing up of the 540 radicals in Xu Shen's *Origin of Chinese Characters* reveals the existence of this system to some extent. Zheng Qiao wrote *Xianglei Shu* (郑樵,《象类书》) in which he defined '330 primary signs as pictographic components and 870 secondary signs as phonetic components. These 1200 components can generate numerous characters'.[15] The original book is now non-extant, so we cannot be

---

[15] Zheng Qiao (郑樵) (from the Southern Song dynasty), 'On Character Roots and Radicals', in *An Outline of the Six Script Categories*.

sure that it divides the basic pictographic components and the phonetic components into two interdependent systems, but it definitely contains some awareness in this respect. The study of the 'radicals and the origins of characters', taking the radicals from the *Origin* as the essential formation elements of the Chinese character system, started as early as the Tang and Song Dynasties and prevailed in the Qing Dynasty.[16] The Japanese scholar Shima Kunio in his *Classified Anthology of Yin-Xu Oracle Bone Inscriptions* (岛邦男:《殷墟卜辞综类》) and Mr Yao Xiaosui in his *Classified Compilation of Yin-Xu Bone and Tortoise Shell Inscriptions* (姚孝遂:《殷墟甲骨刻辞类纂》) made bold adjustments of the radicals in the *Origin* by using the ancient script material and reclassified the radicals, respectively, into 164 and 149. They paid much attention to the basic pictographic units of the character structural formation.[17] The aforementioned studies are mainly focused on the basic forms and radicals of the Chinese character formation, and thus they are unable to raise the concept of the 'pictographic component system' in regard to the pictophonetic structure. We have summed up the pictophonetic components of the ancient pictophonetic characters and come up with over 110 common pictographic components. Generally speaking, most of the basic forms of the Chinese character formation can be used as pictographic components. Thus, the basic forms Shima Kunio and Yao Xiaosui summed up as radicals generally fit the pictographic component system of the pictophonetic structure. Although the research in this area is far from sufficient, it is a fact that over a long period of time, the pictographic component system has developed and demonstrated, in its formation, different functional roles. The formation of the pictographic component system corresponds to the phonetic component system, signifying the increasing improvement of the pictophonetic formation mode.

Third, the pictographic components are finalized and positioned. In the development of the pictophonetic structure, the changes of the pictographic components gradually decreased. Through a long period

---

[16] Huang Dekuan (黄德宽), *A History of Chinese Philology*, 159.

[17] Yao Xiaosui (姚孝遂), *Xu Shen and His Origin of Chinese Characters* (Beijing: Zhonghua Book Company, 1983); Yao Xiaosui, 'Preface', in *Classified Bone and Tortoise Shell Inscriptions* (Beijing: Zhonghua Book Company, 1989).

of selection, some variants of the pictographic components of the pictophonetic structure were generally eliminated and their structures were finalized. In addition, the pictographic components developed to be mainly positioned on the left side from the previous changing sides from all directions. Some pictographic components determined their structural positions according to their origins and formation needs. For example, '艹, 网, 竹, 雨' were positioned above and '皿, 皿' were positioned below. The finalizing and positioning of the pictographic components are also important conditions to strengthen the character formation power by the pictophonetic formation mode and regulate the character forms and signs.

In summary, after the three stages of development, the pictophonetic formation mode has been much optimized, and its character formation power has been much strengthened.

The internal development of the basic formation mode shows the following: the two formation modes of the simple indicatives and pictographs started to dwindle and decline after the Western Zhou Dynasty. The associative formation mode began to transform after the Spring–Autumn period. Meanwhile, the pictophonetic formation mode, with its internal optimization and adjustment and with its increasing power of formation function, gradually became a much improved formation mode. Thus, as a dynamic and evolutionary system, the rise and fall of different formation modes have shaped the basic pattern of the development of the system. The development of the general formation mode system reflects the synthesis of the changes of various formation modes.

The development and evolution of Chinese character formation modes, in fact, fundamentally reflect the changes of the whole Chinese character system. In the following, we will conduct further analysis of the concerning elements of the Chinese character system that affects the development of formation modes so as to expound the definite trends of the development of Chinese character formation modes revealed previously.

First, the signification of Chinese character forms has shaken the early character formation basis of the basic modes of pictographic and associative characters. The formation thoughts and modes, over a long period of time, have been reformed accordingly. Written characters are signs in nature, so the so-called 'signification' refers to the progress and degree by which Chinese characters rid themselves of their primitive forms. As Chinese characters developed until the Yin-Shang period, the signification of their forms reached a considerably high degree. The oracle bone script, as the main tangible forms by now, representing the character features of the Yin-Shang period, made themselves far ahead of the character forms cast as bronze inscriptions of the same period, thanks to the special characteristics of their writing instruments. Their character forms are arranged by even and single lines, and some common characters tend to be highly simplified by their strokes. After the Western Zhou Dynasty, the Chinese character forms further followed the path of simplification. The curving lines gradually developed into the combinations of dots and flicks, and the character forms were much regulated, resulting in the signs purely made of the abstract dots and flicks. The early pictographic formation mode formed characters by depicting the outlines of objects. Once the characters broke away from the realm of depicting objects and followed the path of drawing straight lines, the basis of the pictographic formation would become non-extant. The early associative and simple indicative formations of the type of added signs were based on pictographs. Once the pictographic formation lost its basis, the pictographic features of the pictographic characters would disappear, the marking signs could not be added and the pictographic combinations would lose their reliance. As a result, with the increasing signification of the character forms in the Chinese character system, the early pictographic and associative formation modes were bound to recede from the historical stage. Although the signification of the character forms is the external development of the Chinese character system, it has become an important element that affects the internal development of the formation modes of the Chinese character system.

Second, the common occurrences of phonetic loan characters have a great impact on the early formation modes, accelerating the leap from the pictographic–semantic relationship to phonetic–semantic relationship in the character formations. The Chinese characters are the sign system recording the Chinese language and their homophone loans are the important means by which the early Chinese characters fully record the functions of the Chinese language. The picto-semantic mode cannot make a fully recorded character system of the Chinese language, which is a most obvious fact. The means of homophone loans is the only effective mode by which the early Chinese characters compensate for their own defects. Almost with no exception, different ethnic groups make extensive use of the method of the homophone loans in their primitive character material. According to the sampling analysis, the number of homophone loans can be as high as 70 per cent in the oracle bone script,[18] which shows that the phonetic loan characters are important phenomena that occurred in the development of the Chinese characters. Some scholars conducted the analysis of over 120 homophonic or phonetic loan characters with stable relationship in the oracle bone script, and they found out that these homophonic loans were originally pictographic, simple indicative and associative characters.[19] This shows that homophonic loaning is the important means to compensate for the early pictographic and associative character formation modes. Homophonic loaning expands the possibilities of the Chinese character formation modes, making the intentional separation between the character forms and the meanings they represent, with the character forms purely as the signs to record speech sounds. This opens up the direct connection between the character components and the word syllables, which makes the hub for the transformation from the pictographic–semantic to the phonetic–semantic orientations in the Chinese character formation modes. On the other hand, extensive homophone loaning has a great impact on the early pictographic–semantic Chinese characters, causing the discrepancies of homophones in written forms as well as difficulties for readers who are used to reading characters by their pictographic–semantic functions. Thus, the pictophonetic formation mode has naturally become an ideal choice, which inherits the pictographic–semantic advantage

---

[18] Yao Xiaosui (姚孝遂), 'The Structures and Developmental Stages of Ancient Characters', in *Studies in Ancient Characters*, vol. 4 (Beijing: Zhonghua Book Company, 1980).

[19] Li Xiaoding (李孝定), 'The Origin and Evolution of Chinese Characters', in *Bulletin of the Institute of History and Philology, Academia Sinica* (Taipei: Academia Sinica, February and May 1974).

and eliminates the homophonic disadvantage. The large number of phonetic loan characters in the oracle bone script forcibly promotes the development of the pictophonetic formation mode. In addition, the large number of pictophonetic characters based on homophonic loans and generated by pictographic markers should not be underestimated in freeing the pictophonetic formation mode from its primitive state and in strengthening the phonetic function of the phonetic character components. Therefore, the prevalence of homophone loaning is also an important factor to promote the change from the pictographic–semantic mode to the phonetic–semantic mode.

Third, the requirement for the Chinese character system by the development of the Chinese language system is an important drive for the development of the Chinese formation modes. There are serious defects in the earlier simple indicative, pictographic and associative formation modes which are difficult to adapt themselves to the requirement for the development of the Chinese character system by the language development. These earlier formation modes are primitive in their approaches, which 'take various parts of the body in the nearest distance and various objects of the world in the farthest distance' as the character components, modelling themselves on objects and images, forming the signs recording the language by the pictographic and semantic relationship. Such formation modes only fit the early stage of the development of written characters. Once the written characters are free from their primitive stage and truly become the implement to record language, their defects will be fully exposed. Furthermore, the advancement of language and the increasing number of new words accelerate the decline of such formation modes. There must be new approaches by which the written character system fits the need of language. The pictophonetic formation mode opens up the deep relationship between Chinese characters and the Chinese language in that it makes the character formation by recording speech sounds. It makes the character system and language system develop in harmony to fit the requirement for the character system by the language development. Thus, as the pictographic–semantic formation mode starts to decline, the pictophonetic formation mode can replace it and gain lasting vitality.

Fourth, the written character system as a sign system follows the principle of optimization for sign formation. The pictographic–semantic formation mode is not strong in its regularity of forming signs, with its deep contradiction between limited forms and unlimited meanings. By this mode, it is difficult to form the sign system that is both operative and orderly, which is against the 'principle of simplicity' in semiotics. However, the pictophonetic formation mode has great advantage in forming signs, which is manifested in the following aspects: First, the pictophonetic mode is clear in its types and limited in its combination modes, only including several structural modes such as the left–right, above–below, internal–external and semi-circular combinations. Thus, the sign formation easily becomes regular. Second, in the formation system of the pictographic and phonetic character components, the basic character components are limited in number. The limited types of the structural combinations and the limited number of basic character components make both the formation and application more convenient. Third, it has the great power to generate regular signs. The pictographic, simple indicative and associative formation modes are all limited in their power to generate regular signs, and they are not as strong in regularity. The pictophonetic formation mode makes the formation by one pictographic component and one phonetic component to create a character with sign combinations of strong regularity, and it also has strong generative power. The matching between the basic pictographic component system (Xn) and the phonetic component system (Sn) can theoretically form the pictophonetic system of a great number of variants. The combination of the same pictographic component and phonetic component can generate more than one character, such as '忠' and '忡', '吟' and '含', and so on. Thus, the number of new characters generated by the pictophonetic system can be expressed by the following mathematical formula:

$$N > N_1 = Xn \times Sn$$

Computed by this formula, the combination of 150 pictographic components and 1,000 phonetic components can theoretically produce a huge number of 150,000 various pictophonetic signs. The pictophonetic characters in the Chinese character system will never ever actually reach that extreme number. However, from this, we can see the great advantage of the pictophonetic formation mode in terms of sign formation. It has the basis for a major formation mode development with incomparable advantage over other formation modes and can thus replace other modes with its supremacy.

The aforementioned four aspects reveal the close relationship between the Chinese character system and its formation mode system, and the changes of various modes are the inevitable results affected by the development of the Chinese character system.

By statistically analysing the distribution of the various structural types of Chinese characters, investigating the internal development of various formation modes and revealing the determining influence of the development of the Chinese character system on the development of its formation modes, we hold the view that the Chinese character formation modes are a diachronic evolutionary system. This fact is unquestionable. In the philological research, we should not neglect this important theoretical issue hidden in the structural types. We hope that the exploration and conclusion of this chapter will benefit the present theoretical research of Chinese characters, Chinese character teaching and the related application research.

A Dynamic Analysis of the Chinese Character Formation Modes[20]

The Issue of Dynamic Analysis

The study of the Chinese character structures has been one of the most essential issues in Chinese philology as well as the most contributive aspect in traditional philology. The theory of 'six categories', which has been influencing Chinese philology for nearly 2,000 years, is the earliest generalization of the Chinese character structures. Although unprecedented achievements have been made in Chinese philological studies

---

[20] In November 2002, I was invited to the Institute of History and Philology, Academia Sinica, for an academic visit. The present paper is part of my academic speech 'The New Discoveries of Ancient Characters and the Theoretical Study of Chinese Characters' delivered in the morning of 28 November 2002 at the institute. It was published in the 2003–04 issue of *Anhui University Journal*.

in the last hundreds of years, there is still no fundamental breakthrough in the theoretical study of the Chinese character structures. We believe that in the present theoretical study of Chinese character structures, what we need to do is threefold: the first is the full use of the ancient script material; the second is the improvement of research methods and approaches; the third is the adjustment of the theoretical perspective and the elevation of the explication level. The 'dynamic analysis' is duly proposed on the basis of the aforementioned considerations.

The study of Chinese character structures involves the concern on three levels: formation modes (or the methods of creating characters), characters of different structures and structural types. Formation modes refer to the modes of generating character signs, or the methods of forming character signs. Characters of different structural features can be created by different formation modes; different structural types can be generalized by summing up and classifying the characters of different structural features. The study of the character structures is usually conducted from the analysis of individual character forms to the generalization of structural types and then to the awareness of the formation modes corresponding to the structural types. In reality, the previous monographs on Chinese character structures are primarily the diachronic and static analysis and induction of individual forms and signs of the character system instead of the clear distinction of structural types and formation modes. Mr Li Xiaoding (李孝定) pointed out: 'The study of Chinese philology is two-fold: the static and the dynamic. The main objects of the static study is character structures'.[21] This assertion basically reflects the reality of the analysis of Chinese structures in Chinese philology. Our view is that the conclusion of the diachronic and static inductive analysis is only on the different structural types of Chinese characters. Although this typological conclusion is no less than the basic means to study the character structures, it neglects the historical evolution of the Chinese character system and conceals the changes of the character formation modes. The Chinese

---

[21] Li Xiaoding (李孝定), 'A General Comment on the Collation of Chinese Characters from the Perspective of the Chinese Character Structures and Evolutionary Process', in *A Symposium on the Origin and Evolution of Chinese Characters* (Taipei: Linking Publishing, 1986).

character structure theory based on this conclusion can only be a general and obscure theory.

Over a long period of development, the Chinese character system, with the discovery of the Yin-Shang bone and tortoise shell inscriptions, and the excavation of large numbers of the bronze inscriptions from the Zhou Dynasties, the characters from the Warring States period, and bamboo slip and silk inscriptions from the Qin and Han Dynasties, has clearly revealed its evolutionary progress and historical outlook. As far as the whole system is concerned, Chinese characters are a sign system of sequential accumulation and gradual completion with the historical development. The system is not only, in general, historical in its developmental stages but also dynamically evolutionary in its forms and signs within its system. It is obviously problematic to study such a historical and dynamic system with the diachronic and static analytical approach. Therefore, we believe that the scientific study of the Chinese character structures should be based on dynamic analysis.

Dynamic analysis cannot only be used to investigate the historical evolution of the different forms and signs within the Chinese character system, their structural adjustments and finalization but also to analyse the formation modes of these individual forms and signs.[22] The Chinese character formation modes are a deep system concealed behind the Chinese character semiotic system, which is manifested with the help of the surface system of the character structural types. This is exactly why researchers mix up the structural types with the formation modes. Although previous scholars did not provide explicit explanations on the development and changes of the formation mode system, in fact, there have already been related discussions. The 'Preface' of the *Origin* reads as follows:

> When Cang Jie started to create scripts, he made pictographs according to types of objects, so they were called *wen* (文: carved pattern). Then pictophonetic characters increased, so they were

---

[22] We have specific papers devoted to the discussion of the diachronic development of the formation mode system. Based on the previous discussion, the present paper is focused on the methodology. Cf. 'The Chinese Character Formation Modes: A System of Diachronic Evolution' in this book.

called *zi* (字: phonetic character), and they multiplied in large numbers of derivatives.

This comment from *wen* to *zi* involves the development from the 'pictographic' to the 'pictophonetic' in the formation modes. Afterwards, many scholars in their study of the 'six categories' also discussed the development of the formation modes to some extent. Zheng Qiao from the Song Dynasty held the view:

> The Six Categories are based on pictographs. When pictographs no longer serve the purpose, there appear simple indicatives; when simple indicatives no longer serve the purpose, there come associative compounds; when associative compounds no longer work, there emerge pictophonetic characters which are all in harmony. When the five categories become insufficient, then there arise phonetic loan characters.[23]

Dai Dongyuan from the Qing Dynasty clearly pointed out:

> Generally speaking, in the beginning, the Chinese characters were based on nothing but the things and objects in the universe. When they referred to things, the characters were called self-explanatory characters such as '一, 二, 上, 下' (one, two, above, below). When they generally resembled certain objects, the characters were called pictographs such as '日, 月, 水, 火' (sun, moon, water, fire). When the characters were created, the pronunciations were embodied in the character components and the characters could be tuned in their pronunciations. When the associative meanings were embodied in the characters, the characters could be comprehended. These are the two major functions of the characters. Extended in such manner, the characters in phonetic harmony are called pictophonetic characters; those not in phonetic harmony but in semantic harmony are called associative compounds. These four types are the final forms of characters.[24]

---

[23] Zheng Qiao (郑樵) (The Southern Song dynasty), 'Preface to the Six Script Categories', in *An Outline of the Six Categories, General Annals*, vol. 1.

[24] Dai Zhen (戴震) (The Qing dynasty), 'A Reply to Mr Jiang Shenxiu on Philology', in *The Complete Works of Dai Zhen*, 3 vols. (Hefei: Huangshan Press, 1994).

These discussions on the history of the 'six script categories' demonstrate that they already became aware that the various character formation modes (methods of creating characters) originated on different historical stages and they were complementary in their formation functions, except that this awareness was still on its hazy stage. In the 1960s, Li Xiaoding conducted the statistical classification of the 'six script categories' of the oracle bone script. He did not only conclude with the statistical results of the various proportions in the classification of the 'six script categories' of the oracle bone script but also quoted the classification of the 'six script categories' of the *Origin* by Zhu Junsheng (朱骏声) from the Qing Dynasty (see *The Illustrated Changes of the Six Script Categories in the Origin of Chinese Characters* 《说文六书爻列》) and the classification of the 'six script categories' of the Song characters by Zheng Qiao from the Song Dynasty (see *A Brief Account of the Six Script Categories* 《六书略》). Thus, he compared the oracle bone script, the small seal script in the *Origin* and the Song characters according to the classification of the 'six script categories' and by this comparison discovered considerable increase and decrease of the percentages of various script forms. In addition, he conducted detailed investigations of 'the confusions in the phonetic tendencies of characters and in the process of their transformations'.[25] What Li Xiaoding conducted was the enlightening work of dynamic analysis of the Chinese character formation modes. His research work not only revealed the necessity of the dynamic analysis of the character structures but also illuminated to us the possibility of the analysis.

The Dynamic Analysis of the Formation Modes

The Chinese character formation modes, as a deep system, have been developing with the manifestation of the changing distribution of different character structural types. The dynamic analysis of the evolutionary development of the Chinese character formation mode system

---

[25] Li Xiaoding (李孝定), 'On the Characters in the Oracle Bone Script from the Perspective of the Six Script Categories', in *A Symposium on the Origin and Evolution of Chinese Characters* (Taipei: Linking Publishing, 1986).

should, first of all, be based on the analysis of different character structural types and on the different levels of the historical evolution of the Chinese character system, and the changes and distribution of different types of the characters are to be revealed, so that from different structural types, the development and changes of the character formation mode system can be explored. This is just opposite to the process of generating the signs of Chinese characters, which is a reversal tracing process. Therefore, the basis of the dynamic formation modes is still the analysis and typological generalization of the features of individual character sign formation.

At present, there are several new different views concerning the analysis of the Chinese character forms. According to our research, the four script categories of 'pictographs, simple indicatives, associative compounds and pictophonetic characters' are generally in accordance with the reality of the generation of the Chinese character signs and are appropriate for the study of the character structures and the dynamic analysis of the formation mode system. In the analysis of the Chinese character formation modes, we have added new interpretations to the 'four script categories'. We define the 'pictographic formation mode' as the mode of generating characters by depicting the features of objects or their profiles. Signs generated by this mode are 'pictographs' and the cluster of various pictographs is of 'pictographic structural types'. 'Simple indicative formation mode' refers to the mode of generating characters by adding marking signs to the existing characters or by combining abstract signs. 'Associative formation mode' refers to the mode of generating a character by combing more than two character components. 'Pictophonetic formation mode' refers to the mode of generating characters by employing phonetic marking, pictographic component marking and differentiation.

By the different aforementioned formation modes, the Chinese characters are formed of different structural features and are classified into different structural types accordingly. The various phenomena in the Chinese character development and the process of the formation, development and finalization of each individual character make the Chinese character structural analysis very complicated and sometimes even uncertain. However, generally speaking, by close discernment and analysis, we can classify the concerning characters into different structural types and investigate the formation mode system.

The basis for the dynamic analysis of the formation mode system is to place the investigation of the distribution of different structural character types on different levels in the historical development of Chinese characters. By the comparative analysis of the distribution of the Chinese characters in different historical periods, we can demonstrate the changes of the Chinese character formation mode system. Although the previously quoted comparison by Li Xiaoding is not focused on the investigation of the development of the Chinese character formation modes, it testifies the plausibility of his method. Now we are to select the representative materials from the different historical periods of Yin-Shang, the Western Zhou, the Warring States, Qin–Han and the Song Dynasties to examine the distribution of the characters of different structural types. The materials from the Yin-Shang period are the oracle bone script. According to the latest statistics, the total individual characters from the oracle bone script are around 4,000,[26] one-third of which can be identified. Based on the *Collected Yin-Zhou Bronze Inscriptions* (《殷周金文集成》), which records the Western Zhou bronze inscriptions representing the materials from the Western Zhou period, the characters used in this period amount to 2,488, of which 1,753[27] can be identified. As for the character materials from the Warring States period, we select the Guodian Chu bamboo slips from the mid-later Warring States period as representatives. The characters used in this period total up to 1,293, of which 1,257[28] can be identified. The Qin–Han characters are represented in the small seal script in the *Origin*, with the total number of 9,353. The Song regular script

---

[26] Shen Jianhua and Cao Jinyan (沈建华、曹锦炎), *A Newly Compiled General Chart of the Forms of the Oracle Bone Script* (Hong Kong: Chinese University of Hong Kong Press, 2001).

[27] The statistical work of the bronze inscriptions in Western Zhou dynasty on which the present paper is based is completed by my doctoral student Juang Xuewang (江学旺), 'A Study of the Bronze Inscriptions in the Western Zhou Dynasty' (a dissertation at Nanjing University, Nanjing, 2001).

[28] This statistical work is completed by my doctoral student Zhang Jing (张静), 'A Study of the Guodian Chu Bamboo Scripts' (a dissertation at Anhui University, Hefei, 2002).

is based on *A Brief Account of the Six Script Categories* (《六书略》) with 23,266 characters. We analyse and classify the characters from the aforementioned materials according to the four structural types.[29] The proportion of each type can be seen from Table 1.4.

The statistics in Table 1.4 only concern the analysis of the recognized characters of the Yin-Shang oracle bone script and the Western Zhou bronze script. Besides, there are inaccuracies in the analysis and classification of the character structures from different periods. However, they generally reflect the distribution of different types of characters in the different periods of Yin-Shang, the Western Zhou, the Warring States, the Eastern Han and the Song Dynasties. Over about 2,500 years from Yin-Shang to the Song Dynasties, the Chinese characters had undergone the development from the ancient script to the modern script. From the statistical data, we can see the changes in the distribution proportions of the four structural types of Chinese characters: the simple indicative type decreases from 4.29 per cent to 0.53 per cent; the pictographic type decreases from 28.28 per cent to 2.07 per cent; the associative type decreases from 37.50 per cent to 3.53 per cent; and only the pictophonetic type increases from 29.11 per cent to 93.87 per cent. If we have it in mind that more than two-thirds of the unrecognized oracle bone script and over one-third of the unrecognized Western Zhou bronze script mainly belong to the three types of the simple indicatives, pictographs and associative compounds, then the increasing and decreasing changes of the distribution of the four structural character types will be more prominent. Despite all those, they clearly demonstrate that there occurred major adjustments and changes in the character-forming functions of different formation modes in this historical process. The character proportions, formed by the three picto-semantic formation modes of the simple indicative, pictographic and associative types, decreased from more than 70 per cent in the period of the oracle bone script to around 10 per cent in the Song Dynasty. On the contrary, the character

---

[29] The oracle bone script statistics in this paper are in reference to Li Xiaoding's 'On the Characters in the Oracle Bone Script'. The statistics, analysis of the characters and the treatment of the related issues in Mr Li's paper are all based on the principles of the present author. They may not be absolutely accurate, yet they will not affect the discussion and results in the present paper.

Table 1.4

Period / Category	Oracle Bone Script		Western Zhou Bronze Script		Warring States Script		Small Seal Script		Regular Script	
Distribution	Number	%	Number	%	Number	%	Number	%	Number	%
Simple indicatives	47	4.29	57	3.25	24	1.84	117	1.25	123	0.57
Pictographs	310	28.28	224	12.78	118	9.06	347	3.71	481	2.07
Associative compounds	411	37.50	333	19.00	148	11.36	819	8.76	821	3.53
Pictophonetic characters	319	29.11	1,051	59.95	909	69.76	8,070	86.28	21,841	93.87
Uncertain	9	0.28	88	5.02	104	7.98	0	0	0	0
Total	1,096	100	1,753	100	1,303	100	9,353	100	23,266	100

proportion formed by the pictophonetic formation mode increased from less than 30 per cent to more than 90 per cent. These decreases and increases complemented each other.

Many scholars have long been aware of such adjustments and changes of the Chinese character formation modes, and yet limited by the research materials; none of them have provided clear and definite explanations.[30] If this statistical analysis over a wide range of historical periods only reflects the development of the character formation mode system on a macro level, then to conduct the more detailed analysis by using the materials that can be divided into historical periods can more reflect the degree and track of such changes. Dr Jiang Xuewang (江学旺) divided the Western Zhou bronze inscriptions into early, middle and late periods and then conducted the statistical analysis of the distribution of the four structural types of Chinese characters. The results can be seen from Table 1.5.

From the division statistics in Table 1.5, we can see the obvious changes of the distribution of the four structural types of Chinese characters. The first three types are gradually declining in their respective

Table 1.5 *The Obvious Changes of the Distribution of the Four Structural Types of Chinese Characters*

Period / Distribution Category	Early Period		Middle Period		Late Period	
	Number	%	Number	%	Number	%
Simple indicatives	45	4.46	43	4.08	42	4.05
Pictographs	170	16.83	158	15.00	150	14.45
Associative compounds	225	22.28	219	20.80	199	19.17
Pictophonetic characters	506	50.10	575	54.61	586	56.45
Uncertain	64	6.33	58	5.51	61	5.88
Total	1,010	100	1,053	100	1,038	100

---

[30] The present author discusses the topic for the first time in 'The Chinese Character Formation Modes: A System of Diachronic Evolution' included in this book.

proportions but the pictophonetic structural type is steadily rising in its distributive proportion. This situation generally reflects the changes of the character-forming functions of different formation modes in the Western Zhou period. Such changes are quite rapid, compared with those in the Yin-Shang period.

All the previous statistical analyses are focused on general discussions on Chinese characters in a particular period. The Chinese characters of the different periods, in fact, include both the inherited characters and the newly added characters of the period. Although the changes of the distributive proportion of different structural character types reflect the developments of the formation mode systems of different periods and the adjustments of the character-forming functions of different formation modes, owing to the mixture of the inherited characters accumulated in different periods, the distributive proportion of the characters formed by different formation modes cannot accurately reflect the actual functions of the formation modes in the periods. Only the newly added characters in each different period can reflect the actual character-forming functions of the formation modes in the period. However, to determine the newly added characters in a particular period is rather difficult work. First of all, it is required that all the character systems prior to the period be collated. Second, only by comparison can the inherited characters and newly added characters be distinguished. Third, due to the limited number of character materials in different periods, particularly in the ancient script period which can most fully reflect the development of Chinese character formation modes, the existing materials may not be the totality of the characters in the particular period or previous periods. The confirmation of the inherited characters or newly added characters can only be based on the existing materials, and therefore the conclusions may not be very reliable. Despite all that, the relatively confirmed newly added characters are the most direct manifestation of the formation functions of the Chinese character formation modes in different periods. Let us take the Western Zhou bronze script as an example. We have compared the distribution of the characters of different structural types reflected by the newly added characters in the period with the distribution manifested by the totality of the Western Zhou bronze script in Table 1.4. The results are shown in Table 1.6.

Table 1.6 *The Distribution of the Characters of Different Structural Types Reflected by the Newly Added Characters in the Period*

Category		Simple Indicatives	Pictographs	Associative Compounds	Pictophonetic Characters	Uncertain	Total
Total	Number	57	224	333	1,051	88	1,753
	%	3.25	12.78	19.00	59.95	5.02	100
New	Number	10	22	97	765	35	929
	%	1.08	2.37	10.44	82.35	3.76	100

The comparison in Table 1.6 does not only reflect the wide discrepancy between the general statistical analysis and the distribution statistics of newly added characters but also demonstrates the fundamental changes of the function of the formation modes in the Western Zhou period. Statistics show that more than 82 per cent of the newly added characters in the Western Zhou period were formed in the pictophonetic formation mode as the character-forming functions of the simple indicative and the pictographic formation modes had declined, and the function of the associative formation mode had not been strong. The newly added characters are more definite in the Yin-Shang oracle bone script, and more than 70 per cent of the recognized characters from the oracle bone script are formed in the simple indicative, pictographic and associative formation modes. However, only less than 14 per cent of the newly added characters in the Western Zhou period are formed in the aforementioned three modes. This long negligence of the enormous change prevents us from truly understanding the important adjustment of the internal formation function of Chinese character formation modes. As a result, we are unable to make accurate evaluation on the important development of the pictophonetic formation mode in the Western Zhou period and its impact on the Chinese character formation mode system in the same period.

By investigating the distributive changes of different character structural types and analysing the distribution of the structural types of the newly added characters in the Western Zhou period, we have somewhat clearly revealed the development and changes of the Chinese character formation modes. The different Chinese formation modes form a complementary system. From a diachronic and dynamic perspective, we can see the rise and decline of different formation modes within the system, each playing its role in different historical periods and experiencing its internal function adjustment. In the Yin-Shang period, the picto-semantic formation modes of the simple indicatives, pictographs and associative compounds had strong formation power, while the pictophonetic formation mode was still on its developmental stage. The newly added characters in the Western Zhou period show that the pictophonetic formation mode had rapidly become the dominating formation mode in this period, when more than 80 per cent of the new characters were formed in this mode, while the other three modes gradually lost their formation functions or their functions had become extremely weak. This demonstrates that the dynamic analysis of the Chinese formation modes is the effective approach to reveal the adjustment and changes of the formation mode system.

The Theoretical Significance of the Dynamic Analysis of the Formation Modes

The results of the dynamic analysis have posed a series of new questions for the Chinese character formation mode analysis and the study of the history of Chinese characters, which have strong theoretical significance.

First of all, the adjustment and development of the Chinese character formation mode system have their own deep internal and external causes. To reveal such causes is the main task for the research of the Chinese character formation theory. We hold the view that the advantages and limitations of different formation modes are the internal causes for their development or decline; whether they can adapt themselves to the demands of the Chinese character development is the external cause for their constant development or gradual elimination.[31] From the perspective of the formation modes proper, there exist deep internal causes for both the decline of the pictographic formation

---

[31] Cf. 'The Chinese Character Formation Modes: A System of Diachronic Evolution' included in this book.

mode and the rapid rise of the pictophonetic formation mode. In the simple indicative formation mode, new signs are formed mainly by the markers made up of abstract signs or their combinations. In the Yin-Shang period, this formation mode still retained certain formation power. However, after the Western Zhou period, it basically lost its formation power except when there was a need for form differentiation. Now it is still hard to decide whether or not the simple indicatives in the oracle bone script are, to a large extent, inherited from the characters before the Yin-Shang period. Generally speaking, it is primordial and backward to form characters by relying on the existing characters to indicate the meaning or form differentiation. As the signification of the Chinese character forms increased, the image features of the pictographs gradually disappeared. The appearance of the multiple-stroke signs with the signification of Chinese characters forms makes it hard to recognize the objects on which the sign marking relies and the distinguishing features of the signs proper. It is easy to recognize them only when the same character forms grow somewhat differentiated. As a result, the simple indicative formation mode is bound to decline. The pictographic formation mode is the foundation for the Chinese formation system, the single character component being mostly of the pictographic structure. Seen from the characters in the Yin-Shang period, the pictographic formation mode had already reached perfection. Almost all the pictographs in the Chinese character system appeared in the form of single characters or character components in the oracle bone script, and the high linearization of the oracle bone script made it no longer feasible to form written signs by drawing the profiles of objects. It can be predicted that by the Yin-Shang period, the pictographic formation mode had already passed its golden time and it had primarily lost its power to form new characters. Seen from the early pictographic characters, the simple indicative formation mode had a long history. It still retained certain formation function in the Yin-Shang period or even the Western Zhou period. New characters were formed in the simple indicative formation mode by the directions, positions and semantic relationships of different character components, the formalistic features and combination relationships of which play a dominating role in the formation process. Up until the Western Zhou period, the simple indicative formation mode had still retained this primitivity. Owing to the over-reliance on their formalistic features and combination relationships, the simple indicative are often complicated in form, which is their obvious limitation. After the Western Zhou period, there appeared a type of simple indicatives by the combination of semantic relationships, as is the so-called 'human words forming integrity' (人言为信) recorded in the *Origin*. This adjustment of the simple indicative formation mode proper somewhat eliminates the restrictions caused by reliance on the formalistic features and therefore acquires new formation power. However, the adjustment of the simple indicative formation mode seems insignificant in comparison with the improvement of the pictophonetic formation mode. As the three aforementioned formation modes were declining, the pictophonetic formation mode accelerated its pace. In the Yin-Shang period, a considerable number of pictophonetic characters were formed by adding pictographic components to phonetic loan characters, and they gradually developed into the stage where new characters were formed by adding phonetic components and by combining pictographic components to phonetic components. After the Western Zhou period, the rapid growth of the formation function of the pictophonetic formation mode was closely related to the internal adjustment and optimization of the pictophonetic formation mode. By such adjustment and optimization, two relatively divided character component systems were formed from the pictophonetic structure—they were pictographic component system and phonetic component system. The function of the phonetic components was gradually focused on recording the pronunciations of characters, and the function of the pictographic components was gradually extended and focused on differentiation and marking, thus providing multiple possibilities of forming new character forms. Meanwhile, the combinations of pictographic components and phonetic components began to be formulated, their forms beautified more and differentiated more easily. Thanks to this internal adjustment, it becomes very easy to create new character forms by the pictophonetic formation mode. Furthermore, the rich resources accumulated in the Chinese character system provide multiple possibilities of selecting pictographic components and phonetic components and even of creating new characters. Thus, the prosperity of the pictophonetic formation mode has become an inexorable trend.

From the perspective of the development of the Chinese character system, the external factors have impact on the formation modes in at least the following aspects: (a) The signification of the Chinese character forms has fundamentally shaken the foundation for the picto-semantic type of formation modes. The present literature shows that the Chinese character forms were the image signs grounded by 'drawing the objects'; however, as the Chinese characters progressed, such image signs gradually lost their image features and transformed into different sign patterns, the process of which was the progression of the signification of Chinese character forms. Once the Chinese characters entered the stage of signification and linearization, the picto-semantic type of the pictographic and associative formation modes, as well as the simple indicative formation mode which relies on the formalistic features, started to lose its basis for development. It is this surface change of the character forms that alters and determines the adjusting direction of the Chinese character formation mode system. (b) The prevalence of phonetic loan characters makes recording pronunciations the main choice of recording language functions by written signs. The homophonic loan mode was widely used in the Yin-Shang oracle bone script.[32] This phenomenon is not only the remedy the ancients adopted to compensate for the limitations of the characters, but it has also illuminated people to take the approach of constructing forms according to the pronunciations, and thus promoted the development of the pictophonetic formation mode. In fact, large numbers of pictophonetic characters were formed by loaning from homophones and adding pictographic components. The homophonic loaning accelerated the transformation of the Chinese character formation modes from the picto-semantic to the phono-semantic, naturally leading the ancients to abandoning the picto-semantic formation mode which had already been at the end of its tether, and to being focused on the employment of the pictophonetic formation mode, and eventually to constantly improving the pictophonetic structure and making it the sole formation mode. (c) The large numbers of new characters have also played a determining role in the selection of the Chinese character formation

---

[32] Yao Xiaosui (姚孝遂), 'The Structures and Developmental Stages of Ancient Characters'.

modes. Written signs are created to record languages, and they develop with the development of the objects being recorded. After the Yin-Shang period, the Chinese civilization had much advanced. The social spirit and material life had much refined and enriched the Chinese language, and the Chinese vocabulary system had accelerated its pace accordingly. The Chinese character system had been adapting itself to the development of the Chinese language to continue creating new characters in order to record the actual changes of the language, and thus it acquired rapid development as well. This made it possible for the pictophonetic formation mode to play its full role with its formation advantages, and large numbers of new characters were formed in this mode. In contrast, the picto-semantic type of formation modes then declined further, which had already lost its formation power.

Second, the results of the dynamic analysis of the formation modes have provided us with new perspectives in understanding the history of the Chinese characters more clearly. The origin and development of the Chinese characters are the main research areas in the history of the Chinese characters and the history of the Chinese civilization. In recent years, with the new archaeological finds of many pottery characters and signs from the New Stone Age, significant progress has been made in these research areas. The dynamic analysis shows that the simple indicative, pictographic and associative formation modes had already reached their mature stage by the Yin-Shang period, which indicates that the Chinese characters must have experienced a long developmental stage before the Yin-Shang period. This conclusion can confirm the fragmentary materials of the archaeological finds to some extent and vice versa, providing some internal evidence for the discussion of the origin of the Chinese characters.[33] The formation modes as a dynamic system and the rise and decline of various formation modes during different historical periods are of great significance in the study of the development of the Chinese character system. By the Western Zhou period, the pictophonetic formation mode had already become

---

[33] Li Xiaoding (李孝定), 'The Relative Position of the Oracle Bone Script in the Developmental History of Chinese Characters', in *Bulletin of the Institute of History and Philology, Academia Sinica* (Taipei: Academia Sinica, December 1993).

the main mode of Chinese character formation, which indicates that we should give higher assessment of the development of Chinese characters in the stage of their ancient script period. The Chinese character formation had already entered the pictophonetic-oriented period by the Western Zhou period. This fact reveals to us that the advantage of the pictophonetic structure had been acknowledged by that period and the pictophonetic character formation mode had been established as the Chinese character system matured. Since the Western Zhou period, there had generally been no more fundamental changes in the Chinese character formation modes. The prosperity of the pictophonetic formation mode and the decline of the ideographical formation mode have never been revealed by previous scholars in terms of their early dating. As a result, the idea of defining Chinese characters as 'ideographical characters' obviously cannot be supported from the perspective of the formation mode system development.

Third, through the historical fact of the diachronic development of the formation modes revealed by the dynamic analysis, we are informed that it is very necessary to have a comprehensive review of the results and approaches of the theoretical research of Chinese character structures. Almost with no exception, the analysis conducted by researchers on the Chinese character structures is based on the totality of the characters, such as the 'six script categories theory', the 'four script categories theory' or 'the three script categories theory', none of which has included the idea that Chinese characters originated at different historical levels and they should be researched at different levels. General categorical conclusions are vague and ambiguous and the follow-up theories and claims based on those conclusions may not be correct and scientific, although they may also reflect the general characteristics of the Chinese character structures. The results of the dynamic analysis of Chinese character formation modes require us to not only conduct the typological and general analysis of Chinese character structures but also conduct the research at different historical levels. Only in this way can we gain the comprehensive and correct understanding of the features and functions of different formation modes and the Chinese character formation mode system, and make sound judgement of the Chinese character structure theory and the basic theoretical issues, such as the features and nature of the Chinese characters.

In regard to the methods of the Chinese character structure research, the static analysis is the basis of the dynamic analysis; however, if we only stop at this level, we cannot clearly reflect the historical aspects of Chinese character structures, nor can we reveal the rise and decline of the character formation modes as a whole system. By the dynamic analysis of the formation modes, we start with the analysis of the single character structure, make typological conclusions according to its different periods, conduct statistical analysis of the distributions of different types of characters at different historical levels and compare the distribution changes of the same types of characters in different periods so that we can reveal the historical development of the formation mode system. With the macro comparative analysis, by the analysis and generalization of the structural types of the newly added characters in different periods, we can not only directly observe the character-forming functions of the various formation modes in different periods and the state of the whole formation system but also compare and confirm the results of the analysis and the general dynamic analysis and conclusions. By the dynamic analytical approach, we can not only verify many scholars' basic assumptions on the historical development of Chinese character structures but also avoid the impressionistic approach of description they adopted, and build the research conclusions on the basis of scientific statistical analysis.

In addition, the research conclusions by the dynamic analysis are significant in the research of the issues related to Chinese characters and even some issues of the ancient Chinese language in general. As the Chinese character formation had entered the pictophonetic-oriented stage by the Western Zhou period, the research of many phenomena and issues concerning Chinese characters should be considered in combination with the rise and rapid growth of the pictophonetic characters. For example, there exists the phenomenon of 'homophonic loans'[34] prevalent in the use of the ancient Chinese characters, the research

---

[34] Cf. 'Homophonic Loans: The Contradiction and Unity of the Chinese Character Formation and Usage' included in this book.

of the development of pictophonetic characters with the derivations of Chinese characters and the characters of the same origins, and the development of the pictophonetic characters with the explications of the newly added characters after the Western Zhou period. The pictophonetic characters have been the important materials in the research of the ancient phonology. The results of the dynamic analysis can provide us with the materials which are more distinct in the division of the time periods and they can also help simulate and reconstruct the ancient phonology before the Han period.

Homophonic Loans: The Contradiction and Unity of Chinese Character Formation and Usage[35]

The unity between form and sense is the basic principle observed in Chinese character formation and usage. The awareness and understanding of the principle is, to some extent, the foundation on which Chinese philology is established. However, when we fully examine the reality of the Chinese character development and usage from the Western Zhou period to Qin and Han periods, we discover that this principle is not, in fact, as distinctive at the beginning in the process of Chinese character formation and usage. Many characters are not stabilized and do not eventually fulfil the requirements of the principle until they undergo the contradiction and unity of formation and usage. The phenomenon of 'homophonic loans' prevalent in the ancient script is the typical manifestation.

The so-called 'homophonic loans' or phonetic loan characters refer to the situation in which the pictographic characters with the same phonetic components are used interchangeably. The 'homophonic loans' occupy a considerable proportion in the excavated characters, which is fairly impressive. Mr Qian Xuan (钱玄) has given a statistical account of the homophonic loans used in the Zhou bronze script, the Qin and Han bamboo slips and silk manuscripts, and the pre-Qin classics still existent. In about hundred homophonic loans, on average,

---

[35] Originally published in *Journal of Chinese Linguistics* 9 (1999; Beijing: The Commercial Press.

there are 15 or 16 such loans in the Zhou bronze script, about 6 in the Qin and Han bamboo slips and silk manuscripts, and 1 in the pre-Qin classics. In addition, in the homophonic loans in the Zhou bronze script, the loans of the same phonetic components take up more than 79 per cent of the total.[36] We have conducted a comprehensive survey of the loans interchangeably used in the Qin-Han bamboo slips and silk manuscripts from the bamboo slips from the Shuihudi Qin Tombs (《睡虎地秦墓竹简》), *Laozi Version A* and some lost texts attached at its end from the Mawangdui Han Tombs, *Spring and Autumn Accounts* (《春秋事语》), *Laozi Version B* and some lost texts at its beginning, *Manuscripts of the Political Strategists in the Warring States Period* (《战国纵横家书》), the Yinqueshan bamboo slip version of the *Art of War* (银雀山简本《孙子兵法》) and *Wei Liaozi* (《尉缭子》). We have collected 1,675 commonly used interchangeable loans, of which 1,344 loan characters have the same phonetic components, taking up more than 80 per cent of the total. This very likely reflects the real situation of the use of interchangeable homophones from the pre-Qin period to the Qin-Han period. Some interchangeable homophones in the existent ancient classics may have been corrected back to the original characters. Such being the case, interchangeable homophones are still very prominent in some classics. For example, in *Mozi*, many interchangeable homophones are preserved, as is said, 'Many of the ancient characters and expressions remain unchanged as loan characters'. According to the research, there are over 540 interchangeable homophones in the book, 453 of which can be determined as common and rare characters.[37] In the statistical analysis, the interchangeable loans with the same phonetic components take up about 66 per cent of the total. Mr Gao Heng's *Collection of Ancient Interchangeable Homophones* (高亨《古字通假会典》), based on most of the related works from the pre-Qin and Han periods (with a few quotations after the Wei–Jin period), fully reflects the whole situation of the interchangeable homophones in the existent classics. According to

---

[36] Qian Xuan (钱玄), *Interpretations of the Interchangeable Homophones in Bronze Script* (Draft) (Nanjing: Nanjing Normal University, 1981).

[37] Zhou Fumei (周富美), *Collected Interchangeable Homophones in Mozi* (Taipei: The School of Arts, Taiwan University, 1963).

our random statistics, in the 30 speech sounds with the '东' (dong) radical, there are 432 interchangeable homophones, 248 of which are phonetically interchangeable loans, taking up over 57 per cent of the total. This also demonstrates the prevalence of the interchangeable homophones. Compared with the bronze script in the Zhou periods and the bamboo slips and silk manuscripts in the Qin-Han period, this proportion declines to some extent, which has something to do with the revision of the classics by the later generations, and from which we can see that generally speaking, there are fewer interchangeable homophones in the works in the Han periods than in the pre-Qin and Qin-Han periods, which has something to do with the development of the Chinese character system.

The aforementioned 'homophonic loans' can be classified into three types. The first type is the pictophonetic character in which the phonetic component is used as the loan character. For example, '且' is used as the loan character for '祖', '屯' for '纯', '每' for '敏', '折' for '誓', '田' for '甸' (see the bronze inscriptions from the Zhou periods), '又' for '有', '直' for '置', '翏' for '戮', '耤' for '藉', '辟' for '臂, 避, 壁' (see Shuihudi Qin bamboo slips), '失' for '佚', '兹' for '慈', '立' for '位', '耆' for '嗜', '合' for '答', '正' for '政', '古' for '固' (see Mawangdui silk manuscripts), etc. These examples with phonetic components as loan characters take up a considerable proportion in the homophonic loans. According to our statistics, the number of such cases reaches more than 72 per cent[38] of the homophonic loans in the bronze inscriptions from the Zhou periods, while they take up 45 per cent in the Qin-Han bamboo slips and silk script. The second type is the character with the phonetic component in which the pictophonetic character with the same phonetic component is used as the loan character. For example, '譬' is used for '辟', '啻' for '帝', '迈' for '万', '囿' for '有', '征' for '正' (see the bronze inscriptions from the Zhou periods), '有' for '又', '贼' for '则', '诱' for '秀', '造' for '告', '苞' for '包', '投' for '殳', '溉' for '既', '蔡' for '祭' (see Shuihudi Qin bamboo slips), '智' for '知', '视' for '示', '氣' for '气', '浴' for '谷', '畸' for '奇', '静' for '争', '宵' for '肖' (see Mawangdui

---

[38] For these statistics, we have consulted Qian Xuan's *Interpretations of the Interchangeable Homophones in Bronze Inscriptions*.

silk manuscripts), etc. The loan characters with the pictophonetic characters as their phonetic components are just contrary to the first type. This phenomenon is difficult to be satisfying by the traditional theory of homophonic loaning. It only takes a small proportion in the homophonic loan characters, 5 per cent of the bronze inscriptions from the Zhou periods and less than 5 per cent of the bamboo slips and silk manuscripts in the Qin-Han periods. The third type is the interchangeable loans between the pictophonetic characters with the same phonetic components. For example, '悔' for '敏', '朕' for '媵', '哉' for '载', '赢' for '嬴', '阳' for '扬' (see the bronze inscriptions), '治' for '笞', '幅' for '福', '福' for '幅', '组' for '祖', '择' for '释', '避' for '僻', '臂' for '壁', '适' for '敌', '俗' for '容', '绾' for '棺' (see Shuihudi Qin bamboo slips), '侍' for '待', '请' for '情', '渴' for '竭', '检' for '俭', '贤' for '坚', '依' for '哀', '格' for '客' (see Mawangdui silk manuscripts), etc. The interchangeable loan characters with the same phonetic components take up more than 22 per cent of the homophonic loans in the bronze inscriptions from the Zhou periods and over 50 per cent of those in the Qin-Han bamboo slips and silk manuscripts.

How do we explain the prevalent phenomenon of homophonic loans? Zheng Xuan (郑玄) had a very famous comment on homophonic loans: 'At the beginning of writing script, with no exact characters available but in urgent need of them, phonetic interchangeable characters are then used by homophonic analogy, approaching the approximate meanings'. See the quotation from Lu Deming's *Preface to the Annotations of Classics* (陆德明《经典释文序》) in the Tang Dynasty. 'With no exact characters but in urgent need of them' is the cause by which homophonic loaning originated. This is the consensus by both the ancients and moderns on homophonic loaning. However, it is not the case if we try to verify Zheng Xuan's comment by the phonetic interchangeable characters in the ancient script, especially those in the Qin-Han bamboo slips and silk manuscripts. It is not uncommon that in the same piece of writing, we can see that some original characters are loaned as other characters and the other characters loaned still as others. For example, in *The 18 Decrees of the State of Qin* (《秦律十八种》), the character '被' is used as '柀' and then '柀' is used as '罢'. When commenting on the Mawangdui silk manuscripts of *Laozi*, Mr Gao Heng and others said, 'There are many instances of loan characters in the silk manuscripts of *Laozi*.... The main reason is that there were not as many characters in the ancient times'. They also said:

> There are generally four cases in which loan characters are used in the ancient script: 1. There are no original characters at all, so other characters are used as the loan characters, and later the original characters are never created. 2. There are no original characters at all, so other characters are used as the loan characters, and later the original characters are created. 3. There are original characters, but the writers do not know them or are unfamiliar with them, so they use loan characters (like the errors in character usage). 4. There are original characters, but the writers intend to simplify the characters due to too many strokes of such characters, so they use loan characters (like the simplified characters). These four cases are naturally all present in the silk manuscripts of *Laozi*.[39]

However, they do not seem to completely match homophonic loaning reflected in the ancient script. First of all, in the homophonic loan characters, many of the 'original characters' are not used. Second, some other characters are used instead of the original characters. Third, some homophonic loan characters are used not exactly due to not knowing or being unfamiliar with the original characters, or 'simplification of characters'. On the contrary, the second kind of homophonic loan characters are nothing but 'complication of characters'. Thus, the common theory of homophonic loaning can hardly well explain the phenomenon of 'homophonic loaning' in the ancient character script.

When we examine homophonic loaning together with the pictophonetic structure and its development, we discover the close relationship between them. We once pointed out: since the Western Zhou period, the picto-semantic formation mode had gradually declined and the pictophonetic formation function had been increasing, but in the Spring–Autumn and Warring States periods, the pictophonetic structure had

---

[39] Gao Heng (高亨), 'On the Silk Manuscripts (Laozi) from the Mawangdui Han Tombs', *Cultural Relics* 11 (1974).

prospered.[40] The occurrence of homophonic loaning mainly started from the Zhou periods. The Qin bamboo and wooden slips represent parts of the materials from the Late Warring States period to the Qin period, while the bamboo slips and silk manuscripts excavated from Mawangdui and Yinqueshan are the works in the prosperous period of the characters of pictophonetic structures, though they are in fact the manuscripts from the early Han period, such as *Laozi*, the *Art of War* by Sunzi, the *Art of War* by Sunbin, *Manuscripts of the Political Strategists* in the Warring States period and *Wei Liaozi*. They may reflect how the written characters were actually used and developed during the periods. From the Zhou periods to the early Han period, the large number of homophonic loan characters coexisted with the development of the characters of pictophonetic structures.

How do we regard the relationship between the development of pictophonetic structures and homophonic loaning? Many pictophonetic characters are formed by adding pictographic components to the interchangeable homophones. The purpose of adding pictographic components is to form the sole original characters and reduce interchangeable homophones. Thus, on the surface, the development of the pictophonetic structures should have suppressed the use of interchangeable homophones in large numbers instead of producing more interchangeable homophones. Such being the case, it seems contradictory to link the prevalent occurrence of interchangeable homophonic loaning to the development of the pictophonetic structures. However, after our further analysis of the three categories of interchangeable homophonic loaning, the truth of the matter is revealed.

The first category is to use the phonetic components as the loan characters for the pictophonetic characters of the same phonetic components. It can be explained to follow the general homophonic loaning theory of simplification. Nonetheless, to determine such kind of homophonic loaning usually depends on the existent original characters within the established Chinese character system. In the Zhou periods, such kind of characters amount to over 70 per cent, and they

---

[40] Cf. 'The Chinese Character Formation Modes: A System of Diachronic Evolution' included in this book.

can be classified into two situations: the first is that there were original characters at the time but they were not used, such as '且' used as '祖' and '畐' as '福', taking up more than half of the total. The second is that the original characters were not found and we can assume that the original characters were later created, such as '堇' used as '勤', '各' as '略' and '巩' as '鞏', taking up about half. In the former case, the pictophonetic characters are mostly formed by adding pictographic components to phonetic components. This reveals the historical and etymological relationship between the original characters and the loan characters. The phonetic components already had the function of the pictophonetic characters before such characters came into being. Such historical advantage and usage habit still qualify them for replacing the added pictographic components and forming pictophonetic characters. When the pictophonetic characters formed by added pictographic components are not yet consolidated as original characters as a whole unit and have not yet gained the qualification for their special usage, the added pictographic components can sometimes be disregarded. Therefore, it becomes a common phenomenon that the phonetic components are used as the loan characters for the pictophonetic characters. In the latter case, before the pictophonetic characters come into being as forthcoming characters, the phonetic components used as such characters are in fact the predecessors of those so-called original characters. Strictly speaking, it may not be appropriate to assume that this situation is also interchangeable homophonic loaning by using the established character system as the reference. Before the original characters come into being, they are at most only a kind of homophonic loan characters with no predecessors. However, this kind of homophonic loaning can reveal the forming process of the succeeding original characters, which cannot be ignored in the research of the pictophonetic structure development. By the time of the Qin-Han periods, the proportion of the phonetic components as the loan characters drastically declined in the related materials, demonstrating that the pictophonetic structure had gained much progress in the historical process. Many phonetic components became consolidated after the pictographic components were added to them. The phonetic components usually do not have the function of replacing them, and some other phonetic component loan characters with no original characters in the past also formed the characters with special usage after pictographic components were added to them.

The second category is somewhat difficult to explain. The pictophonetic characters as phonetic component loan characters are more complex than the original characters from the perspective of character forms, and they are more recent than the original characters in terms of the usage history. So why not use the original characters simpler in form and longer in usage history? Why use the loan characters of more complex forms and later periods instead? Does it reflect the individual or regional habit of character usage? The usage of some interchangeable homophones in a book may indeed reflect the habit of character usage; however, if the same phenomenon frequently occurs in different texts, we can no longer conclude it with the 'habit of character usage'. For example, the character '智' is frequently used as '知' on the Qin bamboo slips, but it also appears in *Laozi*, *Manuscripts of the Political Strategists* in the Warring States period, Sunzi's *Art of War*, Sun Bin's *Art of War* and *Wei Liaozi* on the Mawangdui bamboo slips and silk manuscripts. '有' used as '又' occurs over 10 times on the Shuihudi Qin bamboo slips, but the same usage also appears in *Some Accounts of the Spring and Autumn Periods*, *Laozi*, *Manuscripts of the Political Strategists* in the Warring States period, Sunzi's *Art of War*, Sun Bin's *Art of War* and *Wei Liaozi*. Although '视' for '示' is not so frequently used as '智' and '有' for '知' and '又', the same usage occurs on the Shuihudi Qin bamboo slips, *Stories of the Spring and Autumn Periods*, *Manuscripts of the Political Strategists* in the Warring States period, Sunzi's *Art of War* and Sun Bin's *Art of War*. Meanwhile, there also exist the cases of '知' for '智', '又' for '有' and '示' for '视'. Such mutually interchangeable loaning shows that the functions of the original characters and loan characters only exist in the relative distinctions in usage, but they are not completely consistent with the unity between form and sense reflected in their formation. However, more interchangeable homophones may not demonstrate such corresponding relationships. For example, in the Mawangdui silk manuscripts, the characters '静', '挣' and '净' are used as '争', and '清' is used as '静'. On the Shuihudi Qin bamboo slips, both

'清' and '精' are used as '青'. Meanwhile, '精' is also used as '清'; and in the Mawangdui silk manuscripts of Laozi, '请' is also used as '清'; '请', '睛', '青' and '清' as '精'; and '请' as '情'. This kind of usage shows that no matter whether the pictophonetic characters with '争' and '青' for their phonetic components as loans for '争' and '青' or, reversely, the characters with the same phonetic components are used interchangeably, they do not manifest themselves in a mutually distinctive corresponding relationship. In fact, the same phonetic components seem the only condition on which they become interchangeable. Based on this analysis, we believe that the convention of character usage is not the main reason for the phenomenon of such homophonic loaning by using pictophonetic characters as loan characters with such phonetic components. After investigating the developmental history of pictophonetic structures, we believe that the occurrence of such situation should be the natural response of the pictophonetic system in its rapid developmental period. First of all, the large number of pictophonetic characters and the formation of specific characters by adding pictographic components became a fad for a period of time, and with this influence, the characters as phonetic components without the pictographic components added might also be replaced by the pictophonetic characters with pictographic components added in the hands of the users who did not know the rules of character formation. Second, the appearance of the large number of new pictophonetic characters with pictographic components added and other types of pictophonetic characters broke through the established pattern of the character system, and it would take quite some time for the new characters to be stabilized. Under this circumstance, there would inevitably be a short period of disorder in character usage. It became commonplace for the characters with the same phonetic components to be interchangeable loans, and it was no wonder that there occasionally appeared the loan characters with the phonetic components of the pictophonetic characters with the same phonetic components. Third, the flourish of pictophonetic characters is, in a sense, the reverse of the abuse of interchangeable homophonic loan characters. However, they are the same in that both record language by the principle of phonetic representation. Although the pictophonetic characters, by the adjustment of pictographic components, did not completely rid themselves of the pictographic–semantic tradition in the development of Chinese characters, the function of pictographic components lay in differentiation and marking, taking the secondary and subsidiary position in the pictophonetic structure. Therefore, we point out that the pictophonetic structure is a kind of character sign of quasi-phonetic nature.[41] Such being the case, both interchangeable loan characters and pictophonetic characters are the signs that record language by phonetic representation. Therefore, the occurrence of the loan characters for the characters with the pictophonetic characters of the same phonetic components as their phonetic components, similar to the other two situations, is the result of the tendency of enhancing phonetic representation in the Chinese character system. Thus, the sameness of the phonetic components becomes the sole condition in homophonic loaning. There are surely various factors that determine character usage. The phenomenon of complication instead of simplification, which is to use the succeeding characters as loan characters, does not comply with the principle of economy in character usage. Thus, it takes a very low percentage in the whole homophonic loaning, and it mainly appears in the flourishing period of pictophonetic structures. As new pictophonetic characters in large numbers become stabilized and their functions distinct, such phenomenon of interchangeable character loaning becomes rarer and rarer.

In the third category, the pictophonetic characters with the same phonetic components are interchangeably used without distinction. In some material, there seem certain rules in the interchangeability. For example, on the Shuihudi Qin bamboo slips, '幅' is used as '福', '福' as '幅', '俗' as '容' and '容' as '鎔'. Such cases of interchangeability or successive loaning do exist but they are not prevalent. The more common cases of usage are the interchangeability and indistinction of the characters with the same phonetic components. For example, on the Shuihudi Qin bamboo slips, the common usage for the phonetic system of character '辟' goes as follows: '避' is used as '僻', '辟' as '臂', '避' as '壁', '臂' as '壁' and '廦' as '壁'. For the phonetic system of

---

[41] Cf. 'The Combinations, Characteristics and Nature of the Pictophonetic Structure' included in this book.

character '皮', '被' is used as '柀', '波' as '破', '彼' as '破' and '柀' as '破'. In the Mawangdui silk manuscripts and Qin bamboo slips, the characters of the phonetic system of '青' can be interchangeably used. All these typically reflect the irregular state of the interchangeability of the pictophonetic characters with the same phonetic components. However, the prevalent interchangeability of the characters with the same phonetic components follow the same rule, that is, as long as the characters share the same phonetic components, they are interchangeable and indistinct from each other. The third category of the interchangeability of the characters with the same phonetic components more typically reflects the usage of pictophonetic characters in the development of the pictophonetic structure. On the one hand, the appearance of new pictophonetic characters in large numbers reduces the cases of using phonetic components as loan characters, and a batch of succeeding original characters becomes the new members of the pictophonetic system. On the other hand, these new characters, in the process of usage, must gain acceptance of the character users in the whole society, and then gradually become unified in form, sound and sense, stabilized in structure and district in function. Only by then can the newly created pictophonetic characters really acquire the qualification of exclusiveness, and the homophonic interchangeability declines or even disappears. After the Western Zhou period, the character formation entered the pictophonetic-structure-oriented stage. From the Spring–Autumn period to the Warring States period, the pictophonetic characters increased in large numbers as the social politics, economy and language developed, and the interchangeability and indistinction of the pictophonetic characters with the same phonetic components became inevitable under such circumstances.

As seen earlier, the prevalence of homophonic interchangeability is in essence with the result of the pictophonetic structure in its prosperous developmental stage as well as the scenario manifested in the evolution and development of the Chinese character system. The traditional philological theory of homophonic loaning alone cannot fully and rationally explain this phenomenon.

The prevalence of homophonic loaning not only concerns the pictophonetic structure in its developmental stage, but it is also determined by the features of such structure.[42] First of all, the pictophonetic structure is centred on the phonetic components and it is the basis for the prevalence of homophonic loaning. The phonetic components, as the major part of the contradictory unity of the pictophonetic structure, with their leading role in the character formation, make it possible for the 'same phonetic components' to be the sole condition for homophonic loaning. The function and nature of pictographic components, with their instability and indeterminacy in the consolidating process of the pictophonetic combination, make themselves insignificant in the actual usage and they often become easily ignored factors. As a result, they enhance the rationality of the interchangeability of homophonic characters. Second, the homophonic loaning reflects the internal contradictory nature of the pictophonetic structure. The functions of pictographic components and phonetic components reveal the unity of contradictions in the formation concept of the pictophonetic structure. In the usage of pictophonetic characters, the interchangeability of the characters with the same pronunciation serves as the complete negation of the function of the pictographic components. This shows that the ideal of specific usage for specific characters pursued in the pictographic formation contradicts the reality of 'sound' as the focus over 'form' in actual usage. This contradiction reflects the internal contradiction of the pictophonetic structure in actual usage. Due to the fact that the pictophonetic structure is a whole unifying entity, the contradiction of its formation and character usage eventually reaches unity after the pictophonetic characters gradually become stabilized and accepted by the social members in their development.

The discussion of the 'interchangeability of homophonic characters' in this chapter demonstrates the following. Some phenomena in the use of Chinese characters are often closely related to the state of their formation and development. When we analyse the phenomena of the use of certain Chinese characters, we should delve into the structures and historical development pertaining to such characters in order to seek more rational explanations. When we analyse the Chinese character formation, we should also investigate the actual

---

[42] Cf. 'The Combinations, Characteristics and Nature of the Pictophonetic Structure' included in this book.

usage pertaining to the characters in order to reveal their natural features and rules from the dynamic and historical perspectives.

The Shang Characters Before the Oracle Bone Script from the Yin Dynasty Ruins[43]

In the historical process of the formation and development of Chinese characters, the Shang Dynasty plays an extremely important role. 'Duoshi' in the *Book of History* mentions: 'The Yin ancestors alone had canonical works'. This is the record from the existent literature that the Yin ancestors already had canonical works. The excavation of the Yinxu oracle bone script recovers the actual situation of the use of characters in the late Shang Dynasty. The archaeological finds from the Shang Dynasty and particularly the discovery of the ruins of the early middle Shang capital in Zhengzhou and the early Shang capital in Yanshi[44] provide very favourable background materials for the exploration of the early Shang characters. As one of the important subjects in the study of the history of the Chinese civilization, many scholars are much concerned about the study of the origin and development of Chinese characters.[45] We think that in the study of the formation

---

[43] This paper was delivered at the Workshop on Chinese Civilization at University of British Columbia, Canada, in March 2005. Jing Zhichun (荆志淳) et al., ed., *Multiple Horizons: A Study of the Shang Dynasty and Early Chinese Civilization* (Beijing: Science Press, 2009).

[44] Du Jinpeng (杜金鹏) and Wang Xuerong (王学荣), *A Study of the Yanshi Shang Capital Relic Site* (Beijing: Science Press, 2004). The Cultural Relic Archeological Institute of Henan Province, comp., *The Zhengzhou Shang Capital: An Archeological Excavation Report 1953–1985* (Beijing: The Cultural Relics Publishing House, 2001).

[45] Since the publication of the pottery characters and signs from the Banpo Civilization of the New Stone Age in the 20th century, Qiu Xigui (裘锡圭), Li Xueqin (李学勤), Rao Zongyi (饶宗颐) and Gao Ming (高明), all published their papers or monographs. In October 2000, at the Symposium on the Origin of Chinese Characters organized by China Yin-Shang Research Society et al., over 30 scholars from home and abroad met at Luoyang to discuss their results on the origin of Chinese characters. Cf. The Editorial Department of Chinese Calligraphy, 'A Brief Account of the Symposium on the Origin of Chinese Characters', *Chinese Calligraphy* 2 (2001).

and development of Chinese characters, it is reliable to start with the late Shang characters represented by the Yinxu oracle bone script. In the exploration of the formation and development of early Chinese characters, it is a possible approach to trace from the late Yin-Shang period to its early period and then conduct a rational speculation on the whole Shang characters. On the basis of understanding this, the present chapter is an attempt to discuss the Shang characters before the Yin-Shang oracle bone script.

An Observation of the Early Shang Characters from the Perspective of the Development of Yinxu Oracle Bone Script

For over a hundred years since the discovery of the Yinxu oracle bone script, scholars have reached the following consensus: The Yinxu oracle bone script includes the earliest systematic characters known so far for the Chinese race. Although there is no doubt regarding their status as the earliest written system of the Chinese characters, scholars differ in their views on the levels of maturity and development of the oracle bone script. Some hold the view that the oracle bone script is a kind of 'very developed characters'[46] and they have entered the 'stage of mature and complete symbolic characters'.[47] Some think that the oracle bone script is 'still on the way of formation'.[48] Some others take cautious attitudes. For example, Qiu Xigui (裘锡圭) thinks that 'the late Shang characters are not only able to record the language

---

[46] Tang Lan (唐兰), *An Introduction to Ancient Philology*, Extended ed. (Jinan: Qilu Book Company, 1981), 79.

[47] Li Xiaoding (李孝定), 'On the Oracle Bone Script from the Perspective of the Six Script Categories'. The paper was originally published in *The Journal of Nanyang University* 2 (1968). Zhao Cheng (赵诚), *An Outlined Philology of the Oracle Bone Script* (Beijing: The Commercial Press, 1993), 31.

[48] Guo Moruo (郭沫若), 'The Ancient Society in the Oracle Inscriptions', in *Studies in the Ancient Chinese Society* (Beijing: The People's Press, 1954). This view was altered by the author in the 1970s. He then thought: 'As far as the oracle bone inscriptions are concerned, they have become a character system of strict regularities'. Guo Moruo, 'The Dialectic Development of the Ancient Characters', *A Journal of Archeology* 1 (1972).

completely but also show much maturity in some aspects'.[49] The accurate judgement of the developmental level of the oracle bone script has direct impact on our discussion of the development of the early Shang oracle bone script.

We believe that to determine the developmental level of a writing system, we should mainly conduct the respective analysis of its formation of the sign system, level of signification, written form of signs and function of signs. In addition, this analysis must be based on the reliable materials of the system on its mature stage so that correct conclusions can be drawn.

The Formation of the Signs of the Oracle Bone Script

According to the research, there are altogether about 3,700 single characters in the oracle bone script as the Chinese character system, 2,000 of which are recognized and determined.[50] Based on Shen Jianhua's (沈建华) and Cao Jinyan's (曹锦炎) further collation, there are 4,071 single characters in the oracle bone script (including numerals and ancestral names), amounting to 6,051 character variants (including different forms of the same characters, numerals and ancestral names).[51] All these figures are the further collation and addition based on the *Classified Compilation of Yinxu Oracle Bone Inscriptions* by Yao Xiaosui, chief editor.[52] The various views are mainly due to the discrepancies in the treatment of the separation and incorporation of the character forms. As Shen's book was published later, his statistics 'should generally be reliable data, by which we can better evaluate

---

[49] Qiu Xigui (裘锡圭), *An Outline of Philology* (Taipei: Wanjuanlou Book Company, 1995).
[50] Zhao Cheng (赵诚), *An Outlined Philology of the Oracle Bone Script*, 75.
[51] Shen Jianhua (沈建华) and Cao Jinyan (曹锦炎), *A Newly Compiled General Chart of the Forms of the Oracle Bone Script*.
[52] Yao Xiaosui (姚孝遂) and Xiao Ding (肖丁), ed., *Classified Compilation of Yin-Xu Oracle Bone Inscriptions* (Beijing: Zhonghua Book Company, 1989). The book includes 3,551 individual characters. Cf. 'The General Chart of Character Forms'.

the developmental level of the time'.⁵³ The approximate 4,000 single characters in the oracle bone script reflect the basic structure of the sign system of the oracle bone script. Compared with the established ancient character system represented in the *Origin*, various types of characters are already formed in the oracle bone script. The 'four types' (pictographs, simple indicatives, associative compounds and pictophonetic characters) of the traditional 'six script categories' are all present in the oracle bone script. This demonstrates that by the late Yin-Shang period, the Chinese characters, represented by the oracle bone script, had already been established in their basic formation mode and their formation system had gradually developed into maturity.⁵⁴ If we further examine the various formation modes, we can find the respective distinctions already existent in the signifying power of the different formation modes during those periods. Most of the 'pictographs' have early origins, and they should have had full development before the Yin-Shang period. Almost all the pictographs in the *Origin* are present as either single characters or characters in the oracle bone script, and there are hardly any new characters formed later in such formation modes. The 'simple indicatives' are weak in their formation function and by the Western Zhou period they had already dwindled. The 'associative compounds' maintain their early characteristics, still capable of forming new characters. The 'pictophonetic characters' do not only retain various formation modes (pictographic, phonetic and pictophonetic) but also demonstrate the general 'phonetic' tendency of forming characters.⁵⁵ The basic formation elements in the sign system of the oracle bone script can also be further analysed in two categories of concrete pictographs and abstract signs, the former of which include about 150 characters and the latter of which are even more limited in

---

⁵³ Li Xueqin (李学勤), 'A Preface to *A New Compilation of the General Chart of the Oracle Bone Inscription Forms*'. Cf. Shen Jianhua (沈建华) and Cao Jinyan (曹锦炎), *A New Compilation of the General Chart of the Oracle Bone Inscription Forms*.

⁵⁴ Li Xiaoding (李孝定), 'On the Oracle Bone Inscriptions from the Perspective of the Six Script Categories'. Cf. *A Symposium on the Origin and Evolution of Chinese Characters*.

⁵⁵ Cf. 'The Chinese Character Formation Modes: A System of Diachronic Evolution' included in this book.

number, mainly referring to signs for numerals and abstract signs for marking distinctions (also called 'markers'). The formation modes of the oracle bone script are already on an advanced level in that they are capable of forming a whole set of sign systems by a limited number of basic pictographic elements.[56]

The Level of Signification of the Oracle Bone Script

Characters, as a sign system to record language, have experienced the progression of the form signification from the primordial state to the mature stage, that is, these characters have transformed from the primordial pictographs, gradually being simplified, linearized and regulated to the appropriate sign system to record language. This progression of signification and the level it has reached are an important standard by which we can judge the maturity level of an old language system.[57] Yao Xiaosui has extensively investigated the developmental level of the forms of the oracle bone script. He concludes:

> Although a large number of primordial pictographs still remained in the writing forms of the oracle bone script, their forms, as a whole writing system, had already passed the transforming stage of signification. They had considerably developed either in linearization or regularity and had reached a very high level in the differentiating mode and measure of character forms. Afterwards, the various character systems followed the foundation laid by the oracle bone script and made further progress in the differentiating mode and measure of character forms. This is only a process of continuous enrichment and deepening but no more fundamental breakthrough and transcendence.[58]

---

[56] Yao Xiaosui, 'A Structural Analysis of the Oracle Bone Inscription Forms', in *A Philological Study of Ancient Characters*, vol. 20 (Beijing: Zhonghua Book Company, 2000).

[57] Yao Xiaosui (姚孝遂), 'On the Signification of the Ancient Characters', The Editorial Committee for the International Symposium on Chinese Ancient Philology, comp. *Collected Papers on Ancient Philology*, first compilation (Hong Kong: Chinese University of Hong Kong, 1983).

[58] Yao Xiaosui, 'The Structural Analysis of the Forms of the Oracle Bone Inscriptions', in *Studies in Ancient Characters*, vol. 20.

The Writing Forms of the Oracle Bone Script

The writing habits formed in the creation of Chinese characters determine their unique writing forms different from the ancient characters of other races. In terms of single characters, both single signs and compound signs seek balance and stability in their two-dimensional structures. Although their lines vary in different stages, such structural formation principles are consistently applied. As regards the written forms of the language, the arrangement of straight lines and the order of from top down to the bottom have been a long inherited tradition in Chinese characters until the 20th century when the tradition began to change. In regard to the oracle bone script, such tradition was then a prevalent written form. In order to adapt to the requirement of this written form, some character forms turn at 90° at the vertical direction and thus transform the direction of the original pictographic centres. For example, the forms originating from animals 'make their legs above in the air' when taking the vertical direction. Other forms such as '水', '弓' and '床' also change their original structures and become vertical. The two written forms of being 'straight' and 'vertical' show that the writing skills of Chinese characters reached very high level in the period of the oracle bone script, and the straight and vertical patterns of Chinese characters were primarily established.[59]

The Function of the Signs of the Oracle Bone Script

The function of the written sign system to record language is the only criterion by which we judge its maturity level and its distinction from other sign systems, which is determined by the attributes of the written language. There was no complete consensus in the early studies of the oracle bone script regarding the belief that the oracle

---

[59] Qiu Xigui (裘锡圭), *An Outline of Philology*, 40; You Shunzhao (游顺钊), 'The Causes of the Vertical Writing Style of Ancient Chinese Characters', *Chinese Philology* 5 (1992).

bone script is the record of the Chinese language in the late Yin-Shang period. Some scholars thought that the oracle bone script was, in fact, characters for special purposes and they could not reveal the actual linguistic situation of that period. As the studies progressed, especially in the comprehensive research of the syntax and lexicological system of the oracle bone script, people have gradually become aware that the oracle bone script as the record of the Chinese language in the Yin-Shang period proves to be of great value in the studies of the developmental history of the Chinese language.[60] Guan Xiechu (管燮初) conducts research on the oracle bone script from the aspects of syntax and lexicology. He discovers that the sentence structures and types as well as the character categories and their functions are generally close to those of the Chinese of later periods, and he believes that the oracle bone script is the written language based on the spoken language of the Yin-Shang period.[61] This view has become definitive since deeper and more systematic research was conducted by scholars both at home and abroad.[62] As the written language to record the spoken language of that period, the oracle bone script should have naturally developed into the mature stage in their function to record language. Easterling believes:

> The ancient Chinese characters are a kind of 'word-oriented characters.... The word-oriented characters are the type of characters whose signs represent single words.... The utterance represented by the word-oriented characters are divided into words; they often reflect the syntactic order of the words, and under many circumstances, they also reflect the pronunciations of the utterance.

These word-oriented characters as signs of words can be divided into two categories: one category is directly related to the sense of the word;

---

[60] Wang Yuxin (王宇信) and Yang Shengnan (杨升南), *A Hundred Year's Study of the Oracle Bone Script* (Beijing: Social Sciences Academic Press, 1999).

[61] Guan Xiechu (管燮初), *A Grammatical Study of the Yinxu Oracle Bone Inscriptions* (Beijing: Chinese Academy of Sciences, 1953).

[62] Wang Yuxin and Yang Shengnan, *A Hundred Year's Study of the Oracle Bone Inscriptions*, 270–80; Zhang Yujin (张玉金), *Grammar of the Oracle Bone Inscriptions* (Shanghai: Xuelin Press, 2001).

the other category is directly related to the sound of the word.[63] The function of the signs of the oracle bone script generally accords with the theory of the 'word-oriented characters' discussed earlier. From the correspondence between a character and a word, a written sign of the oracle bone script represents a word; from the formation mode and the way the character is related to the sense, these character signs start with the relationship between the form and sense to form the formalistic signs (pictographs, simple indicatives and associative compounds) on the one hand, and on the other, they start with the relationship between the form and sound to form and determine the formalistic signs (pictophonetic and homophonic loaning). In fact, to fulfil the function of recording the Chinese language, in addition to the syntactic structure that complies with the utterance, a large number of function words and abstract concepts enable the oracle bone script to be based on the correspondence between characters and words (or what may be called to use a single sign to represent a single word) and to take the approach to representing the sound, which is typically reflected in the prevalence of the homophonic loans and the pictophonetic characters in the oracle bone script. Out of the most commonly used characters in the oracle bone script, the homophonic loans take up approximately 90 per cent, and by random statistical sampling, they take up about 74 per cent.[64] Although there are not as many pictophonetic characters in number in the oracle bone script, their tendency to combine form and sound and to be 'pictophonetic' is obvious.[65] According to the knowledge from

---

[63] B. A. Easterling, *The Emergence and Development of Characters*, trans. Zuo Shaoxing (左少兴) (Beijing: Peking University Press, 1987), 34–38.

[64] Based on Yao Xiaosui's statistics. He points out: from the perspective of the actual function of the oracle bone script, these inscriptions are the complete system that record the language of the period and that has developed into the stage of phonetic characters. This new view has aroused heated discussions. Cf. 'The Present State and the Prospect of the Research Work in Ancient Characters', in *Studies in Ancient Characters*, vol. 1; Yao Xiaosui, 'The Structures and Developmental Stages of Ancient Chinese Characters'; 'More Comments on the Nature of Chinese Characters', in *Studies in Ancient Characters*, vol. 17; 'The Structural Analysis of the Forms of the Oracle Bone Script', in *Studies in Ancient Characters*, vol. 20.

[65] In the previously quoted papers, Yao Xiaosui has full explanations as for the structural features of the pictophonetic characters and the functions of the pictographic and phonetic radicals.

the present research, the sign function of the oracle bone script has truly advanced to the stage in which they can record the Yin-Shang Chinese language by every word and represent its syntactic rules and features (e.g., word order, function words and basic sentence patterns). They form a writing system of complete functions.

From the four aspects of the earlier investigation, we can assuredly conclude: the oracle bone script is a mature writing system of complete functions developed over a long period of time. It does contain not only the earliest systematic characters but also the character samples of a complete system that has entered its mature stage, which we can be assured of so far. This conclusion does not deny the fact that Chinese characters in the Yin-Shang period retain certain primordial features since they are still in the process of development and change. Certain constituents to be developed and improved in the system do not contradict the maturity of a system because there is still constant change even in a long established and mature writing system. The basic evaluation of the maturity level of the oracle bone script in the late Yin-Shang period enables us to take it as the starting point to measure the developmental level of the Chinese characters in the early Yin-Shang period. The matter is how long and what stages it takes for the Chinese characters to develop into the mature state demonstrated by the oracle bone script. This is what we should explore and answer. After comparing the oracle bone script with the Naxi pictographs (纳西象形文字), Dong Zuobin (董作宾) thinks that it should have been an extremely long period of time between the use of the oracle bone script and the creation of Chinese characters, and this creation should be dated back to the New Stone Age.[66] Guo Moruo even claims: 'There should have been undoubtedly at least two or three thousand years of development before the period of the oracle bone script' in the history of Chinese characters.[67] Qiu Xiwa thinks that 'the time of the formation of Chinese characters is probably no earlier than the Xia dynasty

---

[66] Dong Zuobin (董作宾), 'On the Oracle Bone Script from the Perspective of Naxi Characters', quoted in Li Xiaoding, *On the Origin and Evolution of Chinese Characters*, 40.

[67] Guo Moruo (郭沫若), 'The Dialectic Development of Ancient Characters', *Journal of Archaeology* 1 (1972).

(approx 21st century BC–17th century BC)'; 'it is most likely that Chinese characters were not established as a complete system until the Xia and Shang periods', that is, around the 17th century BC.[68] Although many scholars think that Chinese characters emerged far early before the oracle bone script in the late Shang period, there remains much controversy over the actual period of the creation of Chinese characters and their eventual formation of the complete system.

Some Discoveries of the Clay Characters in the Early Shang Period

The developmental level of the oracle bone script provides us with the basis to speculate the state of Chinese characters in the early Shang period (approx 17th century BC–14th century BC). In addition, the excavated written materials become the most important direct evidence. The published archaeological written finds before the oracle bone script mainly include Xiaotun Yinxu pottery characters (小屯殷墟陶文), Gaocheng Taixi pottery characters (藁城台西陶文), Qingjiang Wucheng pottery characters (清江吴城陶文), Zhengzhou Erligang and Nanguanwai pottery characters (郑州二里岗和南关外陶文), etc. These pottery characters have been analysed by Li Xiaoding (李孝定) and Qiu Xigui in their discussions of the formation and evolution of Chinese characters.[69] In recent years, there have been new important discoveries of the written material in the early Shang period, for which there is a need for a full clarification in the following.

Xiaotun Yinxu Pottery Characters

They refer to the archaeological finds excavated in 1928–36. Their age is in the late Shang Dynasty, approximately the same period as the oracle bone script. There are altogether 82 clay fragments with 62 single characters. According to Li Xiaoding's research, these characters can be classified into seven categories: (a) numerals,

---

[68] Qiu Xigui (裘锡圭), *An Outline of Philology*, 38, 40.
[69] Li Xiaoding (李孝定), *A Symposium on the Origin and Evolution of Chinese Characters*; Qiu Xigui (裘锡圭), *An Outline of Philology*.

(b) characters of locality, (c) pictographs, (d) personal names or state names, (e) heavenly stems and earthly branches, (f) miscellaneous cases and (g) unknown items.[70] These pottery characters mainly originate from the late Shang Dynasty and are very limited in number and rather fragmentary compared with the oracle bone script. However, by examining the features of the pottery characters in the mature stage of Chinese characters and their relationship with the prevalent characters of the same period, we can be much enlightened in our research on the characters in the early Shang Dynasty and particularly the pottery character-oriented materials of the same period. For example, most of these pottery characters are carved on or near the edges or mouths of the utensils, few are carved in the middle or inside and some on the feet. They appear mostly in single characters (some in multiple characters, or even seven characters at the most). Some characters are carved on the greenware before kilning, perhaps made by the potters; some are carved and painted after kilning, probably made by the users. Compared and examined with the oracle bone script, over 50 recognizable pottery characters are almost identical to the oracle bone script. In the late Shang Dynasty when the oracle bone script had already become mature characters, the pottery characters were mainly used in the form of single characters, lines of characters or more than two characters rarely seen on a utensil, their forms similar to the oracle bone script, their content mainly including recording numerals, marking localities and recording names (personal names, family names and state names). These remind us that if the newly excavated pottery characters before the Yinxu period have the similar features as mentioned earlier, we can naturally use them as the Chinese character specimen of their period and then estimate their relationship with the prevalent characters of their period. This is why we do not introduce Xiaotun pottery characters in the early Shang Dynasty.

---

[70] Cf. Pottery Characters: 'Xiaotun Yinxu Implements Part A: Pottery Utensils'. *Chinese Archeological Report Series Part II.* Li Xiaoding fully researched and interpreted these pottery characters and conducted frequent discussions in his research papers on the origin and evolution of Chinese characters. Cf. 'Research and Interpretations of Xiaotun Pottery Characters', pictures of pottery character rubbings and related papers in Li Xiaoding's *A Symposium on the Origin and Evolution of Chinese Characters.*

Li Xiaoding was obviously illuminated by Xiaotun pottery characters in his research on the prehistorical pottery characters and the origin and evolution of Chinese characters.[71]

Gaocheng Taixi Pottery Characters

Taixi pottery characters were discovered at the site of the Shang Dynasty ruins in Gaocheng, Hebei Province. They are earlier than Xiaotun pottery characters, their early period equalling the time between Erligang upper layer and Xingtai Caoyanzhuang lower layer of characters in the early Shang Dynasty and their late period equalling the earlier time of Yinxu early civilization.[72] At the site of the relics in both the early and late periods, altogether 77 pottery pieces were discovered with the characters that had been carved before kilning, usually with only one character or sign, occasionally with two characters or signs. The content can generally be divided into two categories: one category includes numerical signs, such as '一, 二, 三, 四, 五, 六, 七, 八, 九', which seem to indicate the relationship of sets of utensils; the other category contains tribal and personal names, such as '臣, 止, 巳, 己, 丰, 乙, 鱼, 大, 刀, 戈'. In addition, there are some characters that have not been recognized yet.[73] Ji Yun (季云) conducted research on the 12 pieces of pottery characters excavated from the Shang Dynasty relics in Taixi Village in 1973, and compared them with the Shang Dynasty pottery characters excavated from Zhengzhou and Anyang. He thinks that the Taixi pottery characters have some inherited relationship with the Yinxu pottery characters of the same type, and speculates that the Taixi pottery characters basically reflect the features of the characters prevalent in the period of the

---

[71] Cf. Li Xiaoding, 'On the Origin of Chinese Characters Based on the Research of the Prehistorical and Earliest Historical Pottery Characters', 'A Second Thought on the Prehistorical Pottery Characters and the Origin of Chinese Characters' and 'Signs and Characters: A Third Thought on the Prehistorical Pottery Characters and the Origin of Chinese Characters', in *A Symposium on the Origin and Evolution of Chinese Characters* (Taipei: Linking Publishing, 1986).

[72] Taixi Archaeological Team, Department of Cultural Relics of Hebei Province, 'A Bulletin of the Shang Relic Site Excavation at Taixi Village, Gaocheng, Hebei Province', *Cultural Relics* 6 (1979).

[73] Ibid.

Shang relics. Of the 12 pottery character pieces, 7 are from the earlier period and the later 4 pieces are no later than the Yinxu period. In terms of the excavation coverage, the pottery characters are very densely distributed. As a result, he thinks that 'the characters of Taixi period are in fact from the early Yinxu stage'.[74] The Gaocheng Taixi pottery characters are earlier than Yinxu period, the forms of which can verify the oracle bone script. They enable us to see some earlier characters in addition to the Yinxu characters, by which we can speculate that the pottery characters from Gaocheng site are the invaluable relics of the characters prevalent in the place during that period. By the lucid lines, fluent and natural handwriting, we can detect the level of the use and development of the characters during that period.

Wucheng Pottery Characters

The Wucheng pottery characters were discovered in Wucheng Village, 35 km to the southwest of Qingjiang County, Jiangxi Province, in the 1970s. The excavation site is a large-scale site of relics in the Shang Dynasty to the south of the Yangtze River. The first period of the site equals the upper layer of Erligang in the mid-Yin-Shang period; the second period equals the early and mid-Yin-Shang period; the third period equals the late Yin-Shang period. In the three excavations from the winter of 1973 to the fall of 1974, 14 pieces (1 piece collected) of implements with 39 carved characters were discovered from the first period; from the second period, there were 16 pieces with 19 carved characters; from the third period, there were 8 pieces with 8 carved (or pressed) characters. From the three periods, there were altogether 38 pieces of implements with 66 carved characters. Some of the characters on the implements are single characters, some are in combination with more than 2 characters and some others may amount to 12 characters and signs at most.[75] From the fourth excavation in 1975, more characters were discovered, and according to the archaeological report, together with the archaeological finds in the winters of 1974

---

[74] Ji Yun (季云), 'The Pottery Characters Excavated at the Shang Relic Site at Taixi Village, Gaocheng', *Cultural Relics* 8 (1974).
[75] Jiangxi Provincial Museum, 'A Bulletin of the Shang Relic Site at Wucheng, Qingjiang, Jiangxi Province', *Cultural Relics* 7 (1975).

and 1975 and from the three previous excavations, there are altogether 77 characters, 11 of which are carved on 1 piece of pottery, the rest of which are mostly single characters carved on single pieces and only 2 of which are carved or pressed on the pottery in 2 or 3 cases. The characters identical with those in the previous excavations are '五, 矢, 在, 戈, 大', etc., and there are quite some new characters as well.[76] Tang Lan (唐兰) discussed the nature of Wucheng Relics as well as characters discovered there, thinking that in the Shang Dynasty, Qingjiang (清江) might be the habitat of the Yue nationality and some Wucheng characters entirely different from the Shang–Zhou characters are most likely to be another kind of ancient characters long forgotten.[77] Wucheng Relics and the characters on the pottery and stone moulds are invaluable materials for academic research in the development of Chinese characters. They concern our understanding of the features of these relics and of the characters. For example, Dai Jingbiao (戴敬标) thinks that Wucheng pottery characters reflect the written record of the yarrow divination in the southern areas.[78] Li Xiaoding does not agree to Tang Lan's view on these pottery characters but thinks:

> The inhabitants of Wucheng during that period are in fact very close to the Han nationality in both language and characters. These differences are the phenomenon before the characters reach their mature stage and the similarities are the result of their maturity. In effect, these pottery characters have a hereditary relationship with those of previous different periods as well as the oracle bone script and bronze script.[79]

---

[76] Jiangxi Provincial Museum et al., 'The Major Finds of the Fourth Excavation at the Shang Relic Site at Wucheng, Qingjiang, Jiangxi Province', in *A Symposium on the Cultural Relics* 2 (Beijing: Cultural Relics Publishing House, 1978).

[77] Tang Lan (唐兰), 'A Preliminary Exploration of the Cultural Relic Site at Wucheng, Jiangxi Province and Chinese Characters', *Cultural Relics* 7 (1975).

[78] Dai Jingbiao (戴敬标), 'A Preliminary Comment on the Ancient Southern Oracles: Some Identification of Wucheng Pottery Characters', in *Proceedings of the Conference for the Founding of Jiangxi Archeological Society and the Academic Seminar*, comp. Jiangxi Archeological Society (Lushan: Jiangxi Archeological Society, 1986).

[79] Li Xiaoding (李孝定), 'A Second Thought on the Prehistorical Pottery Characters and the Origin of Chinese Characters', 217.

It is true that some of the Wucheng pottery characters differ considerably from the conventional Chinese characters, such as the seven characters on the bottom of the grey pelitic pottery bowl (fall of 1974, T7⑤: 51) and the five characters on the bottom of the yellow pelitic pottery jar (fall of 1974, T7⑤: 58), both from the first period. 'They have unique features that do not seem to belong to the system of the Shang culture'.[80] However, many of the pottery characters undoubtedly belong to the Chinese character system of the Shang Dynasty; some correspond to the Taixi characters and some others are comparable with the oracle bone script and bronze script of the late Shang Dynasty. The correct view would be that in the Qingjiang area of that period, the Shang characters were commonly used with their strong influence and some local cultural elements were also preserved with the characters created by the people who had long lived in that area. Our attention is more focused on the pottery characters which had been used as early as the mid-Shang Dynasty, continued to the late Shang Dynasty and were related to the Shang characters. The most attractive of these characters should be the characters around the shoulder part of the pelitic yellow pottery pot (fall of 1974, T7⑤: 46) and those on the bottom of the pelitic grey bowl (collected at the western dam foundation in 1974) of the first period. They are in lines, eight characters in the former and four in the latter, and they seem continuous. In fact, there are altogether 12 characters and signs with 4 smaller signs, which do not seem to be characters, carved on the upper bow string patterns. Tang Lan thinks that these pottery characters undoubtedly belong to the same system of the Shang–Zhou characters and interprets some characters as '止, 豆, 木, 帚, 十, 中', etc.[81] Li Xueqin (李学勤) reads them as '帚臣燎豆之宗, 仲, 七' and suspects that '帚' is a place name and '燎豆' is a person's name, and it is a sacrificial utensil.[82] The author has then made some changes to this explanation. The interpretation of the

---

[80] Qiu Xigui (裘锡圭), *An Outline of Philology*, 37.
[81] Tang Lan (唐兰), 'A Preliminary Exploration of the Cultural Relic Site at Wucheng, Jiangxi Province and Chinese Characters'.
[82] Li Xueqin (李学勤), 'On the Bronze Ware and the Dissemination of the Shang Culture', in *A Study of the Newly Excavated Bronze Implements* (Beijing: Cultural Relics Publishing House, 1990). Originally published in *Ta Kung Pao* (1 May 1978).

pottery characters also concerns the matter of order. Zhao Feng insists that '中' should be the first character of the line. Xiao Liangqiong (萧良琼) thinks that the line can be read as '中宗之豆, 燎臣帚, 七'. '中宗' is '祖乙', the son of '仲丁' and '燎臣' is an official title. '帚' is related to '帚', the name of the state of Nantufang (南土方国), which is near Wucheng, Qingjiang, today[83] and which is close to '我' recorded in the oracle bone script. Rao Zongyi (饶宗颐) agrees to Xiao Liangqiong's interpretation and repunctuates the line as '中宗之豆, 燎。臣帚七'.[84] Another important collected utensil, the grey pottery bowl from the first period, has four characters in two lines on its bottom. Tang Lan interprets the left line as '帚田', pointing out that 'in the oracle characters, '帚' was often used as '妇'; he takes the right line most likely as '且', for 'in the Shang Dynasty', '且' was often used as '祖'.[85] However, Li Xueqin explains the line as '帚田人土', speculating that '帚' is a place name, '田人' is the official title '甸人' and '土' is a person's name.[86] To this explanation, he has made some changes. Xiao Liangqiong considers these pottery characters as the following: 'The sacrificial utensil used by the official of Dianren (甸人) at the temple in the place of Zhou (帚)'.[87] Although there are differences in reading and understanding the characters on the two pottery utensils, consensus has been reached in two aspects: first, they belong to the same character system as the oracle bone script in the mid-Shang Dynasty; second, the content of the utensils and characters is related to sacrificial activities. In addition to the two pottery utensils on which sentences are formed by the characters, the pink sandstone

---

[83] Xiao Liangqiong (萧良琼), 'The Character 帚 in the Wucheng Pottery Characters and the Southern Territory of the Shang Dynasty', in *Collected Papers for Mr. Zhang Zhenglang's Eightieth Birthday*, ed. Wu Rongzeng (Beijing: China Social Sciences Press, 1996), 92–97. Li Xueqin's and Zhao Feng's views can be seen from the quotations in this paper.

[84] Yao Zongyi (饶宗颐), *Signs: Preliminary Characters and Graphemes—The Tree of Chinese Characters* (Hong Kong: The Commercial Press, 1998), 57.

[85] Tang Lan (唐兰), 'A Preliminary Exploration on the Cultural Relic Site and Characters in Wucheng, Jiangxi', *Cultural Relics* 7 (1975).

[86] Li Xueqin, 'On the Bronze Ware and the Dissemination of the Shang Culture'.

[87] Xiao Liangqiong, 'The Character 帚 in the Wucheng Pottery Characters and the Southern Territory of the Shang Dynasty', 93.

mould (1974, ET13H6: 23) on which two characters are carved is also very important, for the two characters pronounced as '又' and '有' in the Yinxu oracles appear on this stone mould.[88] The characters on the two pottery utensils and the stone mould demonstrate that the Wucheng pottery characters record not only numerals and clan names but also events. This reveals the fact that by the time of the mid-Shang Dynasty, the Chinese characters had already entered the mature stage, which is further proved by the character users of the period as well as the extensive area of the use. Most of the pottery characters are carved or painted on the greenware before kilning and glazing, and their hasty and careless style shows obvious marks of the potters. Wucheng is situated to the south of the Yangtze River. Despite the strong regional colour preserved in its relics, the prevalent use of the Chinese characters there reflects the wide and profound impact brought about by the powerful expansion of the Shang Dynasty.[89]

Xingan Pottery Characters (新干陶文)

These characters were excavated from the Shang tombs at Dayangzhou Village, Xingan, Jiangxi Province (江西省新干大洋洲乡), in 1989. The number of the intact and recovered pottery and protoporcelain utensils amount to 139 pieces. On the zhejian (折肩) pots, brownware urns and hard pottery big-mouthed vats, characters are carved usually in the form of an individual character or two characters, mostly on the shoulders or bottoms of the utensils. They are mainly numerals like '五, 七, 十', and the most repeated character is '戈', whose form is basically the same as that of the Wucheng characters. In addition, there appears the character '晶' on the bottoms of the hard pottery zhejian pot (XDM: 511) and the protoporcelain zhejian pot (Model I, XDM: 503), and there appear the two characters '戈革(?)' written together

---

[88] Cf. Tang Lan, 'A Preliminary Exploration on the Cultural Relic Site and Characters in Wucheng, Jiangxi', Diagram 6. This character was also discovered at Erligang Relic Site, Zhengzhou. See more details in the next paper.

[89] Jiang Hong (江鸿, i.e., Lixueqin李学勤), 'Panlongcheng and the Southern Territory of the Shang Dynasty', in *Library of the Contemporary Scholars' Self Selections: Li Xueqin's Selected Works* (Hefei: Anhui Education Publishing House, 1999), 110–20.

on the shoulders of the brownware urns (XDM: 534 and XDM: 535).[90] On this site, there are abundant excavated relics of 475 pieces of bronze ware and 754 pieces of jade ware with high standards, so it is suspected that the tomb occupants may be very high-ranking rulers. The Xingan Shang tombs have strong regional cultural colour, which belong to the constituent part of the Qingjiang Wucheng culture. The pottery utensils with the carved characters are similar to those from the second period of the Wucheng excavation, with the similar characters and burial time around the early period of the late Shang Dynasty. The discovery of the Xingan Shang tombs proves that there exists highly advanced civilization in the Wucheng cultural region, which is unique of its own features and is also strongly influenced by the Shang civilization on the Central Plain.[91] The correspondence between the Xingan pottery characters and the Wucheng pottery characters demonstrates the influence of the Shang civilization from the Central Plain on the Wucheng regional culture to the south of the Yangtze River, and it also proves the extensive use and prevalence of Chinese characters in this region from the mid-Shang Dynasty to the early period of the late Shang Dynasty. It provides us with new reference in evaluating the developmental level of the characters in the early Shang Dynasty.

Xiaoshuangqiao Pottery Characters (小双桥陶文)

The Xiaoshuangqiao pottery characters were discovered on the site of Shang cultural relics in Xiaoshuangqiao Village, Zhengzhou City, Henan Province. The site was discovered in 1989, and the archaeological excavation took place several times in 1995. It proves to be a very important site of the capital ruins in the mid-Shang Dynasty,[92]

---

[90] Cf. Jiangxi Cultural Relic Archeological Institute et al., comp. *Xingan Shang Tombs* (Beijing: Cultural Relic Press, 1997), Diagrams 83, 84, 85, 86, 87, 89, 90. For the interpretation of '戈革(?)', cf. Li Xueqin, 'Several Issues Concerning Xingan Dayangzhou Shang Tombs', *Cultural Relics* 10 (1991), included in *Library of the Contemporary Scholars' Self Selections: Li Xueqin's Selected Works*.

[91] Li Xueqin, 'Several Issues Concerning Xingan Dayangzhou Shang Tombs'.

[92] Henan Cultural Relic Archeological Institute et al., 'The Excavation of the Relic Site at Xiaoshuangqiao, Zhengzhou, 1995', *Huaxia Archeology* 3 (1996).

and many scholars claim that it is the capital Ao (隞都) that Zhong Ding (仲丁) moved to. Zou Heng (邹衡) thinks that the site of relics can be classified into three periods: the first equals the later Erliguang (二里岗) lower layer, the second equals the Erliguang upper layer and the third belongs to the Baijiazhuang (白家庄) period. The Xiaoshuangqiao site is basically the third period, generally equalling the last Zhengzhou Shang Capital (郑州商城) period when the site was already in ruins and Xiaoshuangqiao succeeded it as the new capital of the King of Shang Dynasty.[93] On the pottery utensils at the Xiaoshuangqiao site, there are not only the carved characters but also the characters are in red. These carved pottery characters are simple in form, some on the outside of the bowl rim, some on the outside of the vat rim or the outside of the vat bottom and on the vat rim, and some on the surface of the basin rim. The pottery characters in red are often written on the surface of the small vat and a few are written on the outside of the big vat rim or the inside of the small vat rim or the surface of the utensil lid.[94] The carving of the characters is simple and spontaneous mostly with numerals and marks, seemingly by the potters' hands. However, the pottery characters in red are an important discovery. In his paper 'The Red Characters on the Pottery Utensils Excavated from the Site of Xiaoshuangqiao, Zhengzhou', Song Guoding (宋国定) publicizes the related materials and conducts the preliminary research. He classifies the written pottery characters into three types according to contents: the first includes numerals such as '二, 三, 七', etc.; the second includes pictographs or emblems, more pictographs concerning the human body; the third includes other

---

[93] There is disagreement on whether this relic site is the capital. Chen Xu (陈旭) strongly upholds the view that it is the capital of the Shang dynasty and he published several papers on this issue. Zou Heng (邹衡) et al. support this view. Cf. Chen Xu, 'On the View that the Shang Relic Site at Xiaoshuangqiao, Zhengzhou Is the Shang Capital', *Zhongyuan Cultural Relics* 2 (1997); Zou Heng, 'A Supplement on the View that the Shang Relic Site at Xiaoshuangqiao, Zhengzhou Is the Shang Capital', *Archeology and Cultural Relics* 4 (1998). They have offered convincing archaeological and documentary evidence and proposal on the time of the establishment of the capital.

[94] Henan Cultural Relic Archeological Institute et al., 'The Excavation of the Relic Site at Xiaoshuangqiao, Zhengzhou, 1995'. See the attached Diagram 19 on the carved pottery signs.

types.⁹⁵ These pottery vats are mainly royal sacrificial utensils, but the meanings of the characters in red need further investigation. The structures and features of these pottery characters have obvious commonalities with the Yin-Shang bone and tortoise shell inscriptions and bronze script. The Yin-Shang characters should be the further development of the early Shang characters represented by the pottery characters. Although the pottery characters are limited in number, most of them are comparable with the oracle bone script and bronze script. Their strokes and lines are lucid, balanced, natural and fluent. Considering that these characters are written by soft writing instruments, we can speculate that the writers had very skilfully mastered the handwriting techniques, which demonstrates that both the characters and the handwriting had developed into a considerably high level, far from the primordial state. Although most of the pottery characters appear in the form of an individual character, some appear in the form of more than two characters. For example, there are two lines and three characters on the pottery piece H43: 21, Section 95ZXV and three characters between the bow string patterns on the pottery piece T105③: 01, Section 95ZXV, which are unfortunately damaged and hard to recognize. The phenomenon of more than two characters linked by handwriting is an important clue that they can record language. This seems to suggest that by the period of the Xiaoshuangqiao site of relics, Chinese characters had already matured and developed into the level of recording language, which is very significant to interpret the information provided by the Wucheng and Xingan pottery characters.

Zhengzhou Shang Capital Pottery Characters (郑州商城陶文)

Since the discovery of the Zhengzhou Shang Capital site of relics in the early 1950s, there have been a series of significant archaeological achievements. This site has rich cultural accumulation, reflecting the progression from the late Longshan (龙山) culture and Luodamiao (洛达庙) culture to the Shang Dynasty culture. The Zhengzhou Shang Capital site of relics should belong to the relics of the early Shang

---

⁹⁵ Song Guoding (宋国定), 'The Red Characters on the Pottery Utensils Excavated at Xiaoshuangqiao Relic Site, Zhengzhou', *Cultural Relics* 5 (2003).

Dynasty capital, originally constructed around the second period of the Erligang lower layer, being continuously used until the first and second periods of the Erligang upper layer and then ruined around the late second period (Baijiazhuang period) of the Erligang upper layer.[96] There is no doubt that Zhengzhou Shang Capital is the site of the capital ruins; however, there is now controversy as to which capital it is.[97] The Zhengzhou Shang Capital pottery characters are mainly distributed in the relics of the Erligang period, in which dozens of pottery characters and signs are carved on the inside of the big-mouthed wine vessel rim of the lower layer and second period;[98] on the inside of the big-mouthed wine vessel rim of the upper layer and first period, there are also dozens of pottery characters and signs.[99] Some of the pottery characters are numerals that record numbers, many of such characters on the lower layer of the second period and the upper layer of the first period being repeated, such as '一, 二, 三, 四, 五, 六, 七, 十', etc.; some are pictographs, such as '矢, 木, 网, 黽, 臣, 鸟', etc.; some signs are not recognizable, but they should belong to a type of characters. These pottery characters and signs appear on the pottery utensils in the prosperous period when the Shang Capital was completed. These utensils are mainly big-mouthed wine vessels, and from the Xiaoshuangqiao pottery characters mainly spread on the sacrificial pottery utensils, we can infer that these big-mouthed wine vessels may also serve sacrificial purposes, or they should at least be utensils for important purposes at the royal court. From the results of the current

---

[96] Henan Cultural Relic Archeological Institute, *Zhengzhou Shang Capital: Archeological Excavation Report 1953–1985* (Beijing: Cultural Relics Publishing House, 2001).

[97] There are mainly two views: Capital Ao (隞都) and Capital Hao (亳都) and Tian Changwu (田昌五) et al. estimated that Zhengzhou Shang capital might be first established in Taijia's reign according to the rise and fall of Yanshi Shang capital and Zhongding's move to the place of Ao. Tian Changwu et al., 'On Zhengzhou Shang Capital', *Zhongyuan Cultural Relics* 2 (1994). The discovery of Xiaoshuangqiao and the determination of its nature have supplied new and important reference to the study of Zhengzhou and Yanshi Shang capital.

[98] Henan Cultural Relic Archeological Institute, *Zhengzhou Shang Capital: Archeological Excavation Report 1953–1985*, Diagrams 449 and 450, Printing Plate 134–1, 2, 4 on page 657; Diagrams 556–2, 3 on page 827.

[99] Ibid., Diagrams 516–20, Printing Plate 49 on 762; Diagram 619–9 on page 928.

archaeological excavation and research, Zhengzhou Shang Capital is a little later than Yanshi Shang Capital but earlier than Xiaoshuangqiao site of relics. Zhengzhou Shang Capital entered the stage of ruins on the Erligang upper layer of the second period, when Xiaoshuangqiao site of relics was right in prosperity. The Xiaoshuangqiao red pottery characters are in the hereditary relationship with the Zhengzhou Shang Capital pottery characters as the important materials of the early Shang Dynasty characters. The Zhengzhou Shang Capital characters and signs are bold and skilful in their carving techniques, reflecting strict structures in their seeming casualness. For example, in *Zhengzhou Shang Capital: Archeological Reports 1953−1985*, we can see such characteristics in Nos. 10, 13 and 19 of Picture 449; Nos. 2, 7 and 15 of Picture 450; Nos. 11, 16, 17 and 18 of Picture 516; No. 14 of Picture 518; Nos. 4, 7, 11 and 14 of Picture 519; etc. In particular, the two characters '臣' and '鸟' in Picture 520 are most skilful in their strokes, and accurate and vivid in their lines despite the hard writing instrument used for the carving. Although these characters and signs appear individually (some few linked in pairs), they all send out the information that by the Zhengzhou Shang Capital period, the Chinese characters and their writing had already developed into a considerably advanced stage.

In addition to the pottery characters from the Zhengzhou Erligang period, there are also other related discoveries. The pattern on the neck decoration of the small-mouthed taotie (饕餮) wooden wine vessel (C8M2: 1) excavated from the upper layer of the first period may be interpreted as the character '黽'. Tang Lan does not only interpret the pattern as '黽' but also points out that there is the character '庸' on a dagger-axe, which combines the two vertical strokes, representing the fortress walls, into one vertical stroke, both '黽' and '庸' being clan names.[100] On the upper layer of the first period, there are also two stone implements carved with characters. One is the specimen C5.3T302①: 93, an oval pebble carved with a very complicated pictograph; the other is the specimen C15T7②: 17, a flat stone spade with a handle

---

[100] Tang Lan (唐兰), 'My Comment Starting from the Early Shang Bronze Ware Excavated in Zhengzhou, Henan', in *Collected Works on the Bronze Scripts* (Beijing: The Forbidden City Press, 1995), 481–93.

carved with an arrow-head-like sign (the character '矢').[101] Two pieces of ox bones with characters were also discovered at Erligang in 1953: one upper joint bone is carved with the common character pronounced as '又, 有' from the Yinxu oracle bone inscriptions; the other rib bone is carved with 10 characters, interpreted as '......又土(社)羊。乙丑贞, 从受......七月'.[102] These fragments of characters reflect the general background in which Zhengzhou Shang Capital pottery characters were used, and record the important information about the development and use of the characters. In particular, the discovery of the bones carved with characters does not only indicate that the Erligang Shang characters were able to record language, but it also traces the origin of Yinxu oracle bone inscriptions to the early Shang Dynasty.

Yanshi Shang Capital Pottery Characters (偃师商城陶文)

Strictly speaking, since the discovery of Yanshi Shang Capital in 1983, not many pottery characters have been discovered in over 20 years' archaeological excavation. Up until now, only two cases of discovery were reported concerning the excavation of the Yanshi Shang Capital palace ruins in the spring of 1984: one case is an arrow-head-like sign (J1D4H24: 52) carved on the inside of a pottery cooking vessel rim excavated from the ash pit; the other case is an arrow-head-like sign carved on the middle of a pottery mug (J1D4H36: 1).[103] Most scholars think that Yanshi Shang Capital is no other than Haodu, the earliest capital of the Shang Dynasty

---

[101] Henan Cultural Relic Archeological Institute, *Zhengzhou Shang Capital: Archeological Excavation Report 1953–1985*, Diagram 557–2, 3. 829.

[102] Pei Mingxiang (裴明相), 'Brief Comment on the Early Shang Bone Characters', in *Collected Papers for the National Symposium on the Shang History*, ed. Hu Houxuan (胡厚宣), *Yindu Academic Journal*, supplementary issue (1985), 251–53.

[103] Henan Team 2, the Archeological Institute of China Academy of Social Sciences, 'Bulletin of the Shang Capital Palace Site Excavation at Shixiang, Yanshi, Spring of 1984', Archeology 4 (1985), later included in *A Study of Yanshi Shang Capital Relic Site*, ed. Du Jinpeng and Wang Xuerong (杜金鹏, 王學榮) (Beijing: Science Press, 2004).

when Chengtang defeated the Xia Dynasty, and it is an extremely important discovery for the Xia and Shang archaeological and historical research.[104] The establishment of Yanshi Shang Capital is linked with the time of the No. 1 palace ruins of the Erlitou late third period (approx 1,600 BC), a time when the Xia Dynasty was declining and the Shang Dynasty was rising. By the Erligang upper layer period, Zhengzhou Shang Capital had reached its prosperous period while Yanshi Shang Capital began to decline. The decline and rise of Yanshi Shang Capital, Zhengzhou Shang Capital and Xiaoshuangqiao are generally linked in an interactive manner. As large numbers of pottery characters and other character materials were discovered in both the ruins of Zhengzhou Shang Capital and Xiaoshuangqiao, why have only two cases of the aforementioned characters been discovered so far in Yanshi Shang Capital? Is it because they have not yet been excavated, or because the people during that period did not have the habit of carving characters on pottery utensils, or because the Shang people before the Zhengzhou Erligang period had not yet well mastered characters? This is a question worth our deeper consideration and requiring our further discussions.

From this, we have conducted a comprehensive collation and analysis of the various pottery characters and written materials from the archaeological finds before Xiaotun period. By these materials, chronologically, we can trace the time to the Shang–Tang period; geographically, we find both the Shang capitals, such as the ruins of Zhengzhou Shang Capital and Xiaoshuangqiao and local places such as Gaocheng Taixi as well as the area to the south of the Yangtze River, much influenced by the Shang culture, such as Qingjiang Wucheng. All these offer reliable first-hand materials for our further discussion of the general development of the characters in the early Shang Dynasty.

---

[104] *A Study of Yanshi Shang Capital Relic Site* includes the published archaeological reports and research papers since the discovery of Yanshi Shang Capital on the topics of its nature, etc. Cf. Zhao Zhiquan's (赵芝荃) paper 'On the Controversial Issues of Zhengzhou Shang Capital and Yanshi Shang Capital' included in this book.

Some Points of Discussion on the Development of the Characters in the Early Shang Dynasty

We believe that the late Shang Dynasty mature oracle bone inscriptions have laid the foundation for tracing the early Shang Dynasty characters; furthermore, the early Shang Dynasty pottery characters offer direct evidence for the substantial exploration of the development of the characters of that period. Meanwhile, the earlier examination and analysis have raised several questions for us to discuss further.

First of all, it concerns the value of the early Shang Dynasty pottery characters for discussing the development of the characters of that period. The early Shang Dynasty pottery characters excavated so far are fragmentary and limited in number. It is somewhat controversial whether or not they can be used as evidence to speculate the developmental level of the character system of their time. We have stressed earlier in the chapter that the illuminating significance of the Xiaotun pottery characters lies in the fact that they are set against the background of mature oracle bone inscriptions. The fragmentation, limited number, carving style, and mode and content of Xiaotun pottery characters can all serve as the reference for evaluating other pottery characters. Since the Xiaotun pottery characters have such features against the background of the advanced system of the oracle bone inscriptions, can other pottery characters sharing the same features imply a mature character system similar to that of the oracle bone inscriptions? If so, the information revealed in pottery characters would be of great value. This is exactly how we look at the pottery characters. By examining the Shang Dynasty pottery characters, we can see some of their general features.

The first is their wide distribution in space. Not only do we find pottery characters from the early capital site of Zhengzhou Erligang relics to the late capital site of Anyang relics, but we also find the same characters in Gaocheng Hebei outside the Shang capital and Qingjiang to the south of the Yangtze River under the influence of the Shang people.

The second is the continuation in time. The aforementioned series of pottery characters from the Xiaotun period all the way to the

Erligang period of the early Shang Dynasty and even to the Yanshi Shang Capital period provide us with the chronology of pottery characters on a larger scale. This chronology is not only proved in archaeology, but it also generally corresponds to the historical records of the Shang Dynasty.

The third is that there are more similarities than differences. There is a span of over two or three hundred years (approx 17th century BC–14th century BC) from the early stage of the early Shang Dynasty to the mid- and late Shang Dynasty. In terms of the carving style and features as well as the simplicity and maturity level, similarities are obviously more than differences among the pottery characters from the Zhengzhou Erligang period, the Xiaoshuangqiao red characters or the Wucheng and Taixi pottery characters. In particular, there appear some characters such as the numerals and pictographs of '臣, 刀', etc. from several groups of pottery characters, which are almost identical. This shows that the character system reflected by the pottery characters developed in a slow and gradual manner, and different groups of pottery characters shared hereditary continuity.

The fourth is that there are frequent discoveries of characters continuously written. The continuous writing of Wucheng pottery characters of the first period shows that they may have recorded the content related to sacrificial activities. There are also more than three pottery characters continuously written from the Xiaoshuangqiao period. Although there is no reliable evidence for continuously written characters from the Erligang period, the discovery of the characters carved on the bones from the same period may serve as important circumstantial evidence.

From the relevance between the Xiaotun pottery characters and the mature system of the oracle bone script, we are rationally aware that the different groups of pottery characters from the early Shang Dynasty are of much value as specimen in the study of the development of the character system of that period. By these specimen, we can infer that there should be a prevalent character system in the early Shang Dynasty, and the Yinxu bone and tortoise shell inscriptions should be the further development and improvement of that system, which is not very far from the system of the oracle bone script in terms of its developmental level in the early Shang Dynasty.

Second, it concerns the relationship between the Shang characters and the Xia characters. At the site of Yanshi Shang Capital first built by Cheng Tang, founder of the Shang Dynasty, almost no pottery characters have been discovered so far, and those discovered in Zhengzhou Shang Capital are mainly after the Erligang second period of the lower layer. What does this phenomenon suggest? Does it suggest that the characters of Yanshi Shang Capital wait to be excavated or they did not get preserved, or the Shang people simply did not use written characters? From the construction level of Yanshi Shang Capital and the developmental level of the early Shang culture, we should exclude the possibility that the Chinese characters had not been used by the early Shang–Tang period. Zhang Guangzhi (张光直) traces the early Shang culture to the New Stone Age culture discovered on the 'East Coast' of Shandong and North Jiangsu, and by the archaeological materials, he reveals that the Yin-Shang civilization is somehow related to the culture of the eastern area.[105] The pottery characters and signs discovered at several relic sites such as Liangzhu culture (良渚文化) and Dawenkou culture (大汶口文化) have been attracting much attention of the scholars in the research of the origin of the Chinese characters.[106] They can provide important evidence to show that the Shang people of the pre-Shang and early Shang periods may have already entered the stage of creating and using characters. King Tang of Shang rose in the east of Henan, as is described in 'Duke Wen of Teng' in *Mencius*: 'Tang fought eleven battles and defeated

---

[105] Zhang Guangzhi (张光直), 'A Key Issue in the Study of the Origin of Yin-Shang Civilization' and 'The Origins of the Shang Capital and Shang Dynasty and Its Early Civilization', in *The Chinese Bronze Age* (Beijing: SDX Joint Publishing Company, 1999), 98–137.

[106] Li Xueqin (李学勤) has frequent discussions of the characters carved on Liangzhu pottery and Jade. Cf. Li Xueqin, *Out of the Period Doubting the Ancient Times* (Shenyang: Liaoning University Press, 1994). Since the discovery of Dawenkou pottery characters, Yu Xingwu (于省吾), Tang Lan, Li Xueqin, Qiu Xigui and Gao Ming, all wrote on the topic. Cf. Chen Zhaorong (陈昭容), 'A General Discussion on the Origin of Chinese Characters Based on the Exploration of Pottery Characters', in *Collected Papers of Historical Linguistics Institute, Academia Sinica*, vol. 57—4 (Taipei: Academia Sinica, 1986). Li Xiaoding (李孝定), 'Signs and Characters: A Third Consideration of the Origin of Prehistorical Pottery Characters and Chinese Characters'.

all his enemies'. At last he annihilated the Xia Dynasty and founded the Shang Dynasty.[107] Yanshi Shang Capital, as the founding capital, is the direct material evidence for the civilization of the Shang–Tang period. The archaeological discovery of the Shang Capital makes it hard to imagine that in the Shang–Tang period, the development of its characters was still at such a low level, or its characters were not even created. This can neither accord with the general rules of the development of civilization nor explain the development of the characters in the Erligang and Xiaoshuangqiao periods or even the late Shang period. Thus, the reason why not enough characters were discovered at the site of Yanshi Shang Capital is perhaps that the conditions for the preservation are inadequate or more relics need to be discovered. As a result, we believe that by the time when the Shang Dynasty was founded by Tang, its characters should have entered the mature stage.

If we assume that the Shang Dynasty entered the mature stage for its characters, then what is the relationship between the Shang characters and Xia characters? This is another important topic worth further research. Limited by space, we will only conduct a brief discussion here. The relationship between the Shang characters and Xia characters, first of all, concerns the relationship between the Shang Dynasty and the Xia Dynasty, or the relationship between the Shang Dynasty, the Xia Dynasty and the Western Zhou Dynasty. In traditional Confucianism and the old school of historical scholarship, these 'three dynasties' were described as being in the hereditary relationship chronologically replacing one another, while the contemporary scholars find new clues from the archaeological materials and use comparative sociological views to reassess the historical records and discuss the formations of the Xia, Shang and Zhou Dynasties as ancient states as well as the diachronic and synchronic relationship between the three dynasties. Zhang Guangzhi shows in his research:

> The relationship between the Xia, Shang and Zhou dynasties is not only a hereditary relationship between the dynasties succeeding one another, but also a relationship between the different states

---

[107] Sun Miao (孙淼), in *A History of Xia and Shang Dynasties* (Beijing: Cultural Relics Press, 1987).

coexisting and competing with one another. Considering the whole situation of North China, we take the latter as the main relationship between the three states while the successions of dynasties only represent the rise and fall of the powers of the three states.[108]

'Based on the material relics, the cultures of the three states are very close: even if they may not be the same nationality, they are of the same type of nationalities'.

Based on the political systems, 'the government forms and the governance resources of the three dynasties are also similar'. 'All the three dynasties are the components of the unique ancient Chinese civilization, and their differences are secondary in importance in terms of culture and ethnicity'.[109] This new awareness provides us with the theoretical basis for our general command of the relationship between the Xia and Shang characters. According to this view, the Xia, Shang and Zhou characters should have more 'closeness' or 'similarities' than differences. They belong to the same system. 'The view that the Xia, Shang and Zhou characters belong to the same system' can also be proved by the actual characters of archaeological excavations. For example, the relationship between the Shang and Zhou characters is clearly revealed due to the discovery of the Zhouyuan oracle bone inscriptions (周原甲骨文). The Zhouyuan oracle bone inscriptions are mainly the works in King Wen's reign of the Western Zhou Dynasty, characters of which are hereditary with the Yinxu oracle bone inscriptions, except that their style is a little different and their usage is slightly differentiated, which fully proves that the Shang and Zhou characters belong to the same system.[110] Examined from the early Western Zhou Dynasty bronze relics, the inscriptions of King Wu's and King Cheng's periods, such as the Bronze Victory Gui Inscriptions (利簋铭) made on the eighth day when King Wu of Zhou defeated

---

[108] Zhang Guangzhi (张光直), 'On the Relations Between the Xia, Shang and Zhou Dynasties and the Formation of Chinese Ancient States Based on the Archeological Excavations of the Three Dynasties', *Chinese Bronze Age*, 66–97.

[109] Ibid., 42–65.

[110] Wang Yuxin (王宇信), *An Exploration of the Western Zhou Oracle Bone Characters* (Beijing: China Social Sciences Press, 1984).

King Zhou of Shang, are similar in content and writing style to the bronze inscriptions of the late Shang Dynasty.[111] This is the clear proof that the Shang and Zhou characters belong to the same system. Although the relationship between the Xia and Shang characters does not reveal the similar powerful evidence for that between the Shang and Zhou characters, there are still traces of interconnection between them. All kinds of evidence, either from historical legends or documentary records or archaeological finds, show that the Xia Dynasty should be the beginning of Chinese civilization and that as a sign of the origin of civilization, the Xia characters should have already been formed.[112] Li Xiandeng (李先登) discussed the topic of the Xia characters quite a few times. In the 1981 archaeological excavation of Wangchenggang (王城岗) relics, he discovered a character '共' carved on the greenware, the form of which is similar to the Shang and Zhou character '共'. He considers it as the Xia character and then further argues that the early Xia Dynasty had already entered the stage of using characters and that the Chinese characters were created by the Xia people in the early Xia Dynasty.[113] At the relic site of Yanshi Erlitou (偃师二里头) representing the Xia culture, more than 20 pottery signs were discovered, most of which were carved on the rims of big-mouthed wine vessels and curling-rimmed basins after kilning. In terms of the style and structure, they should belong to the same system with the Erligang pottery characters and Xiaoshuangqiao red characters, many of which may correspond with the oracle bone script.[114] Based on our judgement of the value of the pottery characters,

---

[111] Zhu Fenghan (朱凤瀚), *Ancient Chinese Bronzeware* (Tianjin: Nankai University Press, 1995), 454–55.

[112] The Xia–Shang–Zhou Chronology State Research Project was initiated in 1996. Many important results on the Xia civilization will be subsequently published. Cf. Li Xiandeng (李先登), 'A Review and Prospect of the Pre-Qin Archeological Discovery and Research in the Past 20 Years', in *An Exploration of the Xia, Shang and Zhou Bronze Civilization* (Beijing: Science Press, 2001), 116–18.

[113] Li Xiandeng (李先登), 'A Tentative Study of the Origin of Chinese Characters', *Journal of Tianjin Normal University* 4 (1985), *An Exploration of the Xia, Shang and Zhou Bronze Civilization* (267–73).

[114] Du Jinpeng (杜金鹏), 'On the Issue of Carved Signs and Characters in Erlitou Civilization', *Chinese Calligraphy* 2 (2001).

this should also be very valuable materials to prove the developmental level of Xia characters. To infer the relationship between the Xia and Shang characters by that between the Shang and Zhou characters and base ourselves on these materials, we can judge that 'the view that the Xia, Shang and Zhou characters belong to the same system' is well grounded. As King Tang of Shang built the capital in Yanshi right in the centre of the Xia Dynasty, due to their cultural affinity, the Shang Dynasty easily integrated and continued the Xia culture, and naturally inherited and developed the Xia characters. There are no fundamental differences between this and the Western Zhou's inheritance and development of the Shang culture.

Third, it concerns the issue of 'only the Yin ancestors having books and canons'. The formation of the bamboo and wooden script system is the result of the maturity and extensive use of the Chinese characters. The two characters '册' and '典' are the direct reflection of the character forms in the bamboo and wooden script system.[115] The use of '册' and '典' in the Yinxu bone and tortoise shell inscriptions shows that by the late Shang Dynasty, the bamboo and wooden script system had already been established and the prevalent writing materials then were bamboo and wooden slips and not bones and tortoise shells. This has already been pointed out by many scholars. Meanwhile, there are also other clues in the oracle bone script that prove this point. Based on the writing of the oracle bone script, the features of straight lines and vertical directions as mentioned earlier are the obvious manifestations on the oracle bone script, characteristics formed after the long-term writing on the bamboo and wooden slips. You Shunzhao (游顺钊) thinks that the determining factor for the formation of straight lines and vertical directions in Chinese character writing is the bamboo slips. This view is undoubtedly correct.[116] In the mid-Shang Dynasty, there even appeared some evidence that the bones and tortoise shells were linked according to how bamboo slips

---

[115] Qian Cunxun (钱存训), 8, *Scripts on Bamboo Slips and Silk* (Shanghai: Shanghai Bookstore Press, 2002).

[116] You Shunzhao (游顺钊), 'The Causes of Vertical Writing of Ancient Chinese Characters: An Exploration Outside the Six Script Categories', *Studies of the Chinese Language* 5 (1992).

were linked together.[117] This shows that the bamboo and wooden slips were not only the prevalent writing materials, then but they also enjoyed a long history by the late Shang Dynasty. The prevalence of the bamboo and wooden script system requires two conditions: one is that bamboo as the material was easy to obtain and the other is that soft pens and dye were invented for writing instruments and material. In the oracle bone script, there are characters written with writing brushes and red ink, and there grew abundance of bamboo material in ancient North China.[118] The Xiaoshuangqiao red characters made the history of writing characters with writing brushes and dye as early as Zhong Ding's reign (仲丁之世) of the mid-Shang Dynasty. In addition, the skilful and fluent character lines reflected in the Xiaoshuangqiao red characters are by no means the primordial stage for brush writing. Therefore, we speculate that writing brushes were already used as prevalent means of writing on bamboo or wooden slips. In fact, the patterns and signs on the coloured pottery in the New Stone Age show that the history of using writing brushes (or soft pens) can be dated as early as before the formation of the Chinese civilization.[119] These provide archaeological evidence for the record of 'only the Yin ancestors having books and canons' in 'Duoshi' from *The Book of History*. The fact that the 'ancestors' of the Yin people could have 'canons and books' obviously reveals the fact that the characters then had developed into a mature stage, which was consistently supported with the information indicated by the Erligang pottery characters and Xiaoshuangqiao pottery characters. However, in this sentence, the 'ancestors' are indefinite reference and who they refer to concerns the definite time when the Yin people started to have 'canons and

---

[117] Li Xueqin, 'A Preliminary Investigation of the Bone and Tortoise Shell Oracles at Daxinzhuang, Jinan', *Literature, History & Philosophy* 8 (2003), *Ten Lectures on Ancient Chinese Civilization* (Shanghai: Fudan University Press, 2003).

[118] Hu Houxuan (胡厚宣), 'Climate Change and the Examination of the Climate in the Yin Dynasty' and 'Introduction to the Studies of Oracle Bone Characters', in *Collected Papers on the Studies of the Oracle Bone Characters and the History of the Shang Dynasty* (Shijiazhuang: Hebei Education Publishing House, 2002).

[119] Qian Cunxun.

books'. When taking the statement as a whole: 'as you know, only the Yin ancestors had books and canons, and the Yin overthrew the Xia', we may interpret that 'having books and canons' is related to 'the Yin overthrowing the Xia'. Then it can be understood that in the books and canons, the historical fact of 'the Yin overthrowing the Xia' is recorded, or it may also be understood that the Yin ancestors 'had canons and books' because they 'overthrew the Xia'. Although most people interpret the statement as having the former meaning, the latter meaning cannot be excluded. The Western Zhou Bronze Victory Gui records: '武征商, 唯甲子朝, 岁鼎, 克闻, 夙有商'. (King Wu of Zhou went to subjugate the Shang Dynasty. In the morning of the first lucky day of the lunar year when the Star of Jupiter was high in the sky, King Wu won the victory and had the Shang.) '有' here means '占有' (possess) or '拥有' (own). If we take the second interpretation, then '殷革夏命' and '有册有典' mean Cheng Tang 'possessed' the canons and books of the Xia Dynasty instead of the Yin 'ancestors' making their own 'canons and books'. 'Xianshilan' of *Lü's Spring and Autumn Annals* records: King Jie of the Xia was to lose his kingdom, so Taishiling Minister Zhong Gu took his canons and ran for the Shang. Can this be another circumstantial evidence for Cheng Tang owning Xia's 'canons and books'?[120] No matter how it is interpreted, there should be 'canons and books' in the transformation period from the Xia Dynasty to the Shang Dynasty, that is, the maturity period of the Chinese characters can by all means be traced to the world of Shang Tang of the early dynasty.

Conclusion

By investigating the developmental level of the oracle bone script in the late Shang Dynasty, collating and analysing the excavated early Shang Dynasty pottery characters, we can draw the following general conclusions about the development of the Chinese characters in the early Shang Dynasty.

---

[120] *Taiping Imperial Encyclopedia*, vol. 618 quoted 'Tufa' (图法) as 'Tushu' (图书 books). 'Taishiling' (太史令) here refers to the imperial official in charge of documents and books, which is the evidence that books existed in the Xia dynasty.

First of all, there are considerable common features between the cultures of the Xia, Shang and Zhou Dynasties. The characters of the three dynasties belong to the same system, the Western Zhou Dynasty characters being hereditary with those of the late Shang Dynasty and the early Shang Dynasty characters inheriting and developing the Xia characters. The 'coexistence relationship' of the three dynasties in history demonstrates that the Chinese characters then may have already possessed the function of communication and recording events as prevalent characters. All the three dynasties made contributions to the formation and development of the Chinese characters. However, they had different shares of contributions in the different periods of their development due to 'the rise and fall of strong and weak forces' and the early and late stages of civilization.

Second, the early Shang Dynasty pottery characters may serve as valuable specimen to investigate the development of the Chinese character system. Their value to measure the various developmental stages of the characters lies in the fact that we can detect the coming of autumn by a falling leaf and infer the whole leopard by spying a spot. Thus, we must pay full attention to the true value of this kind of pottery characters. Our systematic collation and analysis show the following: by these pottery characters, we may gain a general understanding and correct judgement of the development of the early Shang Dynasty characters.

Third, the early Shang Dynasty characters already entered the mature stage, after which the pottery characters in different periods shared more similarities than differences. Despite the constant development, their basic style and writing manner had no fundamental changes. From the early Shang Dynasty to the late Shang Dynasty represented by the oracle bone script, what took place in the Chinese character system was only the process of enrichment and constant development and improvement. This process continued until the Western Zhou Dynasty, the Spring–Autumn and Warring States periods and even the Qin-Han period. The Chinese characters had been in such a constant process, which is the necessary requirement for the system to maintain its constant optimization and vitality.

Fourth, the bamboo and wooden script system had already been a mature system by the early Shang Dynasty. That 'canons and books' already existed during the Xia and Shang periods should be the fact that can be inferred and partly proved, which also further proves that the characters of that period had already developed into a systematic and mature stage. The fragments of the Xia characters offer important reference for understanding the development of the early Shang characters, and the assessment of the development of the early Shang Dynasty characters is also a very meaningful fundamental work to further explore the formation and development of the characters in the Xia Dynasty.

CHAPTER 2

The Main Body of Chinese Characters
The Pictophonetic Structure

The Types of the Pictophonetic Structure[1]

The pictophonetic characters formed in the pictophonetic formation mode are the main body of Chinese characters. The period of ancient Chinese characters is when the pictophonetic structure was gradually evolving, new pictographic characters were constantly emerging and the pictophonetic system was in a state of dynamic development. This is a truly complex situation. As a result, it is becoming a particularly important fundamental work to do research on some classification of pictographic characters.

The ancients worked on the classification of pictographic characters from various perspectives. Jia Gongyan (贾公彦) in the Tang Dynasty followed the combinations of the pictographic component and phonetic component in their respective positions and classified the

---

[1] This chapter is selected from the second part of 'On the Pictophonetic Structure of the Ancient Characters'. The whole chapter is included in *A Library of PhD Dissertations and MA Theses of China Humanities and Social Sciences, A Continuation Volume, Literature*, vol. II (Hangzhou: Zhejiang Education Press, 2005).

pictographic characters into the types of the 'pictographic component on the left and phonetic component on the right' (左形右声) (e.g., 江, 河) and the 'pictographic component on the right and phonetic component on the left' (右形左声) (e.g., 鸠, 鸽). This kind of classification is still mentioned today.² However, just as Lu Simian (吕思勉) said, this classification 'is not of great significance'. 'In terms of the combinations in Chinese characters, the positions for components are generally not quite restricted except for the self-explanatory functions of characters'.³ Zheng Qiao's (郑樵) *An Outline of the Six Script Categories*, in the Song Dynasty, classified the pictophonetic characters into two categories: direct reproduction (正生) and indirect reproduction (变生). Indeed, Mr Zheng's classification reflected some features of the pictophonetic structure. Yang Huan's (杨桓) *A Genealogy of the Six Script Categories* in the Yuan Dynasty classified the pictophonetic characters into 18 types such as the 'heavenly imagery, heavenly movement, earthly principle, human body' (天象, 天运, 地理, 人体) and so on, and four styles such as the 'original phonetic component', 'concordant phonetic component', 'close phonetic component', 'concordant and close phonetic component' (本声, 谐声, 近声, 谐近声). Zhao Guze's classification in the Ming Dynasty was 'the same as Yang's except that his was more specific'. Meanwhile, Zhao also classified pictophonetic combinations into five cases of the 'phono with meaning and without meaning' (声兼意不兼意) 'two styles and three styles' (二体三体) 'combinations of positions' (位置配合) (e.g., pictographic on the left and phonetic on the right), 'scattered position' (散居) (e.g., the phonetic component 黄 scattered above and below the character 田) and five examples of the 'omission of phonetic components' (省声).⁴ Up to the Song and

---

²Ruan Yuan (阮元 from Qing dynasty), 'Baoshishu' (保氏疏) in *The Rites of Zhou. Thirteen Classics Explanatory Notes and Commentaries* (Beijing: Zhonghua Book Company, 1980), 731.

³Lü Simian (吕思勉), 'A Brief Commentary on Some Examples of Characters', in *Four Essays in Philology* (Shanghai: Shanghai Education Press, 1985), 183.

⁴Zhao Guze (赵古则 from the Ming dynasty). The Original Meaning of the Six Categories of the Chinese Script. See Hu Yunyu (胡韫玉), "General Commentary on the Six Categories', in *Introduction to the Six Categories,* included in Ding Fubao (丁福保), *Annotations of the Origin of Chinese Characters*, First Compilation, vol. II (Beijing: Zhonghua Book Company, 1988).

Yuan Dynasties, the pictophonetic classifications had already become extremely detailed, including various aspects of pictographic features, categories of character meanings, phonetic relationships and so on. In the Qing Dynasty, the research on the classification of the pictophonetic characters generally never surpassed the aspects above. Mr Zhen Shangling summarizes the previous research on the classification of pictophonetic characters into two schools of the 'phonetic orientation' and 'semantic orientation' with seven types of classifications. He points out:

> All those views either focus on the combination between the pictographic component and phonetic component in their positions, or on such combination in their ingredients, or on the relationship between the phonetic component and the pronunciation of the character, or on the relationship between the phonetic component and the meaning of the character. We may put aside the strength and weakness of such classifications, but one disadvantage all those views share is obvious that they all based their theories on the established characters instead of tracing their origins.[5]

Mr Zhen's comment hits right on the drawback of the research on the classification of pictophonetic characters. Due to the fact that the previous research on Chinese characters is based on the small seal script preserved in the *Origin of Chinese Characters*, with reference to ancient scripts, large seal script and bronze inscriptions, the starting point of which was to testify the origin of Chinese characters, their research on the classification of pictophonetic characters could only be to 'base their theories on the established characters'. The deficiency of this research is often to place the various phenomena in the long evolution of characters into the same historical phase and do oversimplified synchronic analysis so as to draw some superficial conclusion but conceal the fundamentals that play decisive roles behind these phenomena.

---

[5] Zhen Shangling (甄尚灵), 'An Analysis of the Pictophonetic Characters in the *Origin of Chinese Characters*' in *Collection of Chinese Cultural Studies*, 2 volumes 9 (1942).

Mr Zhen attempts to discuss the categories of pictophonetic characters by the history of the 'formation of characters', and classify the pictophonetic characters in the *Origin of Chinese Characters* by the sequence of the combinations between the pictographic components and the phonetic components. This is a very commendable effort. Unfortunately, the materials in Mr Zhen's research are rather limited. Although he has used much of the materials from the ancient scripts and tried to 'examine [them] from the historical facts',[6] the use of such materials is selective and it is not yet the complete and systematic investigation of the ancient pictophonetic characters. As a result, his research has not called the attention as it should have. In Chapter 2 of *A Survey of the Yinxu Oracles*, Mr Chen Mengjia (陈梦家) interprets 'pictographic components and phonetic components enhancing each other' (形声相益) as: (a) pictographic components and phonetic components enhancing each other; (b) pictographic components enhancing each other; (c) phonetic components enhancing each other. He also classifies the pictophonetic characters formed by the increase of pictographic components and phonetic components in the oracle bone inscriptions into five different modes, which is in fact a kind of research on classification. Mr Wu Zhenwu's (吴振武) research on the classification of ancient pictophonetic characters is similar to Mr Zhen's analysis in many ways. He believes that 'from the perspective of the ancient characters, there are generally three types of pictophonetic structures in Chinese characters', that is, the semantic type of pictophonetic characters directly formed by semantic components and phonetic components, the phono-added pictophonetic characters formed by adding phonetic components and the semantic-added pictophonetic characters formed by semantic-added pictophonetic characters.[7] By the full investigation of the ancient pictophonetic structure, we believe that their research results are worth considering.

The purpose of the classification research is to systemize thousands of pictophonetic characters so as to reveal the essence through the various complex phenomena, not just to provide simple descriptions

---

[6] Zhen Shangling, 'An Analysis of the Pictophonetic Characters'.

[7] Wu Zhenwu (吴振武), 'A Study of the Pictophonetic Categories in the Ancient Characters', *Collection of Graduate Papers of Jilin University* 1 (1982).

of the superficial phenomena. Therefore, we believe that the classification work of the ancient pictophonetic structure should start from the different approaches by which pictophonetic characters originated. Classifying pictophonetic characters according to their different origins will help us explore and understand the reproduction, development and nature of the pictophonetic structure. From this perspective, based on the research by Mr Zhen Shangling, Chen Mengjia and Wu Zhenwu, we classify the pictophonetic structures into the following modes.

1. Picto-added Mode: The picto-added mode of pictophonetic structures is to add pictographic components to the established characters. This mode of pictophonetic characters has very diverse origins. Some of them add pictographic components to the original characters to make the meanings of the original characters clearer and more precise, or derive from the original characters to form some specific characters for new meanings; some others add pictographic components to the phonetic loan characters to specify the meanings and to form new pictophonetic characters or to create new specific characters.

   (a) The Examples of Pictographic Components Added to the Original Characters
   The character 祖 is originally used as '且' in the bone and tortoise shell inscriptions and then is used as '祖'. '祖' is still used as '且' in '祖考' in the bronze script from the Western Zhou Dynasty. In the Warring Sates period, the pictographic component '示' was added to '且' and therefore became '祖'. The *Origin of Chinese Characters* says: '示 foretells good or ill luck by the heaven and therefore it means to show people something'. It then says: '示 means divine matter'. '且' is originally pictographic, and as it is the object for sacrifice, the pictographic component '示' is added to indicate the scope of its meaning. Xu Shen (许慎) analysed the formation of '祖' as 'following 示 with the pronunciation of 且', which is a typical pictophonetic structure. This character is a picto-added pictophonetic character. Many of the characters with the radical 示 included in Volume I of the *Origin of Chinese*

Characters are formed by adding the pictographic components to the original characters.

The character 禮 does not follow '示' in either the bone and tortoise shell inscriptions or the bronze script from the Zhou Dynasties. Its original form is like '玨' in a utensil, to indicate the meaning of 'reaching happiness by serving gods', which is an associative compound. In the Warring States period, there appeared 禮 with the added '示' to clarify its meaning.[8]

The character 福 is originally used as '畐' without '示' and it is a pictograph for a wine vessel. The ancients filled up the wine vessel to worship gods for their happiness or gratitude, so they added '示' to form '福' and specify its meaning.

The character 神 is originally used as '申'. In the bone and tortoise shell inscriptions, '申' is like the shape of twisting lightening. In the entry of '虹', the *Origin of Chinese Characters* says: '申 means lightening', and in the entry of '申', it says: '申 means gods'. Thus, the original meaning of '申' is lightening and the extended meaning is '神' (gods). In the descriptions of '其用各百神' (it is being used for all gods) on the Ning Gui (宁簋 food vessel in the Western Zhou Dynasty), the pictographic component '示' had already been added to '申' to form the pictophonetic character with '示' as the form and '申' as the pronunciation. Then '申' was borrowed as a character in the Earthly Branches, '电' was added with the pictographic component '雨' to become the pictophonetic character '電', so '申', '電' and '神' are differentiated three characters.

The character 祭 does not follow '示' in the bone and tortoise shell inscriptions, but is an associative compound in the form of 'holding meat' for sacrifice. Then '示' is added to emphasize the function of sacrifice and it is also defined as an associative compound in the *Origin of Chinese Characters*. Statically speaking, Xu Shen's analysis is not mistaken, but compared with '祖, 禮, 福, 神', '示' is also a pictographic

---

[8] Or perhaps the character uses 玉 (玨 jade) and 鼓 (drum) as instruments to worship the god for happiness.

component added later, and there are no fundamental differences between them, and it therefore also belongs to the picto-added pictophonetic mode. However, as the upper part of '祭', which means to hold meat, did not develop into a phonetic component but became a different component for other characters, it is habitually classified as an associative compound.

Similarly, '祝' is also a picto-added pictophonetic character. In the bone and tortoise shell inscriptions, it is in the form of '兄', like a person on the knee praying (different from '兄' in '兄弟' in the form of a standing position). To indicate the character is related to worshiping gods, '示' is added as a pictographic component to form the character '祝', the formation mode of which is no different from that of '祖, 福'. The lower part of the original '兄' that forms '祝' on the Xiaomeng Ding (小孟鼎 a cooking vessel from the Western Zhou Dynasty) is no longer different from '兄' in '兄弟' after its transformation. The *Origin of Chinese Characters* says: 'It follows 示 and 人 and 口, or it follows 兑 with some omission'. Thus, it is also defined as an associative compound. The two differentiated characters '兄' (祝) and '兄' in '兄弟' in the bone and tortoise shell inscriptions later became fused into one. As a result, it cannot be determined that '兄' is the original character of '祝', and it is why the pronunciation of '祝' is fixed.

社 is the same character as '土' in the bone and tortoise shell inscriptions. '社' is the god of earth, and therefore '土' is also pronounced as '社', such as '邦土 (社), 唐土 (社)' in the bone and tortoise inscriptions. Not until the Warring States period was '示' added to '土' and became '社', the same as '祖', so it should also be a picto-added pictophonetic character. The *Origin of Chinese Characters* says: '社 follows the forms of 示 and 土'. It defines it as an associative compound, for '土' and '社' were already pronounced very differently in the Han Dynasty, and '社神' meant '土地之神' (the god of earth), the characters and meanings closely related, so Xu Shen considered it as an associative compound. In fact, '土' and '社' both belonged to the radical of 鱼 in the ancient times, their places of articulation were close and

'土' could also be treated as the phonetic component of '社'. For example, '郸, 惮' with the pronunciation of '单' are in the group of 端, but '阐, 禅' are in the group of 章. The same phonetic component is pronounced in two different groups that are close in their places of articulation, so '土' and '社' follow the same pattern. However, according to some scholars on ancient phonology, the group of 端 and the group of 章 should have been combined into one in the ancient times.[9]

Starting from the analysis of '祖', we have exemplified the group of characters that followed the same formation process under the radical of 示 such as '礼, 福, 神, 祭, 祝, 社'. We believe that they are all pictophonetic characters formed by adding pictographic components to the original characters. However, in the *Origin of Chinese Characters*, '祭, 祝, 社' are defined as associative compounds, and although the pronunciation of '神' as '申' is deleted in Xu Xuan's (徐铉) edition, the character is also considered as an associative compound. In addition, 禮 was defined by Xu Shen as 'following the form and pronunciation of '豊'. Thus, as adding pictographic components to the original characters was much related to associative compounds, Xu Shen would often confuse such kinds of pictophonetic characters with associative compounds or would treat them both as pictophonetic characters and associative compounds. If we ignore their formation process and only analyse their structures in one dimension, they are indeed not very different from associative compounds. However, from the perspective of their reproduction and formation process, when a pictographic component is added to a character with its complete meaning and pronunciation, as the conventional relationship is firmly established between the character and its pronunciation through a long process of usage due to the mental set in the usage of the character, the character will naturally become the phonetic component

---

[9] Li Zhenhua and Zhou Changji (李珍华, 周长楫), 'An Outlined History of Chinese Phonology', in *An Ancient and Modern Phonetic Diagram of Chinese Characters* (Beijing: Zhonghua Book Company, 1993).

that records the originally firmly established pronunciation of that character. We classify the original character with the pictophonetic component added to it as a pictophonetic character and not as an associative compound, also because these kind of characters have always been believed to be of typical pictophonetic structures in traditional philology, on the one hand, such as the analysis of '祖' in the *Origin of Chinese Characters*, and on the other, associative structures refer to the character formation completed at one time, that is, all the elements of the associative structures participate in the formation of these kinds of structures in the same historical dimension, and not in a diachronical process. Xu Shen classified some of the pictophonetic characters formed by the original characters with pictophonetic components added to them as associative compounds. This is exactly due to the result that he treated all the formation elements of such pictophonetic characters in the same historical dimension owing to his limitations in all respects. All discussed earlier becomes clearer by the following illustrations of the pictophonetic characters formed by the original characters with pictographic components added to them.

鼓 is originally in the form of a drum in the bone and tortoise shell inscriptions, and then '攴' is added to it to mean 'beating the drum' (击鼓). It is the same usage as '壴', and then '鼓' is used to replace '壴, 鼓', which means the name of a drum as well as the action of 'beating the drum'. The *Origin of Chinese Characters* says: '鼓 means beating the drum. It follows 攴 and 壴 with 壴 as the pronunciation'. '鼓 means 郭, the sound of spring equinox when all living things come to life, and therefore it is called 鼓. It follows 壴 and 攴, like hands beating something'. The two characters Xu Shen defined are included under the radical 攴 in Volume III and 壴 in Volume V, respectively, the former as a verb and the latter as a noun, both based on the later character forms and becoming two character variants from the same character. Duan Yucai (段玉裁) thinks that in Xu Xuan's (徐铉) edition of the *Origin of Chinese Characters*, the reason why the former character is pronounced in the *fanqie* (反切) formula of '公户' (pronounced as the consonant in 公 and the vowel in 户) is that the character form is very close to '鼓' and therefore is mixed up, so it should be propounded as '属'. In the ancient script, to follow '攴' or '殳' is interchangeable and the two are no different, so we believe that Xu Xuan's edition is not mistaken, but due to the two usages of a verb and a noun, Xu Shen differentiated them by taking the variants. In the oracle bone script, there are clear differences specified between following 殳 and following 攴, while the form following 支 is derived from an error in the later bronze inscriptions. In the ancient characters, they are in fact the three variants of the same character.

鄙 is '啚' in the oracle bone script. It is an associative compound which means '边邑' (border), such as '东啚' (eastern border) and '西啚' (western border). The *Origin of Chinese Characters* says: '鄙 follows 邑 and is pronounced as 啚'. '邑' is also an added pictographic component to indicate the meaning of '边邑' (border). Related to this character, '啚 follows 口. '亩 亩' looks like the form of '仓廪' (granary) in the oracle bone script. In the bronze inscriptions, '禾' is added to make '' (as on the bronze food vessel 召伯簋 Zhaobo gui). '米' is added to make '' (as on the bronze wine vessel 睘卣 Huanyou). They are both the variants of '亩', following 禾 and pronounced as (米), but Xu Shen defined them as associative compounds. '亩' in the *Origin of Chinese Characters* may have the form of the character '廩'. It follows '广 and 禾'. '广', which is related to the meaning of 仓廪 (granary), should have been added to the top of '稟'. From the perspective of its developmental process, it should be analysed as 'following 广 and pronounced as 稟'. From '亩' to '稟' and then to '廩', it is exactly the differentiating process of adding pictographs. As for the original characters, all the new characters are pictophonetic characters formed by adding pictographs.

国 is '或' in the early bronze inscriptions (as on Bao You 保卣, the bronze wine vessel). The *Origin of Chinese Characters* says: '或 means 邦'. '域' takes its form as 或.

'国' in the bronze inscriptions is originally '或', and then the pictographic component '邑' to make '⿰阝或' (as on Shi Yuan Gui 师寰簋, the food vessel). '匚, 囗' are added to 或 to make '⿷匚或' (as on Marquis of Cai Bell 蔡侯钟 the bronze bell）and '国' (as on Lu You 录卣 the bronze wine vessel). '或, 域, 国' are originally the same characters, and '域, 国' should be originally picto-added pictophonetic characters. In the *Origin of Chinese Characters*, '国 means 邦, following 囗 and 或'. It is meant as an associative compound. This character has the same formation process as '员' for '圆' and then '囗' is added to make '圆'. However, when analysing the structure of '圆', Xu Shen defined it as 'following 囗 and pronounced as 员'. Accordingly, '国' should be analysed as 'following 囗 and pronounced as 或'. '国' in the early ancient times belongs to the radical of 职 and it is pronounced as the consonant in 见 and the vowel in 纽, while '或' also belongs to the radical of 职 and it is pronounced as the consonant in 匣 and the vowel in 纽, both having the vowel similar to 纽, and thus very close in pronunciation.

盧 is '⿱虍𠙹' in the oracle bone script, and it is in fact a pictophonetic character formed by adding a phonetic component to the early character '𠙹'. In the characters of the Warring States period, there appeared the character '盧' formed by adding the pictographic component '皿' to it (as the monetary script), or the character '鑪' by adding '金'. The *Origin of Chinese Characters* says '盧, food vessel, following 皿 and pronounced as 𥂝'.

往 is originally '⿱止王' in the oracle bone script, following 止 and pronounced as 王. It is a pictophonetic character. In the *Origin of Chinese Characters*, '㞷' means grass and trees growing presumptuously, following 止, on the top of 土. It is pronounced as '皇'. Xu Shen defined the character by the erroneously changed form. Obviously, he was mistaken. In the characters of the Warring States period, '往' and '⿺辶㞷' were formed by adding '彳' or '辵'. In the *Origin of Chinese Characters*, '往 means 之, following 彳 and pronounced as 㞷, and it follows 辵 in the ancient script'.

持 in the *Origin of Chinese Characters* 'means 握, following 手 and pronounced as 寺'. '寺' is the early form of '持', and in the bronze script, 'it follows 又 and is pronounced as 之'. In the *Origin of Chinese Characters*: '寺' means 廷. It means being lawful, following 寸 and pronounced as 之'. This is not the original form and meaning of '寺'. '寺' is a pictophonetic character formed by adding the pictographic component '手' to the original character.

In general, adding pictographic components to the original characters is an important approach to form pictophonetic characters. In the paper 'Added Components in Characters', Yang Shuda (杨树达) elaborates on this phenomenon. However, his belief may not be appropriate that 'characters with added radicals are a kind of unique characters in addition to the six script categories'.[10] Adding pictographic components (or radicals) concerns the formation process of character signs while the 'six script categories' refer to the analysis and conclusion of the established character signs. In fact, the traditional analytical method represented by the *Origin of Chinese Characters* generally excludes the formation process of individual signs in that it focuses on the static induction of the Chinese character system. These characters with added pictographic components are mainly classified as pictophonetic type by Xu Shen. Owing to the fact that for these pictophonetic characters with added pictographic components, the parts to which the components are added are original characters themselves, their historical inheritance in pronunciation and meaning will, in many ways, affect the analysis of the formation of the characters with the added components. When the meaning of the character sign to which the component is to be added is easily felt by the analyst, this newly formed picto-added pictophonetic character may be analysed as an 'associative compound' or 'associative compound plus phonetic character'. When the pronunciation

---

[10] Yang Shuda, 'The Added Components of Characters', in *Commentary on Philology from Jiwei Studio*, vol. 5 (Beijing: Zhonghua Book Company, 1983).

of the character to which the component is to be added and the pronunciation of the picto-added pictophonetic character are difficult to be grasped by the analyst due to the gap in time or space, the analyst is more likely to find the connection in terms of meaning according to the rationality of Chinese character formation mode and treat the character as the structure of an associative compound. When some characters to which the components are to be added deviate further from their original forms and meanings due to erroneous forms or in the process of usage (e.g., used as other characters), the analyst will also make various mistakes. It is exactly because of those causes that we find that Xu Shen was rather inconsistent with his analysis of such type of pictophonetic characters. To form picto-added pictophonetic characters on the basis of the original characters, due to the variations or deviations, the added pictographic components mainly serve the functions of exhibiting the formal features, marking the semantic scope or differentiating some meaning. As a result, in terms of the picto-added pictophonetic structure, the parts to which components are added are always the core of such structure. As the predecessors of new characters, these parts take full advantages in form, pronunciation and meaning due to historical inheritance. However, such advantages will gradually disappear in the process of usage. Without carefully tracing their origins, we can hardly feel their advantages. Then they will be mixed up with the pictophonetic characters formed by other means and will be difficult to be discerned. Thus, we can see the limitations of the one-dimensional analysis of pictophonetic characters without differentiating their origins.

(b) The Examples of Loan Characters with Added Pictographic Components

Adding pictographic components to loan characters is another important source of picto-added pictophonetic characters. Their prevalence in usage and significance in the development of pictophonetic structure go far beyond the characters formed by adding pictographic components to original characters.

Many female names in the oracle bone script of the King of Yin period are obviously pictophonetic characters formed by adding pictographic components to loan characters. There are such names as '妇井, 妇良, 妇多, 妇羊, 妇丰' and so on. The female names of '井', '良', '多', '羊', '丰' and so on are all loan characters. The pictographic component '女', which means the female gender, is added to form the proper names of pictophonetic characters such as '妍', '娘', '够', '姅', '姇' and so on. The *Origin of Chinese Characters* includes '妍, 够' and so on and defines them as the pictophonetic structure.

In the group of characters with the radical of 示, some of the characters in the earlier ancient script materials originally did not follow '示' but borrowed other characters for substitution. Later on, the pictographic component '示' was added to them all to form the proper names of the pictographic characters. For example, '禄' in either the oracle bone script or the bronze script does not follow '示' but borrows '录'. Song Ding (颂鼎, a bronze food vessel with inscriptions made by a histographer called Song in the Western Zhou Dynasty) inscription says '通录(禄) 永令(命)' (success in officialdom and longevity). Qiang Pan (墙盘, Qiang's bronze basin) inscription says '福怀祓录 (禄)' (embraced in happiness and officialdom). In both cases, '录' is borrowed for '禄'. '录' originally looks like the form of the shadoof fetching water, and it is the early form of '漉'. In the *Origin of Chinese Characters*, '录' means carving wood to record information. It is a pictograph. '禄 means happiness, following 示 and pronounced as 录'. This is a pictophonetic character formed by adding the pictographic component to the loan character. '佑' borrows '又' originally in the oracle bone script. '又' is the original character of '右', which looks like the form of the right hand. In the usage of '福佑' and '侑祭', it is a loan character and becomes a pictophonetic character formed by adding '示' as the component. In the *Origin of Chinese Characters*, '祐 follows 示 and is pronounced as 右'. '祀' borrows '巳' in the original oracle bone script, and then the component '示' is added to it. In the *Origin of Chinese Characters*, '祀 means that the offering of sacrifice does not end'. 'It follows 示 and is pronounced as 巳'. '祶' borrows '帝' in both the oracle bone script and the bronze script. In the *Origin of Chinese Characters*, '祶' means worshiping heavenly gods and ancestors, following 示 and is pronounced as 帝'. '示' is also an added pictographic component. '禄, 祐, 祀, 祶' are all formed by adding pictographic components to the loan characters.

In the group of radical 邑, there are many characters for place names or state names in the ancient script, which clearly reflect the development from the loan characters with added pictographic components to pictophonetic characters. Take, for example, Xu Zhongshu's (徐中舒) *A Diagram of the Ancient Chinese Character Forms*, Vol. 6, Chendu City, Sichuan Province: Sichuan Lexicographical Press, 1980. The characters in the group of radical 邑 clearly show the prevalence of how characters for place or state names developed into pictophonetic characters by adding pictographic components to loan characters. They are, for example, 啚—鄙, 豊—酆, 奠—鄭, 北—邶, 井—邢, 甘—邯, 無—鄦, 匽—郾, 登—鄧, 咢—鄂, 朱—邾, 會—鄶, 余—䣍, 寺—邿, 取—郰, 丕—邳, 炎—郯, 曾—鄫 and so on. In the *Origin of Chinese Characters*, all these characters are treated as pictophonetic characters in their formation. The pictographic components in these characters only indicate very general meanings. Despite all these, adding '邑' forms a special group of pictophonetic characters.

The pictophonetic characters, formed by adding pictographic components to loan characters, can only be differentiated from large numbers of other pictophonetic characters by large amount of unearthed ancient script literature and its historical formation process. Previous researchers on pictophonetic characters have already noted this category and many scholars believe that this mode of pictophonetic formation is the origin of the pictophonetic structure. Although the origin of the pictophonetic structural formation mode is indispensably linked with the reproduction of pictophonetic characters in the pictophonetic system, we still believe that the pictophonetic formation mode as a sign formation mode is in a different dimension from the pictophonetic characters of the same formation. Compared with the pictophonetic characters formed by adding pictographic components to original characters, adding pictographic components to loan characters to form pictographic characters has greatly enhanced the development of the pictophonetic structural mode. First of all, adding pictographic components to original characters to form pictophonetic characters has to some extent retained the primordial form of the pictophonetic structure. In the previous chapter, we point out that the 'phonetic component' of this type of pictophonetic structure is passively formed. The meaning from the concentration of the original character very much affects the way people treat it as the true pictophonetic structure. If we neglect the historical dimension in which such a structure is created, it will be very difficult to distinguish the structure from the associative compound. The loan character as it is, to which the pictographic component is added, only temporarily forms the relationship between form, pronunciation and meaning in the specific context by means of the phonetic connection. Once it is out of such a context, the loaned meaning and the character sign will have no relationship at all. This relationship between form and meaning established by pronunciation concerning loan characters cannot transcend the context and concentrate until pictographic components are added. As a result, these types of pictophonetic characters, with the added parts as phonetic components, have more purity in representing pronunciation. Even the pictophonetic characters especially formed for the original meanings by the original characters with loaned meanings gain certain accordance with the phonetic components of the pictophonetic characters formed by loan characters as pictographic components when these types of characters become phonetic components of picto-added pictophonetic characters due to the fact that the original characters become specialized signs for common loans and their relationship with the original meanings is somewhat loose. For example, adding the pictographic component '竹' to '其' makes '箕'; adding '手' to '叟' makes '搜'; adding '手' to '爰' makes '援'; adding '艸'

to '盍' makes '盖'; adding '日' to '莫' makes '暮'; adding '手' to '寺' makes '持' and so on. Second, the starting point of adding pictographic components to original characters is to solve the problem of 'representing meaning by form', which is not fundamentally different from the formation approach of representing meaning by form in the early stage of Chinese characters. The starting point of adding pictographic components to loan characters is to 'mark differentiation' and to solve the problems of forming by pronunciation and recording pronunciation by differentiating meaning. The two points mentioned demonstrate the great significance of adding pictographic components to loan characters in the pictophonetic structural development.

Adding pictographic components is the main approach to the derivation and growth of pictophonetic characters. Large numbers of new pictophonetic characters are created by adding pictographic components. This widely-used approach in the period of the ancient script also formed a group of special characters later abandoned or not commonly used.

For example, they include the following characters in the Warring States period: '䥆 (弋), 䤾 (戈), 邡 (江), 㤱 (附), 㓜 (幼), 㝃 (少), 𢁫 (世), 䡐 (乘), 𦙾 (肯), 㪍 (摄), 䰩 (鬼), 郕 (成), 𨛬 (秦), 鄵 (曹), 鄾 (鲁), 䣛 (胡), 䜣 (齐)' and so on. The appearance of these special characters shows that the approach of forming pictophonetic characters by picto-added mode has become a commonly used method that people are aware of.

2. Picto-phono-combined Mode: Adding pictographic components to form pictophonetic characters is a reasonable extension of the early associative compounds developing into the pictophonetic formation mode. From the perspective of the use of character signs, the constant extension of the meanings of characters and the prevalent occurrence of homophonic characters are bound to promote the differentiation of adding pictographic components and the pace of forming new characters. When adding pictographic components as a common formation approach is prevalently used, then it becomes a natural course that people will be prompted to directly take a phonetic component and a pictographic component

to form a pictophonetic character. Such kind of pictophonetic characters are what we call 'picto-phono-added mode'. In terms of the pictophonetic characters formed by the picto-phono-added mode, the combinations of their pictographic components and their phonetic components are completed at one time. In the research of the historical characters, it is very risky to claim that the formation of a pictophonetic character is completed at one time. No materials, either on the ground or under the ground, will provide the claim with absolutely accurate evidence. Nonetheless, inferred from the facts of the later newly formed pictophonetic characters and the internal logic of the development of the matter, this is a type that will inevitably appear after the pictophonetic structure develops into a certain stage. The following examples under discussion are based on two conditions. The first is that we have not found any traces of these pictophonetic characters developing in different stages, that is, they appeared in a complete pictophonetic structure at the very beginning. The second is that the formation of these characters has closely related specific linguistic and cultural background—for example, in a certain period the linguistic and cultural phenomenon related to these pictophonetic characters was very prevalent, the creators of these characters were immersed in it and they could very easily fulfil their wishes of forming characters; or in a certain period, the appearance of certain new things induced a large number of new characters, which did not undergo a long and hard period of formation and development.

For example, in the oracle bone script, the pictophonetic characters '柳, 杞, 榆, 柏, 桼, 桷, 㝱, 柄' following the radical '木' are mostly proper nouns and these oracle characters mainly refer to places. The pictophonetic characters '河, 涂, 洛, 汝, 淮, 洧, 洣, 洹, 淇, 演, 潘, 沚, 潢, 潦, 涵, 淫, 洒, 涛, 沌, 洱, 滴' following the radical '水' are also used as proper nouns. Such proper nouns are so commonly formed by the same pictographic component and different phonetic components, and these proper nouns are all closely related to the people's activities in the Yin period, so it is most likely that these characters are formed by the combination of pictographic components and phonetic components at one time. Characters, such as '(骊), 驳, 鴷, 騽' following '马', and '斦, 献,

狂, 猶, 狼, 狐, 狈' following '犬' should also be considered as pictophonetic structures. '马' and '犬' are both early domesticated animals, and they are closely related to the life of the ancients. As a result, they had closer investigation and deeper understanding of these animals. This group of pictophonetic characters following '马' reflects certain accordance with the names and differences of a variety of horses recorded in 'Definitions of Animals' in Er Ya (《尔雅·释兽》). The frequent hunting also advanced the ancients' naming and understanding of various animals. Thus, quite many pictophonetic characters followed '犬' in the oracle bone script. As can be seen, the pictophonetic structural type of picto-phono-added mode might be mainly used to form the most familiar proper nouns in the earliest period.

In the characters of the Warring States period, there emerged a group of new pictophonetic characters, many of which were of the picto-phono-added mode. For example, the radical 竹 includes '箭, 簬, 簜, 箸, 節, 筥, 篆, 简, 范, 符, 箪, 箸, 筐, 策, 篓, 篇, 箸' and so on. These characters are mostly seen in the Chu script because bamboo implements were very common in the south and '竹' was used as a pictographic component to form a group of special pictophonetic characters. In the oracle bone script and the bronze script of the Zhou Dynasties, there were very few pictophonetic characters with '糸' as the pictographic component, but then in the characters of the Warring States period, there appeared many new pictophonetic characters with '糸' as the pictographic component, such as '绎, 绪, 绐, 纺, 纡, 紫, 红, 缫, 纷, 绣, 紊, 綊, 缰, 绊, 缃, 络, 输, 缪, 绸, 练, 纬, 绕, 襆, 绲, 缋, 缕, 缇, 缓, 绵, 纰, 绣, 纷, 约' and so on. The appearance of the large number of pictophonetic characters with '糸' as the component is obviously related to the large production of the silk and linen textiles in the Warring States period. On the bamboo slips of the Baoshan Chu Tombs (包山楚墓), there are nearly 70 (without counting the use of frequency) characters with '糸' as the component, many of which are new characters. This is closely related to the high development of the silk worm industry and silk textile industry in the Chu regions from the Spring and Autumn period to the Warring States period. The pictophonetic characters with '竹' and '糸' as components, which newly appeared in the characters of the Warring States period, are the reflection of the contemporary social life in language and written characters. These characters primarily belong to the picto-phono-added mode.

It is undoubted that this category of picto-phono-added new pictophonetic characters appeared in the oracle bone script. The large numbers of such characters in the Warring States period are related to the development of the pictophonetic system of this period. The appearance of the picto-phono-added mode is a momentous sign of the pictophonetic structure ridding itself of the primordial state and developing into a mature stage. In the whole pictophonetic system, the picto-added pictophonetic characters maintain a considerable proportion, and they have been accompanying the development of the pictophonetic structure as an important measure in regulating the relationship between the extension of meanings and the derivation of new characters within the character system as well as the relationship between language and characters (character loaning) in the use of characters; however, the picto-phono-added mode truly reflects the advantages of the pictophonetic structure. This mode overcomes the limitations that the formation of Chinese characters must start with the relationship between form and meaning or go through certain transforming stages so that they enter the kingdom of freedom to select phonetic components to record pronunciations and pictographic components to mark meanings and to develop the pictophonetic structure with a wide prospect.

3. Phono-added Mode: After the pictophonetic structure developed into the self-conscious stage of the 'picto-phono-added mode', users of Chinese characters became more aware of the importance of the 'pronunciation' in the formation of Chinese characters. To seek the 'unity between form and pronunciation' in Chinese character formation seems to have emerged in the oracle bone script, that is, the appearance of the 'phono-added' pictophonetic characters. The so-called phono-added pictophonetic character is formed by adding a purely phonetic component to the original character so as to transform the original character and form a new character. As this type of structure contains a clear and definite phonetic component, the original character habitually inherits its meaning

(even its pronunciation). By nature, such characters should belong to the type of pictophonetic structure. The 'phono-added mode' as a type of pictophonetic formation has been continuing since the period of the oracle bone script. Although there are not as many pictophonetic characters formed by this mode, their importance must be fully recognized from the perspectives of the description of the pictophonetic system and the development of the pictophonetic structure.

雉 looks like a pheasant in the original oracle bone script (combination no. 354, 合354), and then the pronunciation of '矢' or '夷' is added. What is followed by '雉' in '雉众' on the oracle bones of Tunnan nos. 2320 and 2328 (屯南 2320, 2328) is still different from '隹'. Later, it is gradually assimilated and becomes a pictophonetic character following 隹 and pronounced as 矢 (夷). The origin and development of '鸡' is the same as in this case.

斧 is originally '⟨?⟩' in the oracle bone script, resembling the form of an axe in a parallel position, which is the primary character of '斧'. In the third period of the oracle bone script, it is formed as '⟨?⟩'; adding the phonetic component '午' makes it a pictophonetic character, and in the small seal script, it 'follows 斤 and is pronounced as 父' and becomes a newly created character.

耤 looks like a man holding a farm tool (耒耜) to plough in the oracle bone script, in the form of '⟨?⟩', and also in the simplified forms of '⟨?⟩, ⟨?⟩', in the oracle bone script. '⟨?⟩, ⟨?⟩' are '巛' (灾) and '昔' as added phonetic components in the oracle bone script. '昔' also has '巛' as the phonetic component. In the Ling Ding (令鼎) inscription, it is in the form of '⟨?⟩'. In the *Origin of Chinese Characters*, '耤 follows 耒 and is pronounced as 昔'. The pictographic component 耒 comes from the simplification of the original character.[11]

蛛 is a pictograph in the oracle bone script in the forms of '⟨?⟩, ⟨?⟩', as well as '⟨?⟩', to which the phonetic component is added. In the bronze script, the pronunciation of '束' is changed to the pronunciation of '朱' as '⟨?⟩'. In the ancient pronunciations, '朱'

---

[11] Liu Zhao (刘钊), 'An Interpretation of the Oracle Bone Characters 耤, 羲, 蟺, 敖,' in *Jilin University Journal of Social Sciences* 2 (1990).

belongs to the group of 章纽侯 and '束' belongs to the group of 书纽屋, which are close to each other. In the *Origin of Chinese Characters*, the pictographic part of the original character in the small seal script is transformed into '黾', or to the form of '蛛', and the pictographic component is further changed to the more simplified form of '虫'.[12]

翌 borrows from the original '羽' in the oracle bone script in the form of '𦏲', or as it is said, the character is like the form of wings. In the oracle bone script, the pronunciation of '立' is added to make '翌', that is, the primary form of '翌'. In the *Origin of Chinese Characters*, '翊 means flying (飞), following 羽 and pronounced as 立'. 'Shiyan' in *Er Ya* (《尔雅•释言》): '翌 means bright (明)'. '翊, 翌' are originally the same characters, following '羽' and coming from the pictograph of wings in the assimilated form.

鑪 is '爨' in the oracle bone script, as the primary character of 炉. The phonetic component '卢' is in the form of '鹵'. When it becomes a pictophonetic character, a series of pictographic components such as '皿', '金', '火' are added to it, and then appear the forms of '盧, 鑪, 爐' and so on.[13]

在 is in the form of '才' in the oracle bone script, as well as in the form of '𡉉' (合371反) and '𡉉' (英1989), and then the pronunciation of '土' is added. In the *Origin of Chinese Characters*, '在 means being (存), following 土 and pronounced as 才'. This is a definition based on the erroneous form. In the inscriptions on the bronze vessels of both Meng Ding (孟鼎) and Qi Zun (启尊), '在' follows '士', and not '土'. For example, in both '贤士' and '士大夫', it is in the form of '在'. Or perhaps the phonetic component '才' is added to '士', and what the oracle bone script '𡉉' follows may also be '士', but later '在' and '士' begin to be differentiated.[14]

The examples above are all phono-added pictophonetic characters in the oracle bone script. In the bronze script of the Zhou periods and the characters of the Warring States, Qin-Han period,

---

[12] Liu Zhao, 'An Interpretation of the Oracle Bone Characters'.

[13] Yu Xingwu, *Interpretations of the Oracle Bone Characters* (Beijing: Zhonghua Book Company, 1979).

[14] Lin Yun (林沄), '王 and 士 Sharing the Same Origin and Related Questions, in *Symposium on Ancient Characters* (Guangzhou: Zhongshan University, 1994).

such phono-added formation mode was still frequently used. For example, 髭 looks like the moustache on the upper side of the mouth in the early bronze script and oracle bone script, in the forms of '㲋, 㕚'. On Meng Ding (盂鼎), it is inscribed as '㲋, 㕚', and then the phonetic component '此' is added. In the small seal script, the original pictograph is assimilated and changed to '须', and becomes the pictophonetic character 'following 须 and pronounced as 此', the pictographic component of which is later changed, and it becomes 髭.

盾 is '✚, ⊕' in the primary forms, like the shape of a shield. In the inscription on the food vessel Dong Gui (䇂簋), it is in the form of '㪷'. When the phonetic component '豚' is added, it becomes a pictophonetic character that follows the pronunciation of '豚'.[15] '豚' is pronounced the same as '盾' in the ancient pronunciation and the variant of '遁' is '遯'.

曼 is '㬎' in the oracle bone script. In the food vessel Man Gong Fu Xu (曼龔父盨) bronze inscriptions '㬎'. When the phonetic component '冃' is added to it, it is simplified as '曼'. 宝 is '㝉' in the oracle bone script, or '㝌' in the Shang bronze script. After the phonetic component '缶' is added, 宝 changes from an associative compound to a pictophonetic character. In the *Origin of Chinese Characters*, '寶 follows 宀, 王, 貝, and is pronounced as 缶'. From the historical perspective, the character '宝' in the bronze script should 'follow 寶 and be pronounced as 缶'. Later, it is further simplified as '㝌' (on the food vessel Zaifu Gui 宰甫簋), and then when 貝 is omitted, it becomes '㝌', pronounced as 宀, 缶, which can be seen in the bronze inscriptions on Jiyaomu Ding (姞䍃鼎) and Zhong Basin (仲盘).

There are quite many phono-added pictophonetic characters in the bronze script and Warring States characters. For example, often quoted are '裘' plus the phonetic '又' (then changed to 求), '疑' plus '牛', '俯' plus '府', '星' plus '生', '鼻' plus '畀', '绅' plus '东', '绝' plus '卩', '齿' plus '止' and '圣' plus '壬' and so on, all commonly recognized phono-added pictophonetic characters.

---

[15] Tang Lan, 'The Study of the History of the Western Zhou Dynasty by the Bronze Inscriptions', in *Cultural Relics* (1976): 6.

There are still many phono-added pictophonetic characters unrevealed in the ancient script. As a result, the characters that can be recognized are in fact not all recognized.

The appearance of phono-added pictophonetic characters is much worth noting in the development of the pictophonetic structure. To fully understand its significance, we must first of all theoretically confirm that they belong to the category of pictophonetic characters. Yang Shuda (杨树达) is insightful in discerning the differences between such characters formed by 'adding components' (including adding pictographic components) and the picto-phono-added pictophonetic characters such as '江, 河'. He points out that in the characters '江, 河', between '水 and 工可', one is pictographic and the other is phonetic, complementing each other like the two wheels of a cart and two wings of a bird, both indispensable', and yet the characters with added components often encounter the pitfall of repetition, either repeated pictographically when adding pictographic components or repeated phonetically when adding phonetic components.[16] These views are undoubtedly correct in some ways, but if we expand our investigation of the critical reviews of the *Origin of Chinese Characters* to all the ancient script materials, from the perspective of the formation and development of the pictophonetic structure, 'adding components' is one of the indispensable sources of the constant development of the pictophonetic system. 'Adding pictographic components' not only makes some characters transform to the pictophonetic structure, but has always been an important means for creating Chinese characters and forming pictophonetic structures, as is discussed in the previous chapter. 'Adding phonetic components' further reflects the development of the Chinese character system and the pictophonetic system. The adding of 'phonetic components' undoubtedly reflects the ancients' pursuit of using characters to record the pronunciations in character formation. This is a change of great significance to the early Chinese system creating signs mainly by means of expressing meanings by pictographs. Seen from the

---

[16] Yang Shuda, 'The Added Components of Characters', in *Commentary on Philology from Jiwei Studio*, vol. 5 (Beijing: Zhonghua Book Company, 1983).

above phono-added character examples of the oracle bone script and bronze script, the participation of 'phonetic components' facilitates the simplification of the original characters or the abstraction of the pictographic components by change and assimilation. This is an intentional adjustment for 'expressing meanings by forms' and 'conveying meanings by pictographs'. '凤, 雉, 斧, 耤, 卢, 髭, 宝' are all originally pictographs or associative compounds, but after the phonetic components are added, by recreating the original characters (by simplification or assimilation), they all transform into purely pictophonetic characters.

The creation of the 'phono-added mode' may be based on two reasons: first of all, since the pictophonetic structure as a formation mode had matured and advanced, the Chinese character formation started to transform from using forms to express meanings to recording pronunciations to express meanings, the influence of which made people intend to change the non-pictophonetic characters to pictophonetic characters; second, the forms of Chinese characters had already been highly linearized up to the oracle bone script period, and there appeared a break in the relationship between the signs formed by primordially drawing the outlines of objects and the direct images of the actual objects, or the external objects changed and differed greatly from the realities when the characters were created, resulting in the 'pictographs unlike the objects', so that people started to recreate the unlike pictographs by the advanced mode of recording the pronunciations to express meanings. Besides, due to the differentiation of the regional pronunciations and forms, new characters are also created by marking regional pronunciations or phonetic marking mode.

Phono-added pictophonetic characters are indeed obviously different from the picto-phono-added mode and picto-added mode. The objects for adding phonetic components as primary script are independently used entities in form, pronunciation and meaning. As the pronunciation as an added element is very easy to fall off, only by means of simplification and assimilation to weaken the dominating features of the original characters and making them lose the status of independent use can the 'phonetic components' truly complete the intervention of the original characters and form new characters. The characters, which later became typical pictophonetic structures, have mostly experienced such a progress, such as '凤, 耤' and so on. Although the objects for adding pictographic components are also independently used entities and the consolidation between the added components and the original characters takes some time, it is only a matter of time and convention in that the parts to which components are added gradually complete the transformation into phonetic components in the process of use without having to be especially recreated. Only by recreating the original characters to make them passive pictographic components and lose their central position in the pictophonetic structure can the 'phonetic components' of the phono-added pictophonetic characters, as the attached elements, accordingly become the focus of the phono-added pictophonetic characters. The finalizing process of such characters is exactly the process of the transfer of such a focus. There is, however, no such a problem for adding pictographic components. The parts, to which pictographic components are added, condense both the meanings and the pronunciations of the original characters, the added pictographic components remain attached elements, and the 'focus' of the picto-added pictophonetic structure is still on the parts to which components are added. Therefore, it is more convenient and efficient to create new characters by the picto-added pictophonetic formation approach. It is easy to complete the formation of new characters by differentiating the extended meanings of the original characters or by adding pictographic components to phonetic loan characters, which is the major means to change the existent characters into the pictophonetic structure. In fact, it is more difficult to create new characters by the phono-added pictophonetic approach. Although the wish to record pronunciations by pictographs can be well reflected by this approach, the difficulty to recreate new characters by the existent characters makes it very inconvenient to apply the approach. The characters to which components are added have long been finalized and they pose strong resistance to the recreation for adding phonetic components, so many of the characters to which phonetic components have been added remain the same and then these phonetic components are eventually abandoned. In the picto-phono-added mode as a more improved type, form and pronunciation emerge in contrast and coexist in unity in the formation process. However, it does not mean that the two maintain the balance like 'the two wheels of a cart and two wings of a bird'. In the picto-phono-added structure, the focus is still on 'pronunciation'. By recording the pronunciation of the character in 'sound' and by indicating the scope of meaning of the character in 'form', this formation mode can come into existence. The status of 'sound' is far more important than 'form'. In the same structure, they are by no means in the equal relationship with each other as they seem to be.

In conclusion, we hold the view that the pictophonetic structure can be classified into three basic types. The picto-added pictophonetic structure appears the earliest. It is formed by adding the pictographic component to the original character or phonetic loan character. The part to which the component is added gradually reduces the pronunciation and meaning condensed in the original and relatively transforms itself into the phonetic component. Adding the pictographic component to the phonetic loan character rids the pictophonetic structure of its primordial state and transforms it in the direction of recording pronunciation purely by the phonetic component, which is an important stage in the development and improvement of the pictophonetic structure. The picto-added mode is also a major means to create new pictophonetic characters, which has very strong function for forming new characters. The picto-phono-added pictophonetic structure is the product of the pictophonetic structure in its mature stage. By selecting the representative pictographic components and phonetic components which form new pictophonetic characters once for all, Chinese character formation completes the true leap from using the pictograph to express the meaning to recording the pronunciation to express the meaning. This has great significance. Such a type of character formation makes it convenient to create new characters and therefore it becomes the most frequently used means for forming new characters, gradually playing a major role in the pictophonetic system. The phono-added pictophonetic structure appears later. It is an important sign for the advanced development of the pictophonetic formation mode and for the conscious pursuit of the Chinese character formation to record the pronunciation to express the meaning. The phono-added mode forms new pictophonetic structures by renovating the old characters. Although this mode plays a certain role in marking pronunciations, differentiating regional pronunciations and some characters, generally speaking, it does not have a very strong function for character formation. However, undoubtedly, it should take an important position in the pictophonetic system. According to our research on the pictophonetic system, the mentioned three basic types are the somewhat complete description of the pictophonetic system.

The Pictographic Components of the Pictophonetic Structure[17]

The pictographic component is one of the two elements of the pictophonetic structure. Studying the pictographic component is the key to understanding the nature and features of the pictophonetic structure. The pictographic component and the phonetic component play their respective roles in the whole organic unity, having close relationship with each other and complementing each other. To discuss them separately[18] is only for the sake of convenience in exploring the relevant issues, and in the research process, we have been conducting the examination and analysis through the pictophonetic structure as a whole. The pictophonetic structure of the ancient Chinese characters was right in the developing and improving stage. By the research on the features of the pictographic component and its relationship with the meaning in this stage, we believe that it is not accurate to say in the past that the function of the pictographic component is 'to express the meaning' or 'to express the meaning of categories'. The main function of the pictographic component should be 'differentiation' and 'marking'. Such a component is only a conventional and distinguishing sign that is related to the meaning of a character.

---

[17] The original title of the paper is 'On Pictographic Components'. *Journal of Huaibei Coal Mining Teachers College* 1 (1986).

[18] Phonetic components are discussed in another paper. Cf.: 'The Phonetic Components of the Pictophonetic Structure' included in this book.

The pictographic component continues changing in the ancient script stage. There are many variants with ambiguities and close meanings in the same pictographic component structure. These are dominating characteristics.

1. The Continuous Change of the Pictographic Component: From the perspective of the pictophonetic characters of high frequent use, the continuous change of the pictographic component is mainly manifested in the following three aspects: first, such a component may be used or may not be used. For some pictophonetic character, under many circumstances, only its phonetic component is actually used while the pictographic component becomes mobile element that may be used or may not be used. For example, in Figure 2.1, the character '匜' may follow '皿' or may be used as '也'. '盤' may or may not follow '皿'. '盨' can be used as '须' or '盨'. Second, it may be added or reduced. The pictographic component may be consecutively added to some character. For example, in Figure 2.1, '匜' follows '皿' and then the pictographic component '金' is added to it. The pictographic component '米' or '金' is consecutively added to '盨'. Such an added part may be deleted at any time. Neither does its addition introduce too much complexity nor does its reduction affect the function of the character use. Third, it may be replaced. Replacement may happen to some pictographic component due to different times, different regions and different scriptwriters such as the pictographic components of '盂, 盤, 盉' in Figure 2.1. The aforementioned three aspects are the causes of the characteristics of the continuous change of the pictographic components of the pictophonetic characters. Such characteristics are reflected not only in the whole pictographic system but also in the pictographic component of the same character. The characters exemplified and discussed earlier clearly reflect several modes of the continuously changing pictographic components.

2. Sharp Differences of the Pictographic Components of the Same Pictographic Structure: There are often differences among the variants in the pictographic structure of ancient Chinese characters, and they are mainly manifested in the differences of the pictographic components while the phonetic components are relatively stable elements. *Houma Covenants* (《侯马盟书》) are the written

The Main Body of Chinese Characters **121**

Figure 2.1

materials of the same period and the same region, in which the differences of the variants are predominant and typical. For example, '殹' follows 支 and is pronounced as 殹 (又 omitted). Its phonetic component remains unchanged but the pictographic component may follow a big variety of forms such as 支, 卜, 口, 心, 止, 彳, 示 and so on, and with their combinations, the variants may reach over 11. With the additional differences caused by decorative marks, changes of phonetic components and the simplification of handwriting, the deviations of the variants are increasing.[19] Take

---

[19] '殹' as a pictophonetic character is based on character form materials on Shiqiang Basin (史墙盘) and Maogong Ding (毛公鼎) from the Western Zhou period.

another example. The number of the variants of '腹' can even reach over 97,[20] of which the variants caused by the differences of the pictographic components reach 24. The basic pictographic component is '肉' and the increased or changed pictographic components are 口, 心, 勹, 厂, 止, 彳, 辵, 攵 and so on. '亞, 腹' have many variants which are typical and predominantly reflect the characteristics that the same pictophonetic character can produce many variants due to its different pictographic components. If we disregard the boundaries of times and regions, the differences of the pictographic components of the same pictophonetic structure are prevalent and more obvious. Take '造' as an example. While the pronunciation of '告' remains the same, there are dozens of variants of different pictographic components (see Figure 2.2). The differences of the variants are prevalent in the same regions and times as well as in different regions and times, which shows that the pictographic components are very active elements in the stage of the ancient Chinese characters.

3. The Interchangeability of the Pictographic Components with Close Meanings: The pictographic components of the ancient Chinese characters are often interchangeable due to the same

颂鼎	颂簋	颂簋	御侯之戈	郜造鼎	申鼎
羊子戈	高密戈	宋公栾戈	曹公子戈	郑竝果戈	
邦之新造戈	滕侯戈	新郑兵器	古玺 2550		

Figure 2.2

---

[20] The character forms can be seen in the character diagram of Zhang Han's *Houma Covenant* (Beijing: Cultural Relics Press, 1976). This diagram lists all kinds of variants.

origin or some links between the meanings of their pictographic components.[21] This is another characteristic of the pictographic components. For example, the pictographic components '人', '女' and '儿' are interchangeable: '嬴' may follow '卩' (Yingji Gui 嬴季簋 food vessel inscription) or follow '女' (Yingshi Ding 嬴氏鼎 cooking vessel inscription); '姓' may follow '人' (Qi Bell 齐镈 bell inscription) or follow '女' (Zu Chu script 诅楚文); '允' may follow '女' (Buqi Gui 不期簋 food vessel inscription) or follow '儿' (Shigu script 石鼓文); '卩', '人', '女' and '儿', except '女', which has gender difference, all deviate from the form of '人' and therefore are interchangeable. '止', '辵', '走' and '彳' are also interchangeable: for example, in the oracle bone script, '逆' follows '辵' (*Yin Qi Remnants* no. 725 佚 725) or '止' (*Yin Ruins Inscriptions Yi* no. 4865 乙4865); '边' follows '辵' (San Family Basin 散盘 inscription) or '彳' (YuDing 盂鼎 cooking vessel inscription); '趄' follows '辵' (ShiHuan Gui 史趄簋 food vessel inscription) or '走' (Fengzhong Gui 封仲簋 food vessel inscription). These four pictographic components are closely related in meaning. '止' is the pictograph of the toes and often denotes the meaning related to human action in the ancient character structure; '辵' denotes a person 人 (止) walking on the road, '彳' being the simplification of '行' and '行' being the pictograph of the main road; '走' denotes a person striding on the road, retaining an early form of '彳' (Shuduofu Gui 叔多父簋 food vessel inscription), the two forms are interchangeable in meaning.[22] '口, 言, 心' are interchangeable: '哲' follows '口' or '心' (Zengbo Fu 曾伯簠 grain receptacle inscription) or '言' (Fansheng Gui 番生簋 food vessel inscription); '誉' follows '心' (Marquis of Cai Bell 蔡侯钟 bell inscription) or '言' (Covenants 盟书); '德' follows '心' (Maogong Ding 毛公鼎 cooking vessel inscription) or '言'

---

[21] Gao Ming's (高明), 'Common Examples of the Pictographic Radicals with Similar Meanings in the Ancient Chinese Characters, *Chinese Philology* 4 (1982), Hong Kong collects most of the interchangeable pictographic components.

[22] The explanations in Xu Shen's *Origin of Chinese Characters* are based on the small seal script. None of the explanations of the four pictographic components above is accurate.

(Shisong Ding 史颂鼎 cooking vessel inscription). In the *Origin of Chinese Characters*, '口 is that by which people speak and eat'. '言 means to speak directly'. '心 means human heart, belonging to the organ of the earth element, dwelling in the centre of the body'. 'Definitions of 亲' in *Guangya* (《广雅•释亲》): '心 means 任 (undertaking)'. *Baihu tongyi* (《白虎通义》*The White Tiger Temple Debates of Classics*): 'The heart must be expressed by the undertaking of speech and this undertaking comes from thought.' As can be seen here, '口, 言, 心' are related in meaning and therefore are interchangeable. Here are some more interchangeable pictographic components due to their relatedness in meaning: '衣' is interchangeable with '巾, 糸', identically following '糸', '索', '素' and '鬲', interchangeably following '米' with '食' and '禾', '皿' with '缶' and '瓦', '飞' with '羽' and so on.

In addition to the three main characteristics above, the interchangeability of the pictographic components close in form is also worth noting. For example, the three pictographic components '月, 夕, 肉' are often interchangeably used due to their closeness in form. In the oracle bone script, the three are relatively different. '月' and '夕' are the two characters that deviate from the same form. In the early period, there is no such a stroke in '月' while there is a stroke in '夕'; however, in the late period, the situation is just the opposite. In the bronze script, the two are differentiated, but they are often interchangeable. In the oracle bone script, '肉' is differentiated from '月, 夕' while in the bronze script, '肉' is no different from '月', and in the small seal script and Shuihudi Qin Slips (《睡虎地秦简》), it is the same (see Figure 2.3 for the examples).

Figure 2.3

Take '肖' as an example. The *Origin of Chinese Characters* says, 'Ii follows 肉 and is pronounced as 小'. This is a misunderstanding because it follows '月' and '肉' in the small seal script, and it is difficult to be differentiated. From the ancient seal character '肖' or '夕', the component '肖' in '宵' in the Xiao Gui inscription (宵簋) follows the form of '月', which proves that '肖' 'follows 月 and is pronounced as 小'. As can be seen above, the confusion is very troublesome between '月' and '肉' due to their closeness in form. During the Warring States period, to avoid the confusion between characters due to their closeness in form, some compensations were made by adding some differentiating strokes. For example, a stroke is added to the right upper side of '肉', and a stroke is added to the opening parts of '月' and '夕', as illustrated in Figure 2.3. Exactly owing to the prevalence of this confusion, there is the demand for the differentiation.

The characteristics of pictographic components show that in the ancient character stage the pictographic components were still developing and changing. 'Continuous changes' and 'different forms' are the common phenomena in the development of the pictographic components. In the changes and differentiations, such components were selected, eliminated and finally determined in one fixed written form or differentiated into several fixed written forms to denote different meanings. Compared with the activeness and complexity of the pictographic components, the phonetic components are stable and unitary, which shows that the pictographic component does not play a predominant role in the pictophonetic structure, and a pictophoetic character may exist with it or without it. The 'different forms' and 'interchangeability of characters with similar meanings' also reflect the uncertainty of the roles played by the pictographic components and therefore their weakness in function.

It was thought in the past that the function of the pictographic component was to be 'ideographic' and 'meaning oriented' or 'half-meaning oriented'. However, from the perspective of the characteristics of the pictographic component in the ancient character stage, these views overestimated the function of the pictographic component. Compared with the phonetic component, the pictographic component is closely related to the meaning of the character. It mainly affects the meaning of the character and therefore it may as well be called the 'semantic component'. Yet some scholars even claim that 'the meaning of the pictophonetic character derives from its pictographic part'.[23] This is truly a misunderstanding. Some other researchers find that the pictographic component cannot play the ideographic role.[24] Some say that it only denotes 'semantic classification' or 'semantic categorization'. There is much progress in these views, but they are rather general and one-sided. To further clarify the function and nature of the pictographic component, there is a need to explore the relationship between the pictographic component and the meaning of the character. As for the ancient Chinese characters, such a relationship is mainly four-fold.

Completely or Basically Meaning-oriented Pictographic Component

First of all, let us look at several groups of characters:

1. '晶' and '星': In the *Origin of Chinese Characters*, '星' denotes the essence of all things. Its upper part is asterism. It follows 晶 and is pronounced as 生. It is also said to be a pictograph, following the form of 口 as the image of the star. In the ancient script, a dot is added in the centre of 口. As a result, it is confused and identical with 日. 㿕 is 星 in the ancient script. The pictographic component '晶' in the *Origin* means 'the light of the essence (精光也)'. Xu Shen uses '精' to denote '星'. *Lü's Spring and Autumn Annals* uses 精 as 星.[25] '精光' is the same as 'the light of the star (星光)'. In the oracle bone script, '晶' and '星' are originally the same characters. '晶' is the pictograph of the stars and then the phonetic component '生' is added so that there emerges the character '星' with '生' as the pronunciation and '晶' as the pictographic

---

[23] Ma Xulun (马叙伦), *Collected Papers of Ma Xulun*, (Beijing: Science Press, 1958).

[24] Yao Xiaosui (姚孝遂), 'The Structures and Developmental Stages of Ancient Characters', in *Studies in Ancient Characters*, vol. 4 (Beijing: Zhonghua Book Company, 1980).

[25] Yang Shuda, 'The Added Components of Characters', *Commentary on Philology from Jiwei Studio*, vol. 5 (Beijing: Zhonghua Book Company, 1983), 37.

component. Thus, '晶' is the same as '星' in meaning, but later they are divided into two characters.

2. '勹' and '匍', '匐': In the *Origin*, '匍 means to crawl on hands. It follows 勹 and is pronounced as 甫'. '匐 means to fall prostrate. It follows 勹 and is pronounced as 畐'. '勹 means to wrap, like a person bending to hold something'. Xu Shen's definition is inaccurate. According to Mr Yu Xingwu's research, this character originally looks like a person crawling on the side with hands. Then '甫' and '畐' are added as phonetic components and they become two pictophonetic characters, and then they develop into '双声謰语'.[26] '勹' originally denotes the same meaning as '匍, 匐'.

3. '邑' and '邦, 都': '邦' appears earlier in the bronze script. In the *Origin*, '邦 means state, following 邑 and pronounced as 丰'. '邑 means state, following 囗. In the former kings' system, there are high and low ranks, so 阝 is used as a component of a character'. According to Xu Shen's definitions, the two are the same in meaning; however, Duan Yuchai (段玉裁) makes the following annotation: 'In the ancient times, the place where there are city walls is called 国 or 邑 but not 邦. 邦 refers to the fief'. This shows that the pictographic components '邑' and '邦' are slightly different in meaning. In the *Origin*, '都 means the place where there are ancestral temples. It follows 邑 and is pronounced as 者'. '邑' and '都' are also close but different in meaning. In the exemplified characters, the pictographic components in group (a) and (b) are identical, both in the meanings of the components and the characters, while those in group (c) are close in meaning. Those characters '星, 匍, 匐' with the identical meanings of both components and characters are all formed as pictophonetic characters by adding phonetic components to the pictographs. It is very rare to see that the pictographic components are originally those characters. Generally speaking, the earlier pictophonetic characters have close meanings in their pictographic components and characters. As the pictographic components are more widely used and their ideographic scope continues to expand, their ideographic

---

[26] Yu Xingwu, *Interpretations of the Oracle Bone Characters* (Beijing: Zhonghua Book Company, 1979), 374–375.

function is relatively weakened in the early pictophonetic characters. For example, '都' and '邦' that follow '邑' emerge earlier and their pictographic components have very close meaning with their characters; however, after the Spring and Autumn period, the pictographic component was added to almost all place names and there appeared a large number of new pictophonetic characters. By then '邑' became very limited in expressing its meanings and its ideographic function was also relatively weakened in characters such as '都' and '邦'. Besides, it is not very frequent that the pictographic components are close in meaning with the concerning characters. Thus, in general, the pictographic components that can be fully or basically ideographic only take a very small proportion in the pictophonetic system.

The Pictographic Components that Express Categorization

These pictographic components indicate the categorization of the concepts contained in the pictophonetic characters, occupying a large proportion in the pictophonetic system. They appeared as early as the Yin-Shang period and were widely used. Nonetheless, such categorization is not strict but general and sometimes even seems confusing. When analysing pictophonetic characters, Xu Shen would use the mode that the character 'follows the form of a certain character or component and is pronounced as a certain character or component'. This, in fact, indicates the fact that some pictographic components express the meaning of categorization. However, from the objective perspective, Xu Shen's mode that the character 'follows the form of ...' mainly reflects his ideas of division: 'Methods are grouped together by their commonalities and objects are divided by their differences. Characters are categorized by their characteristics and commonalities go through them all. Complexity is maintained but overpassing is avoided. All characters are linked by their forms'.[27] He did not intend to explore the relationship between the pictographic component and

---

[27] Xu Shen (the Eastern Han dynasty). 'Preface to the *Origin of Chinese Characters.*'

the character. There are many character examples of the pictographic components that show the meanings of categorization, which have long been clarified by researchers. For example, those characters that follow '马' such as '驹, 驷, 雅, 骅, 骝, 鴽' all belong to the category of '马'; those that follow '木' such as '杞, 杜, 柏, 柳' all belong to the category of '木'. What is worth noting is that in the ancient pictophonetic characters, the interchangeability of the pictographic components with close meanings often breaks the boundary of the categorization between certain pictographic components and causes some confusion, such as the interchangeability of '艸, 木, 禾' and so on, which shows that in the ancient Chinese character stage, the pictophonetic characters are sometimes not very strict in their requirement of the pictographic components indicating categorization.

The Connection Between the Pictographic Component and the Meaning of the Character

Some scholars think that the relationship between the pictographic component and the meaning of the character are of only two kinds as listed earlier.[28] Either from the perspective of the ancient pictophonetic characters or from the perspective of the pictophonetic characters as a whole, the issue is not so simple. Many pictographic components form a certain relationship by a particular mode or character meaning, and such a relationship is highly complex and subtle. For example, the pictographic component '手' in '抉, 择, 掸, 扡' is also formed as '又' in the ancient script. It only indicates that the meanings of these characters are related to '手'. In other words, the pictographic component only indicates that these actions are conducted by '手' (hands). The pictographic '人' in '依, 倍, 偶' is the doer of the action; the pictographic '玉' in '琱, 理, 琢' is the recipient of the action; the pictographic components '戈, 刀, 尃, 殳, 戬, 割' only indicate the weapon or tool to be used; the pictographic components '金, 木, 糸, 革' in '钟, 棺, 组, 勒' are the materials for making these objects. In addition, some pictographic components represent the settings where

---

[28] Liang Donghan (梁东汉), *The Structures of Chinese Characters and Their Changes* (Shanghai: Shanghai Education Press, 1959), 130–31.

things exist or actions take place, and some others indicate the scope of meanings and the characteristics of the objects, the relationship of which is very complicated. This is because the concept contained in the pictographic component may interact with different meanings of characters from different perspectives, while the meaning of the same character may also interact with different pictographic components from different perspectives, resulting in the prevalent existence of the ambiguities of the pictographic components and the complexities in the relationship between the pictographic components and the meanings of characters. The different relationships between the pictographic components and the meanings of characters reflect the features of the human 'psychological association' when characters are formed, the differences of the pictographic selection and the different directions of the psychological association. Generally speaking, the meaning of the same character may interact with many pictographic components in their relationship of association; however, owing to the social nature of characters and the 'convention' and 'experience' in character formation, the association tends to have an 'orientation', which then acquires relative stability, avoids the limitlessness of the selection of pictographic components and makes it possible for us to seek the relationship between pictographic components and character meanings. This involves the psychological aspect of Chinese character formation, which will not be further explored in this part. From the above, we can be aware of the causes for the complexity in the relationship between pictographic components and character meanings and meanwhile we can avoid one-sidedly and over-simplistically seeing the relationship between pictographic components and character meanings.

The Obscurity in the Relationship Between Pictographic Components and Character Meanings

The analysis discussed earlier shows that the selections of pictographic components are mostly rational and we can find the various links between pictographic components and character meanings from different perspectives. Nonetheless, we cannot deny that the selection of some pictographic components may just follow a certain convention and it is originally obscure in the relationship with character meanings. For example, why '風' in the small seal script follows '虫' is a question difficult to be explained. Xu Shen's definition is hardly convincing despite all his efforts to explain.[29] Another example, '唐' in the oracle bone script follows 口 and is pronounced as 庚. Why does it follow '口'? '黔' in the oracle script does not follow '雲' but follows 隹 and is pronounced as 今. Why does it follow '隹'? These are all incomprehensible. The selections in this type of pictographic components or character formation derive from a kind of obscure consciousness, or owing to various limitations today, we cannot yet find the exact links between the pictographic components and the character meanings. On all accounts, their relationship with character meanings is obscure from today's perspective. The rationality of pictographic components is often damaged or some changes frequently occur that make the relationship obscure between pictographic components and character meanings, due to the social, mental and linguistic developments, and the differentiation, simplification, mistakes and interchangeability of character forms. We speculate that in forming characters some pictographic components may only play the role of the obscure representation of meanings but it is hard to be further proved. However, it is not to be doubted that some developments and changes lead to the obscurity of the meanings in the system of pictographic components. When discussing the ideographic role of pictographic components, we should, on the one hand, explore the motivation of the selections of pictographic components, and on the other, study the objective ideographic effect of pictographic components. We should also note the decorative signs and differentiating signs that are not pictographic components, for sometimes they may also enter the system of pictographic components, be accepted and become parts of the obscure elements within. For example, '口' is often used as a differentiating sign in the ancient script; in both '君' and '右', '口' is used to differentiate them from '尹' and '又'. If '口' is considered as a pictographic component to represent meaning, it becomes an obscure element. '口' is also used as a decorative sign in the stage of ancient Chinese characters. For example, in the Western Zhou period, in the same inscriptions on the two Chesanfu Kettle (车散父壶), '姞' on

---

[29] The *Origin of Chinese Characters*: 'When the wind comes up, the insect (虫) is born; the insect will be gone in eight days. It follows 虫 and is pronounced as 凡'.

Kettle B is the original character but '口' is added to the lower part of '姞' on Kettle A. '口' is sometimes added to the lower part of '巫' and '口' may also be added to the lower part of '元' in '冠' on *Houma Covenant Tablets* (《侯马盟书》). '口' is added to the lower parts of '纪' and '青' in Changsha Silk script (长沙帛书) as well as to the lower part of '大' in Knife Money script of the State of Qi (齐国刀币文). '口' is also added to the lower parts of '今' and '余' on King Zhongshan's Ding (中山王大鼎). Some scholars mistake them as '含' and '舍' for the use of '今' and '余' with '口' as the pictographic component. However, seen from '念' and '後' with the decorative component '口' on the same vessel, '口' is only a decorative sign with no meaning. Once these kinds of decorative signs and differentiating signs spread and are used for long, they may enter the system of pictographic components and become the elements of the obscure representation of meaning, such as Xu Shens explanations of '君' and '右' following '口'. As for '台' following '口', the *Origin* mistakes it as a pictographic component and takes it as the original character of '怡'.[30] In fact, in the Western Zhou period, '台' did not yet follow '口'. In the Spring and Autumn period, there appeared the addition of '口' to it, but this character without '口' still co-existed in the Warring States period. '口' only plays a decorative function. In the ancient script, some meaningless strokes out of handwriting habits became decorative strokes (羡画) and then further developed as integrated elements of the character structures. These strokes might become the obscure representation of meanings. For example, in the *Origin*, '元' and '丕' are included under the radical entry of '一'. They are both treated as pictophonetic characters. However, the stroke above '元' and the stroke below '丕' are both decorative strokes. In the ancient script, the traces of decorative strokes are clearly seen. The mistake of treating strokes as pictographic components will surely result in far-fetched claims.[31] Certainly, the elements of the obscure representation of meanings caused by character form evolution, decorative and

---

[30] See the explanation of the character '台' in the group of radical 口 in the *Origin of Chinese Characters*.

[31] See the explanation of the characters '丕' and '元' in the group of radical 一 in the *Origin of Chinese Characters*. '元' in the Xu Xuan's edition lacks '声'. It should follow Duan's annotation.

differentiating signs or decorative strokes are essentially different from the obscure elements caused by the irrationality in the selection of the pictographic elements. However, seen from the objective effect, they all cause the incomprehensibility between certain pictographic components and character meanings in the system of the pictophonetic system, and they all become pictographic components of the obscure representation of meanings. Although these obscure elements cannot well represent the meanings, they play the role of differentiation and marking under many circumstances. For example, '尹—君, 又—右, 厶—台, 兀—元, 不—丕' and so on, they all make use of these elements for the differentiation of character forms. We infer from the various relationships between pictographic components and character meanings that their selection is often restricted by character meanings. No matter how they interact with each other and to what degree they interact with each other, such a relationship can generally be found out. 'Representing meanings by pictographic components' partially reveals this fact. However, this generalization obviously cannot exactly point out the actual function of pictographic components, for the pictographic components that can indicate meanings or generally indicate meanings are very limited in number. Most of the pictographic components only loosely indicate the categorical meanings or are somewhat related to the meanings in some aspect. In addition, some obscure elements enter the system of the pictographic components and therefore reduce their ideographic function. In the ancient character stage, there are prevalent changes and different forms of pictographic components, and the interchangeability of pictographic components with close meanings or close forms. All these show that the pictographic components, as active and unstable elements, basically have not acquired distinctive ideographic functions. These characteristics demonstrate that the pictographic components in this stage could not produce the desirable effects. By the investigation of the characteristics of the pictographic components and their relationship with character meanings, we hold the view that in terms of the whole system of the pictographic components, the pictographic components are related to character meanings but their ideographic functions are rather weak.

Under most circumstances, the pictographic components have distinctive functions of marking and differentiation. Seen from the origin of the pictographic components, the picto-added pictophonetic characters appeared the earliest and became prevalent, by adding a marking or differentiating sign to the original character or phonetic loan character. We realize that the introduction of the pictographic components first only served the purpose of marking the meaning of a particular character or differentiating the semantic entry of ambiguous characters. For example, '冓' originally has several semantic entries but later by adding '辶, 女, 言' they are written as '遘, 媾, 讲'. Thus, by the differentiation of the pictographic components, several special characters are created with distinctive functions and these new characters cannot be confused with each other by the restraint of the pictographic components. Seen from the same pictophonetic pedigree, the differentiating function of the pictographic components seems more important. For example, in the ancient characters, there are the following pictophonetic characters with '工' as their phonetic components, such as '仜, 仛, 巩, 项, 恐 (following 心 and pronounced as 公 on Zhonghshan Square Kettle 中山方壶), 虹, 堆, 红, 杠, 邛, 江, 攻' and so on. Without the attached pictographic components, this group of characters will be impossible to be differentiated in form. Although not every single pictographic component can accurately indicate the meaning, '仜' will not be mistaken as '堆' which follows '隹' because it follows '人'. '江' follows '水' so that it will not be confused with '虹' which follows 虫. The pictographic component here can at least stipulate and direct us that the characters pronounced as '工' with different meanings can be differentiated according to different modes of association. As a result, the pictographic component can play its role in its differentiating function in the pictophonetic pedigree.

The characteristics of the pictographic components in the ancient character stage, their relationship with character meanings and the facts of their emergence and development, all give us reason to make the following judgment: in terms of the function, the pictographic component, by the material sign, stimulates human eyesight, stipulates and directs the orientation of human association so as to make the differentiation of the same phonetic signs; in terms of the nature, it is only a kind of conventional and differentiating (directional) sign which is related to character meaning.

The Phonetic Components of the Pictophonetic Structure[32]

The emergence of the phonetic components of the pictophonetic characters as the key structural elements is of profound significance in the development of Chinese characters. Its emergence signifies the significant transformation from the picto-semantic orientation to the phonetic-semantic orientation in the structural mode of the ancient Chinese characters, resulting in the decisive impact on the shaping and improvement of the Chinese character system. Thus, studying the phonetic components is an important topic in the study of the pictophonetic structure and even the whole Chinese character system. However, compared with the study of the pictographic components, there is a lot more to be explored in the study of the phonetic components, and there is a need for further research in the important issues of the characteristics of the phonetic components, their function of representing pronunciations, their relationship with the meanings and their role in the pictophonetic structure. This chapter conducts the preliminary discussion on the issues above by the use of the ancient character materials.

There are over 500 basic phonetic components of the ancient characters of the pictohonetic structure.[33] We may think this way that in the pictophonetic structure, the characteristics of phonetic components are basically in contrast with those of pictophonetic components. Compared with pictographic components, phonetic components are predominantly stable in a relative sense. The pictographic components in the ancient characters of the pictophonetic structure are often in a

---

[32] The original tile of this paper is 'A Preliminary Exploration of the Phonetic Components of the Pictophonetic Structure of the Ancient Characters' published in *Journal of Anhui University* (Edition of Philosophy and Social Sciences) 3 (1989).

[33] The approximate number of the basic phonetic components are analysed and calculated according to the recognized ancient pictophonetic characters, so the actual number may be larger, for some of the characters have not received the consensus and therefore are not included in the statistics. The present author has made *Diagram of Basic Phonetic Components*, which is too long to be attached here.

state of change while the phonetic components remain unchanged. For example, in the characters for vessel names that often appear in the bronze vessel inscriptions, '盉', '盘', '盨', '匜' and so on, their pictographic components can be optional or changeable; however, no matter how the pictographic components change, their phonetic components, such as '禾, 般, 须, 也', remain stable elements. In the pictophonetic structure, differences in the variants of the pictographic components are very prevalent. For example, the number of the variants of the characters '巫', '腹', '造' can reach dozens. However, the relative stability of their basic phonetic components makes the structural links between all kinds of variants. Consequently, in terms of the ancient characters, it is the relative stability of the phonetic components that maintains the system of the pictophonetic structure. If this stability is destroyed, it is hard to imagine how the pictophonetic structure can exist as a system.

There are multiple possibilities in the interaction between pictographic components and character meanings, which inevitably lead to the prevalent occurrence of the differences and ambiguities of the pictographic components. Theoretically, there are also multiple options for a phonetic component as a sign to record the pronunciation and therefore there occur variants of the same phonetic component. However, from our investigation of the pictophonetic system of the ancient Chinese characters, the variants of the same phonetic component are in fact rarely seen. Although there occur variants for the phonetic components of some characters, these variants are essentially different from those of pictographic components. The variants of pictographic components often reflect differences in the thinking of the structural formation and they are obviously different in the modes of interacting with concepts and in degrees. However, the variants of phonetic components do not affect their commonality to record the pronunciation. Despite the difference in the forms of components, their nature of recording the pronunciation remains the same, which is another aspect of the singularity of the phonetic component. For example, the following characters have the same effect in recording the pronunciation despite their different forms of the pictographic components.

In the oracle bone script, either '夷' or '矢' may be used as the phonetic component for 雉. In the same inscriptions on San Family

Basin (散盘) and the materials of the same period and region with *Houma Covenant* (《侯马盟书》), either '首' or '舀' is used as the phonetic component for 道. These are the interchangeable phonetic components that are very close in pronunciations.

In the ancient Chinese characters, besides the variants caused by differences in selection, some other pictophonetic characters with the variants of phonetic components should be considered as changes of phonetic components. Such changes are different from those of pictographic components, for they are often caused by regional accents and historical phonetic changes. The purpose of such changes is to adapt them to the actual pronunciations. For example, in the characters of the states of Zhao, Wei and Han (三晋, 战国时期赵、魏、韩三国), '铸' is formed as '钊' and the pronunciation of '寿' is changed to '寸'. In the characters of the state of Yan (燕文), '者' is not used as the phonetic component for '都', but '旅' is used instead as the pronunciation. All these cases are perhaps due to the differences in regional dialects. '疑' changes from the pronunciation of '牛' to that of '子' (The Qin Measurement Edict Plate 秦诏版). '脊' (King Wei of Qi's Grain Receptacle 陈侯因齐敦) changes its phonetic component and becomes '齌' and the pronunciation of '次' changes to that of '齐'. Don't all these reflect some traces of the phonetic development? Owing to the limited materials and the lack of the present accurate conclusion of the dialects and phonetic systems in the Yin-Zhou periods, we cannot carry on the discussion further. However, the changes of phonetic components are restricted by the actual pronunciations, which is undoubted theoretically. The singularity of phonetic components succumbs to that of their function to record pronunciations. Therefore, the relative stability and singularity are the predominant characteristics of phonetic components.

The issue of the function of phonetic components representing pronunciations has always been the focus in the study of pictophonetic characters. The interaction of any character system with the linguistic physical representation—the pronunciation—is the result of conventionality. Although people attempt to accurately reflect pronunciations by written signs, the result is far from satisfying. Even the more advanced phonetic written system cannot accurately record the actual pronunciations. Consequently, it is only relative for the written signs to record pronunciations. The ancient pictophonetic structure, as a kind of written signs representing pronunciations, thus, can only relatively reflect the pronunciations of the ancient Chinese language. What we want to discuss is the following. To what degree does the phonetic component as a sign to record the pronunciation match the pronunciation represented by the pictophonetic structure? That is, can the phonetic component truly play the role of accurately representing the pronunciation in terms of the pictophonetic structure?

Scholars earlier pointed out the differences between the phonetic component and the pictophonetic character, that is, the phonetic component cannot completely represent the pronunciation. Mr Zhou Youguang statistically surveyed the actual state of the phonetic components representing the pronunciations of the commonly used pictophonetic characters and drew the conclusion that the validity of the phonetic components representing the pronunciations is 39 per cent.[34] However, in terms of the ancient pictophonetic characters, we cannot conduct the statistical survey scientifically, demonstrate the phonetic function of the phonetic components by numbers and compare it with the validity of modern pictophonetic characters representing pronunciations, because we cannot grasp the exact pronunciation of a particular character of that time. Theoretically speaking, at the beginning of selecting the phonetic component, the phonetic component should have matched the pronunciation of the character, or they should have been very close; otherwise, the phonetic component would lose its function. In terms of the picto-added pictophonetic character, the phonetic component is originally the predecessor of this type of characters and there is no doubt that it is identical with the pictophonetic character in the pronunciation. The other two types of pictophonetic characters should be the same.[35] 'When studying the rhyming works of the Zhou

---

[34] Zhou Youguang (周有光), 'On the Phonetic Function of the Phonetic Components of Modern Chinese Characters', *Studies of the Chinese Language* 3 (1978).

[35] According to different formation approaches, we believe that the ancient pictophonetic characters can be classified into three basic types of the picto-added, phono-added and picto-phono-added characters. Cf.: 'Types of the Pictophonetic Structure' included in this book.

and Qin Dynasties, we find that the phonetic components match the pronunciations perfectly and they are so subtle in their relationships that they should never be confusing'.[36] Duan Yucai (段玉裁) first verified the Zhou and Qin rhyming works and then pointed out the fact that the characters with the same pronunciation share the same phonetic components. This is not only a great contribution to the study of the ancient Chinese phonology but it is also significant in the study of the pictophonetic structure. According to the principle that 'the same pronunciations must share the same phonetic components', the pictophonetic characters with the same phonetic component all belong to the same rhyme category, the phonetic component of which must be at least in the relationship of vowel rhymes with the pictophonetic characters. Then what about the initial consonants of Chinese characters? This is a question that has never been fully verified. The scholars of the ancient Chinese phonology generally assume that the pictophonetic characters of the same pedigree share the same (or similar) initial consonants. The pictophonetic characters are in the relationship with not only vowel rhymes but also alliteration with the phonetic components. The study of the early ancient phonological categories by pictophonetic characters is based on this assumption. Mr Huang Kan (黄侃) once claimed: 'The phonetic component must correspond to the pictophonetic character; otherwise, there must be means for interchangeability. If it does not comply with the vowel rhyme, there must be multiple pronunciations for the initial consonant'.[37] According to this view, the phonetic component conforms to the pronunciation of the pictophonetic character.

---

[36] Duan Yucai (段玉裁 from the Qing dynasty), "Diagram 2 of the Phonology of the Six Script Categories', in *Annotations of the Original of the Chinese Characters* (Shanghai: Shanghai Classics Publishing House, 1981), 818.

[37] In the quotation, '子' refers to the pictophonetic character and '母' refers to the phonetic component of the pictophonetic character. Mr Huang Kan (黄侃) holds the following view: 'A phonetic character must come from a non-phonetic character, and then the phonetic character becomes the non-phonetic pictophonetic character and the non-phonetic character becomes the phonetic component.' 'Phonetic and rhyming Differences' refer to the differences of 'rhyming categories'. See Huang Kan, *Notes on Characters, Phonology and Interpretation* (Shanghai: Shanghai Classics Publishing House, 1983), 36.

As for the function of the phonetic component representing the pronunciation, we can offer some proof by using the phonetic loan characters and rhyming dictionaries related to the ancient script. For example, according to Mr Wang Li's (王力) view, the characters in the category of '止' with 32 early ancient initial consonants and 30 vowels can be classified as follows:

1. The initial consonant of 章 and the vowel of 之: 止, 沚, 芷, 志.
2. The initial consonant of 昌 and the vowel of 之: 蚩, 齿.
3. The initial consonant of 禅 and the vowel of 之: 侍, 恃, 时.
4. The initial consonant of 定 and the vowel of 之: 待.
5. The initial consonant of 邪 and the vowel of 之: 寺.[38]

Their basic phonetic component is '止'. Although they all belong to the category of the vowel of 之, differences exist in their initial consonants. 章, 昌, 禅 are the lingual-palatal consonants, close to the initial consonant of 定 while 邪 is the apical front consonant. When following this initial consonant system, the phonetic component '止' can only be regarded as the basic phonetic representation, for the phonetic component is the same in pronunciation with some characters but only close with others. If we believe that the characters of the same phonetic component must be the same in both initial consonants and vowels, then these characters are either wrongly classified or this early ancient system is irrationally estimated. This is a problem that has not yet been well solved now. Seen from the ancient phonetic loan characters, the characters that follow '止' for their pronunciations are all interchangeable, which shows that there are no big differences in their pronunciations. For example, in *Shuihudi Qin Slip Script* (《睡虎地秦简》), '侍' is interchangeable with '待'. In *Laozi* A version (《老子》甲本) in Mawangdui Silk script, '寺' is interchangeable with '恃', '待', and '之' with '志'. In *Spring and Autumn Accounts* (《春秋事语》) in Mawangdui Silk script, '志' is interchangeable with '恃'. In *Laozi* B version (《老子》乙本), '寺' is interchangeable with '志', '待', and '侍' with '待', '恃', and '之' with '蚩'. In *Manuscripts of*

---

[38] Wang Li (王力), *Chinese Phonology* (Beijing: Zhonghua Book Company, 1963).

the Political Strategists in the Warring States Period《战国纵横家书》, '侍' is interchangeable with '待' and '持' with '恃'. In *Sun Zi's Art of War* (《孙子兵法》) from Yinqueshan Han Slips (银雀山汉简), '侍' and '寺' are interchangeable with '待'. In *Sun Bin's Art of War* (《孙膑兵法》), '侍' is interchangeable with '待' and '恃'. Yang Shuda (杨树达) once used the existent classics to prove that '寺, 持, 时, 恃, 侍 and 之' were all pronounced as '待'.[39] As a result, the characters in the category of '止' should all belong to the phonetic component of 定 and the pictophonetic character of '之' in the ancient character stage.

Take other examples of the characters in the category of '㠯 (台)':

1. The initial consonant of 透 and the vowel of 之: (台), 胎.
2. The initial consonant of 定 and the vowel of 之: 给, 怠.
3. The initial consonant of 喻 and the vowel of 之: 㠯,诒, 饴, 贻.
4. The initial consonant of 书 and the vowel of 之: 始.
5. The initial consonant of 邪 and the vowel of 之: 似, (姒).[40]

All the characters with the phonetic component of '㠯' share the same vowel and the differences in their initial consonants are very similar with those in the category of '止'. However, in the material of the ancient phonetic loan characters, all the characters with '㠯' as the basic phonetic component are interchangeable. For example, in *Shuihudi Qin Slip Script*, '治' is interchangeable with '笞'. In *Laozi* A version in Mawangdui Silk Script, '始' and '治' are interchangeable with '似', '怡' with '始', and '台' with '始'. In the silk script of *Spring and Autumn Accounts,* '台' and '怠' are interchangeable with '殆'. In *Laozi* B version, '怡' is interchangeable with '始' and '殆', '殆' and '台' with '怠'. In *Sun Bin's Art of War* (《孙膑兵法》) from Yinqueshan Han Slips (银雀山汉简), '骀' is interchangeable with '怠'. In *Wei Liaozi* (《尉缭子》), '台' is interchangeable with

---

[39] Yang Shuda, *Commentaries on the Bronze and Stone Inscriptions from Jiwei Study*, Enlarged Edition, (Beijing: Zhonghua Book Company, 1983) 90–93.

[40] '台' is derived from '㠯'. They are in fact the same characters. The pronunciation differs according to Mr Wang Li's proposed ancient phonological system, so it is represented by the form of '()'. '(姒)' and '始' are also the same characters in the ancient character stage, so '()' is also added.

'胎'. Thus, it can be seen that all the characters following the same basic phonetic component can be indirectly interchangeable. Mr Yang Shuda also proves that '诒, 怡, 贻, 饴, 始' are pronounced as '台' in the ancient times.[41] Then, the characters in the category of '㠯' all belong to the initial consonant of 透 (or 定) and the vowel of 之 in the ancient times.

The characters in the two categories of '止' and '㠯', which appear in the bronze rhyming script, also rhyme with the vowel of '之'. For example, '之' on Mengjiang Yi (孟姜匜 Mengjiang washing basin) rhymes with '熙' and '期'. '台' on Cai Houlu (蔡侯卢) rhymes with '亥, 祏, 子, 巳, 母'. '寺' on Zhugongjing Bell (邾公牼钟) rhymes with '忌, 堵, 士'. '以' on Qizi Zhongjiang Bell (齐子仲姜镈) rhymes with '鄙, 改, 忌' and so on.[42]

It is unquestionable to prove the relationship of the same rhyming categories by the rhyming script; however, to prove how much the phonetic component represents the pronunciation within the pictophonetic system by the phonetic loan materials is based on the premise that 'the phonetic loan characters' share the same pronunciations. Does the phonetic character loaning indicate the possibility of close pronunciations? Can alliteration and assonance alone be interchangeable? Opinions differ on these issues. Testifying such issues must be based on the early ancient pronunciations. However, phonetic loan characters and pictophonetic characters are used to study the early ancient pronunciations to affirm that either the characters of the same phonetic components or the phonetic loan characters must share the relationship of the same pronunciations.[43] This leads to the paradox and contradiction in methodology, which cannot be solved

---

[41] Yang Shuda, *Commentaries on the Bronze and Stone Inscriptions from Jiwei Study*, 90–93.

[42] Cf.: Wang Guowei, 'The Rhymed Reading of the Bronze and Stone Inscriptions in the Zhou Dynasties'; Guo Moruo, 'Continuation of the Rhymed Reading of the Bronze and Stone Inscriptions', in *Combined Compilation of the Bronze Script and Rhyming Script* (Jilin: The History Department of Jilin University).

[43] Wei Jiangong (魏建功), *Studies of Ancient Phonology* (Beijing: Beijing University Press, 1935).

at present. If we agree to the methods of the scholars on ancient phonology to affirm that phonetic loan characters are in the exactly same phonetic relationship, then it can be testified that the ancient pictophonetic characters of the same phonetic components share the same pronunciations. For example, as shown above, the characters in the two categories of '止' and '冒' are interchangeable because they have the same phonetic component. This proves that the characters following the pronunciations of '止' and '冒' are pronounced the same respectively. It is very common to see that characters with the same phonetic components are interchangeable in the ancient characters. We cannot elaborate more on these examples but the following statistics are very revealing. According to Qian Xuan's *Exemplifications of the Interchangeable Loan Characters in the Bronze Script*, the number of interchangeable characters in the bronze script in the Zhou Dynasties takes up 79.1 per cent of the total of the phonetic loan characters. We have conducted a preliminary statistical calculation of dozens of slip and silk script characters such as *Shuihudi Qin Slip Script* during the Qin-Han period. There are altogether 1,675 pairs of phonetic loan characters, of which 1,344 pairs are interchangeable, taking up 80.2 per cent.[44] The percentage is very close to that of the bronze script in the Zhou Dynasties. This shows that the interchangeability of the characters with the same phonetic components is a very prevalent phenomenon in the ancient script stage. If the phonetic loan characters must be in the relationship with the same pronunciations, then it proves that the pictophonetic characters with the same phonetic components must be pronounced the same. As can be seen hereby, in the ancient script stage the phonetic components have the function of accurately representing the pronunciations, or we can assume at least that even if the relationship of the phonetic loan characters indicates the closeness in their pronunciations, these materials also show that the phonetic

---

[44] Based on Shuihudi Qin Tombs Bamboo Slips, Mawangdui *Laozi* A Version and the Lost Articles after the Version, *Laozi* B Version and the Lost Articles before the Version; Mawangdui Silk Script: Spring and Autumn Accounts, *Manuscripts of the Political Strategists in the Warring States Period*; Yinqueshan Han Bamboo Slips: *Sunzi's Art of War, Sunbin's Art of War, Wei Liaozi*. The present author has written *Chart of Interchangeable Characters*, which is too detailed to be attached here.

components of the pictophonetic characters have strong function of representing pronunciations. This is because if the discrepancy is huge within the pictophonetic system, there will not occur the prevalent phenomenon of the interchangeability of the characters with the same phonetic components.

With the phonetic development, the pronunciations within the pictophonetic system gradually differ and the function of the phonetic representation of phonetic components starts to weaken. Such differences had started to occur no later than the Eastern Han Dynasty. The material concerning 'being read like...' (读若)[45] in Xu Shen's the *Origin of Chinese Characters* reflects such changes. They are manifested in the following three situations:

1. The character follows a certain pronunciation and then it is read like another similar character. For example, 珣 'follows 王 and is pronounced as 句. It is read like 苟. '珪' follows 王 and is pronounced as 隹. It is read like 维. '句' is originally used as the phonetic component for '苟'. '隹' is originally used as the phonetic component for '维'. As Xu Shen already indicates that one character is 'pronounced as 句' and the other is 'pronounced as 隹', and then he indicates again that one character 'is read like 苟' and the other character 'is read like 维', this reveals the fact that the actual pronunciations of the phonetic components '句' and '隹' have already deviated from the pronunciations of '珣', '苟', '珪' and '维' with '句' or '隹' as its phonetic component. Otherwise, he has no need for such redundancy.
2. In addition to the indication of the phonetic component, another character is used as a similar pronunciation. For example, 呴 'follows 王 and is pronounced as 句', and it 'is read like 宣'. 珛 'follows 王 and is pronounced as 有', and it 'is read like 畜 in 畜牧'. As these phonetic components are common characters, these

---

[45] As for '读若', the present views differ. Duan Yucai thinks: '"读若" means the imitation of the pronunciation.' Qian Zhuting (钱竹汀) says: 'It refers to the phonetic loan characters in the ancient script.' Wang Yun (王筠) claims: 'It may refer to the pronunciation and it may also refer to the phonetic loan character. Both are possible.' We take Duan's view.

similar pronunciations are not used to notate difficult characters but to indicate that the actual pronunciation of character has already deviated from its phonetic component despite the indication of their structural subordination.

3. 'It is pronounced as and read like the same character'. It indicates that the character follows a certain character, is pronounced as a certain character and is read the same as the character. For example, 瑂 'is pronounced as 眉 and is read like 眉'. Dozens of more characters follow the same pattern. This mode of phonetic notation is not noted in Duan Yucai's annotated *Origin of Chinese Characters*. Despite the elaboration on the expression 'being read like...' in Wang Yun's (王筠) *Exemplifications of the Origin of Chinese Characters*, it is still puzzling. Our speculation is that perhaps there were differences between their phonetic components and their actual pronunciations at that time. If they were read according to their changed pronunciations, they would not fit their phonetic components. However, Xu Shen still insisted that the phonetic components should be the correct pronunciations and they should be not ignored to cater the changed pronunciations. Thus, he made such indication to correct the mistakes during that period.

The three situations of 'being read like ...' related to the picophonetic characters indicate that there were considerable phonetic discrepancies within the pictophonetic system in the Eastern Han Dynasty. The phonetic discrepancies of the pictophonetic characters with the same phonetic components are the reflection of the phonetic changes and developments. The interweaving 'diachronic phonetic changes' and 'synchronic phonetic changes' of the actual pronunciations make it possible that the pronunciation recorded by the same phonetic component changes asynchronously. As a result, there must appear discrepancies in reading pronunciations within the pictophonetic system. The longer the 'diachronic phonetic changes' last and the more frequently the 'synchronic phonetic changes' occur, the more discrepancies there will be in reading pronunciations within the pictophonetic system. This occurrence has something to do with the character of the language as a sign system. The relative stability of language signs and their agreement with speech make it impossible to accurately reflect phonetic changes. In terms of any language sign system, the longer its history is, the bigger the gap is between the system and the actual pronunciations it records and the more obvious the discrepancies are. Even the Western phonetic languages are no exceptions, which cannot completely and accurately record the actual pronunciations. Seen from this perspective, it is no wonder that there are so many phonetic differences within the pictophonetic system. Because of such differences, some people deny the progressiveness of the phonetic representation by the pictophonetic characters. This is unscientific methodologically. Consequently, despite the phonetic discrepancies of the phonetic components, the basic viewpoint is undeniable that the pictophonetic structure in the ancient Chinese characters has the strong function of phonetic representation.

Each of the two elements (the phonetic component and the pictographic component) of the pictophonetic structure has its own distinctive function, complementing each other and forming a whole unity. In the pictophonetic structure, are the two elements in equal proportion or are they in the primary or secondary position? This is an unavoidable question in the study of the pictophonetic structure. It would affect our understanding of the nature of the pictophonetic structure whether we consider the two elements as 'equally important' or 'the pictographic component as the primary' or 'the phonetic component as the primary'. In the history of the study of the pictophonetic structure, the view of the pictographic component as the primary or the view of the two elements 'as equally important' is immensely influential.[46] From the perspective of the respective character of pictographic components and phonetic components, we believe that the pictographic instability and semantic uncertainty of the pictographic components place them in the secondary position, while the relative stability and unitarity of the phonetic components and their strong function of phonetic representation help them take a leading role in the pictophonetic structure. This can also be testified from the perspective of the derivation of the pictophonetic characters.

---

[46] Hu Pu'an (胡朴安), *A History of Chinese Philology* (Shanghai: The Commercial Press, 1937).

'Preface to the *Origin of Chinese Characters*' said, 'When Cang Jie started to create the script, he made pictographs according to types of objects, so they were called wen (文: carved pattern). Then pictophonetic characters increased, so they were called zi (字: phonetic character), and they multiplied in large numbers of derivatives'. Thus Xu Shen realized that the pictophonetic structure was the major means by which Chinese characters were derived. The number of the pictophonetic characters in the oracle bone script takes up about 10 per cent, the number in the bronze script in the Zhou Dynasties takes up 35 per cent and the number in the *Origin of Chinese Characters* exceeded 80 per cent, almost rising perpendicularly.[47] For the increase of the pictophonetic derivatives, there are four major causes.

1. *Differentiation of character forms*. It refers to the increase of pictophonetic characters derived from the differentiation of the same character. For example, '孚' is the original character of '俘'. To strengthen its semantic function, '亻' is added to make '俘' and the erred form in the small seal script is '俘'. The occurrence of '俘' is only the differentiation of the character. '各' and '佫', '迶' are originally the same character. To add the pictographic component to them is to strengthen the semantic function of '各', and thus two new pictophonetic characters of '佫' and '迶' are derived. '寺' and '持' are the same characters. '持' is derived from '寺' by adding '手'. The pictophonetic characters derived from the differentiation of character forms are only different from the original characters in the formalistic structures in the beginning and can be used interchangeably, but over a long period of time, they start to coexist with different meanings or some are eliminated.

---

[47] These are only approximate statistical data. The oracle bone script and the bronze script are compared with the recognized pictophonetic characters and the total number of their individual characters. Among the total number, there must be some pictophonetic characters that have not yet been recognized. Therefore, the percentage of the pictophonetic characters of the two kinds of materials should be higher than the present statistics. The characters included in the *Origin of Chinese Characters* are neither the total of the Qin characters nor do they represent the total of the characters of the Eastern Han Dynasty. However, these characters may reflect the general tendency of the pictophonetic development.

2. *The extension of the character meanings.* The extended meanings often result in multiple semantic entities of the same character and they contradict the ideal of specific characters for specific usage in the Chinese character system due to the lack of semantic clarity out of the overburden. As a result, they lead to the increase of new derivatives. For example, '冓' is the original character of '遘', from which '媾', '遘' and '觏' are derived. They are formed by differentiation, whose original meaning is 'encounter' (交遇), with the extended meaning of '媾', '觏', '讲' and so on, from which several new pictophonetic characters are then derived.
3. *Homophonic loaning.* The frequent homophonic loaning makes many characters acquire various semantic entities and they easily cause conceptual confusions. Consequently, pictographic components are added to create new pictophonetic characters. For example, '䜌' (on Luan Shu Jar 欒书缶), '䜌' (on Luan Ren Zhen Pot 欒人朕壶), '䜌' (on Xi Jia Plate 兮甲盘), '䜌' (on Song Ding 颂鼎) are originally borrowed from '䜌' and then when the pictographic components are added, such as '木, 女, 虫, 金' and so on, there appear new pictographic characters accordingly.
4. *To strengthen the phonetic representation.* The occurrence and development of the pictophonetic structure strengthens the phonetic function of Chinese characters. Some non-phonetic structures are affected and some phonetic components are added to them to create new pictophonetic characters. For example, '立' is originally used as '位', and then on King Zhongshan's Square Kettle (中山王方壶), '胃' is added as a phonetic component to '立'. '麋' in 麋鹿 (elk) is originally a pictograph, and then the phonetic component '米' is added to it. Some familiar terms like '凤', '鸡' and so on are also formed by adding phonetic elements on the basis of pictographs. We used to call them 'phono-added pictophonetic characters'.[48]

The new characters derived from the above four factors are created by adding pictographic components or phonetic components to

---

[48] According to different formation approaches, we believe that the ancient pictophonetic characters can be classified into three basic types of the picto-added, phono-added and picto-phono-added characters.

the original characters. There is another direct method of creating new characters, that is, to form a pictophonetic character by taking a pictographic component and a phonetic component simultaneously. By the process of creating pictophonetic characters, phonetic components have been taking dominating positions. In cases of the pre-differentiation, 'extended meanings' and 'homophonic loaning', in fact the phonetic components afterwards are used as the new pictophonetic characters to be created, that is, the phonetic components for the newly created pictophonetic characters function as such characters. Such being the case, in the creating process, phonetic components take very prominent positions. Except for some small number of pictophonetic characters created to strengthen the phonetic function, most of the characters are created on the basis of phonetic components by adding pictographic components. The character of the pictographic component places it in a secondary and complementary position. Meanwhile, the phonetic component makes itself acquire the condition of taking the dominating position in the structure due to its relative stability and unitarity. In addition, its relationship with language also establishes itself. Due to the constant change of language, such change is predominantly reflected in the accelerating increase of pictophonetic characters in the Chinese character system, and the phonetic component of the ancient Chinese pictophonetic character, in most cases, represents a phonetic form of an ancient Chinese character. This is the internal reason why the phonetic component plays a dominating role in the creation of characters. Even the pictophonetic creation to 'strengthen phonetic representation' by adding phonetic components can also reflect its due role of the phonetic component in its creation. The parts that become pictographic components because of the phonetic addition originally have their relative independence of form, sound and meaning and they are the predecessors of the created characters. Their independence can exist alone without the phonetic component and therefore the phonetic components have the tendency of attachment from the very beginning. However, through simplification and replacement, the parts that passively become pictographic components are often weakened, which therefore stabilizes the pictophonetic structure. For example, the changes of '鸡', '耤', '宝' and so on clearly demonstrate this viewpoint.

The process of the pictophonetic creation and the role phonetic components play in the creation naturally become the pictophonetic pedigree with phonetic components as the core. Dai Dongyuan (戴东原) first proposes the concept of 'pedigree'.[49] This is truly a big discovery in the research of the pictophonetic structure. According to the pictophonetic pedigree, we can trace the evolution of the pictophonetic characters and their close or distant relations. This is of great significance for the research in the etymology of characters and expressions. The pictophonetic characters of the same pedigree, if from the same origin, must have certain connection in their phonetic components. Wang Shengmei's (王圣美) 'Theory of Right Phonetic Components' (右文说) from the Song Dynasty partially reflects this fact.[50] This theory is incomplete, and it creates controversy for a long period of time, with no consensus even today. In our view, despite its defect of taking parts as a whole, its rational elements should be affirmed. The value of this theory mainly lies in the research on linguistics. The idea of 'making sense from the phonetic components' in philology is exactly the extension and development of its rational elements. Then it is developed into 'interchangeability of sense from close phonetic components' and the study of etymology, both of which exceed the category of philology.[51] From the philological point of view, the meaning of 'sound' pointed out in the theory can be used to infer the origins of the pictophonetic characters, helping to correctly understand the peculiar phenomenon of 'both pictophonetic and associative' functions in the character structures. However, it must be pointed out that this 'meaning' is only the historical trace left by the creation of pictophonetic characters, or it is the residue in the development of pictophonetic characters. In term of the pictophonetic structure, it is only focused on recording speech and therefore reflects its semiotic function to record language by characters. It does not need to or it

---

[49] Dai Zhen (戴震 from the Qing dynasty), 'A Reply to Duan Ruoying's View on Phonology', *Works of Dai Zhen* (Beijing: Zhonghua Book Company, 1980).

[50] Shen Kuo (沈括 from the Northern Song dynasty), *Brush Talks from Dream Brook*, vol. 14.

[51] Shen Jianshi (沈兼士). 'The History and Supposition of the "View of the Components on the Right" in Philology', *Collected Papers of Shen Jianshi* (Beijing: Zhonghua Book Company, 1986).

cannot represent concepts by its original meaning. The meaning of the 'phonetic' (component) left due to the creation of the characters is an entirely different matter from the 'meaning' (concept) of recoding speech and language by phonetic components. They should be treated differently. As a result, we should limit the discussion of the meaning of 'phonetic' components in philology to the minimum scope (discussing the issues of the derivative relations and etymology), and strictly distinguish it from the relationship between 'sound' and sense in the category of linguistics so as to avoid the confusion in our research work and correctly understand the character of phonetic components and the pictophonetic structure.

From the above discussions, we hold the following views: the basic function of phonetic components is to record speech, and it only exists as the material sign to record speech. Its development and change are closely related to those of language. The character of relative stability and unitarity of phonetic components, their strong function of representing speech and their dominating role in the pictophonetic structure can all demonstrate this viewpoint. In other words, the character, function and position of phonetic components are all determined by their semiotic nature of recording speech.

The Combinations, Characteristics and Nature of the Pictophonetic Structure

The Combining Relationship of 'Form' and 'Sound'[52]

The combination of a pictographic component and a phonetic component forms a pictophonetic character. The respective positions of the two components should be fixed according to the requirement of the relative stability of the form of the character sign. However, in the ancient character stage, it is very common that form and sound change freely. If we take the phonetic component as a fixed position, we can see the following: the pictographic component can be on the left or the right, above or below, inside or outside. The

---

[52] Originally published in *Journal of Anhui University* 3 (1997).

uncertainty of the pictophonetic position shows that the relationship of the pictophonetic combination is still unsettled, which is directly related to the period when the pictophonetic structure of the ancient characters was still in the developing stage. It would take quite a process for the forms of the character signs to settle down. Only by a long period of selection and elimination can the character structure be relatively stabilized.

In some characters, the pictographic component and phonetic component seem unstable in their relationship. It often occurs that the pictographic component falls off, which is the main manifestation of their unstable relationship. Such pictophonetic characters are mainly formed by adding pictographic components. It shows that after the pictographic components are added, it still takes time for the combination of form and sound to settle down. The falling off of the pictographic component exists in the whole process of the development of the pictophonetic structure. The early pictophonetic structures may settle down in usage and convention but then the new structures will still cause similar unsettlement. If the history is ignored in the development of pictophonetic structure, after the falling off of the pictographic component, the phonetic component is usually considered as the phonetic loan character. From forming the pictophonetic character by adding the pictographic component to maintaining only the phonetic component when the pictographic component falls off, in the development of the pictophonetic character, the process seems a reduction. However, such changing results are fundamentally different. By adding the pictographic component, the original part of the character is changed into a phonetic component, forming a new pictophonetic structure, a leap from one essence to another, while, when the pictographic component falls off, it becomes a necessity that the new essence changes and improves itself.

We need to further explain here that in the ancient character stage, the 'unsettlement' and 'instability' reflected in the combination of the pictophonetic structure only concern the comparison of the settled character system. In reality, the two elements of the pictophonetic structure still retain their own character in the forms of their combination and follow some universal principles. When the ancient characters developed into the system of the small seal script, such characters and principles became more obvious and graspable. For example, the 'right component', as was discussed by the ancients, refers to the fact that in the combination the phonetic component is placed on the right of the pictographic component, that is, the pictographic component is on the left and the phonetic component is on the right. This is a very characteristic combining principle of the pictophonetic structure in the settled small seal script system. The pictographic component of '水' in the oracle bone script reveals the tendency of the pictographic component to be on the left. Take *The Compilation of the Oracle Bone Script* as an example. In the oracle bone script, there are 68 characters with '水' as the pictographic component (perhaps it cannot yet be determined whether some of them are pictophonetic characters), in which the script form of '水' goes as follows: 𔓱, 𔓲, or in the form of a drop of water. 38 characters have '水' on their left, taking up about a per cent; 2 characters have '水' on their right and 6 characters have it on either left or right; 20 characters have '水' on both left and right or have dots across them. Besides, in two characters '𔓳', '𔓴' (following 水 and pronounced as 麋), the former takes '水' as the main part with the phonetic component '又' (有) on the lower position, and the latter takes '水' right below '麋', both of which are positioned naturally in the characters in accordance with the features of the forms of the pictographic component and the phonetic component. Regarding the group of characters with this radical, although '水' as a pictographic component, still needs to be fixed and unified, it is obvious that its position tends to be on the left. *The Compilation of the Bronze Script* includes 64 pictophonetic characters with '水' as the pictographic component from the Zhou Dynasties to the Warring States period, among which 50 characters have '水' on the left, taking up more than 78 per cent, 5 characters have it on the right, 8 have it below and 1 has it either on the left or the right. As can be seen, from bronze script from the Zhou Dynasties to the Warring States period, the pictophonetic characters with '水' as the pictographic component generally have the tendency of having the pictographic component on the left and the phonetic component on the right in their combining forms. Shuihudi Qin Slips, as the specimen of Qin characters, have 46 pictophonetic characters with '氵' as their pictographic components, all of which are positioned on the left.⁵³ It shows that the characters in the small seal script included in the *Origin of Chinese Characters* are in line with the Qin characters. The other pictophonetic series with the combination of the pictographic component on the left and the phonetic component on the right similar to those with '氵' as the pictographic component include the following: '示, 王(玉), 牛, 口, 走, 辵, 彳, 齿, 足, 言, 革, 目, 羊, 歹, 骨, 月, 角, 食, 缶, 韦, 木, 日, 禾, 米, 人, 石, 豕, 豸, 马, 犬, 火, 鱼, 手, 耳, 女, 弓, 糸, 虫, 土, 田, 金, 车, 阜, 酉' and so on. The pictophonetic structures formed by these pictographic components, in the ancient character, from 'unsettlement' to settlement, have gradually the structures of the pictographic component on their left and the phonetic component on the right. Due to the large proportion of the pictophonetic series formed by these pictographic components, people have formed the conventional concepts of the pictophonetic characters with the phonetic components on the right and the pictographic components on the left, and they generalize such phenomenon by 'right component'. Although 'the pictographic component on the left and the phonetic component on the right' reflect the formalistic features of the pictophonetic combination of most of the pictophonetic characters, they are not the basic principles to be followed by the character formation and development.

The forms of the pictophonetic combinations are never completely consistent. In terms of the structures of the pictophonetic combinations, the principles for such combinations to follow, whether the pictographic component is on the left and the phonetic component is on the right, or up and down, are a matter of equilibrium in the structures of the character forms. The balance of character structures depends on the features of the original formation or deformation of the characters and their script conventions. As is mentioned above, in the bronze script during the Western Zhou Dynasty and the Warring States period, the pictographic component '氵' is primarily settled down on the left, but in quite some characters, it is not on the left. Let us make an analysis of the features of the eight exceptional character

---

⁵³ Zhang Shouzhong (张守中), *A Compilation of Shuihudi Qin Bamboo Slip Script* (Beijing: Cultural Relics Press, 1994).

Figure 2.4

forms with '水' on the lower position, so that we can see these issues clearly. These eight characters are given in Figure 2.4).

The eight characters above include '河, 涂, 汉, 滛, 脊, 湘, 谦, 灛'. This group of characters has the pictographic component '水' in the lower position, which is obviously related to the features of the forms of their phonetic components. The phonetic components of the previous six characters all have the left–right structure. The phonetic components of the latter two characters form the harmonious balance. '水' on the left undoubtedly overthrows the whole structure, but when it is placed below, the combination of the whole character seems balanced. '水' as the pictographic component is mostly placed on the left; however, when it is later placed below, it predominantly shows that the pictophonetic combination follows the principle of balance in character formation but not just sticks to the 'pictographic component on the left and the phonetic component on the right'. Since five out of the eight characters come for E Junqi Passes (鄂君启节), does it mean that they are formed by individual or regional script convention? Our answer is negative. The pictophonetic character '瀞' with the pictographic component '水' on the right can provide us with the evidence. The character is written as '𩰚', where '水' as the pictographic component is most appropriately written on the right position below in the character. We cannot find a better rationale to explain why '水' is placed on the right if it is not because of the principle of balance. When the characters are stabilized in the left–right structure, except for '湘, 溓', the rest of them adjust their phonetic components so as to keep balance with their pictographic components. Similar cases can be provided as typical material in Baoshan Chu Slips (包山楚简). For example, in these slips, in the 18 pictophonetic characters with '水' as the component, except for '渐' as '𤃇', '湘' as '𣲚', '沼' as '𣲖', '没' as '𣳏', 水, the rest of the characters all have '水' on the left and the phonetic component on the right. In the 60 pictophonetic characters with '糸' as the component, '糸' is generally placed on the left, and only '繁(绷), 鬓(滕), 絫(絩), 㬅(缘)' are exceptions, which are similar to the character forms with '水' below. In the same group of slips, the pictographic component '木' on the left is very consistent with the exceptions. Thus, this phenomenon can only be fully explained by the principle of structural equilibrium in the form of pictophonetic combination.

By the exceptions of one group of characters, we have examined the principles that the pictophonetic combinations follow in structure. If we take the features of the pictophonetic combinations as a whole, in the process of the gradual settlement and certainty of the pictophonetic characters, it is also true that the principle of equilibrium determines the combining positions of the pictographic components and the phonetic components of various characters in the pictophonetic system. For example, '艹, 竹, 宀, 网, 彡, 雨' and such pictographic components are usually placed above the phonetic component; '皿, 虫, 蟲' and so on as components are placed below the phonetic component; '鬥, 门, 口, 匚' usually include the phonetic components within themselves. (If they are used as phonetic components, they include pictographic components within. '问, 闻' are the examples'.) When '广, 疒, 厂, 𠂆, 尸' are used as pictographic components, their phonetic components are half enclosed; when '鬲, 贝, 巾, 衣, 心' are used as pictographic components, they are either placed on the left or below, depending on the features of their phonetic components. '羽, 鹿, 山' are mostly placed on the left or occasionally placed above; however, '殳, 攴, 隹, 鸟, 刀, 虎, 邑, 见, 欠, 页, 戈, 刀, 斤, 斗' as pictographic components are normally placed on the right. Such examples all follow the principle of equilibrium of the character structures according to the features of the pictographic and phonetic components in the character forms so as to make the character forms meet the aesthetic requirement.

In general, when we historically investigate the combining relationship of the ancient pictophonetic characters, we do not only grasp the features of their unsettlement and instability, but we are also assured, through their developmental trend and the process of their settlement and certainty, that the formalistic features of the pictophonetic combinations are the manifestation of the harmony and unity between the pictographic components and phonetic components in the Chinese characters, which follows the principle of equilibrium in the character formation.

The Features of Pictophonetic Structures

After the discussion of the features in the combinations between pictographic components and phonetic components, we need to delve into the inner layers of the pictophonetic structures to analyse the features of the pictophonetic structures in their formation so as to better understand this structural mode.

As a structural mode, the dominating features of the pictophonetic structures are that they break through the thinking pattern of the picto-semantic representation of the early Chinese characters in the formation of new characters, and base the links between character formation and the characters recorded thereby on the medium of 'phonetic' components. The formation modes such as pictographs, simple indicatives and associative compounds mainly rely on the formalistic features and combinations and flexible means to make the semantic representation of the linguistic expressions recorded thereby by the character forms, so as to establish the fixed relationship between character signs and linguistic expressions. As a result, the links between the basic formation modes and the 'phonetic' representation of the linguistic expressions are gradually established by repeatedly emphasizing the relationship between form and meaning. In the characters formed by the modes of pictographs, associative compounds and simple indicatives, every formation component or sign starts from the link between form and meaning, participating in the formation of the language sign. There is no inevitable and definite phonetic connection between the characters formed by these modes and the expressions recorded by them. Once the sign is formed to record a certain expression from the picto-semantic relationship, the 'sound' of the expression accordingly establishes the relationship with the sign. The pictographic component in the pictophonetic structural mode, as a formation element, is somewhat similar to the formation components employed by pictographs, associative compounds and simple indicatives; however, the phonetic component as a sign to record the pronunciation of the expression is entirely different from these formation components. The appearance of the phonetic components as new elements for Chinese character formation leads to the features of the pictophonetic structure different from the other three basic formation modes.

1. In the pictophonetic structure, the two formation elements have their respective roles and distinctive formation functions. In the structures of the pictographs, associative compounds and simple indicatives, each formation element is in the same dimension, having the same function in the formation of new characters. Even the abstract signs in the structure of the simple indicatives play their roles in the relationship between the character form and meaning. For example, '寇' is composed of three formation components: '宀' in the shape of a house, '元' referring to a person (a human head) and '攴' indicating holding an instrument. The combination of the three components indicates the meaning of '寇'. If we seek the association of every component with the meaning of the character '寇', we can follow the implied association of these components of 'committing violence with weapons in the house' to understand the whole meaning of the character. Therefore, to a certain degree, all the components of the associative compound have more or less connection with the meaning of the character. The pictograph carries the meaning of its recorded expression with its formalistic features. In the early stage of the formation, the connection between its form and meaning is obvious. As for the abstract signs of the simple indicatives, such as the dots and strokes in '乀, 人, 木, 夊', although the abstract dots and strokes cannot clearly point out concrete contents, the indicative signs, based on the pictographs, adequately indicate the meaning of the simple indicative, making the abstract dots and strokes of no substantial meaning acquire the connection with the meaning of the character within the restraint of the character form. Thus, in essence, the indicative sign still reflects the relationship between form and meaning. In the pictophonetic structure, the pictographic component still participates in the formation from the sphere of the

meaning of the character. What needs to be particularly stressed is that the pictographic component is weak in indicating the meaning of the character. The pictographic components of most of the characters in the pictophonetic structure are only limited to a certain degree in their implication of the meanings of the characters. It is unlikely that they have the capacity of representing the whole meanings of the characters. Despite all these, they, as the formation element, have distinctive roles to play. In the picto-phono-added type of pictophonetic characters, the selection of the pictographic component starts from the indication of the meaning from the very beginning. The picto-added pictophonetic character, by the intervention of the pictographic component, indicates the meaning represented by the added part. The pictographic component of the phono-added pictophonetic character is formed passively. The added part does not only have the capacity of recording the meaning of an expression, but also consolidates its pronunciation. This 'pictographic component', if it is the original character, is naturally semantic; if it is the phonetic loan character, it records the meaning according to the phonetic association. At any rate, it seems that its function is different from the pictographic component in a real sense. Consequently, the pictographic component of the phono-added pictophonetic character acquires the function of a general pictographic component after its renovation and assimilation. If few pictophonetic characters formed by loan characters plus phonetic components still retain their 'pictographic components' (the added parts) as they are, then they are often regarded as an attached category of the pictophonetic structure, which is called 'both components as being phonetic' (两体皆声) or 'character of double phonetic components' (两声字) or 'double pictophonetic character' (二重形声), such as '薔, 訋, 雩, 虖, 悟, 闵, 箕, 貦, 萠, 夔' and so on. In fact, this pre-existing 'sound' of 'both components as being phonetic' habitually records the meaning of the original character; only the 'sound' added afterwards has the function of recording the pronunciation. Since the former has already lost its function of recording the pronunciation, it becomes an altered 'pictographic component' that gathers the loaned meaning. Phono-added characters of such kind are very few, so they serve as a special category and do not affect the basic features of the pictographic components in the pictophonetic structure. The function of the phonetic component in the pictophonetic structure is to record the pronunciation of the character. In terms of the picto-phono-added and phono-added pictophonetic structure, it can be assumed that the only function of the phonetic component is to record the pronunciation. A phonetic component is selected on the basis of being pronounced the same as the expression being recorded. It does not need and cannot concern the relationship with meaning. Meanwhile, we also need to acknowledge that under certain circumstances, the selection of the phonetic component may be enlightened by the meaning. When multiple components with the same pronunciation coexist, perhaps it is not unlikely to select a component that is associative in both pronunciation and meaning. However, in most cases, it may not be a prevalent fact. If the phonetic component in the pictophonetic structure has both the phonetic and semantic function, the formation will become very difficult and the pictophonetic structure will lose its progressive significance. As for the phonetic component of the picto-added pictophonetic character, if the picto-added mode comes from the loan character, the function of the phonetic component is still phonetic; if it is the case of adding the pictographic component to the original character, the part that passively becomes the phonetic component in effect inherits the 'meaning' recorded originally. Such phonetic component, in a sense, is not purely phonetic. The so-called meaning within the phonetic component (声中有义) refers mainly to this category. Nonetheless, we must acknowledge that seen from the reproduction and differentiation of characters, the 'meaning' recorded by this category of 'phonetic components' has already been far different from that of the original character, or the original character is rather ambiguous in its meaning and thus the relationship between its form and meaning becomes hard to discern, resulting in the inner requirement of indicating meaning by 'added pictographs'. In essence, the addition of the 'pictograph' widens the separation between the added part and the meaning of the original character, making it equal to a phonetic component in actual usage. If we do not consciously seek and examine the relationship, the connection will have already been disrupted between the meaning of the original character and the part that has become the phonetic component due to the addition of the pictograph. As a result, in the pictophonetic structure, the two formation elements have distinctive roles to play: the pictographic component, through the interaction with the meaning of the character, indicates the semantic scope; the phonetic component, through the recording of the pronunciation of the character, carries the meaning of the character; both rely on each other to form new characters.

2. *The formation duality of the pictophonetic structure.* Written characters as signs to record language are a whole unity composed of different components on the same level. This whole unity of signs has three elements of form, sound and meaning: 'form' being the material subsistence, 'pronunciation' being the phonetic sign carried and recorded by the 'form' and 'meaning' being the semantic content of the linguistic expression recorded by the sign. These are the features shared by any writing system in a strict sense all over the world. The Chinese characters, as a writing system, are no exceptions. Every Chinese character has the three elements of form, sound and meaning in a general sense. In terms of the formation of a writing system, all the formation units of the western alphabetic writing systems participate in the formation of the linguistic signs on the level of the 'sound'. However, the Chinese characters have their own features. They are formed by the structural modes such as associative compounds, pictographs and simple indicatives, and every formation component (unit) participates in the formation of the linguistic sign on the level of 'form−meaning'.[54] As for the alphabetic writing system that spells the words purely by recording the pronunciations, every spelling unit (letter) only serves its function as the phonetic symbol. As

---

[54] The 'simple indicatives classified by their phonetic features' pointed out by Mr Yu Xingwu has gone beyond the level of 'form–meaning'. However, this is a kind of 'simple indicatives' came into existence only afterwards. They may be influenced by the differentiation formation mode of the picto-added pictophonetic characters. See Yu Xingwu, 'A Case Study of the Simple Indicatives Classified by Their Phonetic Features in the Ancient Characters', *Interpretations of the Oracle Bone Script* (Beijing: Zhonghua Book Company, 1979).

for the early Chinese characters that represent meaning purely by forms, every formation component serves its function of representing meaning by form and the other original content of every component does not participate in the formation. The pictophonetic structure is neither a purely phonetic symbol nor purely a semantic symbol, but it has the dual features. In the pictophonetic structure, the pictographic component participates in the formation on the level of 'form—meaning', maintaining its consistency with the function of the formation component in the associative structural mode. The phonetic component participates in the formation on the level of recording the pronunciation, acquiring the same function of the spelling unit in the alphabetic writing system. This duality of the pictophonetic structure actually determines the direction of development of the Chinese character system different from other writing systems. On the one hand, it inherits the tradition of Chinese character formation, utilizes the existing sign resources to form new characters and maintains the continuity and stability of the Chinese character system; on the other hand, it rids itself from the dilemma of representing meaning by form, develops the Chinese character signs into the stage of the phonetic formation and thus expands the approach for the Chinese character formation. The duality of the pictophonetic structure is also reflected in the inner complementary relationship of this formation mode. The attachment of the pictographic component to the phonetic component, its indication of the meaning of the character, the reliance of the pictographic component for its distinctive function on the phonetic component and the dominant position of the phonetic component in the pictophonetic structure, all are the direct manifestation of the complementary relationship in the pictophonetic structure. In fact, the duality of the pictophonetic structure, in the pictophonetic development and different types of the pictophonetic structure, is not manifested as clearly. In some of the picto-added pictophonetic structure, the phonetic component as a sign to record the pronunciation has more or less the primordial nature, which cannot be considered as the 'purely' phonetic sign; in the phono-added character, the added part that becomes the 'pictographic component' at the beginning is not the 'purely' semantic indicative sign, either.

However, after the development and evolution, these two types of pictophonetic characters gradually grow away from the primordial state and acquire the duality of the pictophonetic structure. Thus, we believe that for either type of the pictophonetic characters, it can be rationally testified that the pictophonetic structure has the characteristic of the duality in its formation.

3. *The pictophonetic structure is a paradoxical unity.* The pictographic component participates in the formation on the level of 'form—meaning', reflecting the features of the pictographic–semantic representation and rational formation of the early Chinese characters. The phonetic component records the pronunciation and breaks the longstanding tradition of the Chinese character formation by the 'sound' as the media, so as to adapt itself to the most general requirement of the written signs in the language system. In this semiotic system of the pictophonetic structure, the pictographic component and phonetic component do not only coexist in contrast in form but also coexist in paradoxical unity in essence. The pictophonetic structure, as a paradoxical unity, does not only reflect the mutual reliance and contrast of 'from' and 'sound' in general sense, but also the contradiction and unity of two formation concepts on a deeper level. The early ideographs as the semiotic system to record language inevitably end up in predicament. In fact, it is objectively impossible to establish a semiotic system that forever adapts itself to the development of the language and accurately records the language by the concept of ideography although in the early stage of civilization, ideographs carried out such a mission in a certain period and within a certain scope. However, 'ideography' has serious defects. For example, (a) it is difficult to express words of general or abstract meanings or proper nouns by the early characters; (b) as a semiotic system of numerous signs, it cannot meet the demand of tens of thousands of words by ideography; (c) it cannot well express the syntactic forms of the language by ideography; (d) the gap is widened in the connection with the development of the language.[55] These defects

---

[55] Cf.: B. A. Easterling, *The Emergence and Development of Characters*, trans. Zuo Shaoxing (左少兴) (Beijing: Peking University Press, 1987).

lead to the transformation of the early ideographic conception. It becomes a necessity to make connection with the pronunciation, and thus the emergence of prevalent homophonic loaning and pictophonetic structure is an inevitable result in which the ideographic system rids itself from the predicament. In particular, the pictophonetic structure is both closely related to the early ideographic conception, and it also reflects the formation of the pictophonetic conception. In a sense, phonetic loaning makes the signs lose their functions within the writing system. These signs, as the phonetic reliance, are endowed with a new capability—the capability of recording the sound and expressing the word. Their transformation is more thorough in the conception of their formation. However, the duality of the pictophonetic structure, to a certain degree, reflects the conflict and unity of the two formation concepts. In the early pictophonetic characters, the added formation by loaned characters is obviously a restraint and correction of phonetic loaning, and the added formation by original characters is the natural manifestation and emphasis of the ideographic formation concept. The combination and differentiation of the two elements of the pictophonetic structure are the manifestation of the contradiction and unity of the two formation concepts. This relationship of paradoxical unity, between the new and old features in the process of the development of written signs, makes the pictophonetic formation mode unique. The actual use of the pictophonetic characters also reflects the inner paradoxical unity of the pictophonetic structure. For example, we believe that homophonic loaning exactly reflects the dual features of the pictophonetic structure in terms of its specific role due to the pictographic component on the one hand and in terms of its void role due to the phonetic loan on the other hand. This typically shows the inner contradiction and conflict of the unity of the pictophonetic structure in its formation process.

The analysis of the three features of the pictophonetic structure above may deepen our understanding of the relevant issues. It must be acknowledged that these features of the pictophonetic structure in the semiotic formation truly reveal different nature from the other structural types in the Chinese character system.

The Nature of the Pictophonetic Structure

In terms of the pictophonetic structure as the most prominent structure type in the Chinese characters, the assessment of its nature directly concerns the evaluation of the nature of the Chinese characters as a whole. The published works on Chinese philology more or less involve the nature of pictophonetic characters in their discussions of pictophonetic characters and the nature of Chinese characters. For example, Mr Tang Lan says, 'Once the pictophonetic characters appear, they immediately take advantage over pictographs.... Then pictographs gradually become obscure, their high time passes away and the whole writing system is dominated by pictophonetic characters despite some few remains of pictographs'.[56] He continues, 'Although pictophonetic characters are phonetic, they also indicate the semantic categories, which may be truly assumed as perfect characters'.[57] Due to the combination between his evaluation of pictophonetic characters and the evolutionary history of Chinese characters, and his thought that pictophonetic characters are 'phonetic characters' and 'perfect characters', he insists that the reform on Chinese characters should be on the track of 'new pictophonetic characters'.[58] Mr Zhou Youguang (周有光) points out the following:

> The characters that synthesize the modes of both semantic and phonetic expressions can be called 'ideophonograph', of which Chinese characters are one kind. In the process of the development of Chinese characters, ideographs (including indicatives, associative compounds and non-pictographic pictographs) have been dwindling in proportion, and ideographic and phonetic pictophonetic characters have become the backbone of the repertoire of Chinese characters. In the Chinese dictionaries, the proportion of pictographic has reached 90% in the far early times. From the oracle bone script to modern Chinese characters, the combining

---

[56] Tang Lan, *Chinese Philology* (Shanghai: Shanghai Classics Publishing House, 1979), 98.

[57] Tang Lan (唐兰), *An Introduction to Ancient Philology*, Extended Editing (Jinan: Qilu Book Company, 1981), 123.

[58] Tang Lan, *An Introduction to Ancient Philology*, 287–300.

principles are the same, that is, over the three thousand years of the recorded history, our Chinese characters have always been following the ideophonographic system. The differences between the ancient and modern times are only the changes in the number of pictophonetic characters and semiotic styles.[59]

What he proposes as the principle of 'ideophonographic system' is based on the nature of the pictophonetic formation and the proportion of pictophonetic characters in the whole Chinese character system. Mr Jiang Shanguo (蒋善国) further believes,

Due to the fact that Chinese characters took the pictophonetic characters as the major forms since their transformation into the clerical script, the pictophonetic characters opened the path to the later ideophonographic characters, changed the nature of the pictographs and became a form between the pictographic and phonetic characters, a blended ideographic and phonetic form, that is, ideophonographic characters. Consequently, since the transformation into the clerical script, the Chinese characters neither simply use the formalistic structures (pictographs) to represent meaning nor employ the alphabetic and phonetic system, but combine the two ideographic and phonetic elements as the basis for the Chinese character formation, which becomes the new stage of Chinese characters and alters their nature. The Pre-Han Dynasty is the period of pictographic and ideographic characters and the post-Han Dynasty is the period of ideographic and phonetic characters.[60]

Mr Jiang here makes his unifying comment on the pictophonetic features of characters and the features of Chinese characters as a whole. When commenting on the features of Chinese characters, Mr Qiu Xigui (裘锡圭) points out, 'The features of a written language are determined by the features of the signs employed by the written language'. By the

---

[59] Zhou Youguang, 'The General Principles of the Evolution of Characters', *Studies of the Chinese Language* 7 (1957).
[60] Jiang Shanguo (蒋善国), *Studies of Chinese Characters* (Shanghai: Shanghai Education Press, 1987) 122–123.

comprehensive analysis of the 'ideographic components', 'phonetic components' and 'written signs', he thus concludes:

> In the early period when Chinese characters were mostly pictographic (generally, before the Western Zhou Dynasty), they were primarily a writing system of ideographic and phonetic components (strictly speaking phonetic loan components). Later with the changes of character forms, pronunciations and characters meanings, they gradually evolved into a writing system of ideographic components (mainly semantic components), phonetic components and markers (The formation of clerical script can be considered as a sign of such evolutionary completion). If we must name the two periods of Chinese characters, the former may be called the characters of ideographic components and phonetic components, or abbreviated as ideophonographs as some philologists call them, and the latter may be called the characters of ideographic components, phonetic components and markers. Considering the fact that in the latter period almost all the markers evolved from ideographic components and phonetic components, and most of the characters were still composed of ideographic components and phonetic components, we may also call the characters of this period the characters of post-ideographic-phonetic components or post-ideophonographic characters.

When commenting on ideographic components and phonetic components, he clearly asserts: as for the pictophonetic characters, their pictographic radicals are ideographic components and their phonetic radical are phonetic components.[61] As can be seen, the pictophonetic characters as the features of a type of formation signs are also the basis on which he draws the preceding conclusion.

Among the aforementioned scholars, only Mr Jiang Shanguo clearly points out the 'features of pictophonetic characters', but when he discusses this topic, he does not explain it explicitly. He seems to indicate that the features of pictophonetic characters are included

---

[61] Qiu Xigui (裘锡圭), 'Chapter II: The Features of Chinese Characters', in *An Outline of Philology* (Beijing: The Commercial Press, 1988).

in 'using types of objects as pictographic components and adding phonetic components', and being 'both ideographic and phonetic'.[62] As most scholars, when discussing Chinese characters as 'ideophonographs', use pictophonetic characters as their basis and think that pictophonetic characters are a kind of ideo-phono structure, it seems also to reflect their views on the features of the pictophonetic structure. After investigating the pictographic components and phonetic components of the pictophonetic structure and their characteristics, we conclude that this view on the features of pictophonetic characters still needs to be further explored.

The features of the pictophonetic structure depend on the characteristics and nature of their formation elements of pictographic components and phonetic components. In terms of the pictographic component of the pictophonetic structure of the ancient Chinese characters, it is only a conventional marking (differentiating) sign associated with the character meaning; in terms of the phonetic components of the pictophonetic structure of the ancient Chinese characters, it indeed participates in the formation as the sign to record the pronunciation. As a result, the pictophonetic structure is in fact a kind of written sign that represents pronunciation by pictographic marking, and this is the nature of the pictographic structure. Different from all the scholars discussed earlier, we emphasize 'pictographic marking' but not 'ideographic representation'. In fact, as early as the ancient character stage, the ideographic function of pictographic components is very limited, whose major use is to imply the semantic scope of the character by the pictographic marking and lead people to differentiate the pictophonetic characters with the same phonetic components by reasonable association. Although the different roles of the pictographic components in the pictophonetic structure are related to character meanings, they cannot effectively highlight the character meanings to serve the purpose of 'semantic representation'. The phonetic component functions as representing the pronunciation and it takes the dominating position in the pictophonetic structure, so the pictophonetic structure mainly serves as a sign to represent the pronunciation. As the pictographic component is

---

[62] Jiang Shanguo (蒋善国), 'The Nature and Function of Pictophonetic Characters'.

related to the character meaning, it may also be called an ideographic sign according to the function of the pictographic component. However, the view of being 'both ideographic and phonetic' and 'ideo-phono' equals the function of the pictographic component with that of the phonetic component, and therefore in effect exaggerates the function of the pictographic component. It cannot reflect the true nature of the pictophonetic structure as the phonetic sign. My mentor Yao Xiaosui (姚孝遂), based on his comprehensive research on the ancient character materials and starting from the function and use of the written character signs, conducted an in-depth discussion of the developmental stage and nature of the formalistic structures of ancient characters and analysed the formalistic structures and nature of the pictophonetic characters. He believes that the pictographic component does not have much of the function of semantic representation. Instead, it is only a sign for differentiation while the phonetic component is a sign representing speech. The pictophonetic structure, as a whole unity of the sign, serves its function and feature as representing speech.[63] This conclusion is correct and recommendable. Mr Sun Changxu (孙常叙) discussed the features of the pre-Qin characters based on the phonetic loan characters and pictophonetic characters, but he believes that in the pictophonetic character only the phonetic component that 'enters the character structure as a phonetic element in the word script' represents speech while the phonetic component of the 'picto-added' pictophonetic character does not represent speech, the two kinds of pictophonetic characters from different sources being different in nature. Consequently, we cannot use the pictophonetic characters as the evidence to prove that the pre-Qin characters are phonetic characters.[64] It is commendable that Mr Sun Changxu pays attention to analysing the formation processes of different types of pictophonetic structures and treats them differently.

---

[63] These views are fully discussed in Yao Xiaoshui's papers: 'The Structures and Developmental Stages of Ancient Chinese Characters', in *Studies of Ancient Characters*, vol. 4 (Beijing: Zhonghua Book Company); 'More Discussion on the Nature of Chinese Characters', in *Studies of Ancient Characters*, vol. 17 (Beijing: Zhonghua Book Company).

[64] Sun Changxu (孙常叙), 'Phonetic Loan and Pictophonetic Characters and the Features of Pre-Qin Characters', in *Studies of Ancient Characters*, vol. 10 (Beijing: Zhonghua Book Company, 1983).

However, he separates the formation of the pictophonetic structure from its development and ignores its function and use as a whole unity. As a result, it becomes difficult to elevate from the analysis of the sources of the forms to the correct judgment of the features of the pictophonetic structure. Nonetheless, it should be acknowledged that the pictophonetic structure is a kind of primordial sign of phonetic representation. It is due to the following causes. First, this kind of phonetic sign must always be complemented by the pictographic component. The intervention of the pictographic component makes it inseparable from the character sign in terms of the formation conception. Such a character sign was formed in the early period by the pictographic means, on which the phonetic sign was dependent for its growth. Second, the phonetic component of the pictophonetic structure is not a pure sign to record speech. Then the phonetic component is actually taken from the ideographic sign, and in the same sign system, the sign as the phonetic component represents either meaning or speech, with different functions, interacting with each other. Some signs are even used both as pictographic components and phonetic components, which inevitably interferes with the phonetic function of the phonetic component. This is the first reason. As for the pictophonetic character formed by the picto-added original character, the phonetic and semantic functions of its phonetic component become interwoven due to historical factors, and, due to the etymological relationship, some phonetic components become interchangeable in speech and meaning, affected by the original characters as the phonetic components (such as '填' and '真', '珥' and '耳'). It also makes some phonetic components both phonetic signs and somewhat connected with the 'meaning'. This is the second reason. Different pronunciations of the same phonetic component coexist due to historical phonetic change and regional dialectical change, and the same pronunciation is recorded with different phonetic components due to the differences in their formation, time and space, leading to one 'phonetic' (sign) with multiple pronunciations and one pronunciation with multiple 'phonetic' (signs), and thereby affecting the results of the phonetic components and enlarging the system of phonetic components. This is the third reason. The three above reasons make the phonetic components of the pictophonetic structure unable to develop into a pure phonetic sign. In consequence, the pictophonetic structure can only be called a 'quasi-phonetic' written sign that borrows pictographic marking. Although its emergence and development reflect the new formation mode by speech in the Chinese character system, it is not a thorough phonetic formation concept. To a certain degree, it has some elements inherited from its parents—the ideographic system. Despite all these, the emergence of the pictophonetic structure undoubtedly reveals the transformation from the ideographic representation of meaning to the phonetic representation of meaning in the Chinese character formation.

After the appearance of the pictophonetic structure, Chinese characters have been maintaining such a pattern. They have become an ideographic and pictophonetic system of signs and an aggregation of signs of variants, and therefore it is difficult to provide an adequate account of the features of Chinese characters by any simple means. As to the question of why Chinese characters did not develop further into a purely phonetic written system after the pictophonetic structure, many scholars have conducted discussions. We believe that it is related to various factors such as the features of Chinese characters, the historical and cultural traditions of the Chinese nation and the relationship between Chinese characters and Chinese language. Thus, we need to seek satisfactory answers from these aspects rather than limit ourselves to the development mode of the 'common direction of the development of world written languages' designated by some foreign philologists.

The Dynamic Analysis of the Pictophonetic Structure[65]

We have discussed the pictographic and phonetic components of the ancient pictophonetic structure,[66] and we have primarily examined the pictophonetic structure as a relatively stable system. The ancient character stage is exactly the period when the pictophonetic structure was developing and improving, in which every character had its own

---

[65] Originally published in *Journal of Huaibei Coal Mining Teachers College* 1 (1987).

[66] Cf.: The two papers 'The Pictographic Components of the Pictophonetic Structure' and 'The Phonetic Components of the Pictophonetic Structure' included in this book.

history of occurrence and development, the whole pictophonetic system was changing, and the development of the society, thinking, language and the Chinese character system had impact on the pictophonetic structure. Consequently, it is insufficient to conduct the static analysis alone. We must carry out the dynamic analysis and multi-faceted observation from the perspective of the development of the pictophonetic structure and the various aspects of the impact on it so that we can provide a rational explanation of the various complex phenomena in the pictophonetic system.

The true history of the early years after the pictophonetic structure occurred is unknown to us due to the lack of actual materials. By the oracle bone period, the pictophonetic structure had obviously already developed into its conscious stage.[67] However, seen from the situation reflected from the Chinese character system, the pictophonetic structure was not yet the main formation mode. During the Western Zhou Dynasty, the pictophonetic structure had developed to a certain extent, but generally speaking, the development was gradual and slow. During the Spring and Autumn and Warring States periods, the pictophonetic structure prospered. It can be assumed that since the Western Zhou period, the new elements in the Chinese characters had been created primarily by means of the pictophonetic structure. Seen from the present ancient character materials, from the Yin-Shang period to the Warring States period, there were over 2,000 recognizable pictophonetic characters, about 17–18 per cent of which appeared in the Yin-Shang period and about 25–26 per cent of which appeared in the Western Zhou period, and nearly 60 per cent of which appeared in the Spring and Autumn and Warring States periods.[68] It shows that since the Spring and Autumn and Warring States periods, the rapid

---

[67] Cf.: 'An Exploration of the Origin of the Pictophonetic Characters' included in this book.

[68] The numbers of characters differ in *A Compilation of the Oracle Bone Script* (by the Archaeological Institute), *A Compilation of the Bronze Script* (by Rong Geng 容庚), *A Classified Compilation of the Ancient Characters* (by 高明 Gao Ming), *A Chart of the Forms of Ancient Chinese Characters* (by Xu Zhongshu 徐中舒), etc. In addition, the present interpretations of some characters vary, and the bamboo slips of the Warring States period, the silk script and the bamboo slips of the early Han period have not yet been systematically collated. Thus, these figures are only relatively accurate but they do reveal the general tendency.

development of the Chinese society and the increasing progress of the Chinese thinking and culture had also indirectly promoted the development of Chinese characters, which was also predominantly reflected in the rapid increase of the pictophonetic characters.

To adapt to the general tendency of the pictophonetic system, the internal pictophonetic structure was also under constant change. The pictographic components of the pictophonetic structure in the oracle bone script are primarily pictographs of simple forms, which 'are taken from various parts and objects, both nearby and in the distance'. They mostly have something to do with people's daily lives, material production and spiritual activities. Even the pictographic components representing the natural world of animals, plants, heavenly bodies and landscape take their subjects that are most closely related to human activities. In the early Western Zhou period, there were no major changes in the pictographic formation, in the middle and later periods, new situations appeared, and then by the Spring and Autumn and Warring States periods, obvious changes appeared. Apart from the new development and differentiation of some existent pictographic components, since the middle and later Western Zhou periods, many new pictographic components had appeared, mainly including '走, 页, 见, 言, 竹, 玉, 金, 巾, 羽, 角, 草, 韦, 邑' and so on. Then the new pictographic characters were no longer simple pictographs. They also included some associate compounds such as '邑, 走 and 韦, and the selection of the pictographic components transformed from simplicity to complexity. More advancement was made in the pictographic components such as '糸, 竹, 金 and 玉', and they became active elements for character formation. For example, in the oracle bone script, there were very few pictophonetic characters with '糸'. In the Western Zhou period, there was a gradual increase of such characters, and in the Spring and Autumn and Warring States periods, there were a large number of them. '金' could be seen as a pictographic component in the middle of the Western Zhou period,[69] such as '鉴' on (录伯簋)

---

[69] Mr Hu Houxuan (胡厚宣) discovered that there were pictophonetic characters that followed '金' in the oracle inscriptions in the fifth period. However, the lower parts of the characters were fragmented and therefore could not be determined, and there was only one such evidence, so now we still think that there is no such a pictographic component as '金' in the oracle bone script.

and '鉈' on (史頌匜). After the late Western Zhou period, there were more pictophonetic characters with '金'. The character formation capability of '竹, 玉' also gradually increased. The addition of new pictographic components indicates the change of the formation in the number of the pictographic components, while the increasing capability of the existent pictographic components is the main indicator of the development of the pictographic components. On the other hand, there appears some differentiation in both the old and new pictographic components, such as '尸' and '卩' differentiated from '人', '立' from '大', '寸' from '又', '音' from '言' and so on, which also led to certain adjustment in the system of the pictographic components.[70] Since the Yin-Shang period, the phonetic components have also been developing. Due to their stability and singularity,[71] their development was mainly manifested in terms of quantity. For example, our primary analysis shows that in the ancient character stage, there were 501 basic phonetic components, 183 from the Yin-Shang period, 157 from the Western Zhou period and 161 from the Spring and Autumn and Warring States periods.[72] The constant increase of the phonetic components offers the basis to form the pictophonetic components to record different pronunciations.

We have only briefly outlined the development of the pictophonetic structure of the ancient Chinese characters above. The development of the pictophonetic structure has been influenced and restricted by various factors, and this is what we emphasize on in the following analysis.

The pictographic component of the pictographic structure is directly associated with conception. Human intellectual activities will

---

[70] The present author has also written *A Diagram of Basic Pictographic Components* to reveal the origin, evolution and differentiation of the pictographic components. However, they are not easy to be printed and therefore are not attached here.

[71] Cf.: 'The Phonetic Component of the Pictophonetic Structure' included in this book.

[72] The present author has also written *A Diagram of Basic Pictographic Components* to reveal the origin, evolution and differentiation of the pictographic components. However, they are not easy to be printed and therefore are not attached here.

inevitably leave overt traces in the system of the pictographic components. As a result, the development of pictographic components is closely related to human intellectual activities.

The increasing power of abstraction and generalization in thinking makes the transformation from concreteness to abstraction and generalization in the semantic representation of pictographic components. The manifestation goes as follows: the semantic scope gradually widens in the pictographic components whose early semantic scope is quite definite; the pictographic components of concrete semantic representation tend to be categorized or more general through change and replacement.

The pictographic component of '邑' was mainly used to mean capital in the Western Zhou Dynasty, which had very concrete meaning in the characters of '邦, 都', etc. From the late Western Zhou period to the end of the Spring and Autumn period, the semantic scope of '邑' gradually widened so that any vassal land name or general place names would take '邑' as their pictographic components, and there appeared a large number of new pictophonetic characters with '邑' as their pictographic components such as '邗, 邛, 郼, 邖, 鄂, 邾, 邿, 郐, 郢, 郜, 都 and 郓' all from the Spring and Autumn period, and more from the Warring States period, such as '邜, 邜, 邜, 邡, 邡, 邛, 邟, 邢, 鄂, 巷, 郢, 郡, 郯, 聊, 鄙 and 鄄'. Many of these characters were originally only the substitutes borrowed from the later phonetic components, such as '邻, 邻, 邦, 邢, 鄂, 郯, 聊, 鄙 and 鄄', which were originally used as '戈, 寺, 井, 哭, 炎, 取, 嗇 and 厭', and then offered conditions for their transformation into pictophonetic characters due to the enlargement of their scope of semantic representations. '邑' extended its meaning from '都邑' (capital) to all vassal land and general place names. It is a process from the 'concrete and specific to abstract and general', reflecting the influence of human thinking on pictographic components. The semantic scope of most pictographic components tends to expand as human thinking develops, and therefore there appears the phenomena that the meanings of many pictographic components in the ancient Chinese characters are only associated with the meanings of the characters, and the same pictographic component can indicate multiple meanings relevant to it, causing various complicated relationships between pictographic components and characters meanings.[73]

The increase of the power of abstraction in thinking has another impact on pictographic components, that is, the change of the actual pictographic components for the semantic representation, which shows the same tendency as the widening scope of semantic representation of pictographic components. In the oracle bone script, there still remain some traces of the early pictographic components representing the actual meanings. For example, in the oracle bone script, '臽' (i.e., '陷' in the original, a way of hunting) with the phonetic component '凵' (坎) unchanged, its pictographic component can be '人', or it can also be written as '鹿, 麋, 犬, 牛' and so on, and it changes, depending on the different subjects of '臽'. Different pictographic components represent different subjects and their semantic representation is very concrete. Later on, the character variant becomes obsolete, '臽' is taken as a fixed form, and the pictographic component '人' substitutes and generalizes different subjects.[74] The *Origin of Chinese Characters* says 牝 means 'female animal, and it follows 牛 and is pronounced as 匕'. In the oracle bone script, depending on the different subjects referred to, the pictographic component '牛' may also be changed into '羊, 豕, 犬, 马' and so on, and finally it takes '牛' as the pictographic component to generalize the rest of them. The development of the pictographic components of characters '臽' and '牝' show the progress of the pictographic components from representing concrete meaning to general meaning. Compared with seeking concrete semantic representation in the early stage, to represent and generalize different subjects with only one pictographic component is obviously the active influence of the progressing thinking capability on the pictophonetic structure. In fact, this situation is rare. The more common situation is that certain pictographic component of concrete semantic representation changes into the more abstract pictographic component, or similar changes occur in different pictographic components of different pictophonetic characters, and they are categorized into the same

---

[73] Cf.: 'The Pictographic Component of the Pictophonetic Structure' included in this book.

[74] Yu Xingwu *Interpretations of the Oracle Bone Script*, 270.

more general and abstract pictographic component. '城' originally does not follow '土' but follows '𩫏'. This pictographic component is originally the pictograph of town or city (on Yuannianshidui Food Vessel: 元年师兑簋). Not until the late Spring and Autumn period did '城' (on 郐鎛, 尹钲, 驫羌钟) change to follow '土'. To take '土' as the pictographic component is due to the fact that the ramparts which protect the city or town from external invasion is built by a wide pile of earth. The change of the pictographic component from '𩫏' to '土' indicates that its semantic representation tends to be abstract. Corresponding to the evolution of the pictographic component of '城', the pictophonetic characters following '𩫏' are all categorized to follow '土'. For example, '坏, 坒, 垣, 堵, 堈' and so on in the script materials of Jing You (竞卣), Bi You (坒卣), Lv Zhong (吕钟), Shi Song Gui (史颂簋), Zhou Wen (籀文) originally all take '𩫏' as the pictographic component, and then in the materials of Qin Gong Gui (秦公簋), Zhao Yu Tu（兆域图）and the *Origin*, they all change to follow '土'. Let's take another example. In the oracle bone script, '镬' follows '鬲' and changes to follow '金' on the Ai Chengshu Ding (哀成叔鼎). In the bronze script, '釜' follows '缶', '匜' originally follows '匚' in the bronze script, '盨' and '盘' follow '皿'. In the Spring and Autumn and Warring States periods, they were all categorized to follow '金', or the pictographic component '金' was added. The pictographic components '鬲, 缶, 皿, 匚, 金' are originally all the pictographs of implements, and as pictographic components for semantic representation, they are concrete and different, but when they are categorized to follow '金', the semantic representation changes from being concrete to being general. This categorization reflects the consistent human understanding of different implements as a result of thinking in the abstract. It is true that not all these characters follow '金', which shows that the development of pictographic components is also affected by other factors; however, in the accent character stage, the development of pictographic components from concrete to general and abstract semantic representation undoubtedly demonstrates the promoting force of thinking advancement on pictographic components. The more the thinking, as the advanced stage of understanding, develops, the more profoundly it delves into the nature of subjects and the wider connections it can discover among different phenomena. In the pictophonetic structure, the strengthening of the generalization of the pictographic component, the categorization between different pictographic components and the association of the same pictographic component with multiple concepts, all are the direct manifestation of such development of thinking.

The increasing precision of thinking leads to the overlapping and complication of the pictographic components in some of the pictophonetic structures. On the one hand, the development of thinking makes pictographic components more general and abstract; on the other hand, the Chinese characters, in formation, seek rational precision of thinking, make more accurate and concrete semantic representation in the selection of pictographic components, and make compensation by adding other pictographic components when a certain pictographic component is not clear and concrete enough for the semantic representation. In 'The Pictographic Components in the Pictophonetic Structure', we have analysed the situation of 'added pictographic components', in which the additions of '盉, 盘, 盈, 匜, 簋' and so on are exemplified.[75] The additions of pictographic components are special cases due to the influence of the development of thinking. In fact, the development of thinking is limited in affecting Chinese characters and its influence cannot surpass the restraint of their own rules of Chinese characters. In addition, the added pictographic components do not go in line with the general development of pictographic components but they go contrary to the rules of Chinese characters from complexity to simplicity. Therefore, this phenomenon is not very common in the ancient pictophonetic system of ancient Chinese characters but they only appear in some specific inscriptions, not widely practiced and mostly eliminated in the end.

The impact of pictographic components on thinking development is one of the reasons that led to the complexity of the pictophonetic system. We will here discuss only two major aspects. Meanwhile, we should also note that this influence is only external, and it must succumb to the features and nature of the pictophonetic structure itself, and thus the thinking development and the development of characters cannot correspond to each other.

---

[75] Cf.: 'The Pictographic Component of the Pictophonetic Structure' included in this book.

The pictophonetic structure, as the most important part of Chinese character system to record the Chinese language, is inevitably influenced by the development of Chinese characters. This influence is manifested in the following three aspects.

1. The development of the phonetic system leads to pronunciation differences of the pictophonetic characters in the same category. We have pointed it out when discussing the function of the phonetic representation of the phonetic components.[76] The constant development of speech is a prevalent fact of language development. Differences in time and region shape linguistic differences in terms of archaism and contemporaneity, vulgarity and elegance. Although written characters change as language changes, they never follow as closely, especially characters of the pictophonetic structure. Once they form their pedigree, their phonetic components become relatively stable, and their internal restrictive relations make them unable to quickly adapt to the phonetic change. Thus, the differences between the pronunciations of phonetic components and the actual pronunciations represented by the pictophonetic characters as signs become inevitable, and the complexity of the phonetic change makes the pronunciation differences more complicated within the pictophonetic pedigree. If we examine the pronunciations from the perspective of the whole pedigree of Chinese pictophonetic characters, the changes caused by the speech change become most obvious. It is enough for us to give sufficient note of understanding of this point as at present we have no conditions for more detailed analysis.

The speech changes make differences of pronunciations in the pictophonetic pedigree and lead to the corresponding changes of the phonetic components in the pictophonetic structure so as to adapt to the actual speech changes. For example, the characters following '羸' for pronunciations are differentiated into two categories '羸, 贏, 臝', and '嬴, 蠃'. The former belongs to the initial consonant of 来 and the rhyme class of 歌; the latter belongs to the rhyme class of 喻 (四, etc.) and the rhyme class of 耕. The early

---

[76] Ibid.

scholars were very much baffled about this case; however, Mr Yu Xingwu (于省吾) has provided rational explanations from the perspective of the ancient phonetic transformation.[77] After '赢', as a phonetic component, is differentiated into two kinds of pronunciations, the characters following its pronunciation are also naturally affected in their structure and are adjusted accordingly. For example, on both Lieji Vessel (鼠季鼎) and Qiaojun Zheng (乔君钲, a bell-shaped percussion instrument), there is the character '赢'. On '赢' the phonetic component '呈' is added. '呈' belongs to the initial consonant of 定 and the rhyme class of 耕, and after the addition, it is pronounced the same with two forms so as to avoid the confusion with the pronunciation of '赢' with the initial consonant of 来 and the rhyme class of 歌. Furthermore, it eliminates '赢' and takes '衣' as the pictographic component, from which '裎' is derived. '赢' included in the *Origin* follows 衣 and is pronounced as '赢'. In the ancient classics, it is often written as '赢', and due to the phonetic change, '果' is added as the phonetic component to indicate the initial consonant of 来 and the rhyme class of 歌. Later, it eliminates the pronunciation of '赢' and takes '衣' as the pictographic component and changes into the character '裸' included or manifested in the *Origin*, following 衣 and is pronounced as 果. The appearance of '裎, 裸' is caused by the self-adjustment within the pictophonetic system after the pronunciation ambiguity of the phonetic component due to the speech change. Their production modes and causes are the same. In Mencius, '袒, 裼, 裸, 裎' are all used, and in the *Origin*, '裸' and '裎' are defined the same way, which can prove that the two are of the same origin. Let's take another example. When the characters with '古' as the phonetic component are differentiated into the initial consonant of 见 and the initial consonant of 母, there appears variant of '匫', the common implement name in the bronze script. This character usually follows 匚 and is pronounced as 古, but Lushi Gu (鲁士匫) changes the phonetic component '古' into '害', and Jigongfu Hu (季宫父匫) changes the phonetic

---

[77] Yu Xingwu, 'An Interpretation of 能 and 赢 as Well as the Characters Following 赢', *Studies of Ancient Characters*, vol. 8 (Beijing: Zhonghua Book Company).

component '古' into '猷'. '古' is originally pronounced as the initial consonant of 见 and '害' belongs to the initial consonant of 匣. '猷' in the ancient classics is usually written as '胡', for example, the name of King Li (厉王) of the Western Zhou Dynasty is '猷', which is written as '胡' on the bronze bell named 'Zongzhou Bell' (宗周钟). '猷德' on 师龢鼎 is '胡' in the ancient classics, such as '胡福'. The 致簋 '戎猷' is written as '戎胡' in the classics. They all show that '猷' is also pronounced as the initial consonant of 匣. It can be seen that the appearance of the two variants of '匡' is the intentional change to adapt to the phonetic ambiguity in the phonetic component '古'. Their appearance in the implements in the Spring and Autumn period shows that they followed the phonetic component '古' as early as the Spring and Autumn period, but were pronounced differently as the initial consonant of 见 and the initial consonant of 匣.

The speech change is relatively slow, and therefore, in the ancient character stage, the appearance of such phenomenon due to phonetic differences is not very frequent. It shows that in the ancient character stage, the pronunciation differences of phonetic components are still limited, and the phonetic components can generally meet the demand to record speech.

2. The semantic development promotes the reproduction and differentiation of the pictophonetic structure. The semantic development is a major aspect of language development. The 'extended meaning of the character', as one of the causes of pictophonetic reproduction, refers to the impact of semantic development on the pictophonetic structure.[78] The ancient Chinese words and characters are identical in their written forms, so the 'extended meaning of the character' is the same as the extended meaning of the word. The word meaning is constantly being enriched by extension, causing one written sign to record multiple relevant semantic entities. Each semantic entity is closely or distantly related to the original meaning, depending on when the entity occurs. The distant semantic entity may be differentiated into an independent word of its own and thus a new recording sign occurs

---

[78] Cf.: 'The Phonetic Component of the Pictophonetic Structure' included in this book.

accordingly. In addition, when the same written character records too many semantic entities and contradicts the structural intention of specific words for specific usages, there is a need to differentiate between the written characters and therefore new characters appear. Most of the new characters produced due to the extended meaning in the ancient Chinese characters are created by the mode of the pictophonetic structure. The semantic development promotes the 'reproduction of pictophonetic characters', as is shown in the following examples.

In the oracle bone script, '启' is shaped as opening the door with hands, meaning 'open' (开). The *Origin* defines '启' as 'open (开)', which is the original meaning. In the oracle inscription, apart from using '启' as '开', it is also used to define 'clear up' (启晴), which is the extended meaning. Then comes '晸', which is written as '啓' to mean 'it clears up after the rain'. It is also extended to mean 'in front' or 'taking the lead' (see *Yinqi Conjugated Compilation* no.471), as is annotated in 'Xiang Shi' in *The Rites of Zhou* (《周礼·乡师》): 'When the army is in front, it is called qi (启)'. Thus, the army vehicle in front is called '棨', which is obvious in its extended relationship. The *Origin* also defines the character '瞽' as 'look carefully'. Mr Duan annotates it as 'bright as daytime or clear sky'. This also includes '瞽' and '啓' in the relationship of reproduction and differentiation. '啓, 瞽, 棨' are all the new pictophonetic characters reproduced to adapt to the semantic development of '启'.

The creation of the characters '听, 声, 圣, 廷(庭)' and so on also typically reflects the impact of the semantic development on the reproduction of pictophonetic characters. '听' in the oracle bone script is written as '耴', whose form is still preserved in the *Book of History* in the Wei Stone Inscriptions (魏石经《尚书》), associated with mouth and ear.[79] There are two semantic entities of '听闻' (listen to know) and '听治' (listen to judge) in the oracle bone script. 'Speak by the mouth, and what the ear picks up is speech'.[80]

---

[79] Guo Moruo, *A General Compilation of the Oracle Inscriptions* (Beijing: Science Press, 1983), 489.

[80] Yu Xingwu, *Interpretations of the Oracle Bone Script*, 83.

Therefore, the meaning of '听闻' is extended to the semantic entity of '声', and the pictographic component '殸' is added to '耴' to reproduce a new pictophonetic character. The meaning of '听治' is further extended into the meaning of '圣', (sacred) as is stated in 'Sishi' in Guanzi (管子·四时): 'what is heard and believed is called sacred'. Then the phonetic component '耴' is added to '壬' to reproduce the character '圣'. In the oracle bone script, '听治' is also extended into the place name '廷' (庭) where the listening and judgement are conducted, and thus the pictographic component is added to make '聑', '廷' in the bronze script and the derived character '庭'. In the oracle bone script, '听' may be used as '廷' (庭). '圣姜' in Zuo's Commentary on the *Spring and Autumn Annals* is written as '声姜' in Gongyang Commentary on the *Spring and Autumn Annals* and in Lianggu Commentary on the *Spring and Autumn Annals*. In the Mawangdui Silk Script, in Laozi A '圣' is written as '声' and in Laozi B it is written as '听', both of which can prove the phonetic interconnection among '听, 声, 圣, 廷 (庭)'. Here, their reproduction approaches are obvious.

The semantic development is one of the important causes to boost the pictophonetic reproduction, by which a large portion of the pictophonetic characters is created. The pictophonetic characters, created due to the semantic development, are mostly cognate characters, which can provide reliable materials for the research on etymology.

3. The rapid reproduction of new words accordingly induces large numbers of new pictophonetic characters. The fast development of social reproduction and the increasing human material and spiritual enrichment first influence the vocabulary development of the language system. Humans must use large quantities of new words to reflect human progress in various aspects. In addition, the large quantities of new words require that new characters be created to record them, and then they boost the reproduction of more new characters. For that matter, most of the new characters after the mid and late Zhou Dynasties are created by the formation mode of the pictophonetic structure. For example, in the Spring and Autumn and Warring States periods, textile industry was much advanced, particularly with the southern state of Chu taking the

lead, where fine textile fabric remains were excavated several times in Changsha, Jiangling and Xinyang. The funeral objects lists show numerous textile items in the tombs together with a large number of written materials of that period. From the materials of Chun bamboo slips and Changsha silk script in Jiangling, Yangtianhu, Xinyang and Wangshan, we can see that in the state of Chu alone there are nearly a hundred new pictophonetic characters following '糸' concerning the textile industry. The Spring and Autumn and Warring States periods were a glorious epoch, when progress was rapidly advancing in all social aspects and the Chinese language was fully developing. Accordingly, it was also the time when Chinese characters were changing and developing at the fastest pace. The emergence of the pictophonetic structure is the inevitable result of the development of the society, language and its written system. Meanwhile, the social progress is not synchronous with the linguistic progress, and the linguistic progress is not synchronous with the progress of its written system either.

As one of the formation modes of the ancient Chinese characters, the pictophonetic structure is also affected by the general rules of the progress of Chinese character forms, which in fact it must observe. The evolution, simplification and normalization of the character forms all affect or restrict the development of the pictophonetic structure. Let us look at the influence from the following three aspects.

First of all, we will discuss the 'erroneous form' and 'erroneous sound' caused by the evolution of the character forms. Seen from the development of over a thousand years from the Yin-Shang period to the early Han period, the forms of ancient Chinese characters had undergone tremendous changes. Such changes are most obvious when we survey the written materials of the oracle bone script, the bronze script of the early and mid-Western Zhou periods, the carved or cast inscriptions and bamboo slips after the Eastern Zhou period, and the silk script and bamboo and wooden slips of the early Han period. In particular, the generation of the clerical script in the Qin period had structurally shaken the whole ancient character formation system and had significant impact on various structural modes. As a result, to study the structure of the ancient Chinese characters, we must fully estimate the impact of the evolution of Chinese character forms. The 'erroneous form' and 'erroneous sound' are the result of the impact of the evolution of character forms on the pictophonetic structure. The 'erroneous form' and 'erroneous sound' do not refer to the tricky and unrecognizable phenomena caused by the accidental occurrences of the ancient Chinese characters. The accidental erroneous changes have something to do with bad casting or mistaken carving, which usually occurs as negligence in the process of making inscriptions. However, the 'erroneous form' and 'erroneous sound' occur in the natural evolution of character forms. Their changes have connections and bases in form. They inherit their erroneous changes and become 'pictographic components' and 'phonetic components', which eventually gain structural validity. For example, '者' in the *Origin* 'follows 白 and is pronounced as 米'. The pictographic component '白' is exactly the 'erroneous form' grown out of the evolution of character forms. In the bronze script, '者' follows the form of '口' and not '白'. After the evolution of the forms, there are three different forms of writing: '曰, 其, 白'. The small seal script takes on '白' and then erroneously forms the pictographic component, whose evolutionary traces are most obvious (see Figure 2.5).

'丧' in the *Origin* means '亡 (death)'; it is an associative compound following 哭 (weep) and 亡 and is pronounced as 亡 (wang)'. This is based on the small seal script. '丧' is originally the same character as '桑',[81] which in the oracle bone script is used as human names or place names and then is borrowed to mean

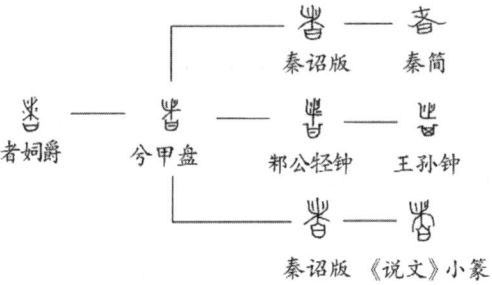

Figure 2.5

---

[81] Ibid., 75.

'丧' (death) as in '丧亡' (loss and death). In the bronze script, there appears the erroneous form of '亡', which is erroneously derived from the base of '桑'. On the three utensils of Qizuofuwu Ding (旂作父戊鼎), Maogong Ding (毛公鼎), Lianghou Gui (量侯簋), the character has a long and curved stroke all the way downward, which retains the shape of the trunk connecting the root in a mulberry. On the Qihou Pot (齐侯壶), the lower part of '亡' had already been separated from its main part to make '亡'. On the same utensil, the omission of '亡' on the lower part more obviously shows that undoubtedly it erroneously followed '亡' in that period. The erroneous use of '丧' as '亡' has also something to do with its borrowed meaning of '丧亡', which should be the erroneously changed pictographic component. The *Origin* treats it as an associative compound and phonetic compound in consideration of its semantic association (see Figure 2.6).

'鬲' is originally a pictograph, and in the bronze script it is mistaken as '羊'. The lower part of '鬲' originally looks like three feet. The change takes place with the middle foot and then '羊' is erroneously derived from it, the evolutionary process of which is very clear (see Figure 2.7).

The evolutionary changes of '者, 丧, 鬲' and so on all erroneously result in the elements connected with pictographic components as erroneous examples. The 'erroneous sound' comes into being due to the increasing growth of pictophonetic characters, the strengthening phonetic quality of Chinese characters and the phonetic components erroneously derived from non-pictophonetic

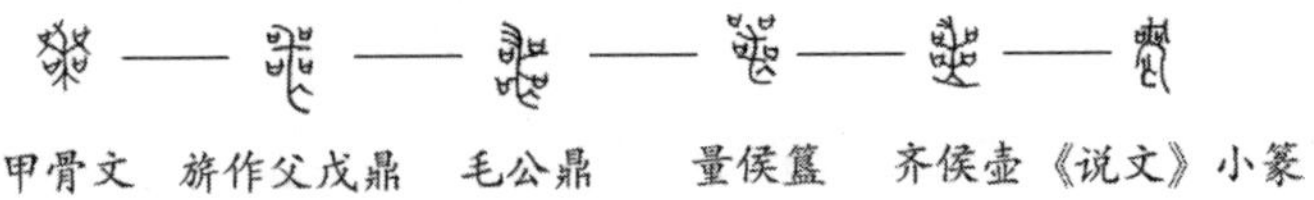

甲骨文　旂作父戊鼎　毛公鼎　　量侯簋　齐侯壶《说文》小篆

Figure 2.6

召仲鬲　　孟鼎　　南姬鬲　　伯姜鬲　　同姜鬲

Figure 2.7

structures. Some of the erroneously derived phonetic components can only be generally close to the pronunciations of the words. The rules of natural evolution of forms cannot be violated, and the subjective elements are only limited even though they may be added, so the 'erroneous sound' can only be symbolic. In the past, not enough attention has been paid to the 'erroneous sound'. Now, let us look at a few examples.

'甫' in the *Origin* means 'to describe a handsome man. It follows 用 and 父 and is also pronounced as 父'. '父' is erroneously derived as a phonetic component. The key for its evolution is the upper curve of a long vertical line in the middle. '父' is pronounced the same as '甫' and they can be interchanged when used to describe a handsome man in the ancient classics. Therefore, Xu Shen says that '甫' follows '父' and is also pronounced as '父'. From the evolutionary history of '甫', what Xu Shen defines as 'following 父' is based on the borrowed meaning to explain the erroneous pronunciation. This is unreliable (see Figure 2.8).

'良' in the *Origin* means 'kind; it follows 畐 and 省 and is pronounced as 亡'. To say that it follows 畐 and 省 is not accurate. '良' has nothing to do with '畐' and the 'pronunciation of 亡' is erroneous. The characters on Jiliangfu He (季良父盉 Jiliangfu Wine Vessel), for example, had already been erroneously changed to be close to 王, and on the Ancient Seal (古玺) it was erroneously changed into a phonetic component (see Figure 2.9). The erroneous pronunciation of 亡 is very similar to the erroneous change

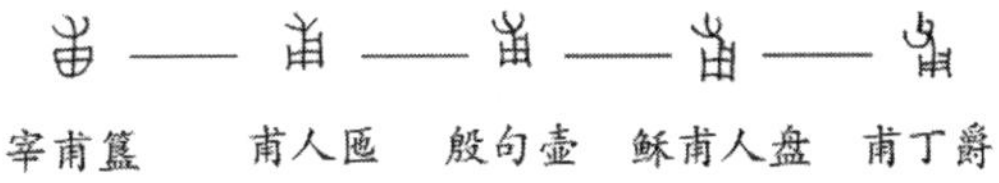

甫 —— 甫 —— 甫 —— 甫 —— 甫
宰甫簋　　甫人匜　　殷旬壺　　穌甫人盘　甫丁爵

Figure 2.8

良 —— 良 —— 良 —— 良 —— 良 —— 良 —— 良
甲骨文　季良父盉　尹氏匜　齐侯匜　　古玺　　秦简　《说文》小篆

Figure 2.9

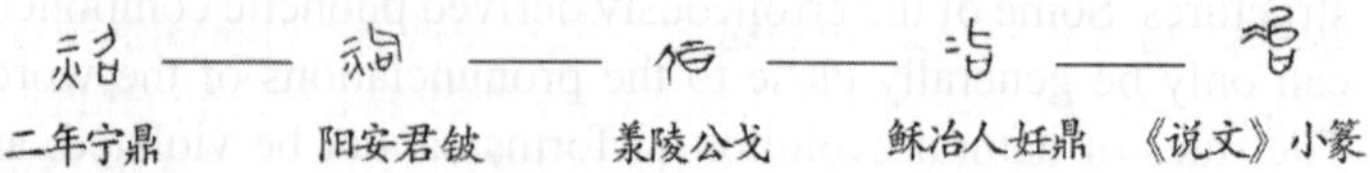

二年宁鼎　　阳安君鈹　　羕陵公戈　　穌冶人妊鼎　　《说文》小篆

Figure 2.10

from 亾 to 亡. As for the original meaning of the formation of '良', opinions differ and it is still undecided.

'冶' in the *Origin* means 'melt; it follows 仌 and is pronounced as 台'. Both the form and pronunciation of the character are erroneous. It is very often seen in the script with dozens of variants in the Warring States period.[82] '冶' is erroneously derived from an abbreviation, changing '二' into '仌' and '㠯' into '台' (see Figure 2.10).

In addition, '匹' erroneously followed the pronunciation of '匕' (on the Large Ding 大鼎); '朢' may have erroneously followed the pronunciation of '王' (on the Ancient Seal); '两' may have erroneously followed '羊', etc.

The 'erroneous form' and 'erroneous sound' are the unique features in the evolution of ancient Chinese characters, which are both the natural result of the evolution of Chinese character forms and the manifestation of the increasing signification and phoneticization of ancient Chinese characters. The existence of the 'erroneous form' shows that it breaks through the limitation of rationality of formation. The pictographic component as a symbolic sign does not in fact much concern the effect of the actual semantic representation. This is in agreement with the writing mode of the Chinese character system based on 'pictographs' and the tendency of symbolic art of lines. The emergence of the 'erroneous sound' is the positive effect of the increasing development of the pictophonetic structure and the strengthening of phoneticization of Chinese characters on the evolution of character forms. Although

---

[82] Huang Shengzhang (黄盛璋), 'A Study of the Structural Types and National Identities of the Character "冶" in the Warring States Period', eds. Editing Committee of the Collected Papers of the International Symposium of the Ancient Chinese Philology, *Paper Collection of the Ancient Chinese Philology* (Hong Kong: Chinese University of Hong Kong, 1983).

the 'erroneous sound' can only achieve the approximate phonetic effect, the whole structure becomes the phonetic-oriented representation of the structural mode due to the change of some parts into phonetic components. Although the 'erroneous form' and 'erroneous sound' as the unique elements in the pictophonetic structure have their negative aspects in terms of the rationality of the structural formation, they also have a positive effect in terms of formation evolution on the pictophonetic structure seen from the general development of Chinese characters. In the process of the evolutionary formation of Chinese characters, it occurred that the pictographic components and phonetic components came to extinction or they mixed up and replaced one another. We will omit this issue here and focus on it when we discuss the erroneous changes of Chinese character forms.

Second, we will discuss the 'pictographic omission' and 'phonetic omission' caused by the rule of simplification. Simplification is an important rule in the development of character forms, the fundamental purpose of which is to make the complex firms simpler for easy use. Simplification has been going on throughout the whole process of the Chinese character development, playing a predominant role during the time when ancient Chinese characters were used. Scholars have noticed this phenomenon long before. Simplification has shaken the rationality of the Chinese character structures and may have affected such structural modes as pictographs, associative compounds, simple indicatives and pictophonetic characters and thus make them lose their original formation. The 'pictographic omission' and 'phonetic omission' are the result of the impact of simplification on the pictophonetic structure. Correctly revealing the process of omission and simplification enables us to gain a rational explanation of the structures after omission and simplification. In his *Origin*, Xu Shen took note of analysing the pictophonetic characters of uncertain structures caused by simplification from the perspective of the 'pictographic omission' and 'phonetic omission'. For example, in terms of characters '籯, 耆', he correctly pointed out that their pictographic components followed the 'omission of certain characters'. In terms of '䏽, 秋', he correctly explained that they followed 'certain phonetic omissions'. The *Origin* points out less of the pictographic omissions but points out more than 300 phonetic omissions. Although due to the limitations of time and materials, Xu Shen might not be very appropriate in his analysis of particular characters, he was very insightful in his revelation of the pictophonetic structure after omission and simplification from the perspective of omission and simplification. There are a lot more cases of pictographic omissions and phonetic omissions that Xu Shen never saw in the ancient characters. For example, '府' may have followed '贝' and on Shaofu Small Utensils (少府小器) '贝' is simplified as '目'. On the Ancient Seal '駒' follows '马' and its body is omitted. '雕, 鸥' on the Ancient Seal follow '隹, 鸟' and their heads are omitted. '昂, 晨, 星' are all simplified from following '晶' to follow '日'. '醜' follows '鬼' and its head is omitted (on the Covenant 盟书). These are the examples of pictographic omissions. The phonetic component of '袭' is simplified as '龙' (Tianxingguan Chu Slips 天星观楚简). The phonetic component '官' of '棺, 馆, 辊, 輨, 绾' is simplified as '㠯'. The phonetic component '石' of '席' is simplified as '厂' (Wei Ding 卫鼎), etc. These are the examples of phonetic omissions. The 'pictographic omission' and 'phonetic omission' have been obviously much noted by researchers. After the 'pictographic omission' and 'phonetic omission', the pictographic components and phonetic components have lost their original functions and the rationality of the pictophonetic structure no longer exists. Now the whole pictophonetic character only as a conventional sign cannot be analysed or explored for its structural intention. Only by seeking the original forms before omission and simplification can we provide a rationale for the omitted and simplified forms. As a result, to study the pictophonetic structure, it is very necessary to fully understand the impact caused by the rules of simplification.

Third, the elimination of character variants by standardization will be discussed. The ancient Chinese characters are in the stage of development and improvement. Due to the differences of times, regions and individual handwriting habits, the same character often has many kinds of variants of complex or simple strokes and structures, or of radicals of uncertain positions, or of lines and parts of unfixed positions vertical or horizontal, left or right, or of ambiguous and interchangeable pictographic components or phonetic components and so on. All these are the manifestations of unsettlement and irregular handwriting of the ancient Chinese character structures in progress. In the Spring and Autumn and Warring States periods, the situation of 'different sounds in speech and different forms in characters' was most prominent. The social nature of written characters requires that they have uniformity and standardization in form. Too diverse character forms inevitably affect their function and role as communication tools, so it is a universal principle that character forms develop from non-standardization to standardization. When the state of Qin was annexing the six states, it officially decreed that the ancient characters of the six states that 'did not conform to the characters of Qin' be abolished and the 'script be standardized'. This action greatly promoted the standardization of the ancient Chinese characters. The characters of the imperial edicts on the measurement instruments are the fine examples of the 'standardized script' of that period. The most powerful impact of standardization on the pictophonetic structure is to eliminate large number of character variants. In the paper 'The Pictographic Components of the Pictophonetic Structure', we point out that in the stage of the ancient characters, the ambiguities of pictographic components are predominant and they cause lots of variants. Their eventual conformity is realized by standardization. Dozens of variants of '造, 巫, 腹' had been eliminated by the time of the small seal script and only one standard form was retained. There are abundant such materials, so we do not need to give more examples. The variants caused by handwriting differences and not structural ambiguities are more prevalent in the ancient Chinese characters. For example, '阳' had over 360 variants in the monetary script of the Warring States period alone.[83] Then by the time of the small seal script, they had conformed to one form. The implementation of the 'script standardization' made

---

[83] Shang Chengzuo (商承祚), *A Compilation of the Pre-Qin Currency Script* (Beijing: Bibliography and Document Publishing House, 1983).

the variants-dominated pictophonetic characters, along with other characters, first of all, to be uniform in the official script. This is a great leap in the development of the pictophonetic structure. On the one hand, standardization makes the variants of pictophonetic structure to be uniform; on the other hand, the uniformity of the pictophonetic structure lays the foundation for the standardization of the Chinese characters.

The impact of the general principles of the development of character forms on the pictophonetic structure reveals the indispensable relationship between the development of the pictophonetic structure and that of the Chinese character forms. Only by examining the whole Chinese character system can we gain a rational explanation of the phenomena of the 'erroneous form, erroneous sound, pictographic omission, phonetic omission and uniformity of variants'.

This chapter takes different perspectives to examine the pictophonetic structure in a dynamic system in order to further reveal the causes by which some complex phenomena are formed in the pictophonetic structure. By the preliminary analysis, we have realized that the pictographic components of the pictophonetic structure are most prone to be affected by thinking and the development of language. The development of thinking directly affects pictographic components, causing their overlap, replacement and complexity of semantic representation. The semantic development promotes the pictophonetic reproduction and the main aspect of the reproduction is to add pictographic components or replace the pictographic components of the original characters. When such new characters are still unable to have independent status, they will serve as the variants of the original characters in a transitional state. This is reflected as the ambiguities of the variants within the pictophonetic system. Consequently, in the ancient character stage, the change and uncertainty of pictographic components seem most striking. Speech develops more slowly. Although phonetic components start to differ or change as speech develops, these changes are not prominent in the ancient character stage. In consequence, phonetic components are relatively stable and unitary. The development of the pictophonetic structure is closely related to the evolution of the whole system of Chinese character forms. The general principles of the development of forms restrict the pictophonetic structure and often make it change in opposition to its internal structural rules, from which arise the phenomena of erroneous change and omission or simplification. The emergence of these phenomena breaks through the rationality of the pictophonetic structure, adds special elements to the pictophonetic system and leads to the complexity of the pictophonetic system.

Part II

Textual Analysis and Interpretation

CHAPTER 3

Method and Practice
The Explication of Ancient Chinese Characters

The Methods of Explicating Ancient Chinese Characters[1]

Studies on the methodology of philology are of great significance as it is now viewed as an independent discipline. For any branch of scientific research, the methods of doing studies diverge greatly in that its objectives are quite different. Authentic conclusions in any study could only be made through reliable methods and approaches, on which the building of the basic framework of a discipline depends. Therefore, the issue of methodology is too important to overlook for philology. Along the cause of philological studies, the achievements that have been made differ in accordance with the discrepancies of the thinking patterns of different scholars of the times. From a diachronic point of view, research methods have grown in an increasingly sophisticated fashion, with those that emerged later turning more and more specific and refined. Synchronically, scholars of the same time may have brought about achievements of different scale, which are largely attributed to the scholars' mindset as well

---
[1] The article was first published in *Cultural Relics Studies,* vol. 6 (Beijing: Huangshan Publishing House, 1990).

as their working methods, if presumably no other reasons are taken into consideration.

As Yu Xingwu points out,

> There has long been a hard fight between the materialist dialectical approach and the idealist metaphysical one when it comes to examine and interpret Chinese ancient script, which is in nature an objective existence, tangible to recognize, pronounceable to read and paraphrasable to explain. The form, sound and meaning are closely related and complementary to each other, while no ancient characters can stand on its own. When doing research, scholars may well examine the interrelation among the form, sound and meaning of a single character, while attaching the same attention to its connection with other script of the same time as well as its own variation and transformation along the time. An objective research result can be generated from such thorough analysis.[2]

Illuminating as the review is, it defines the guidelines, that is, the materialistic dialectic way of doing studies on the ancient script, a summary of Yu Xingwu's decades of practices. It may also well explain the reason how he could reinterpret over 300 oracle bone scripts, generate new findings and correct the errors of previous studies after gurus such as Luo Zhenyu and Wang Guowei. Enlightened by the materialistic dialectic methods, researchers of the present time can summarize practices and experiences of previous generations, sift sand for gold and conduct comprehensive research so as to explore a scientific method to examine and interpret ancient scripts.

Comparing the Forms

The form of the character marks a major tool to interpret ancient scripts and the basis to conduct research. The method of comparing the forms of characters is a simple yet effective way in the examination and interpretation of ancient scripts. Having gone through various

---

[2] Excerpts from the 'Preface' to *Interpretations on Selected Oracle Bone Scripts*. (《甲骨文释林》).

transformations in the long history of mankind, ancient characters, being a historical presentation of certain language may be well connected to or detached from the present linguistic form, and some even have gone in to the discard of time, such as, the hieroglyphs of the ancient Egypt. For whatever reasons, there exist no better ways to interpret the ancient scripts that were once prevalent in history than to develop a system for comparisons. The ground-breaking research done on the Egyptian hieroglyphs and cuneiform scripts of the Mesopotamian are largely attributed to the introduction of the methods of comparison. Take the decipherment of hieroglyphs for example; it started with the comparative study on the bilingual epigraph on the Rosetta stone. The same inscription was recorded on the stone in ancient Greek characters as well as the Hieroglyphic scripts and Demotic scripts, both of which are the forms of the ancient Egyptian language. Thanks to these, the philologists were able to open the door to the mysterious Egyptian characters through close comparison of the three forms of languages.[3]

Studies on ancient Chinese script are blessed with more advantages. First, through the ages, there has been continuous development for Chinese characters with no interruptions or breaks, whose nature and essence remain unchanged as the existing script maintains itself as an intact and integrate comparing system. The initial research on the ancient Chinese script can be dated back to the Han Dynasty when ancient characters had just experienced a transition from the old system to a new one. That period of time was furnished with scholars of great learning, whose accomplishment could be manifested through Xu Shen's book *The Origin of Chinese Characters*. Centred on the small seal script, the book has constructed a relatively comprehensive system by interpreting the forms, meanings of characters and making annotations on the pronunciations while resorting to the large seal script and ancient script for references. Besides, this seal script-centred system, in comparison with the large seal script of the previous dynasty and the clerical script of the upcoming time (also the existing characters

---

[3] Johannes Friendrich, *Entzifferung Verschollener Schriften und Sprachen*, Tr. Gao Huimin (Hong Kong: The Commercial Press, 1979), 36.

of the present day) employ the method of comparing character forms as its primary approach. The clerical scripts—a source of references in this chapter—are viewed only as an underlying system due to the aim of this book. The trilingual stone classics of the Wei Dynasty were inscribed in the ancient script, seal script and clerical script, a clear demonstration of the intentions—to contrast and compare. As the corpus for comparing the character forms, those stone classics make better and more ideal materials than the Rosetta stone, as they are not just large in scale but also represent the three types of scripts of the same language in its different stages of development. Sources such as *Selections of Bamboo Slips* (《汗简》) and *Four Tones of the Ancient Script* (《古文四声韵》) also offer a considerable amount of references to the studies on character forms. It is under such a context that scholars can publish their interpretation by comparing the forms of characters when bamboo slips from the graves of Ji County (汲冢竹书), the bronze script and oracle bone script were first unearthed. However, the form-comparison approach had never been a conscious option for scholars in the philological academia until the Qing Dynasty when Sun Yirang (孙诒让), Wu Dacheng (吴大澂) started to employ it in their research, while some scholars released hypothetical theories based on their own assumptions. The approach came to the academia's awareness in the modern time. Luo Zhenyu (罗振玉) introduced the *Origin* to the systemic textual research of the bronze script, which was later employed as a comparative sample to identify the bone script in his later studies. Just as some philologists have concluded, the methods of interpreting the bone script with the help of/by comparing with bronze script, the *Origins*, and the *Selections of Bamboo Slips* are to decipher the unknown words with a known form of character, which can be categorized into the form-comparison category. Professor Tang Lan defined the comparative approach;[4] yet even up until now, it has not grown into a conscious option for the scholars.

The approach of comparing character forms, to be specific, refers to closely comparing the known character (or a radical of a known character) with an unknown character (or radical) to decipher and interpret the unknown ones by taking advantage of the systemic nature as well

---

[4] Tang Lan, *Guide to Philology* (Jinan: Qilu Publishing House, 1981), 163.

as the diachronic correlation of the Chinese script. Such a comparison can be conducted in a synchronic and diachronic way, with the former meaning connecting the unknown character with the known of the same time so as to conclude similarities of the two, whereas the latter signifying to keep track of the development of a certain character form across the time so as to systemize its writing patterns of different ages, which aims to have better comprehension of the past by relating the present to it. It would be much more convenient if the character forms have few fundamental changes or if it is possible to pin a direct connection between the past and the present despite the long time in between.

As a semiotic system, the Chinese script and its different forms are bound together as the same character, or its radicals remain unified and unchanged across the time. Therefore, an unknown character can be identified through comparing the forms and radicals of the same time span. 肃屯 (hem with embroideries) from *Zaibifu Gui* (Zaibifu food vessel: 宰辟父簋) has been explained as 带束 (girdle or belts) by scholars since the Song Dynasty following Lv Dalin's (吕大临) interpretation. Yet of all the scholars, Sun Yirang was the only one that offered the right explanation. He first compared the two characters' forms in bronze scripts and pointed out that the former had merely fewer strokes while the latter was the result of slips in the process of copying and replication. He then set the characters' forms and designated them with the same pronunciation as 黼纯 (fu chun, the decorative pattern on a piece of clothes made with black and white silk).[5] Such a conclusion is in debt to Sun's synchronic comparison of character forms, which is also accountable to Yu Xingwu's explanation of 心 in the oracle bone script. The form of 心 in the bone script bears large resemblance to that of 贝; hence, scholars of previous generations used to misinterpret it as 贝. Yet, Yu discerned some subtle differences between the two on bone scripts. Yu's analysis on the semantic context of the character 心 and other characters with 心 being a radical leads to the conclusion that the form of 心 features consistency and coherence in different contexts and in compound characters. In this

---

[5] Sun Yirang, '*Zaibifu Gui*', *Gu Zhou Shi Yi*, vol. 1 (古籀拾遗, *Relics of Ancient Zhou Scripts*).

way, the character as well as a series of others composed by 心 were set and defined.

To command sources and data of the same character in different times, especially the typical character forms, shall be the prerequisite for conducting diachronic comparison. If systemized in accordance with the time span, these sources would show the evolutionary track of these characters, which naturally connects the unknown with the known ones by bringing the past to the present. Synchronic comparisons function as a method to decipher the unknown, and to summarize fixed patterns with the help of close examination on character forms. Take 宜 as an example; diachronically, it can be listed as following:

宜 —— 宜 —— 宜 —— 宜 —— 宜 —— 宜 —— 宜 —— 宜
甲骨文　　　弋卣　　　秦公簋　　　宜戈　　　盟书　　　玺文　　　楚简　　　小篆

The *Origin* explains, '宜' (Yi) refers to suit. It is written between a 宀 on top and 一 on the bottom, with '多' usually as its phonological symbol. Through the synchronic comparison, we could draw a picture of the character's evolution trace as well as the slips and mistakes in the process, while Xu Shen's misinterpretation of the forms due to his understanding of small seal script would be easy to spot.[6] Reliable interpretations might be achievable through synchronic comparison and large reservoir of relevant materials.

Diachronic comparisons might be omitted if few changes have taken place to the character forms. It is quite popular for scholars for the purpose of interpreting a character, to compare the forms that are preserved in the *Origins* and *Selections of Bamboo Slips* with the characters of the bone script, bronze script and that of the Warring States period. Sometimes scholars even employ the clerical script for comparison as most characters have remained in their original forms in the long course of history. The *Selections of Bamboo Slips* keeps

---

[6] 俎 and 宜 are of the same origin as in the oracle bone script and bronze script, the radical 肉 lies above 且. The *Origin*'s interpretation on 宜's meaning and character forms is considered incorrect.

a large reservoir of the Warring States script, whereas the *Origin* preserves a lot of large seal script and ancient script characters apart from the small seal script which is regarded as the last version of ancient character of the Qin and Han Dynasties. The employment of these characters as a source of references can be categorized as a branch of diachronic comparison that has taken a considerable part in deciphering ancient scripts. Since the interpretation of bronze script started early, it can also be used as a reference to explain the unknown bone script, just as what Sun Yirang did in his *Selected Illustrations of Khitan Scripts* (《契文举例》). When interpreting 甲丙丁戊庚辛壬癸 and some other characters, he listed the bronze script as a comparative resource, and in his explanation of 子申亥亘帝我求, some ancient characters in the *Origin* were introduced for reference, while the seal script in the book was enlisted to interpret 羌启年牢且省禺及受丰京. All are the examples of diachronic comparison.

Textual research of characters could start with the interactive adoption of synchronic and diachronic comparisons. A diachronic comparison helps to decipher the changes of the character form over the time while the synchronic contrast could reveal the synchronism of the changing character forms so as to reinforce the argument. Therefore, a conclusion made on the basis of synchronic and diachronic comparison is more trustworthy. A typical case can be found from Yu Xingwu's way of explaining 屯 in the bone script.[7] 屯 is quite commonly seen in the bone script as the saying 某示若干屯 appeared quite often on the oracle inscription. There are six other explanations apart from Yu Xingwu's.

1. Ye Yusen (叶玉森) suspected it to be 矛 (mao, spear), Wang Xiang (王襄) introduced 㭉 as a reference for comparison, and Dong Zuobin (董作宾) pushed the study even further to the evolution of 矛's character forms.[8]

---

[7] Yu Xingwu, 'On 屯 and 蓍', in *Interpretations of the Oracle Bone Script* (《甲骨文释林·释屯、蓍》), 1.

[8] Ye Yusen, *Selection and Interpretation of Wooden and Bamboo Slips from the Yin Dynasty Ruins* (《殷墟书契前编集释》), vol. 5; Wang Xiang, *Classified Documents from the Yin Dynasty* (《簠室殷契类纂》) vol. 1; Dong Zuobin, 'On the Characters of 帚 and 矛' (《帚矛说》), in *Evacuation Reports on the Ancient Sites of Anyang*, vol. 4.

2. Guo Moruo interpreted it as the ancient form of the character 包, meaning to wrap something up in the shape of a sealed letter.[9]
3. Tang Lan believed it is the upside-down form of 豕 (shi, meaning pigs).[10]
4. Ding Shan (丁山) interpreted it as 夕 (Xi, the Moon) in compliance with 今屯, 来屯.[11]
5. Hu Houxuan (胡厚宣) interpreted it as 匹, based on bone inscriptions.[12]
6. Zeng Yigong (曾毅公) interpreted it as 身 (shen, the body) and further expounded it into symmetric torso as the right and left scapulae make a complete pair, thus can be called a full body.[13]

The scholars mentioned here, except Hu Houxuan and Zeng Yigong, had all conducted close comparisons on the character forms on both synchronic and diachronic terms, and some of their arguments were even made with the bone inscription as the exemplification. Yet, their conclusions varied.

Yu Xingwu listed his references at his command in details about the transformation of 屯, made analysis on the transforming process and specifically explained the word—春 (chun, refers to spring) and corrected previous errors on the interpretation of 楙 (mao, meaning lush). In this way, the synchronic comparison lays a concrete and trustworthy foundation for the conclusions that are definite and credible.

Despite the introduction of the comparative analysis, reliable conclusions would still be beyond the reach of the studies if researchers fail

---

[9] Guo Moruo, *Exploring the Inscriptions on the Oracle Bone Scripts* (《骨臼刻辞之一考察》), excerpts from More on *Bone Slips of the Yin Dynasty* (《殷契余论》).

[10] Tang Lan, *Studies on the Oracle Bone Scripts at Tianrang Pavilion* (《天壤阁甲骨文存》).

[11] Ding Shan, *On the Gens and Gentile Rules Listed on Oracle Bones* (《甲骨文所见氏族及制度》).

[12] Hu Houxuan, 'Exploring the Five Inscriptive Items on Historical Events of the Wuding Age (1250BC–1192BC)' (《武丁时代五种记事刻辞考》), in *On the History of the Shang Dynasty*, vol. 3.

[13] Zeng Yigong, 'The Precious Remains of the Oracle Bonze Script' (《甲骨叕存》), in *Selected Interpretations of the Oracle Bonze Script* (Taipei: Institute of History and Philology, Academia Sinica, 1970), 171–82.

to pay attention to the following issues raised by different scholars in their interpretation of 屯. First, scholars must have in command large quantity of data about the characters. When scholars were interpreting 矛, 包 and 豕, they all compared the forms of these characters and were confronted with the same shortcoming—the data for synchronic comparison were neither sufficient nor systematic while their use of some single character form as reference source made their research findings unreliable since such a comparison was too random to be trustworthy. Yu Xingwu's conclusion was generated on the basis of a comprehensive corpus and systemization of the character forms in accordance with the passage of times, thus presented the track of the gradual evolution of 屯. Generally speaking, authentic findings of a study depend on accumulated data about the same character's various forms in different times, as well as impersonal comparative analysis, whereas randomly chosen references overlooking hierarchical order of the time only lead to conclusions that can only be defined irrelevant, inadequate and shallow.

Second, the comparability of scripts deserves much prudence when employing the method of comparison. This method refers to synchronic/diachronic comparisons of the same character radical with a certain and concrete comparative reference. References and character forms that cannot be introduced for comparison include those that are too dim to recognize, or yet to be deciphered with settled explanation, or the results of mistakes and slips from copying and duplicating, or suffering damage in casting. As a matter of fact, there exist distinct differences between 楸, following the same pattern of 矛 in the bronze script and the character 春. Yet a diachronic comparison between the two would be insufficient and easy to raise doubts. Yu Xingwu delved deep into the same character, but resorted to diachronic comparisons of the character forms and of the inscriptions, thus provided more reliable evidences for the studies. The comparative radicals (and components) that Guo Moro employed in his interpretation of 包 can be categorized as misshaped slips in the same period of time, thus unsuitable for synchronic comparative researches. Tang Lan brought the arguments into academia's awareness, yet mistook it as 豕 in his own exploration, which could be attributed to the slurred inscription and dim shapes of the character. To apply the data that share no comparability to comparative studies will inevitably bring about judgmental errors. Hence, in the comparisons of character forms, the feature of comparability shall be the primary principle to abide by.

Lastly, the shape and form of the character shall be the objective criteria for comparative studies. When comparing character forms, scholars shall be highly cautious of first-impression prejudices, strained analogies or imagined proposals. Decent conclusions could only be yielded through rigorous and meticulous comparisons and analysis. Dong Zuobin's examination of 矛 was conducted on the basis of character comparison, yet he coined its original form. Tang Lan believed that 矛 was the upside-down form of 豕 with the footing of the latter omitted. But this explanation does not fit the construction pattern and writing rules of the ancient script, thus is more of a subjective surmise than a trustworthy finding. Ding Shan's interpretation of it as 夕 (the moon) was largely based on the inscriptive items on the oracle bone while that of the character forms was nothing more than literal guesswork. These researchers were all high achievers in the discipline, yet any slips of their mind would lead to subjective mistakes, even for scholars such as Tang Lan, who had attached much value to the accuracy of research methods. It is justified to conclude that scholars should pay close attention to every detail in their studies and stick to the basic principle of objectivity and accountability.

The Method of Analysing Character Radicals

Chinese characters can be classified into the unified single and compounded complex in terms of its composing radicals. The latter is formed based on the former by following certain formation patterns. If we dissect a compounded word, the minimal unit is the phonetic one which can be regarded as a basic component of a character. For the unknown script, conducting analysis to designate its radicals and relating them to the known characters may help define the script and characters under evaluation. This method of analysing components is different from what is previously discussed in the comparison of character forms as the former focuses on to define a character through inner dissection. Therefore, for those that are lacking in sufficient data for systematic radical comparison, or those that are less painstaking to recognize and compare, it is quite efficient to conduct a component analysis.

The analysis of character structures is an important part when it comes to the research on the inner relation among the structures, phonetics and meanings of Chinese scripts. In the infancy of philology, there were sayings such as 'The character of 武 (wu, military forces) comes from the combination of 止 (zhi, to stop) and 戈 (ge, a weapon made with bronze or metal)',[14] '蛊 (gu, a mysterious and poisonous substance raised by humans) is composed of 皿 (min, a vessel) and 虫 (chong, worms)'.[15] Such is the explanation of the interrelation between the forms and phonetics through dissociation of radicals. It was by adopting this method that Xu Shen wrote his famous book and named it literally deciphering a character by dissecting it—*Origins of Chinese Characters*, a typical exemplification of radical analysis. As a matter of fact, this method is derived directly from Xu's book. From interpreting the bronze script in the Song Dynasty to the rejuvenation of studies on bronze and stone inscriptions in the Qing Dynasty, the academia had witnessed a growing popularity of this method. Sun Yirang relentlessly analysed the radical and structure of a character in every interpretation, which can be well manifested in the way he interpreted 静 (*jin*, tranquillity).

After analysing and weighing the radicals of the two characters, 𣉙 𣉛, I personally think that their forms should follow 𣉙. The character is in fact '静' that 'follows "争" and is pronounced as "青"'. Why do I say so? The upper part of 𣉙 obviously follows '生', below which '井' should have '丼' within itself (Yin He 尤盉, the ancient wine vessel, exactly follows 丼; in the 'category of 女' of *Selections of Bamboo Slips*, '静' is formed as 姘 in the ancient script, and it borrows '姘' as '静' according to Yi Yun (《义云章》). '青' follows 生丹, and, in the *Origin of Chinese Characters*, '丹' in the ancient script is formed

---

[14] Zuo Zhuan, 'Year Twelve of King Xuan', in *Commentary on the Spring and Autumn Annals*.

[15] Zuo Zhuan, 'First Year of King Zhao', in *Zuo's Commentary on the Spring and Autumn Annals*.

as 禼, which follows 𠂇 as a replacement of '丹'. It follows 受 on the right and becomes '争'. In the *Origin*, '争' follows '𠂇' and '受 follows 爪 and 又'. This form of 钅 is 爪, also is '𠂇' and '𠂇' and this 朩 is 又 written upside-down. (However, in Xiao Chen Ji Yi 小臣继彝, it is not written upside-down.) Marquis of Qi Yan (齐侯甗 a cooking vessel): in '卑旨卑瀞', the character 瀞 is formed as 䚄; in '齐邦灶静安宁', '静' is formed as 䚄, in which '肖' used as '青' is a different case, while '𠂇' and '𠂇' used as '争' is the definite testimony that 彝 𠂇 is the form of '争'.[16]

By analysing the radicals and making close examination, together with the synchronic comparison of character forms, Sun Yirang (孙诒让) corrected Ruan Yuan's (阮元) misinterpretation of 静 as 继 (ji, to follow).

It is Tang Lan that proposed the radical analysis as a method for interpretation. In his book, *A Guide to Philology*, he specifically expounded on this method with two sets of examples. He in his book says, 'The best part of this method is that we can decipher a lot new words simply by knowing one radical'. As he first defined the meaning of 斤 (jin, a tool that looks like an axe), a radical of the oracle bone script, he went on to interpret about two dozens of other characters with 斤 as its radical, such as, 折 (zhe, to twist), 斫 (zhuo, to hack with an axe), 兵 (bing, army), 炘 (xin, heat), 昕 (xin, brightness), 斧 (fu, axe) and 新 (xin, new).[17] Yu Xingwu adopted the same method to interpret 心 (xin, heart). He first compared the character forms to summarize the meaning of 心, distinguishing it from 贝 (bei, shell). Then analysis of radicals was introduced to identify other characters; thus, those with 心 that were previously misinterpreted or unknown were able to be deciphered.[18]

The method of analysing radicals is based on scholar's correct understanding of the internal structure of Chinese characters, and

---

[16] Sun Yirang (孙怡让), *Relics of Ancient Zhou Scripts* (Beijing: Zhonghua Book Company, 1989).

[17] Tang Lan, *Guide to Philology*, 175, 195.

[18] Yu Xingwu, *Selected Oracle Bone Scripts*, (Beijing: Zhonghua Book Company,1979), 361.

Method and Practice **209**

thus its dissection of the character according to its constituting pattern is soundly justified. Chinese philology has long established its own theory and methodology on character structures, and thus provided a theoretical foundation for the radical analysis. To make the most advantage of this scientific approach that focuses on analytical studies, scholars should pay attention to two aspects.

First, a large quantity of variations of the same radical is of pivotal role in studies. Scholars' comprehensive understanding of the synchronic and diachronic radical variations lays a sound foundation for additional studies as they are equipped with sufficient analytical data to define the unknown ones. Accordingly, an erroneous interpretation would bring about a total disaster to the overall studies. Mistakes made by the Qing scholars were largely due to inadequate data on the radicals in their analytical studies as well as misunderstandings on the variations of the same radical. For example, when interpreting the inscriptions on the chime-bells of Zhu Gonghua (邾公华钟),[19] Ruan Yuan (阮元) mistook 名 (ming, names) as 听 (ting, hear), a direct result of inadequate data on the radical 夕.[20] Although an expert of analytical studies on radicals, Sun Yirang still made many mistakes when it came to inscriptions on the oracle bones. For example, one inscription says that 生 is the ancient form of 往 (wang, going to somewhere), noted as 㞷 in the bone script, following the sound of 止 and 王 (wang, king). Sun Yirang puts it as 'The character is commonly seen yet hard to interpret'. It seems to be the ellipsis of 台 (tai, a high platform). Under the category of 至 in the *Origin*, 台 refers to a platform that stands high from where people can have a bird-eye view of the surroundings. It is the ellipsis of 至 and 高 that bears the same meaning as 室 and 屋 (both refer to rooms) and follows the sound of 之. The upper part of the character follows the pattern of 㞢, used as 之, similar to 市 and 先. The lower part follows the pattern of 土 rather than 大, used as 从高省, similar to the character 就 and

---

[19] Zhu Gonghua, father of emperor Xuan of the Zhu kingdom in the southeast part of Shandong Province, east of China.

[20] Ruan Yuan (Qing Dynasty), *Chime-Bells of Zhu Gonghua*, in *Jigu House Interpretations of Inscriptions on the Chime-bells and Vessels*, vol. 3.

following the pattern of 京, meaning 亦. His misinterpretation of 生 is mainly because that of the radical 王. In the same fashion, the character 既 was mistaken as to follow the pattern of 欠 and 豆 because he apprehended the radical 皀 as 豆.²¹ Thus, a thorough understanding of the radical-analysis method cannot necessarily guarantee the correct interpretation if researchers do not have adequate data on radicals. To some extent, the mistakes that Su Yirang had made are inevitable as when he was writing his *Selected Illustrations of Khitan Scripts*, his only references were data from Liu E's book *Oracle Tortoise Sheltered in Clouds* (铁云藏龟), while his lack of systematic knowledge on the radicals of bone script prevented him from making further progress.

Second, analysing the radicals should follow the same way in which a skilled butcher dismembers an ox—conforming to the natural order and avoiding any arbitrary handling out of subjective speculation. In script analysis, no justified conclusions can be drawn if scholars dissemble a radical or disintegrate it into separate stokes with no unified forms and with no regard to the basic rules of the characters' composing units. It is not a rare scene to spot mistakes in the interpretations of the ancient script caused by inappropriate decomposition of the characters. For example, in the chapter 日壬卣 (Riren You: the drinking vessel) of the book *Reflecting the Past and Recording the Bronze Script* (捃古录金文),²² it says that the character 𐅧 is the name of a person. The author of the book Wu Shifen quoted Xu Yinlin, '𐅧 is also noted as 𐅨, followed by the character既'. 𐅨 resembles the action of raising one hand, follows the sound of 手 (shou, the hand) and 既 (ji, meaning to have eaten up) and bears the features common as 摡 (gai, to cleanse), with 皀 omitted in it. In the book *Phonology* (集韵), 摡 and 旡 were referred as the same, with a note specifying: 'the book *Bo Ya* (博雅) explains it as取 (qu, to fetch), meaning 拭 (shi, to wipe) or 抚'. As a matter of fact, the character is the ancient form of 何 (or 荷), as it looks like a person holding something on his shoulders. Xu Shen dissembled the pictographic radical into two parts and regarded the load as well the man's head as an integral part,

---

²¹ Sun Yirang, *Exemplifications on Bamboo Slips* (Jinan: Qi Lu Press, 1993), 77, 94, 106.

²² Wu Shifen (吴式芬), *Reflecting the Past and Recording the Bronze Scripts*《捃古录金文》. It is a specialized book on epigraphy in the Qing Dynasty.

which deranged the original formation of the character and left him in an embarrassing context where he cannot justify himself despite his strenuous efforts to quote and cite extensively. Radical analysis that splits the unity of characters on no scientific bases will surely meet no other fate than failure.

From those misinterpretations, we may see that researchers cannot justify their own arguments and therefore usually adopt the general saying of 'an omission of…' as a statement of excuses. The ellipsis of radicals can be seen in the composition of a character, yet scholars have to employ sufficient data on radical analysis to prove the objectivity of ellipsis. Otherwise, they are prone to draw forced analogies.

The credibility of radical analysis lies on its scientific methods that require discreet and close examination in every part of the research. Be it dissembling the radical, identifying it or interpreting it, researchers need to constantly remind themselves of the rules of Chinese scripts that value the shapes and forms of the character. Reflecting upon the many mistakes and achievements that Sun Yirang made in his analytical studies may inspire younger generations.

Radical analysis functions to distinguish the structure of the unknown character, yet it is the comparative study of character forms that will determine the relation of structure, phonetics and meaning in a character. The process of identifying a radical is in nature a comparative study on the forms. If references and radicals are not available for the analogy, researchers still cannot pin down the meaning of the word just through analysing the radicals. That is why Tang Lan and Yu Xingwu cannot define the meaning of the word, although they have set apart the radicals that followed the patterns of 斤 and 心, respectively. Therefore, for a thorough and comprehensive understanding of ancient characters, other aiding approaches will be hard to miss due to the limitations of the analytical studies.

Inductive Studies on Oracle Inscriptions

In interpreting the ancient script, it is quite common to have characters that are with radicals missing or too blurred to recognize, or that have experienced special variations, thus indecipherable for the scholars. Some of the characters are quite legible but exert few long-lasting influences to the present day, while some may be endowed with a distinct structure, yet the meanings are nowhere to be deciphered. In conditions like these, comparative studies on character forms or radical analysis would be powerless, unless the method of generalizing the inscription items could come to their rescue.

The method refers to analysing, comparing and concluding a series of inscriptions based on the linguistic context where the unknown characters stand for the purpose of interpreting scripts in a correct way.

All written scripts are signs of languages. As a sign to record the Chinese linguistic items, Chinese character stands for a trinity of forms, phonetics and meanings. Wang Yun of the Qing Dynasty said, 'The profundity of languages lies in the form, phonetics and meanings of scripts'. Our ancestors coined characters to name all things and creatures by complying with the meaning of the object, making sound flowing, which leads to the natural formation of character structure. When doing their research works, later generations defined a character's meaning by clarifying its sound which was pinned through examining the character's forms and structure.[23] The marrow of form comparison and radical analysis is to define a character's meaning and sound through close examination of its form on the basis of interrelation among the form, meaning and sound. On the other hand, Chinese characters, being a set of signs to keep record of oral expressions, present themselves in certain linguistic contexts and concrete inscriptive items. The former refers to an organized sequence in which each expression is meaningfully related, complementary and contradictory to each other. Hence, an explicit linguistic context and inscriptive item can define approximately the semantic scope of the unknown scripts, based on which researchers can be led to deduce the meaning, shape and sound, while at the same time to summarize similar inscriptive items so as to interpret the unknown characters. This method is largely based on the correlation between language and character, as well as the triple unity of character form, phonetics and meanings. Successful interpretations of ancient scripts demonstrated

---

[23] Wang Yun, Exemplifications on the *Origins of Chinese Characters*.

that the method of summarizing is feasible if adopted appropriately. It works in the following two aspects.

1. To distinguish the forms of a character by comparing them with the inscriptive items. Through summarizing the functioning context and inscriptions, the semantic scope of the unknown characters can be defined, while analogies and conclusions of the synonymous or similar inscriptions can bring new thoughts to the interpretation of character forms. There is an inscription on the Zhao Bohu Gui (Zhao Bohu food vessel) that puts '囗余既囗有司'. The first character was usually explained as 月 or 曰 (yue, to say). Sun Yirang started his studies from the inscription, believing that

   > it does not make sense to define it as 月, as in the bronze script 月 and 曰 were not written in this way. Taking a semantic look at this, it should be the variation of 今. 今 and 余 are quite commonly seen in the two-character phrase (连文) of the bronze script.

   He then went on to list eight more examples about 今余 in the bronze script to identify the character as 今, thus corrected the previous mistakes.[24] Such is the case to summarize the inscriptive items to define the variant characters. In the bronze script, the character 讯 takes on a peculiar shape that can rarely be seen in ancient classics or scripts. Scholars' opinions were widely divided concerning its interpretations—some interpreted it as 㚻, some 纬, or 馘 or 绚, all of which were inappropriate. Chen Jieqi, in view of the context of this character 折首五百, 执㰷五十 found that it was equivalent to the 讯 in the phrase 执讯 in the *Book of Songs* and would also show up after the character 执 in other occasions. Besides, what was inscribed on the Guoji Zibai plate (虢季子白盘) happens to be the history of attacking the clan of Yan You (猃狁) dwelling in the northwest of the country. Hence, the character should be defined as 讯 according to the semantic meaning.[25] This viewpoint also

---

[24] Sun, Yirang, 'Zhao Bo Hu Gui (Zhao Bo Hu food vessel)', in *Gu Zhou Shi Yi* (古籀拾遗, *Relics of Ancient Zhou Scripts*).

[25] Wu Shifen, Guo Ji Zi Plate, excerpts from *Selected Recording of Bronze Scripts*, vol. 3 (《捃古录金文》).

earned the support of Wu Dacheng, who believed it followed the patterns of 糸 and 口 and bore the meaning of seizing the enemies and questioning them.[26] Wang Guowei studied the inscription on the Yu Gui (敔簋, Yu food vessel), Guo Ji Zibai plate, Xi Jia Plate, Shiyuan Gui (师袁簋), Buqi Gui (不期簋), compared their semantic context and found that the character always followed the appearance of 执, similar to the phrases in the *Book of Songs*, such as 执讯获丑, 执讯连连. This finding further proved that the character takes on the shape of 讯 and the meaning of captives.[27] It is by summarizing the inscriptive items and comparing it with the ancient classics that the meaning of 讯 was identified. These two examples are all centred on identifying the unknown characters through summarizing the inscriptive items. In the process of interpreting ancient scripts, the comparison and analysis of character forms are of the same importance, with which the summary of inscriptive items need to be compared for a definite and appropriate conclusion.

2. To infer the meaning of a character through summarizing the inscriptive items. Some ancient characters are recognizable as far as the forms are concerned, yet are not included in the dictionaries or classics of the later generations, thus cannot be identified through form comparison. It left the scholars with few options to decipher their meaning except the method of summarizing them. For example, the bone character 㞢 is commonly seen in the oracle inscriptions of the Wu Ding period (1250 BC–1192 BC). Sun Yirang, Luo Zhenyu and Wang Guowei all interpreted it as 之 which as a matter of fact bears great differences with it regarding the character shapes. Hu Xiaoshi, in his books, *On the Ancient Script in the Origin of Chinese Characters* (《说文古文考》) and *Illustrations of Oracle Bone Scripts* (《甲骨文例》), explained that it is equivalent to 又 and 有 in meanings based on the semantic context of this character. He puts in the books,

---

[26] Wu Dacheng, *Supplements of the Ancient Script in the Origin of Chinese Characters*, vol. 1 (《说文古籀补》; Beijing: China Bookstore, 1990), 11.

[27] Wang Guowei, Posthumous Papers of Wang Guowei, (王国维遗书・六・不期敦盖铭考释).

in regards of the 㞢 that the character can be interpreted into 又 as in the case 俘人十㞢六人, which means to have captured 16 people.²⁸ There are some other sayings such as 自今十年㞢 五, which means 15 years since then (俘人十又六人). On the other hand, it can also be translated into 有, such as, in the phrase 允㞢来艰 that can be completed into 允有来艰. Another possible interpretation might be that it is the simplified form of 告, which can be proved from the saying 贞, 㞢于且丁, that is, 贞, 告于祖丁. Its meaning is totally different from that of 之.²⁹ Guo Moruo had the same understanding. 'Whenever the character shows up in inscriptive items, it bears the same meaning with 又 … Yet, the form of this character is yet to be deciphered'.³⁰ Based on the scholars' illustrations of the inscriptive items, conclusions can be drawn that 㞢 in the oracle bone scripts can be deciphered as 有, 又, 佑 and 侑. Yet, its form is still undecided because it gradually disappeared after King Wu Ding, and was substituted by又. The on-and-offs of the character form's evolution brought obstacles to the interpretations. The reason why researchers can reach unanimous agreement on the meaning of 㞢 is proved by the inscriptive item 㞢 that works for both 㞢 and 又. It follows the sound of 又, while 有 is also pronounced in the same way.

In some occasions, the inscriptive item is clear and set, thus its semantic meaning can be defined. However opinions are divided regarding the best interpretation. A typical case can be found in the interpretation process of the character 囮. It was frequently used in the oracle bone script, such as in the phrases of 有～, 亡 (无)～, 旬有～, 夕亡(无)～, 唯～, 不唯～. In consideration of the context, it can no doubt be deciphered as misfortune and calamity. However, different scholars offered different insights into its meanings which include 卜、戾、凶、繇、凸、骨、祸、悔、咎 and so on. Almost

---

²⁸ Jing Hua, 菁华6页, 6.
²⁹ Hu Xiaoshi, *Illustrations of Oracle Bone Script*, vol. 1 (1982), 1.
³⁰ Guo Moruo, 'A Compilation of Oracle Bone Inscriptions', in *Collected Works of Guo Moruo* (Beijing: China Science Publishing House, 2002), 230–31.

all scholars of certain fame in this field have published their opinions on this character; still, no final verdict has been achieved. It can be inferred that the method of summarizing alone is not sufficient enough to define a character. The same semantic context can accommodate several synonyms, thus making researchers deliberate before they can come up with a sound interpretation for it. Employing 卜、戾、凶、繇、冎、骨、祸、悔、咎 to replace 囮 makes sense and can even be justified by examples from the ancient classics. As a matter of fact, 囮 can only be used to substitute one or some aspects of its meaning, thus scholars cannot just depend on the inscriptive items for the credible interpretations. Yu Xingwu pronounced it as 咎 and listed three reasoning.

1. On Marquis of Lu Gui (Marquis of Lu food vessel), there is a line that reads 鲁侯又（有）囮工. Guo Moruo believed it should be 有猷功, with 囮 as the variant of 囮, the same as 猷.
2. The bamboo slips unearthed in the Lin Yi city was carved with the saying 尧问许囮, 许囮. The character appears three times on the slips, and was later deciphered as related to the phrase 许由, with 由 being the equivalent form of 囮.
3. In the book *Long Kan Shou Jian* (《龙龛手鉴》) under the category of the radical 囗, it records a character 囮, following the sound of 其九反. 囮, 猷, 由 and 咎 are all categorized under the ancient tone of 幽.[31]

Based on these arguments, the interpretations related to 戾、凶、悔、祸、卜 are expelled. Nevertheless, its appropriate form is still under evaluation.

Researchers are also baffled by some other characters that are clear with its meanings and semantic context, yet hard to comprehend and recognize as far as the character forms are concerned. Researchers of the Song Dynasty spotted characters such as 乙子, 癸子 in the bronze script. For centuries, these characters are incomprehensible. In the light of the tablet on heavenly stems and earthy branches restored in the bone script of the Shang Dynasty, people can find out that during

---

[31] Yu Xingwu. *Interpretations on Selected Oracle Bone Scripts*, 231.

that time, 子 was often used to stand for 巳. Thus, all the conceptual clouds can be dispelled. 乙子 and 癸子 in nature are, respectively, 乙巳 and 癸巳. Still, another question hangs in the air: Since there existed the character of 巳 in the bone script, why it was written into 子 in the zodiac tablets? Such doubts can also be found in other cases. The bronze pot of King Zhongshan was inscribed with 方数百里 (with a radius of a hundred miles) while the bronze plate that was carved with the layouts of King Zhongshan's grave also bears the inscription of 王堂方二百尺 and so on. In this case, 百 can be interpreted as 全 (full and complete), following the structural pattern of 全. Although the character took on a clear appearance on the plate, its shape and structure were quite peculiar and unexpected that cannot be deciphered even up until now.

Thus it can be seen that the method of summarizing and generalizing can define the scope of a character's semantic meaning, and even its specific meaning. Yet to define the unknown characters is beyond its reach, whereas other approaches are indispensable to define the form of a character.

Moreover, this method is also helpful to distinguish character forms. Some characters are of the same origin in form and thus hard to distinguish. The introduction of inscriptive items in this case is essential. For example, in the bone script characters such as 比 and 从, 月 and 夕, 女 and 母, 立 (替) and 立 (並), 寅 and 黄, 人 and 尸 are of slight differences in form and shape, which can only be differentiated through close examination on the inscriptive items and context. As for the characters that are of various meanings, it would be impossible to seek the characters with the same phonetics yet different forms without the help of inscriptive items. All in all, summarizing the inscriptive items can be of great value in studies, and it makes up for the deficiencies of form comparison and radical analysis.

The Method of Comprehensive Argumentation

The aforementioned three methods could solve some basic problems concerning the interpretation of ancient scripts. Yet to explore the difficult and complicated characters, researchers are required to employ their entire repertoire of all relevant methods, expertise and data so as to conduct comprehensive analysis from all possible perspectives—a comprehensive argumentation as this book would name it. An adequate adoption of this method entails strategic insights, together with in-depth examination based on the philological and linguistic features as well as socio-historical context of the problem.

Both the written and oral languages are important aspects of human civilization. The structure and development of the written language are closely related to the social and historical context of a certain age. Hence, ancient scripts are the embodiment of the materialistic and cultural civilization of the ancient society, from which later generations are able to have a quick peek of the ancestors' conventions, ideas and mindset, hundreds of years ago. Yu Xingwu said, 'Chinese pictographic and ideographic scripts reflect in a vivid way what the ancient Chinese society was like. Therefore the scripts themselves are precious historical documents'.[32] Such a nature of ancient characters shows that by taking advantage of such a nature of ancient characters and exploring the historical, cultural and folk features of the ancient society, scholars may be able to interpret and trace the origin of difficult characters.

Three types of historical and cultural materials can be used to interpret ancient scripts. They are the unearthed scriptures or scripts passed down to the present times which also constitute the most important part in the reservoir; the objects of the Qin Dynasty, which include the relics, historical ruins found through evacuations, archaeological investigations, as well as the ancient customs and conventions that can still be found in ethnic groups. Therefore, the process of deciphering the ancient scripts entails various disciplines, such as, documentation science, histology, archaeology, cultural archaeology as well as folklore, and hence is regarded as a quite comprehensive way of interpreting.

The method of comprehensive argumentation can be categorized as a modern school of methodology in that it represents the dialectic and reflective perspectives in the materialism and on the other hand

---

[32] Yu Xingwu, *Interpretations on Selected Oracle Bone Scripts*.

the overlapping connection between philology and other disciplines. Such a research approach indicates the sophisticated growth of the philological and the encyclopaedic knowledge of the researchers. The ice-breaker in the adoption of this method is believed to be Guo Moruo who had set a distinct objective at the very beginning of his studies. He summarized Wang Guowei and Luo Zhenyu's approaches, and pointed out that Wang and Luo's findings were not reliable for scholars of his time to do research on the Chinese philology and ancient Chinese society. At the same time, he also made it clear that

> the resources we need are not the worn clothes of others as we have already been equipped with the aircraft to escape from the castles constructed by others. We need to take a step back from the so called studies of ancient Chinese classics before we can really figure out the truth of this field.

What Guo implies is to reveal the real ancient Chinese society by taking advantage of the present materials and conducting studies from a new perspective while his aim is to fill in the blanks that China has left in the civilization history around the world. It is under such a context that he wrote his first book on philological studies, *Studies on the Ancient Chinese Society* (《中国古代社会研究》). In the preface of the book's first edition he wrote the following.

> This book could be the sequel to Friedrich Engels' *The Origin of the Family, Private Property and the State*. The book follows his research methodology and elaborates on what happened in the Ancient China about which he failed to provide any information, apart from the American Indians, ancient Greek and Rome in his book.

This is to inform the many pedants of the 'works of Marx and Engels, besides those of Dai Dongyuan, Wang Niansun and Zhang Xuecheng. Without the knowledge of materialistic dialectic as their base, it is even hard for these pedants to talk about their own ideas'.[33] It is clear

---

[33] Guo Moruo, *Studies in the Ancient Chinese Society* (Beijing: The People's Press, 1954).

that Guo Moruo had been greatly influenced by Marx and Engels as well as their scientific worldviews and methodologies. Hence, he was able to achieve great success in the field of philological studies. The way he interpreted ancient scripts had incorporated proficient uses of character comparison, radical analysing and summarizing inscriptive items. Another remarkable feature is that he set his studies against a broad backdrop of global civilization history and ancient Chinese society and evaluated his research questions from the perspective of the evolution of human society. For example, in the passage of *On Chen Zai* (《释臣宰》) he started from the social development and stratification and evolution of the classes, later deciphered the meanings of the 臣民 (officials and ordinary citizens) and 宰 (ministers of the ancient imperial courts) and pointed out that both 臣 and 民 were slaves in the ancient times, and ministers were like any other official. He then went on, 'The essence of a book on the history of the ruling classes can be revealed through a few words, and this fact should be known to each and every philological scholars'. The text of *On Zhi Gan* (《释支干》) explained in detail the origin and meanings of the 10 Tian Gan and the 12 Di Zhi,[34] comparing the Babylonian 12 zodiac signs with the ancient Chinese 12 Di Zhi, the 12 constellations with the 12 Chinese horoscopes. Some unique views were presented on the issue of ancient Chinese calendric system.[35] In the text of *An Explanation of the Graphic Characters in the Yinyi Rules of the Zhou Dynasty* (《殷彝中图形文字之一解》), a conclusion was summarized through a detailed analysis of graphic characters as follows.

> in reference to the common rule of the social evolution and the stylistic features of the signings on ancient vessels, the scripts taking the forms of birds, beasts, fishes and insects are all the totems or the heritages of ancient people. If the form be something other than the above mentioned, it must be the variation of the clans' totems,

---

[34] The Ten Tian Gan (celestial or heavenly stems) are a Chinese system of ordinals as the names of the ten days of the week. The heavenly stems were used in combination with the 12 Di Zhi (the earthly branches, a similar cycle of twelve days) to produce a compound cycle of sixty days (notes by the translator).

[35] Guo Moruo, 'Studies On Oracle Bone Scripts', in *Collected Works of Guo Moruo*, vol. 1 (Beijing: China Science Publishing House, 2002).

which indicates the sophistication of their culture having outgrown its ancient clan insignia.

This provides a breakthrough for the interpretation of ancient graphic scripts.[36] Some other texts such as 'On Gan Lu' (《释干卤》), 'On Huang' (《释黄》) and 'On Bing' (《释鞞》) can be categorized to the same group.[37] When dealing with real questions, these articles provide more than just macro-level inspirations. The adoption of real-life evidence, archives, records from the classics and folk culture in the deciphering process have in the meanwhile offered a broad range of detailed reasoning and arguments, echoing with the approach of comprehensive argumentation.

Yu Xingwu was the first to propose this approach as he pointed out in his article 'On Qiang, Gou, Jing, Mei' (《释羌、苟、敬、美》).

> To trace the roots of the ancient scripts' composing radicals, researchers may be able to acquaint themselves with the lifestyle and customs of the ancestors which constitutes a valuable resources for studies. Moreover, a close examination of the living habits stored in the ancient or ethnographical classics may manifest the authentic meaning of some ancient scripts when they were first created… Of the present moment when we have seen and mastered the meanings of large quantities of ancient characters, any narrowly isolated researching methods should be avoided for anyone. We the researchers should take into considerations of the real-life situations of the ancient society recorded in the ancient world history and ethnographies. This paper is a tentative experiment of this new approach.

Although Yu Xingwu did not name this approach in specific terms, what he proposed and employed was exactly what he meant. His paper can inspire future studies in many aspects. The first part is on the interpretation of 羌, in which he quoted from seven ancient classics and archives on the oracle bones, and examined the connection of the

---

[36] Guo Moruo, 'Studies on Bronze Inscriptions of Yin Zhou period', in *Collected Works of Guo Moruo*, vol. 4 (Beijing: China Science Publishing House, 2002).

[37] Guo Moruo, 'A Collection of Bronze Scripts', in *Collected Works of Guo Moruo*, vol. 5 (Beijing: China Science Publishing House, 2002).

Qiang ethnic group with the Han people, pointing out that 'For a long time, the ancient Han people had maintained with the Qiang people closer relationship than any other ethnic groups in forms of matrimonial connection and close contacts on battle fields'. Such a conclusion has set a grandeur historical–cultural background for future studies. Second, he traced the roots of the radicals of 羌 and proposed that the character originated from the folk tradition of wearing ram's horns. Then, 12 more archival items from home and abroad were introduced to prove that wearing the horns of rams, ox and deer or using them as decoration were a universal tradition of the primitive people across the world. Discussions evolved around these sources unveiled the evolutionary stages of wearing ram horns: hunting disguises, decorations, aesthetic and honorary items, sacrificial and worshipping offerings, deciphering the folk tradition's origination and evolution from the perspective of mankind's materialistic and cultural development. Based on the influence exerted by the materialistic and cultural interactions between Han people and other ethnic groups, a conclusion was drawn:

> Because of the clan's tradition, Qiang people borrowed the image when coining the characters and put the graphic of 羊 (ram) on top of 人 (man). As the Qiang clan was frequently plundered by clans living in the central plain, a rope-shape radical was added to the character to be like 羌. The ram horn-shape radical of 羌 from the inscriptive items and bronze scripts was mis-transformed into 羊, while the small seal script of this character experienced no variations thanks to intact inheritance. Xu Shen then misinterpreted the character based on the misshaped variations as 'following the shapes of 人 and 羊, with the latter indicating the pronunciation.[38]

Yu's exposition on the composing radicals and structural evolution coincides with Guo Moruo's decipherment in terms of researching methods, yet exceeds as it designates this new approach in specific details. Besides, Yu's papers of 'On Fu' (《释孚》), 'On Sheng' (《释圣》) and 'On Shu' (《释庶》) are also great successes derived from this approach.

Given the wide-ranging influence of Guo's works and Yu's further proposals, the approach of comprehensive argumentation has been

---

[38] Yu Xingwu, 'On Qiang, Ji, Jing, Mei', *A Journal of Jilin University (Social Science Edition)* 1 (1963).

recognized and accepted by researchers in their own studies. Works of 'On Wang' (《释王》) by Lin Yun[39] and 'A Tentative Study of the Character 屮 in Oracle Bone Script' (甲骨文 "屮" 字试探) by Huang Xiquan[40] were direct outcomes of this approach. Yet the comprehensive argumentation as a research method is yet to be made available to more researchers in that, on the one hand it requires large repertoire of relevant knowledge and higher level of theoretical attainment, and on the other lacks adequate reasoning and elaboration.

These four methods are a brief summary of former generations' experience on the interpretation of ancient scripts which are all based on materialistic dialectics. The four approaches differentiate from each other as the method of comparing character forms focuses on the diachronic and synchronic correlation of the character forms; the radical analysis method then aims at the inner core of a character by decomposing the character, whereas the approach of generalizing the inscriptive items is in pursuit of the clues that may solve the problems through the phonetic aspects reflected by the linguistic signs. The comprehensive argumentation starts from the viewpoint of cultural anthropology and thus represents a type of in-depth research. As a matter of fact, the four approaches are correlative and complimentary to each other. The character forms are the basic reference for deciphering and interpreting, without which generalization of inscriptive items and comprehensive argumentation would be as rootless as the moon in the mirror. No decent conclusions would be made without the objective base featured by character forms; hence, the generalization of inscriptive items makes the deciphering of character forms as its goal while comprehensive argumentation would achieve at nothing if its beholders deviate from its starting point of a proper analysis of the character forms. Moreover, the findings of these two approaches usually rely on specific inscriptive items as proving evidence. A typical example can be found in Yu Xingwu's way of interpreting new characters. Apart from a close study of the evolution of the character forms, he applied its findings to specific items to check its validity before a final conclusion

---

[39] Lin Yun, 'On Wang', *A Journal of Archaeology* 6 (1965).

[40] Huang Xijin, 'A Tentative Study of the Character 屮 in Oracle Bone Script', in *Studies of Chinese Ancient Characters*, vol. 6 (Beijing: Zhonghua Book Company, 1981).

was drawn. In the interpretation process, these four approaches do not function in isolation. On the contrary, they intermingle and complement each other so as to reveal the nature of a character. For philological researchers, it is important to employ as various methods as possible.

Methodological issues are the loopholes in philological studies. This paper is a mere experimental study on the basis of previous examples. To push the philological academia for further development, it is a prerequisite to establish a methodological system. Yet to make things worse, recent years have witnessed quite a large array of works and papers that have violated the basic rules and principles of philological studies in the pursuit of the so-called new and creative point of view. It is a belief shared by scholars of this generation that methodological studies exert significant and realistic impact on guaranteeing the scientific and unified feature of philological studies. Thus, more books of gravity and objectivity are under earnest expectations.

A New Explication of the Inscription on Zeng Ji Wu Xu Pots (曾姬无卹壶)[41]

In 1930s of the 20th century, a group of bronze wares were unearthed from the tomb of Lord Chu in Zhujia Ji, Shou County, Anhui Province, two of which were Zeng Ji Wu Xu pots with the same inscriptions. Half a century has passed but few scholars, although they did deep research on the inscriptions on the two pots, provided precise explanations on the key words in the inscriptions. Here will be proposed some opinions on those key words and discussed their related issues.

The first one to explain is the character 聖. This character was explained by Liu Jie (刘节) as '望',[42] followed by Yang Shuda[43] and

---

[41] It was originally published in *Research on Ancient Chinese Characters,* vol. 23 (Beijing: Zhonghua Book Company, 1979).

[42] Liu Jie (刘节), 'Textual Criticisms and Explanations on Chu Wares Unearthed from County Shou', in *Textual Research on Ancient History* (Beijing: People's Publishing House, 1958).

[43] Yang Shuda, *Ji Wei Ju Album of the Oracle Bone Script·Postcript of Zeng Ji Wu Xu Pot* (Beijing: Zhonghua Book Company, 1997), 159.

Guo Moruo,[44] and *Anthology of Inscriptions on Bronze Wares of Shang and Zhou Dynasties*, vol. 4 (《商周青铜器铭文选·四》), which explained '望' as '望祭' (watch from afar and do the sacrifice).[45] Tang Lan explained it as '虘'[46] and was followed by Li Jiahao (李家浩) who doubted that this character went with tone of '壬' and was pronounced as '镇' (zhen) in the inscriptions.[47] Liu Xinfang (刘信芳) thought that

> this character should follow Ren '壬' (他鼎切) (referrer note as 壬), 虘 tone, pronounced as Wu (吾). This character was also seen in *Laozi* (《老子》) of Guodian Chu Bamboo slips, told by Mr Cui Renyi (崔仁义) from Museum of Jing Men (荆门市, a city of Hubei Province). I initially thought that this character followed the tone of Ren (壬) and was pronounced as Zhèng (郑), but afterward with many examples, I knew it should follow '虘' tone.[48]

Li Ling (李零) initially thought this character 'served as predicate verb' and probably bore the meaning of 'feeling or compassion', 'sympathizing' and 'relieving'.[49] Afterwards, the clerical script (隶书) made it like '虘' and it was pronounced as 'Fu (抚)' and served as a predicate verb.[50]

This character was also seen in the Xin Yang Chu bamboo slip nos. 1–012 and 1–014, the *Compilations of Ancient Imperial Jade Seal*. The Square Jade Seal nos. 3056, 3411 and 3433, and all the old

---

[44] Guo Moruo, *Textual Criticisms and Explanations on Antique Catalog of Bronze Scripts of Two Zhou II* (Shanghai: Shanghai Bookstore, 1999), 166.
[45] Ma Chengyuan, ed., *Selections of Inscriptions on Bronze Wares of Shang Dynasty and Zhou Dynasty* (Beijing: Cultural Relics Publishing House, 1990), 454.
[46] Tang Lan, 'Textual Criticism on Bronze Wars Unearthed from County Shou', *Journal of Sinological Studies* 4, no. 1 (1934).
[47] Li Jiahao, 'On the Time When Chu Extinguished Zen from Inscriptions of Zeng Ji Wu Xu Pot', in *Wen Shi* (《文史》), vol. 33 (Beijing: Zhonghua Book Company, 1990).
[48] Liu Xinfang, 'Haogong, Haojian and Haoli', in *Chinese Characters*, vol. 24 (Taipei: Yiwen Publishing House, 1998).
[49] Li Ling, 'On Typical Chu Bronze Wares in East Zhou', *Research on Ancient Scripts*, vol. 19 (Beijing: Zhonghua Book Company, 1992).
[50] Li Jing, 'On Reading of Compilation of Characters on Bamboo Slips and Silk Manuscripts of Chu', *Studies on the Excavated Relics*, vol. 5 (Beijing: Chinese Science Publish, 1999).

materials, could not come to an accurate explanation. In the newly unearthed Guodian Chu Bamboo slips, this character can be seen 14 times, 11 of which are pronounced as 'Wu (吾)' and 3 as 'Hu (乎)'; it is thus clear that this character was pronounced more likely as 'Wu (吾)' in the script of the Warring States period. Verified in the Xin Yang bamboo slips and ancient imperial seals, being pronounced as '吾' was also clear and coherent, like Xin Yang 1–012 '🅇 (吾)闻周公'; no. 1–014 '🅇 (吾)几(岂)不智(知)才(哉)'; no. 3056 '🅇 🅇', no. 3433 '🅇' in *Compilations of Ancient Imperial Jade Seal* were pronounced as 'Wu Qiu (吾丘)', a compound surname; no. 3411 '🅇' was pronounced as '分吾',[51] a compound surname.

The use of this character is basically perspicuous, but analysing its form is very difficult. There is a formation phenomenon in the ancient script which might be helpful to form the analysis of this character.

Tang Tuhui (汤涂惠) pointed out that in the ancient script, the herringbone component written at the bottom sometimes can be changed to 土.[52] This formation phenomenon existing in the ancient script made us doubt that '🅇' that the character 𠂇 followed was derived from '🅇🅇🅇', and its evolution process was speculated to be 虎虍. If this speculation was right, then this character should be explained as '虎'. This character was pronounced as 'Wu (吾)' or 'Hu (乎)', which was a phonetic loan character. In ancient Chinese phonology, '虎', belonged to Xiaoniu radical and the Yubu consonant, '吾', belonged to Yiniu radical and the Yubu consonant; the initial consonant (of a Chinese syllable) of these two characters belonged to the guttural sound with the same vowel (of a Chinese syllable), and therefore these two could be phonetic loan characters. Pot inscription '壶 (Hu) (pot)' which was also pronounced as '吾 (Wu)' was the first person pronoun. Commonly seen in the bronze script, '虍' was used as the first person pronoun and

---

[51] Wei Yihui, Shenxian, 'Textual Criticisms and Explanations on Inscriptions of Ancient Emperor Seal', *Culture of the South East* 3 (1999).

[52] Tang Tuhui, 'On Some Issues in Research on Forms of Characters in Warring States Period', in *Research on Ancient Scripts* vol. 15 (Beijing: Zhonghua Book Company, 1996).

followed 虍, and the 鱼 consonant was added. '鱼' and '吾' had the same consonant and vowel in old Chinese phonology, with '虎' being used as '吾', following the same rule, with '虜' being used as '吾'.

The second one to explain is 㝢. This character was on two pots, one having a kind of damage and the other being very clear. Liu Jie explained it as '守',[53] Yang Shuda explained it as '安' and pronounced it as '按 (àn)',[54] Guo Moruo, *Anthology of Inscriptions on Bronze Wares of Shang and Zhou Dynasties* (《商周青铜器铭文选》) and Li Ling (李零) explained it as '安'. Li Ling believed, 'An Zi (安兹), Yang Ling (漾陵) and Hao Jian (蒿间) should be the paralleled names of places'.[55] Li Jiahao proposed a new statement and explained this character as '毋'. He said

> As the side character that '毋' followed was similar with the right-side character followed by the second character of No. 0362 seal in *Compilations of Ancient Imperial Jade Seals*, comparing the right-side character followed by the second character of No. 0362 seal with the side character of '女' in the script of Yan, we could assure that it was '毋'.

Here to present the character of '毋' in the inscriptions on the pots, the second character of no. 0362 seal and the character that followed the side character of '女' in the script of Yan, we make comparison as shown in the following figure:

㝢 曾姬无卹壶
㝢《古玺汇编》63·0362
㝢(妸)《古玺文编》292·0190
㝢(郾)《古玺文编》147·3857
㝢(安)《古币文编》75

---

[53] Liu Jie (刘节), 'Textual Criticisms and Explanations on Chu Wares Unearthed from County Shou'.
[54] Yang Shuda, *Ji Wei Ju Album*, 159.
[55] Li Ling, 'On Typical Chu Bronze Wares'.

Seen from the characters presented in the figure, the difference between the right-side character followed by the second character of No. 0362 seal and the side character of '女' was that the former had one more horizontal stroke, and hence, it obviously should be '毋'.

He also said that '㝯' might be the variant of '庀'.[56]

In the opinions mentioned here, the explanation of '安' is the most influential. Now we would take a look at '安' in the script of Warring States period.

秦 (Qin): ⿳ 宜安戈

楚 (Chu): ⿳ 包山105

⿳ 郭店·老子甲25

三晋 (the states of Zhao, Wei and Hand): ⿳ 《中国历代货币大系》1278

(Extensive Range of Coins of Successive Dynasties of China)

齐 (Qi): ⿳ 陈纯釜

燕 (Yan): ⿳ 《古玺汇编》3900

⿳ 《古玺汇编》0012

⿳ 《古玺汇编》1348

The '女' followed by '安' in the script of Yan was the closest in form to '⿳' followed by '氏'. But '女' or side character of '女' followed by '安' in the script of Yan (like the one followed by 妣, 郾, etc.) was mostly used as 㐆, 㐄, 㐅; the vertical strokes on the left curved to the right and the vertical strokes in the middle mostly went up to pass through, which were obviously different from '氏' (or copied as 氐, an error), and thus to explain this character either as '安' or '㝯' was doubtful.

In the script of the Warring States period, '厇' (宅) was similar to what shown in the following figure.

---

[56] Li Jiahao, 'On the Time When Chu Extinguished'.

楚 (Chu): 斥 包山155
民 郭店、成之闻之34
斥 郭店、成之闻之33
斥 望山1·113
祏 望山1·112
中山 (Zhongshan): 斥 中山王鼎

The '⿱宀' followed by '斥' had a similar form as 民, 斥 and 斥 should be '厇' which was the same as '宅' from the ancient script of the *Origin* and *San Ti Shi Jing* (《三体石经》, inscriptions engraved on stone in three scripts, the ancient script, the small seal script and the clerical script). Guodian Chu Bamboo Slips have the character '乇', and '乇' was often used as '厇' (宅). For example, 忓 (托) emerged 21 times as ⿱宀乇 in 'Zi Yi' (《缁衣》, the first poem of the *Book of Poetry*) and 11 times as ⿱宀乇 in 'Tai Yi' (《太一》, Tao, referring to the origin of the universe). Taking this into account, the script of Chu which followed '乇' could be traditionalized to the tone of 厇 (宅). So, this character should be analysed to follow '⿱宀', the tone of '厇' (宅; equivalent to tone of '乇'), which was the variant of '宅'. In accordance with the formation of the characters which followed '⿱宀' and the tone of '厇' (宅), He Linyi (何琳仪) explained it as '宅',[57] which was correct. As per the Guodian bamboo script '家' was often used as 豕 (《缁衣》 20), and as 豕 (五行 29), which are the same. Therefore, it would be undoubted to explain ⿱宀 in Zeng Ji Wu Xu Pot as '宅'.

Since this character was explained as '宅', what exact meaning does it bear in pot inscriptions? To answer this question, we need to make explicit explanations on '蒿间' in the following paragraphs.

Regarding '蒿间', Liu Tizhi (刘体智) believed that it borne the same meaning as of robbers and bandits;[58] Yang Shuda (杨树达)

---

[57] He Linyi （何琳仪), *A Dictionary of Ancient Scripts of the Warring States Period* (Beijing: Zhonghua Book Company, 1998), 524.
[58] Liu Tizhi (刘体智), *Dictionary of Golden Wares in Shanji Zhai Dictionary of Wares of Rites III* (Shanghai: Shanghai Library, 1998), 55.

read it as '藁榦', meaning the arrow shaft;[59] *Literary Selections of Inscriptions on Bronze Wares of Shang and Zhou Dynasties* (《商周青铜器铭文选》) read it as '告简', meaning sacrifice and pray in bamboo script;[60] Cui Hengsheng (崔恒升) believed that '蒿' was a name of a place, '蒿间' meaning between Hao (蒿) and Yi (邑);[61] Li Jiahao (李家浩) read it as '郊闲 (Jiao Han), meaning a remote inhabitation area;[62] Li Ling (李零), according to Baoshan Chu bamboo script, believed that '蒿间' was a region name which included County Chu, and it was located along the Huai River and its branches;[63] Liu Xinfang (刘信芳) believed that 'it (蒿间) should refer to the tomb area, including the mausoleum, the living area for the personnel and the farming area'. Meanwhile, he also believed that '鄗' in the bamboo script of no. 103 and no. 115 of Baoshan should be pronounced as '蒿间'.[64] Of all the opinions given here, only Liu's could be accepted.

'蒿间' means tomb area, and '宅' should be related to tombs. 'Shi Di' in *Guang Ya* (《广雅·释地》) said, '宅，葬地也 (宅 was the burial ground)'. 'Shi Sang Li' in *Yi Li* (《仪礼·士丧礼》) said, '筮宅，冢人营之 (to foretell the good location of the tomb is that the Zhong does. 冢 means an official who is in charge of imperial tombs)'. Zheng Xuan (郑玄) added the note: '宅，葬居也 (宅 is where to bury)'. 'Sang Qi' in *Xiao Jing* (《孝经·丧亲》) said, 'to foretell for the 宅 so that some measures could be taken'. Xing Bing (邢昺) added the note: '宅, 墓穴也 (宅 is the tomb)'.

'漾陵' was the name of a place, and its location would be discussed in detail later.

'无鴄' was pronounced as '无匹'. Yang Shuda suspected that 鴄 was a phonetic loan of 匹 and thought that 匹 meant 'enemy'.[65] Guo Moruo believed that '无匹' meant being alone and had no one

---

[59] Yang Shuda, *Ji Wei Ju Album,* 159.

[60] Ma Chengyuan, *Selections of Inscriptions on Bronze Wares*, 454.

[61] Cui Hengsheng, *Supplementary Revision on Bronze Scripts Unearthed in Anhui*, (Hefei: Huangshan Book House, 1998), 73.

[62] Li Jiahao, 'On the Time When Chu Extinguished'.

[63] Li Jing, 'On Reading of Compilation of Characters'.

[64] Liu Xinfang, 'Haogong, Haojian and Haoli'.

[65] Yang Shuda, *Ji Wei Ju Album*, 159.

else to tell',[66] and this was followed by Li Jiahao and Li Ling. Cui Hengsheng explained '无匹' as 'no one able to compete or beat',[67] which could be adapted. According to *Zuo's Commentary on the Spring and Autumn Annals*, in the twenty-third year of Xi Gong, '秦晋, 匹也 (Qin and Jin are enemies)'. Du added the note, '匹, 敌也 (匹 means enemy)'.

In conclusion, '虎宅兹漾陵蒿间之无嗎' should be read as '吾宅兹漾陵蒿间之无匹', meaning that 'I will be buried in the best place in the tomb area of Yang Ling 我(将)葬居漾陵墓区的最好地方'. 'I' (我) was referred to Sheng Huan's wife, Zeng Ji Wu Xu (曾姬无卹).

Aforementioned are the explanations we have made on several characters in the inscriptions of the pot. Next, we will roughly discuss several issues that are related to the inscriptions of the pot.

The beginning of the inscription was '隹 (唯)王二十又六年, 圣趄 之夫人曾姬无卹 (in 26th year of the King, Sheng Huan's wife Zeng Ji Wu Xu)'. Most scholars believed that 'the 26th year of the King (王二十又六年)' referred to the 26th year of King Xuan of Chu, which was 344 BC. Sheng Huan's wife (圣趄之夫人) referred to the wife of King Chu Sheng. Their opinions were right. The first year of King Sheng of Chu was 407 BC and he died in the sixth year, which was 402 BC. Li Jiahao (李家浩) once made the following estimation:

> Zeng Ji Wu Xu Pot was made in the twenty-sixth year of the King Xuan of Chu, fifty-eight years after the King died. Even if Zeng Ji Wu Xu was still young when King Xuan was dead, say, she was twenty years old, she would have been almost eighty in twenty-sixth year of King Xuan, why would she go to Yang Ling to relieve the lonely and elderly people?[68]

He then also added the following statement:

> After defeating Zeng, King Xuan was probably concerned about her grandmother Zeng Ji Wu Xu so that he removed the Zeng people

---

[66] Guo Moruo, *Textual Criticisms and Explanations on Antique Catalog of Bronze Scripts of Two Zhou II* (Shanghai: Shanghai Bookstore, 1999), 166.

[67] Cui Hengsheng, *Supplementary Revision on Bronze Scripts*, 73.

[68] Li Jiahao, 'On the Time When Chu Extinguished'.

from Xi Yang to Yang Ling and kept the temples of the ancestors and allowed them to sacrifice their forefathers. But, in order to prevent them revolting, he invited the lady who was the wife of the late King and also was the Zeng people to relieve them.[69]

However, it was kind of unreasonable to have an elderly lady at almost 80-year old to Yang Ling to relieve the widows and orphanage people, while it should be perfectly logical and reasonable to have her to select the best burial ground in Yang Ling. Because the best burial ground was selected, the pot was then made. It was quite natural to have the pot stored in imperial palace for heirs to use.

The last one to discuss is the location of the Yang Ling. Opinions about this are different. Li Jiahao (李家浩) believed, 'Perhaps, "漾陵" should have been "羕陵", and its eponymy had nothing to do with Yang Water'.[70] According to the text criticism and explanations, we have made, as Yang Ling was the tomb area of the imperial family of Chu, it should be close to the capital at the time of King Xuan of Chu. Generally speaking, the tombs of the emperors and other royal relatives were placed near the suburban area. As being recorded in 'Aristocratic Family of Chu' in the *Records of An Historian* (《史记·楚世家》), King Wen of Chu established his capital in Ying (郢) (city of Ji'Nan, Jiang Ling), and in the 10th year of King Ping of Chu, the city wall was built up due to the fear of Wu.[71] In the 10th year of King Zhao of Chu, 'people of Wu entered Ying and settled there'. This proved that the palace was of excellence. The next year when the army of Qin saved Chu and defeated Wu, King Zhao 'moved back to Ying again'. In the 12th year of King Zhao of Chu, Wu invaded Chu again and King Wang abandoned Ying and moved the capital north forward to Ruo (鄀). After the capital was moved, the historical records about when it was moved back were lost, but in the 21st year of King Zhao

---

[69] Ibid.

[70] Ibid.

[71] The story can be seen in 'Duke Zhao Twenty Third Year' in *Zuo's Commentary of Spring and Autumn Annals* and *Book of Han·Geographical Annals*. By archaeological examination, the wall of Jinan City was built up in later spring and autumn period or Warring States period, which could be testified. This can also be seen in Museum of Hubei Province, 'The Excavation of Jinan City as the Capital of Chu', *ACTA Archaeological SINICA* 3, no. 4 (1982).

of Chu, Wu and Yue became enemies and 'Wu blamed Yue for not going west to fight against Chu'. Not long after this, supposedly, King Zhao moved back to Ying from Ruo. This is why there was the story that in the 21st year of King Qin Xiang of Chu, 'Bai Qi, the general of Qin, attacked and occupied Ying and burned the tombs of the late Kings'. From this, during the regime of King Xuan, the capital was still located in Ying. Seen from the facts that 'the people of Wu entered Ying and insulted the tombs of late King Ping' and 'Bai Qi occupied Ying and burned the tombs of late Kings', the tombs of Kings of Chu were all near the suburban area of Ying. Thus, we have reason to believe that the tomb of Yang Ling that was selected by Zeng Ji Wu Xu was also near the Ying.

Yang Ling, as a place name, emerged many times in the bamboo script of Bao Shan. '漾' also noted as '羕' (107, 108), 鄴 (117) were the variants of one character. According to the bamboo script, several official positions were set in Yang Ling, such as, '邑大夫' (senior official in feudal China), '君' (a title of nobility), '正' (a senior officer). There was also a saying like '鄴陵人xx' in the bamboo script. It was recorded in the bamboo script nos. 126 and 127. '漾 (羕) 陵' and '郢' emerged in the bamboo script, and it seems to indicate that these two places were very close. The Eastern Zhou Dynasty emplaced the sovereign at Ying, which indicated that they lived in Ying at the time of King Chu. Ying might be thought as Ji Nan Cheng.[72] '郢' in the bamboo script might generally be called the capital of Chu, which was the short name of Qi Ying at that time.[73] The tomb of Chu in Bao Shan was 16 miles far from Ji Nan Cheng, the former capital of Chu. '漾陵' emerged many times in the bamboo script, and it was even seen in the same place of the bamboo slip with '郢'. These indicate that Yang Ling should be near the suburb of Ying, and it was where the tomb area of King Chu was located. These provide us with important clues to conduct a thorough investigation on the location of Yang Ling.

---

[72] Huang Xijin, 'Analysis on "郢"': Compilation of Research Center of Chu Culture', in *Analects of Research on Chu Culture*, vol. 2 (Wuhan: Hubei People's Publishing House, 1991).

[73] The *Origin*, 郢,故楚都。It is recorded in 'The Aristocratic Family of Chu' in the *Records of an Historian* that '始都郢', '城郢' and '入郢' all referred 郢 as the capital city of Chu.

Disclaimer: This image is for representation purpose only.

A Supplemented Correction of the Interpretation of *The Chu Bamboo Books in the Warring States Period (Part II)*[74]

The Chu Bamboo Books in the Warring States Period, Part II preserved by Shanghai Museum emerged to the public recently,[75] which is a great event in academia. The newly released *The Chu Bamboo Books in the Warring States Period* includes not only a batch of very

---

[74] Originally published in *Research on Bamboo Slips and Silk Manuscripts* on 21 January 2003. Also published in *Academia Sinical* (2003).

[75] Ma Chengyuan, ed., *Chu Bamboo Slips of the Warring Period: A Compilation by Shanghai Museum*, vol. 2 (Shanghai: Shanghai Ancient Books Press, 2002).

important masterpieces of Confucianism such as *Min Zhi Fu Mu* (《民之父母》), *Zi Gao* (《子羔》) and *Lu Bang Da Han* (《鲁邦大旱》) but also the literary pieces such as *Rong Cheng Shi* (《容成氏》), which systematically recorded the legends of kings in early historical times. In regard to the legends of the ancient times involved in *Rong Cheng Shi*, the existent ancient books do not have records on them, and this literary piece is of great value in studying the history prior to King Wu in the Western Zhou Dynasty. The discovery, compilation and release of this batch of bamboo books have profound meaning to research on the academic history of our country. People who arranged the books and studied the books are mostly famous domestic and overseas experts. The whole work, with precise explications and explanations, solves many hard questions and contributes to the further research and exploration on the value of the batch of bamboo books. However, the arrangement of the damaged bamboo clips is really a difficult job, and we could not expect to solve all the questions at one time. After conducting the initial study on these bamboo books, we propose some immature ideas on the original annotations with uncertainty or missing characters as reference for researchers. The quotation is generally based on the annotations of the original books and makes parentheses '( )' marks in the chapter, the number of the bamboo slips and the page numbers of the annotation:

〇奚 (系) 耳而圣 (听) 之, 不可得而闻也; 明目而见之, 不可得而见也 (《民之父母》第六、七简/164页)

'奚' is read as '系' in the annotation, which is not correct. In 'Kong Zi Xian Ju', in the *Book of Rites* (《礼记·孔子闲居》) and 'Lun Li' in *Kong Zi Jia Yu* (《孔子家语·论礼》), this character is all read as '倾; with '奚' being the phonetic loan character of '倾'. The ancient tone of '奚' is the combination of the Xia Niu consonant and the Zhi Bu vowel (匣纽支部), '倾' is the combination of the Xi Niu consonant and the Geng Bu vowel (溪纽耕部), and they both have the consonant of the same type and their vowels are convertible. In 'Significance of Sacrifice', in the *Book of Rites* (《礼记·祭义》), there is '故君子顷布而弗敢忘', and '顷' is explained in *Classical Annotation* (《经典释文》) as pronounced as '跬'. '跬' belongs to the Xi Niu consonant and Zhi Bu vowel (溪纽支部). In 'Radical Yan' in the *Origin of Chinese*

Characters (《说文解字·言部》), '謑' might be referred to as '謕' and follow the pronunciation of Xi (奚). '奚' in the *Origin* is said to follow the pronunciation of Gui (圭), and '圭' belongs to the Xian Niu consonant and Zhi Bu vowel (见纽支部). All of these can prove that '奚' is read as '倾'. '倾耳而听' (lean forward closer to listen) was a common word in the pre-Qin period, but it does not make sense to pronounce it '系耳'. Two characters of '见' in the original bamboo slip were written in 目 and 人 (standing), and this writing, according to Guodian Chu Bamboo Slips and the bamboo slip characters published by Shanghai Musuem, should be read as '视'. In Kong Zi Xian Ju and Lun Li, there is '正明目而视之,不可得而见也', which indicates that the first character should be explained as '视', and the second character of '见' should follow the form of '视' and then be mistaken:

〇亡(无)圣(声)之乐, 亡(无)体之礼, 亡(无)服之丧, 可(何)志(诗)是怎《民之父母》第七、八简/165页)

Pu's notes read the last character as 'Ni (迡)'. Kong Zi Xian Ju and Lun Li have '何诗近之', by which it is reasonable that it is read as '迡' and explained as '近'. The author analyses its forms as 辶 and 匚, and pronounces as 匚, which cannot be seen in the book of characters. '匚' is used as 𠃊 or 𠃋. The black pot added inside is a simple indicative. We then think that it is '匚' in '匚 Radical' in the *Origin* (《说文·匚部》), and its pronunciation can be phonetically loaned by '尼 and 迡'. The 13th bamboo slip of *Cong Zheng I* (《从政》甲) records, '君子相就也, 不必才(在)近𦉢药(乐)'. Zhang produced the annotation in detail and said, '𠃊 should be the mistaken form of "耳"', and therefore he identified it with three forms and believed that '尼' following 匕 is derived from '耳'. Zhang made notes and pronounced 怎 similar to '昵' or '迩', but its form was still under discussion.[76] We think that '匚' and '耳' have their own clear forms and '尼' has its own origin.[77] The possibility of mistaking '耳' as '匕' is small. Pu's notes analyse the character and it is closer to follow the pronunciation of '匚'. Furthermore,

---

[76] Zhang Guangyu made notes that it could be referred to *Cong Zheng I*, and to Ma Chengyuan, *Chu Bamboo Slips of the Warring Period*, 226.

[77] Yu Xingwu, 'Shi Ni', in *Interpretations on Selected Oracle Bone Scripts* (Beijing: Zhonghua Book Company, 1979), 303.

we believe that 㔷 might be the ellipsis of '匿' (dot added to mark). The *Origin* records, '匿, 亡也, 从匸若声' (匿means death, it follows the similar sound to 匸). Duan Yucai (段玉裁) commented: '读尼质切' (it feels authentic to read this) and '㞢, 匿也' (㞢is just 匿)'. Duan added, '㞢之言隐也' (㞢is to mean 隐)'. No. 34 slip of *Zi Yi* (《缁衣》) of Guodian Chu Bamboo Slips records, '言从行之, 则行不可匿', *Zi Yi* of bamboo slips of Shang Bo is the same. '匿' in 'Shi Gu' in Guang Ya (《广雅》) is explained as '藏' and followed 匸. The *Origin* records, '匸, ... 有所侠藏也, 从上有一覆之 ... 读与傒同'. '匿' and '匸' share the same meaning and pronunciation and therefore '匿' could be omitted to be '匸'. So, the 㦣, 㔷 and 㦣 could be identified as 遜, 偐 and 遜. The inscriptions on the slips '可(何)志(诗)是㦣', '㦣'' can be loaned as暱. The *Origin* records, '暱 means the sun is close'. And in 'Shi Gu' in Er Ya, '暱 means close'. '暱' and '昵' can be phonetically loaned by each other, and it is quoted in the *Origin* that '昵' is the variation of '暱'. *Cong Zheng I* has stated, '君子之相就也, 不必才(在)近㦣乐' and '乐' should be understood with its later sentences. '相就' has a coherent meaning with '不必在近暱'. In Duke Xi, 24th year in *Zuo's Commentary on the Spring and Autumn Annals*, it was recorded that 'to reward people with contributions (庸勋), to love one's kinsfolk (亲亲), to be close to courtiers (暱近), to respect a virtuous person (尊贤), people who do these is of great virtue'. '近暱' in the *Cong Zheng* slip is the same with '暱近' in *Zuo's Commentary on the Spring and Autumn Annals*. In Duke Cheng, 13th year in *Zuo's Commentary on the Spring and Autumn Annals*, it is recorded that, 'Duke heard this saying and felt distressed and disgusted, and came close to me (诸侯备闻此言, 斯是用痛心疾首, 暱就寡人)'. '暱就' ('暱' and '就') is used together, which can be testified with '君子之相就也, 不必才(在) 近暱'. No. 17 slip, 'Zun De Yi', in the Guodian Chu slip recorded '察㦣则亡避, 不党则亡怨'. Here '察㦣' is possibly pronounced as '察暱', which needs further verification:

○伊尧之德则甚显与？孔子曰：铃也；舜来于童土之田（《子羔》第二简/186页）

The annotation says that 'it is first time to see the name of 伊尧 (伊尧之称为初见)', which is not true. It is recorded in 'Wu De Zhi', the eighth volume of *Qian Fu Lun* written by Wang Fu in the Eastern

Han Dynasty that '（神农）后嗣庆都与龙合婚, 生伊尧, 代高辛氏, 其眉八彩, 世号唐。作乐大章, 始禅位。'. We can see from this that the name of 伊尧 was still popular in the Eastern Han Dynasty. It also explains that '昷' is '温', which is not true. '愠' in Guodian Chu Slips (No. 35 of Xing Zi Ming Chu) followed 囚 but 日. This character should be analysed to follow 日 and 皿 and be the variation of '盟', and here it should be pronounced as '明'. '盟' and '明' can be loaned by each other, which is quite common to see in the ancient books and records.[78] '铃' is the wrong explanation, and it follows 金 and 勾 but '今'. The characters in Chu Slips that follow '勾', like '均' ('The Nineteenth' in *Guodian Lao Zi I*) and '军' ('The Ninth' in *Lao Zi III*), also follows the same with the form of 钧. This character should be explained as '钧' and pronounced as '均', and it is not the name of Zigao (子羔). '均也！' should be the answer to the question proposed by Zigao. No. 32 slip of Rong Cheng Shi has '天下大和均, 舜乃欲会天地之气, 而听用之'. The use of '和均' could be the reference to the character. The explanation of '来' could be negotiable. Although this character could be identified to follow 从 and 田, it might not be that appropriate to pronounce it as '徕'. Guodian Chu bamboo slip Qiong Da Yi Shi said that '舜耕于鬲山, 陶拍于河浦, 立而为天子'. This slip said that '舜蕃于童土之田'. The character '番' should be related to farming. In No. 1 slip of Guodian Lao Yi, '啬' emerged twice and were used as 嗇. Compared with it, this character could be explained as '啬'.[79] The ancient character of '啬' in the *Origin* could be used as 嗇, which is just the copy of this form. '啬' could be phonetically loaned to '穑'. 'Fa Tan' in the *Book of Poetry* has '不嫁不穑, 胡取禾木三百亿兮', and here '穑' is used as a verb. 'Pan Geng I' in the *Book of History* has '若农服田力穑, 乃亦有秋'. *Zheng Yi* has '种之曰稼, 敛之曰穑。穑是秋收之名, 得

---

[78] Gao Xiang, *Dictionary of Ancient Interchangeable Characters*, vol. 9, Yang Part II (Jinan: Qilu Press, 1989). He Linyi believed that the above character should be read as '盟', which could be loaned by '明' (refer to the 'Speech on Seminar of Bamboo Slips of Shanghai Museum II' on 3 January 2003).

[79] There are many examples to testify that 啬 is interchangeable with 穑 (see Gao Xiang, *Dictionary of Ancient*, vol. 11, 426.). Xu Zaiguo also explained this character as 啬, which can be seen in *Collected Essays of Bamboo Slips (Zi Gao) of Shanghai Museum*.

为耕获总称。'. In short, the annotation of this slip should be '伊尧之德则甚明与？孔子曰: 均也！舜稽于童土之田…'

〇孔子曰: "庶民智（知）说之事, 视也, 不知型（刑）与德"（《鲁邦大旱》第二简/205–206页）

The annotation believes that '说' was one of the sacrifices praying for rain in the ancient time, which is true. But, the annotation of '视' is negotiable. Its character is used as 鬼, and it is undoubted to follow '示'. The part which is identified as '见' is reasonable in terms of its form, but it is not logical to pronounce it as '视也'. We believe that this character should be analysed to follow the pronunciation of 示 and 鬼, and it is the variant character of '鬼'. First, '视' in Guodian and Shangbo Chu Slips follows 目 and 人, and its difference comparing with '见' relies on whether the leg part of '人' is bent or not, which is now the common view, and so far we have not seen '视' which follows '见'. Second, the writing of this character has a similar formation with '畏' used as 鬼 in *Lao Zi II* of Guodian Chu Slips and '威' used as 鬼 in *Min Zhi Fu Mu* of this book. The difference between them is that one is used as Guitou (鬼头) and the other as Mu (目). Actually, it is common to see in ancient characters that '目' was written as '田'. The character '胃' in this book emerged many times, and it might be used as 胃 or 胃. This writing has its correspondence in this book. '胃' in *Min Zhi Fu Mu* is used as 胃, and '威' as 胃 (the thirteenth slip). Thus, we have reason to believe that what is co-called '视' here, '威' in *Min Zhi Fu Mu* and '畏' in *Lao Zi II*, they are the different writing and use of one character. '鬼' in '恭盟鬼神' on Chen Fang Gui (陈方簋) follows the pronunciation of 示 and 鬼, so this character could be pronounced as '鬼'. Therefore, this slip should mean that '庶民只知道求雨而事鬼神, 却不知道刑与德', which is clear and understandable.

〇君卒。太子乃亡闻亡圣 (听), 不闻不命 (令), 唯哀是思, 唯邦之大粤是敬。(《昔者君老》第四简/246页）

The annotation says, 'in 大粤, the character 粤 is not known clearly and needs further examination'. Its character is presented as 粤, which is '烎' and pronounced as '务'. The tenth slip of *Cong Zheng* has '曰从正（政）所务三', and '务' is used as 务; the first slip of *Cong Zheng I* has '曰犯人之务', and '务' is used as 务; *Lao Zi III* of the

Guodian Chu Slip has '其即（次）侮之', and its annotation says that 'its simplified character follows 矛 and 人'. *Gu Wen Si Sheng Yun* (《古文四声韵》) quoted *Gu Xiao Jing* (《古孝经》) that '侮' follows '矛' and '人', which is the same with its simplified character; *'Zun De Yi I* has '为人上者之务也'. The thirteenth slip of Cheng Zhi Wen Zhi has '戎（农）夫务食不强'. All of the '务' follow 矛 and 人. Knowing from aforementioned materials, Guodian Chu slips identify it as '矛', which conforms to the its form, and it is surly pronounced as '务'. *Lao Zi III* of the Guodian Chu slips reads it as '侮', and *Gu Xiao Jing* reads it as '侮', which are all loan characters. '矛' and characters which follow '矛' emerged many times in Chu slips and other scripts of the Warring State period. '矛' is written as 矛, 矛, 矛, and normally it does not follow '人'; the characters which follow 矛 and 人 could be seen as the omitted form of '敄'. In the bronze script, it is presented as 敄, 敄, and its right part follows 攴 and its left part follows the form of the stuff that the person is wearing, which is not the character of '矛' but similar to the form of '矛', and it is falsely spread in the scripts of Warring State period that it follows '矛'. King Zhongshan Square Pot has '敄在得贤', which is pronounced as '务', the upper part of '人' is the same with '矛'; '茅' on King Zhongshang Round Pot being used as 茅 can testify this. In the fourth volume of *Gu Wen Si Sheng Yun*, '务' is used as 敄, which omitted '矛' to the form of '人'. Based on these, we could know that '务' in Chu slips, which follows 人, should be annotated as '敄', so the character of '务' in this slip could be the omission of '敄' and pronounced as '务'. '邦之大务' is just '邦之大事'. The word '大务' emerged many a times in the existing books and records, such as, '为义孰为大务' in 'Geng Zhu' of *Mo Zi*; '不以小功妨大务' in 'Nan Ⅱ' of *Han Feizi*; '粟者王之本事也, 人主之大务' in the fifteenth volume of *Guan Zi*; '五曰先王有大务' in 'Bo Zhi' of *Lü's Spring ad Autumn Annals*; '文王问太公曰: "愿闻国之大务…"' in 'Guo Wu' of *Liu Dao*; '凡南面之大务, 莫急于知贤' in 'Kao Ji' of *Qian Fu Lun*, etc. All of these verify that in this slip, '大务' could be '大务', which is ensured. '邦之大务' equals to '国之大务' in *Liu Dao*. '唯邦之大务是敬' indicates that Prince Ju Sang in his mourning period did not completely 'listen to nothing' but just kept his duty of 'the major task of the county'.

CHAPTER 4

The Cultural Interpretation of Chinese Characters

The Interpretation of Chinese Characters and Cultural Tradition[1]

Chinese culture is the existence of the super organism, which depends on the ability of the Chinese people to use symbols. It includes systems, tools, residence, languages, philosophy, beliefs, customs, patterns of behaviour, etc. It is a dynamic system which is full of vitality, and it is a process which is interacted by various elements. In this process, each of the elements will have an impact on others. Some elements are excluded because of aging while new elements are combined into it from time to time. As a new synthesis of cultural elements, invention and discovery are continuously produced in the process. The 'cultural tradition' in this chapter refers to this dynamic system.[2] Undoubtedly, Chinese characters are one of the fundamental elements of Chinese cultural traditions.

Even dating from the Shang Dynasty, Chinese characters have experienced a history of more than 3,000 years since its occurrence

---

[1] This text is written by Huang Dekuan and Chang Sen, which was originally published in *Academic World 1* (1995).

[2] L. A. White, *The Science of Culture: Research in Humanity and Civilization*, trans. Shen Yuan, et al. (Jinan: Shandong People's Press, 1988), 72, 120; Philp Bagby, *Culture: The Reflection of History*, trans. Xia Ke, et al. (Shanghai: Shanghai People's Press, 1987), 86–112.

and development. However, even by now we have not yet had a clear and comprehensive reflection on its value.

We believe that the value of Chinese characters is not a 'given act' by later generations which is subjective and arbitrary, but a specific history—the inherent connotation of culture. It is shown on two levels which are interconnected but not the same with each other.

First of all, due to its complete symbolic system, Chinese characters have made the cultural elements of the Chinese language transcend time and space limitations to materialize into a form of visual perception which will store and show the changing and accumulating process of cultural tradition. As early as the Eastern Han Dynasty, the value of Chinese characters in this dimension was clearly recognized and expressed. As Xu Shen said in the post face of the *Origin of Chinese Characters*, 'Characters are the foundation of the Five Classics and Six Arts and the origin of benevolent government'. The former generations leave experience and knowledge in characters to later generations who will get an understanding of the ancient history through it. Since Xu Shen, treating characters as the foundation, classics as the key, knowing the mind of sages of the past and the present as the goal, have become the distinctive trajectory to pursue and explore the values of characters in traditional philology.

Second, as a result of the regular development of cultural tradition, Chinese characters are actually the accumulation of the deep mystery in Chinese culture and act as a vivid hint and direction in cultural tradition. For example, according to the inscriptions on bones or tortoise shells of Shang Dynasty, we would find ancient concretization in their culture and psychology. In fact, from the perspective of genetics, the configuration of almost all of the Chinese characters is rooted in the perception of the specific things or phenomena. If people who created Chinese characters did not have a high ability of observing and expressing the characteristics of things and phenomena, it would be impossible for them to present such colourful images of things.

Usually it is difficult for the ancients to abstract common and general characteristics because of the concretization of their thought. Therefore, there are a large number of 'variants' in the early stage of

Chinese characters. The heterogeneous variants of the character '牢' (lao) in *A Compilation of the Oracle Bone Script* is a typical example.[3] Xu Shen explained, '牢 is the sty for cattle, horse and other livestock. So the character 牢 is based on cattle which represent all kinds of livestock and the upper part of character 牢 is the representation of the sty all around cattle'.[4] '牢' in the oracle bone script is indeed just like the sty of livestock, but it focuses not only on the abstract function of the sty itself but also on the specific circumstance of stock farming in sty. For the ancients who invented the characters, there is only the concrete '牢' for cattle, sheep and horse farming rather than the abstract '牢'. It is not reasonable to classify these characters into allographs directly, and the character '牢' which is based on the Chinese character that represents cattle is essentially different from the character '窂' which is based on the Chinese character that represents sheep.[5]

There is no doubt that the oracle bone script is not the initial state of Chinese characters. However, there is a culturological fact in it. That is to say, for the primitive ancients creating civilization, everything around them is concrete and vivid. They just understand objects around them according to their feeling, recognition, judgement and memory of the specific images.[6] This does not mean the ancient ancestors do not have any abstract ability. Take the perception of beasts as an example. It is not possible for humans to produce the same visual image for any two chickens while Chinese characters in the early period could grasp the common morphological characteristics of most chickens. This is a kind of 'abstraction' which is not beyond the concrete level. Historically, all of the human languages have been evolved from the concrete state into the abstract state and all of the original names 'depend on the perception of specific facts and specific activities'. The later generation

---

[3] As for the character shape, please refer to Archaeological Institute of Chinese Academy of Science (AICAS), *A Compilation of the Oracle Bone Script* (Beijing: Zhonghua Book Company, 1965).

[4] 'Chapter 2' of *The Origin of Chinese Characters*.

[5] Yao Xiaosui (姚孝遂), 'Differentiation of '牢' and "窂"', in *Studies of Ancient Characters* (Beijing: Zhonghua Book Company, 1984).

[6] Deng Fuxing, *Art Before the Art: Studies of Prehistorical Arts* (Jinan: Shandong Arts Press, 1987), 104.

will find 'all of the nuances' which had been described in precision and detail by various names.⁷ 'Explaining Beasts' in *Er Ya* tells us that there are more than 50 species for horses and they are named for their colour, ##shape, sex and height.

Chinese characters can reflect not only the specific cultural psychology of the ancients but also tools, residence, systems, languages, philosophy, beliefs, customs code of conduct as well as other cultural elements and their evolvement. Therefore, it can be said that Chinese characters mark the fresh existence of Chinese culture from content to form. Unfortunately, researchers were not fully aware of the cultural value of Chinese characters in the past.

The two values of Chinese characters are different in characteristics. As each Chinese character is in the fixed primitive relationship with cultural traditions, the cultural information which Chinese character itself (Chinese characters configuration or pronunciation) reflects is single; as cultural tradition is constantly endowing new things into languages and so are Chinese characters, the value of Chinese characters as language symbols keep on proliferating. In order to fulfil its symbolic function, the relationship between Chinese characters and cultural traditions has undergone a profound transformation. For example, the character '日' evolves from the pictogram of the sun into the expression of the time concept of 'daytime', and this is an 'extended conversion' of the character '其' that evolves from the pictogram of dustpan into an abstract word and this is a 'phonetic loan conversion'; the characters '甲' and '乙' evolve from the pictogram of fish armour⁸ into the representation of the Ten Heavenly Stems and the movement of Yin-Yang, and this is a 'forced conversion'. In the forced conversion, the relation between characters and cultural tradition is not the natural development of the primitive relation, and

---

⁷ Ernest Cassirer, *Christian Anthropology*, trans. Gan Yang, (Shanghai: Shanghai Translation Publishing House, 1985), 172.

⁸ As for the explanation of 'Jia' (甲), please refer to Zhu Junsheng, 'Shuo Wen Tong Xun Ding Sheng'; for the explanation of 'Yi' (乙), please refer to Guo Moruo, *The Study of the Oracle Bone Script* (Beijing: Science Press, 1982), 169–70.

thus there is no basis in the aspect of the original form, meaning and pronunciation. Through these conversions, Chinese characters would quietly construct or rebuild its adaptation to languages and even the whole cultural tradition.

However, these conversions made the values of Chinese characters based on the dilution of full functions that Chinese characters acquired in language sign system. '其自西来雨' (Qi Zi Xi Lai Yu) is a sentence from the oracle inscriptions on bones or tortoise shells of the Shang Dynasty, and it contains five Chinese characters. Among these characters, there is only character '雨' whose two value functions are the same. Originally, '其' is the pictogram of dustpan, but it is used as a predicate; '自' is the pictogram of nose, but it is used as a preposition; '来' is the pictogram of wheat, but used as a verb; '西' is the pictogram that birds perch on the trees, but used as an orientational noun. It can be seen that when Chinese characters are incorporated into a particular language system, their values are often hidden at varying degrees.

So only through the full attention to values of Chinese characters, we can find that the positioning of Chinese characters in cultural tradition not only relies on its functions as a language symbol but also transcends or partially transcends its own connection with language to independently accepting people's contemplation.[9] In general, a Chinese character can present a relatively integrated cultural connotation, although it cannot convey the complete language information.

There is no absolute alienation or separation between the two values of Chinese characters, and the two can actually be linked together by the intermediary of Chinese character explications. Explications of Chinese characters are based on the interpretations of the original form, original meaning and original pronunciation of Chinese characters. It not only reveals the primitive relations between Chinese characters and cultural tradition but also indicates the extended conversion, phonetic loan conversion and forced conversion of this relation.

---

[9] For example, we can regard the early hieroglyphs as plastic arts. As an 'art', these images are not inferior to the pictographic symbols in Primitive Art written by Franz Boas. Franz Boas, *Primitive Art*, trans. Jin Hui (Shanghai: Shanghai Arts Press, 1989), 153–54.

Traditional philology has several major misinterpretations associated with the explications of Chinese characters. First, it takes character meaning as the sole attributes of Chinese characters. Scientifically speaking, character meaning is ultimately the endowment of cultural tradition. There is no inevitable and irreversible link between the circle and the sun, and the cultural tradition stipulates the meaning (or value) of the circle as a linguistic sign. Second, it takes character meaning as the only thing within the scope of character form, pronunciation and meaning. However, between the character and the character meaning, there is no inevitable and irrevocable connection between the pronunciation and meaning of the character. Both the provisions of the value of character form and provisions of the value of the character pronunciation are cultural tradition.

The explications of Chinese characters are not so much a human behaviour as a cultural behaviour. This does not mean the subject of explications is not 'human', while it means that the explications of Chinese characters cannot be explained accurately or reasonably only from the aspect of the organism. In essence, the explication of Chinese characters is the reaction of the subject to all kinds of cultural guide. It is the synthesis or combination of character form and other cultural elements. Take the character '甘' as an example. According to the character form, we know that '甘' follows 口 and contains 一. Other guides in the cultural elements are (a) '甘' has the meaning of beauty; (2) '一' usually refers to the independent '道' (the way, morality); (c) the morality of Confucianists refers to rite, modesty, fidelity, trust and other moral standards or attributes; (d) the beauty in Confucian tradition does not only mean the sensual pleasure but also the happiness of the subjective heart endowed by the ethics. '甘' was explained in the *Origin of Chinese Characters* as '甘 means beauty and is composed of 口 and 一; 一 means morality'. Although the explanation only uses a few characters, in fact, it is the integration of the aforementioned cultural elements.

It can be seen that the explication of Chinese characters is a complex process of subjective behaviour under the domination of cultural traditions. In this process, explicators can get rid of the constraints of one cultural element, but they cannot transcend the guide or constraints of all cultural elements. Cultural tradition does not only help explicators to achieve the original intention of exploring the primitive connotation but also makes them deviate from their original intention consciously or unconsciously. It can become not only the correct guide for explicators but also the limitations that explicators feel difficult to avoid.

Interpretations of the Oracle Bone Script by Yu Xingwu (于省吾) reflects an important concept that the oracle bone script era is in a class society. 'Class society is a society in political oppression and economic exploitation'. Under the guidance of this concept, Yu Xingwu makes an investigation about the configuration and connotation of the character '尼' in the oracle bone script. He identifies '尼' as a person seating or riding on the back of another person, and it is a 'specific example' to illustrate the oppression and trampling of class society.[10]

From our perspective, Yu Xingwu not only gives a new interpretation of the character '尼', he also provides us with a typical example which illustrates the fact that cultural tradition will restrict the explication of Chinese characters. Xu Shen explains the character '尼' as follows: 'The meaning of this character is drawing near from the rear; it follows 尸 and is pronounced as 匕'.[11] Duan Yucai made a presumption that the sound of the character '尼' is in the 15th phonetic category which is the same as the character '匕', so '匕' (in the fanqie formula of 卑 bei and 屢 lv) can be used as the phonetic component of it. Both Xu and Duan believe that the original form and meaning of '匕' don't have any real function and '匕' just plays a part in the pronunciation of '尼'. Even if we regard the character '匕' as the form component, different schools gold different views. Wang Yun said in *Shuowen Judou*: '"匕" has the same meaning with "比". We all know that if people are compared with each other, it means drawing near; if one person is below another one, it means from the rear'. Lin Yiguang explains that the character '尼' is just like the character '昵' from the perspective of the pictograph. Wang and Lin take the configuration of

---

[10] Yu Xingwu, *Interpretations of the Oracle Bone Script* (Beijing: Zhonghua Book Company, 1979), 303–08.

[11] Xu Shen, *The Origin of Chinese Characters*, Chapter 8.

the character '尼' as the representation of daily experience. Yu Wuxing thinks that the character '匕' is 'a reversed man' and takes '尼' as the image that one person is on the back of another. This inference is close to Wang and Lin. And he further understands the character '尼' as 'one person oppressing another' and 'one person trampling on another'. Rather, Wang and Lin understand it as 'intimacy'.[12] What a difference between them! It shows that if explicators are clearer about the understanding of one cultural element, it will be more difficult to maintain the necessary detachment of this element. In this case, if Yu's ideas are correct, the only reason is that some elements in the cultural tradition has revealed the real connotation of Chinese characters in the subject; if Yu's ideas are wrong, the only reason will be that some elements in the cultural tradition have covered the appearance of the real connotation of Chinese characters.

The dominant role of cultural traditions in the explication of Chinese characters can be divided into the following three main aspects.

First, from the aspect of the character meaning, the explication of Chinese characters is the manifestation of configuration functions of Chinese characters under the specific cultural background. Xu Shen explains '日' as follows:

> '日' means the state which is full of energy. The cream of the sun is inexhaustible and the radiance is shining between the sky and the land forever. The character form is composed of the character "囗" and the character "一" which is like the shape of the sun.[13]

Li Yangbing (李阳冰) in the Tang Dynasty said, 'The external circle of the character "日" is like the shape of the sun and the internal "一" is like "乌"'.[14] Duan Yucai agreed to the later one.[15] Then Xu Shen said,

---

[12] Wang Yun (王筠) interprets it as 'approaching from behind', which implies intimacy.

[13] Xu Shen, *The Origin of Chinese Characters*, Chapter 7.

[14] Xu Kai, *Biographical Annotations of the Origin of Chinese Characters* (Beijing: Zhonghua Book Company, 1987), 320.

[15] Duan Yucai, *Explanations of the Origin of Chinese Characters* (Shanghai: Shanghai Chinese Classics Publishing House, 1981), 302.

'叒 means mulberry where the sun rises from the east in Tang Gu'.[16] Duan Yucai views that the '木' components in the characters 'Gao' (杲) 'Dong' (东) and 'Yao' (杳) all refer to the mulberry, and their overall configuration vividly presents the scene in which the sun shuttles between the mulberry.[17] It is evident that this explanation is not about the character form or the subject itself, but it is related to myths and legends in the cultural tradition. 'The Legend of the Great Eastern Wilderness' in *Classics of Mountains and Seas* said, 'There is mulberry in Yang Gu where the sun carried by the bird come and go'. The long poem 'Tian Wen' (《天问》) by Qu Yuan in the Warring States period is related to the legend of Hou Yi shooting the sun and the Sun Bird's feathers falling off. The concept that the sun was carried by the golden bird has become very popular until the Han Dynasty. Stones with the figures of the Han Dynasty are the intuitional embodiment of this concept. Some of the stones are wheels with a carved bird, and others are birds with a carved wheel. All of them are the intuitive representation of this concept.[18]

Second, from the aspect of the subject, all of the explicators are dominated by the specific cultural tradition. So, in the process of the explication, we tend to regard one kind of cultural elements as the directed content of Chinese characters configuration and pronunciation; the explication process is actually the process in which the subjects will devote its own cultural tradition to Chinese characters. For example, Xu Shen lived in the blood-based, hierarchical Confucian tradition where father is the respected person. As far as we are concerned, if there is only one respected person, it will be peaceful; if there are two respected persons, then the whole family will be in a mess. It is impossible to maintain peace if two respected persons are struggling for power.[19] On account of this, Xu Shen thinks that the character '父' can give us the image that a man holds a sceptre in his hand, which represents the status and dignity in the family.[20]

---

[16] Xu Shen, *The Origin of Chinese Characters*, Chapter 6.
[17] Duan Yucai, *Explanations of the Origin*, 252.
[18] Refer to Wang Jianzhong and Shan Xiushan, *Stones with Figures of the Han Dynasty* (Beijing: Cultural Relics Press, 1990), 179, 269, 271, 275, 279–80.
[19] Discussion of Talents in Xunzi.
[20] Xu Shen, *The Origin of Chinese Characters*, Chapter 3.

Third, from the aspect of character form, the perception of the configuration of Chinese characters needs the 'anticipatory knowledge' of the cultural tradition. For example, why is the character '妇' composed of the character '女' and the character '帚'? Xu Shen explains, '妇 means service, describing the image that a woman sweeps the floor with brooms'.[21] Xu Shen's indication is very accurate that the configuration of '妇' is related to '女' and '帚', but the key point is how to identify the function of this configuration. 'Sweeping the floor with brooms' reflects the division of labour for females in the specific historical period which is not difficult to understand either in modern times or in the ancient times. However, Xu Shen defines its meaning by the character '服'. This definition reveals that the explicators have drifted away from the 'simple' surface of character formation and have entered into the anticipatory knowledge field which is set by the cultural tradition. Using '服' to explain '妇' does not simply reveal the closeness of the two sounds, which is also called the relation of phonetic explanation. Whether the character '服' means 'service' or 'obedience', it indicates that women have lost their independent personality in the family and society. Xu Shen's perception of the character form and his definition of the function of the character form are only the reflection of this common social concept. It proves that it is the anticipatory knowledge of the cultural tradition that makes Xu Shen abandon the common connotation 'the wife of the son' or 'the married woman' which was well known in the ancient times. Then Xu Shen chooses the explanations which will reflect the concept at that time and try to find the relations between it and the character form to reveal the motivation of the configuration of the character '妇'.

In conclusion, Chinese characters cannot be correctly explained if they are detached from the cultural tradition; the explanation of Chinese characters can only be generated in a cultural tradition. Some explanations are a little strange or absurd for the later generations because the relevant cultural elements have been lost in the long history or the cultural tradition has fallen into mystery at that time.

---

[21] Ibid., Chapter 12.

The process of explicating Chinese characters dominated by the cultural tradition can be expressed as the following models:

文化诱导: Cultural Guides 文化抉择: Cultural Options 具体化: Concretization 体悟: Experiencing and understanding 证说: Authenticated explanations.

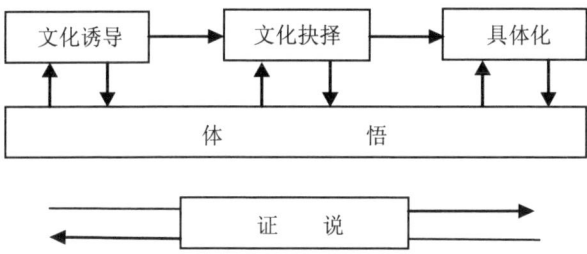

This model includes several important elements.

1. *Cultural guides*: 'Cultural guides' refer to the guiding role of the cultural tradition to explicate Chinese characters which are the invisible hand lurking behind the explication of Chinese characters. In the explication of Chinese characters, the exclusion of cultural guides is not only unscientific but also impossible. On one hand, the connection between Chinese characters and the cultural tradition is an objective fact. On the other hand, the cultural tradition is also the representation of many Chinese characters explicators. For the former aspect, only the cultural tradition could provide various possibilities of the correct understanding of Chinese characters. People will not have a scientific understanding of Chinese characters without a profound understanding of Chinese traditions. As for the later one, whether correct or not, the explication of Chinese characters can be attributed to the identity of a cultural element. In fact, no serious explicator could denounce the guiding role of Chinese traditions.
2. *Cultural options*: 'Cultural options' refer to the choice and selection between different cultural information in the process of explications.

Cultural guides are not always unidirectional, but they are inevitably multidirectional and even reverse. The uncertainty of meaning by form in Chinese characters makes different guides from different cultural elements play a very important role in the perception process. For example, why the character '闽' and '蛮' are composed of '虫' (insect)? The ancient character '虫' vividly presents the physical characteristics of them. But, in addition, it is obvious that it could not present any other connotation related to the character '虫'. The historical totem legacy points out that it is because 闽 and 蛮 are born for the insects that '闽' and '蛮' are composed of '虫', which means they are 'the later generation of snakes'; the humanistic sense of Confucianism reminds us that the nation whose ideograph is '虫' or '犬' or '豸' is in opposition to the nation whose ideograph is '人' or '大'. The fact that '闽' and '蛮' are composed of '虫' reveals that the people of 闽 and 蛮 are not as benevolent as the people of 夷.

Theoretically speaking, explicators should not make different analysis and definitions in the function of Chinese character configuration due to the coexistence of various cultures. At the beginning of creating the characters, people will take various methods to exclude the polysemy of character forms rather than make it play different roles. However, in the explanation of '闽' and '蛮', Xu Shen accepted these two types of guides which are different in essence so that these explanations present a mixture.[22] This case is the same as the explanation of characters representing the Ten Heavenly Stems. In fact, the character '甲' never refers to both 'like the head' and 'the growth of trees and grass' at the same time. I'm afraid that it is not convincing to affirm that Xu Shen did not recognize this simple rule. But certainly, Xu Shen couldn't eliminate the awkward self-contradictory situation. Cultural options are not a relaxing matter, in which, all of the explicators are likely to get into dilemma. After the correct choice, the cultural tradition could become the candles through which people will find the deep meaning of Chinese characters. After the wrong choice, the cultural tradition will become the 'Procrustean bed'. Xu Shen explains the configuration of characters representing the Heavenly Stems and Earthly Branches through the non-stop growth and decline of Yin-Yang in the

---

[22] Refer to the explanation of '蛮', '闽', '羌' (Chapter 4), '狄' (Chapter 10) and '貉' (Chapter 9).

sky, which reflects the 'Procrustean bed' phenomenon in explicating Chinese characters.

Cultural options always follow the relations between Chinese characters and the cultural tradition from one historical aspect: the original relation, secondary extended conversion relation, phonetic loan conversion relation and forced conversion relation. In the final analysis, cultural options are inevitable but they are restricted.

3. *Concretization*: 'Concretization' refers to the process of putting the cultural information of Chinese characters into the configuration and pronunciation of Chinese characters.

The goal of cultural options is to identify the cultural information directed by Chinese characters while the goal of concretization is to seek the specific evidence for the information. For example, Xu Shen thinks that the character '父' indicates the authority in the family. This kind of meaning is not in direct relation with the character form. In the *Origin of Chinese Characters*, 'the character "父" is like the character "又" lifting the sticks'. That is, it is lifting the sticks in hands, which is the experiential representation of authority. It should be pointed out that the concretization in the explications of Chinese characters is not equivalent to the understanding of the concretization (or concreteness) of graphs, which includes three ways in the concretization, abstraction and grammaticalization. In general, the concretization in the explications of Chinese characters means the understanding of the concreteness of the configuration of Chinese characters such as the negative word '不' and the meaning of 'reaching' in the character '至', which has achieved consensus in the Han Dynasty. However, these explanations of meaning are not in complete agreement with the configuration of these two characters, so Xu Shen explains character '不' as 'birds flying to the sky and not declining to the land' and explains '至' as 'birds flying from the sky to the land'.[23] In this way, the character '不' expressing negation has become the negative content in a specific circumstance while the character '至' expressing the

---

[23] Xu Shen, *The Origin of Chinese Characters*, Chapter 12.

meaning of reaching has become a specific sensational way. The closer we get to the occurrence period of Chinese characters, the more proper understanding we reach to the concreteness of Chinese characters. But in the explication process, it is also inevitable to fall into the abstract understanding of character forms. When Xu Shen explains the component '一' in the character '至' and '旦' as the earth,[24] the component '一' in the character '不' as the heaven,[25] and the uppermost stroke of the character '巫' as the heaven and the lowest one as the earth,[26] his understanding of '一' comes from the concretization. But at the same time, Xu Shen also interprets '一' as the independent way of 'creating the world into the heaven and the earth which will be divided into all the things in the world'.[27] He explains '一' in the character '毋, 乍, 甘, 正' as the way to regulate moral behaviour and concept of values.[28] These explanations are from the abstraction of character forms.[29]

In addition, the grammaticalization of character forms cannot be ruled out in the concretization process of explicating Chinese characters. When explicators regard a character as the mark character, or a stroke in Chinese characters or a character as a mark or phonetic sign, they actually refuse the concretization and abstraction understanding of these characters. Their claim means that the figurative or abstract characteristics of these characters fully depend on the character meaning.

Therefore, strictly speaking, the 'concretization' category in explications of Chinese characters summarizes this type of process which in fact means achieving agreement between the configuration function of Chinese characters and some type of cultural information through the understanding of the concretization, abstraction and grammaticalization of character forms.

4. *Experiencing and understanding*: 'Experiencing and understanding' is the explicators' intuitive perceptions about the configuration of

---

[24] Ibid.
[25] Ibid.
[26] Ibid., Chapter 13.
[27] Ibid., Chapter 1.
[28] Ibid., Chapters 2, 5, 12.
[29] As for the configuration of the character '毋', please refer to Duan Yucai's ideas rather than Xu Xuan's. Yucai, *Notes for the Origin of Chinese Characters*, 626.

Chinese characters. Although it is inclusive of cultural guides, cultural options and concretization, it has a distinct relative independence.

First of all, experiencing and understanding can lead other cultural elements to guide the explications of Chinese characters. For example, almost all the explicators agree that the character '乘' in the oracle bone script is like a man standing on the wood.[30] Historically, this experiencing and understanding has led to at least two kinds of guiding elements. One is the daily experience of climbing trees; the other is the historical legends such as You Chao Shi（有巢氏）building the wood nest to avoid beasts, insects and snakes.

Next, in the absence of the guides of other cultural elements, experiencing and understanding character form scan become options for guides. For example, Yang Shuda (杨树达) explains,

> '甬' is like the shape of the bell and it is the primitive expression of the character '钟': the upper part of the character '甬' is like the hanging bell, the lower part is like the body of the bell and the middle part is like the belt of the bell.

Among all of the relevant works, the similar circumstances can be seen everywhere.

Finally, experiencing and understanding greatly influences the concretization process. According to the *Origin of Chinese Characters*, some known relations between the form and meaning of Chinese characters which are far from the original state have become the subjective options from cultural guides. In this circumstance, it is evident that the concretization of cultural options depends on the subjects' experiencing and understanding of character forms.

5. *Authenticated explanations*: 'Authenticated explanations' refer to the proof to illustrate its reasonableness in explicating Chinese characters. It should present the motivation and reliability of the process and result of explications. To this end, explicators should often pursue and explore the configuration in the early stage and various

---

[30] As for the character shape, please refer to AICAS, *A Compilation of the Oracle Bone Script*.

development forms. They should also investigate the time situation and books in all ages which are closely related with Chinese characters. Various cultural elements have become the support to explicate Chinese characters by authenticated explanations.

The five categories including 'cultural guides', 'cultural options', 'concretization', 'experiencing and understanding', and 'authenticated explanations' have formed an integral stereotype process. Although not all Chinese characters cover the whole content of this model, the simplest explanation must include some essence of it.

There are many mysteries in Chinese culture. We do not know the truth about the dragon and taotie yet. In particular, people still do not know the cultural mysteries preserved in Chinese characters, so the explications of Chinese characters are devoted to solving the puzzles of Chinese characters. Therefore, the explications of Chinese characters play a very important historical and cultural role. First, this chapter positions the explications of Chinese characters from the aspect of the values of Chinese characters. Then it discusses the culturological characteristics of the explications of Chinese characters and the complete model in the explication process. The main goal of the chapter is to enhance the sublimation of the explications of Chinese characters from spontaneity to self-consciousness in order to correct some fundamental deviation. By now, people should not regard the explications of Chinese characters as only one kind of specific practice. We should take them as a science and reflect on them from the theoretical perspective.

Historicism: The Principles of the Interpretation of Chinese Characters[31]

As Cheng Shude (程树德) says in the 'Preface' to *Ancient Events Related to Chinese Characters* (《说文稽古篇·凡例》),

> The *Origin of Chinese Characters* is written by Chinese people, in which the explanations of the character meanings would reveal the

---

[31] This chapter is co-authored with Chang Sen (常森), *Journal of Humanities* 2, (1996).

historical records beyond the history, systems and customs before the Han Dynasty. So the *Origin of Chinese Characters* is a way to judge history.[32]

Indeed, the *Origin of Chinese Characters* by Xu Shen is the best work to reflect culture with Chinese characteristics from the perspective of traditional Chinese philology since *Er Ya*.[33] However, when interpreting the Chinese characters as the foothold to prove the 'historical records beyond the history', 'systems' and 'customs', we must exclude the subjective arbitrariness and trace the objective and real connections between Chinese characters and Chinese culture at the specific historical level.

The character '乘' is like the man situated on the wood with expanding legs, so it is said that 'there are more people than beasts in ancient times and people cannot defeat the beasts, insects and snakes'. Therefore, the character '乘' reflects the historical facts in which Youchao built the nest by the wood to avoid beasts, insects and snakes; the seal character '炙' is like the meat on the fire which means '炮肉'. It is also said that people in ancient times devour raw meat and bowl full of stench, and it leads to various diseases in people. The character '炙' reflects the historical facts that Suiren drilled the stone to make fire and to reduce the smell of stench. If this claim can be established, then it must have the following historical and logical premise: either the configuration of these two characters are produced in the historical background of 'building nest by wood' and 'removing stench by fire' or it reflects the memory of ancient people for this historical period. However, the former cannot obtain the necessary evidence of classic literature and archaeological excavation, the latter is in line with the common sense. When climbing the tree and burning the meat become an ordinary and common daily experience, people would rather retain their own familiar experience than pursue the increasingly distant and strange 'history'.

---

[32] Cheng Shude, *Ancient Events Related to Chinese Characters* (Beijing: The Commercial Press, 1957).

[33] Hu Qiguang (胡奇光), *History of the Chinese Fiction* (Shanghai: Shanghai People's Publishing House, 1987).

Chinese characters are a symbolic system whose occurrence and development are accompanied by the historical development. It is endowed with historical hierarchy. However, when they are used as a systemic and complete cultural legacy that has passed down to the coming generations, people can no longer find its implied and orderly historical layers.

Xu Shen explains, '贝 means the worm in the sea and it is a pictographic character; the ancient people treasured "贝" and "龟". Then there was 泉 in the Zhou Dynasty, and then the Qin Dynasty abolished 贝 and issued the currency'.[34] By just these few characters, Xu Shen's definition can be regarded as the summary to describe the evolution of ancient currency. *Discourse on Salt and Iron* says that '贝 was used in the Xia Dynasty while the purple stone was used in the Zhou Dynasty', which means that seashells had been used as the medium of commodity transaction in the Xia Dynasty. During the Yin-Shang period, seashells were still regarded as the equivalent of commodity transaction. However, seashells were difficult to obtain because they originated from the South Sea and were introduced by people of the Southern Pacific. Then they were changed into shells in bone and bronze. In the Zhou Dynasty, both currency and shells were used. Until the Qin Dynasty, pearls, jades, shells and silvers were all treasures and ornaments rather than currency. Six new kinds of currency, including money, gold, silver, tortoise, shells and cloth, were issued simultaneously in the Xin Mang period and 28 items were named as 'treasures'.

The fact that shells were used as the equivalent of commodity made deep influence on the ancient social life, which is manifested in the configuration of Chinese characters. Sales were conducted with shells as the media, so characters 'Mao (贸), Shu (赎), Jia (贾), Fan (贩), Mai (买) and Gou (购)' all took the meaning from '贝'. Characters such as 'Gui (贵)' and 'Jian (贱)' that express the value of goods also took the meaning from '贝'. Characters 'Ying' (赢) and 'Lai' (赖) that express the profit of commodity transaction, characters 'Zhen' (赈) and 'Pin' (贫) that express the wealth of people,

---

[34] Xu Shen, *Origin*, Chapter 6.

characters such as 'Huo (货), Hui (贿), Xian (贤) and Zhu (贮)' which refer to the property and accumulation also took the meaning from '贝'. In addition, shells can be used to express the behaviour of borrowing and that is why 'Dai' (贷), 'Dai' (贷), 'She' (赊) and 'Shi' (贳) contain '贝'. Shells can be used to express mortgage, so characters 'Zhui' (赘) and 'Zhi' (质) contain '贝'. Shells can also be used to give presents and making congratulations, so characters 'He' (贺), 'Ji' (赍), 'Zeng' (赠), 'Lu' (赂), 'Zan' (赞) and 'Bi' (贲) contain '贝'. Some shells can also be used to mean rent and tax payment, so '贝' was used in characters 'Gong' (贡), 'Fu' (赋) and 'Cong' (賨). 'Shang' (赏), 'Ci' (赐), 'Gan' (赣) and 'Lai' (赉) contain '贝' because it can be used to express the meaning of rewarding. 'Zi' (赀) and 'Pi' (赑) also has '贝', as it is used to express the meaning of atonement. '贝' is one of the most important desires of humanity, so character 'Tan' (贪) also has '贝'.[35] There is no denying that '贝' is just the representative of some characteristics in some Chinese characters. It is a very complex question and we do not discuss it further in this chapter.

As for this group of Chinese characters, the *Origin of Chinese Characters* just tells people that character '贝' was produced prior to other characters and it could not show the complex historical relations between them. As for the *Origin of Chinese Characters* (or other works to demonstrate related historical facts such as the *Origin of Chinese Characters*), it is unscientific or unstrict to generally assign this group of Chinese characters and the social phenomenon it reflects to 'the ancient one' or 'the ancient times' because 'ancient and modern' is a relative concept with no definiteness. And that's why we say,

> There is no definite time that can be referred to as either the ancient or the modern time; if the Zhou Dynasty was the ancient, then the Han Dynasty would be modern times while if the Han Dynasty was regarded the ancient, then the Jin and Song Dynasties would be modern times.[36]

---

[35] See the explanations of '贝' in Xu Shen, *Origin*, Chapter 6.
[36] Duan Yucai, *Explanations of the Origin*. Note 94 for character 'Yi' (谊).

Shells were used as the media for commodity exchange through Xia, Shang Zhou Dynasties and even in the Han Dynasty. But there is no confirmation as to in which specific historical stage '贝' and a series of Chinese characters related to '贝' were produced, and there is no confirmation that among those characters, whether '贝' is the pictogram of seashells or the pictogram of shells in the bone or bronze, which was very popular in the Yin-Shang period.[37]

In this aspect, the major drawback of traditional philology is not that it does not point out that it could not reproduce the historical hierarchy of the occurrence of Chinese characters but that it is not intended to reproduce this hierarchy at all. Chinese characters that matured in the Shang Dynasty and its evolution in the later ages as well as the increasingly rich explanations of Chinese characters since the Han Dynasty are used to illustrate the historical facts, such as, 'building nests by wood' and 'removing stench by fire' during the Three Kings period; or, they are used to illustrate the myths in the Five Emperors period. For example, Wang Yu, the Confucianist in the Han Dynasty, thought that the character 'Wu' (无) demonstrates that 'Tian (天) bows to the northwest'.[38] People had used Chinese characters to interpret the historical–cultural phenomenon in almost all periods, which is a surprising fact but has not received careful reflection. It is unacceptable but understandable that Xu Shen's *Origin of Chinese Characters* had taken advantage of Chinese characters in the Yin-Shang period to illustrate the concepts of yin-yang and five elements which had been already fixed during the Spring and Autumn and Warring States period.

It is inconceivable that the early configuration of Chinese characters was explained through some customs in Europe and America. For

---

[37] Luo Zhenyu, in *Catalogue of Yinxu Antiquity*, says that shells in the bone and bronze are different from real shells. According to this book, both the real shells and the shells in Yao were excavated from Yinxu. As far as we all know, the oracle bone script which was the earliest, but most mature Chinese characters was also excavated from Yinxu. This finding in archaeology is thought-provoking.

[38] For explanations about the character 'Wu' (无), please refer to Xu Kai (徐锴), *Guide to the Origin of Chinese Characters*, 248.

example, some people would like to interpret the character 'Zai' (灾) as 'a matchstick unable to light 3 cigarettes'.³⁹ It seems that Chinese characters occurred at the large spatio-temporal background throughout the ancient and modern times and all around the world. So far, the traditional philological theory has no intention to curb the emergence of this modern myth.

The historical hierarchy of Chinese characters is by no means a subjective affirmation. It presents an inherent and inseparable link between Chinese characters and Chinese culture on a diachronic axis. The upper limit of the occurrence of Chinese characters has not been explored, but it is a basic historical–cultural fact that it had grown up in the Shang Dynasty. Of course, the historical hierarchy of Chinese characters is not represented by the replacement of dynasties, but marked by some profound variations in the occurrence and development of Chinese characters. Placing the Chinese characters into the Three Kings period, Five Emperors period or Xia, Shang, Zhou, Spring and Autumn periods and Warring States period at discretion could not reveal the true historical hierarchy of Chinese characters, and it could even hide this hierarchy.

As for the *Origin of Chinese Characters*, Chinese characters are consciously or unconsciously placed in the same historical phase, which will submerge or dilute the fundamental variation in the traditional concept. If we look at the contents reflecting the religious consciousness in the ancient times in the *Origin of Chinese Characters*, it would be clear.

Xu Shen explains,

> 巫 is 巫觋 (someone praying for the deity). Women can serve the mysterious things and can attract the deities through their charming

---

³⁹ In the 11th edition of *Xinmin Evening News* on 22 December 1992, Yao Zhiwei (姚志卫) said in 'There's a kind of habit in China',

> Americans has a kind of habit that if we need to light the third cigarette, the matchstick need to be extinguished. Then we need to light a new one; there had been a habit in China that the image of the traditional character 'Zai' (災) is 'three persons with a fire' which means if three persons light cigarettes at the same time, there will be a disaster. So it means unluckiness which is regarded as a taboo.

singing and dancing. 巫 is just like the image in which a person dances with their two sleeves lifting. It is told that 巫咸 is the first one to use this witchcraft.[40]

'觋 should serve the deities carefully and it is formed by the character "巫" and "见"'.[41] Xu Kai explains the reason why the character '觋' follows '见'. He said, '觋 expresses the meaning of being able to see the deities'. It is an extremely ancient concept of ancestors that the witch (巫觋) could communicate with the deity by sight and hearing. It is said in 'The Chu Dialect' in *Guo Yu* (《国语·楚语》), 'They have good sight and listening abilities so that the deities can come and communicate with them. The man is called 觋 and the woman is called 巫'.

The function of the witch is to communicate between deities and people and to deliver the intentions of deities to the world. Wang Fuzhi, a Confucian scholar in the Qing Dynasty, said, 'The customs of ghosts were very prevalent in the state of Chu. The witch could conjure the presence of the deity and the deity would cling to the witch to pass messages'. This is exactly the same with the saying in *Guo* Yu that the deity falls on the witch. It can be said that witch has two responsibilities in activities serving for the deity: He is a witch at first, and then he could be the representation of the deity. The witch serving the deity has been a long established custom. Some believers hold the view that there had been 巫 named 咸 ever since the periods of the Yellow Emperor, the Yao Emperor as well as the Xia Dynasty and the Spring and Autumn period.

In Chapter 16 ('Legends of the Great Western Wilderness') of *Classics of Mountains and Seas*, 10 witches of Ling Mountain are headed by Wu Xian (巫咸). From this view, the occurrence of Wu Xian was prior to the Xia Dynasty, who was believed to be the first witch by Xu Shen.

During the Yin-Shang period, the most common way to verify the willingness of the deity is divination. According to the record in the

---

[40] In the revised version of the *Origin of Chinese Character*s by Xu Xuan, '巫觋' means blessing.

[41] Xu Shen, *The Origin of Chinese Characters*, Chapter 5.

oracle bone script, people would depend on divination for all businesses, including offering sacrifices to gods, announcements, wars, hunting, behaviour and conducts, years, rains, etc. The main procedure of divination goes as follows: drill several circular holes at the back of the tortoise shell or animal bones, sometimes even dig an elongated slot, burn the slot to crack the tortoise shell, and then determine the good luck or ill luck through the patterns at the front of the tortoise shell. The main purpose of divination is casuistry.

Xu Shen thinks that '卜' is like the shape of burning the turtle; '兆 (which is same as '卜' in the seal script)' refers to the cracks out of burning, and the character '兆' in ancient Chinese prose is the pictogram of crack; the characters 'Ji' (卟) 'Zhen' (贞) 'Zhan' (占) and 'Zhao' (召) refer to forecasting good luck or ill luck by divination.[42]

Divination is the way '卜' is used for the late emperor and '考' is for the deity.[43] The diviner generally thinks that the deity or ghost could express their willingness through the cracks in tortoise shell and animal bones. As a result, the result of divination decides the basic reality choice. In Chapter 32 ('Great Plan') of the *Book of History*, when Yu became the emperor, he put forward nine laws for national governance. The seventh of it 'Ming Yong Ji Yi' (明用稽疑) means burning the tortoise shell to do divination. Since then, there have been lots of descriptions and typical examples about divination. In *Records of the Historian*, Qi Yizhong's marriage with his wife Chen Wan is done through divination; in 'Aristocratic Family Zhao', Zhao Shuai decides to serve Zhong Er through divination; in 'Biography of Emperor Qin', Emperor Qin chooses the tour route through divination. Under the background of this experiential fact, Xu Shen explained the special meaning and configuration of the character 'Yong' (用): '用 means do something in some way and it is an associative compound of "Bu' (卜) and "Zhong" (中)'.[44] In other words, the configuration of the character '用' involves the meaning that we can do something

---

[42] Ibid., Chapter 3.
[43] Note for the character '用' in Xu Kai, *Biographical Annotations*.
[44] Xu Shen, *The Origin of Chinese Characters*, Chapter 3.

according to some way after the divination. Xu Kai understood Xu Shen's ideas and he said, 'Our ancestors do not violate divination'.[45]

The core concept of religious philosophy is 'deity' or 'god', and the core theory of religious philosophy is the characteristics of deity or god and the relation between god and world and humanity. There is a great difference between the Wu Xi and divination at the superficial level, but there is an obvious deity-human relation.[46] Deity or god is something opposite to humanity, so these two activities could present the willingness of deities, but the subject of activities could not merge with deities. As a result, we could classify the aforementioned characters and these two cultural phenomena into the same historical phase.

It is regretful that Xu Shen's explanation of another group of Chinese characters made this historical phase contain another kind of distinct and heterogeneous religious concept.

In Xu Shen's the *Origin of Chinese Characters*, '偠' means the god which follows the character "人" (human) and is pronounced as "身"'. '偠' has the meaning of the god while its form contains '人' which reveals that the god and humans could bridge the connection under certain circumstances and that is what Xu Shen means. In his view, 偠 is both the secularization and humanization of the god and the sanctification and deification of humans; its connotation is closest to the character '仙'. 仙 is the human who has lived a long life and then left the world. The *Origin of Chinese Characters* is 'compiled according to the categorized components of characters. Characters having the same components will be arranged together'.[47] Therefore, the character 偠 and 仙 are arranged together. Xu Shen explains that '"真" means immortals whose body has changed in its nature and then

---

[45] Note for the character '用' in Xu Kai, *Biographical Annotations*. Xu Shen's explanation to the character '用' is not so accurate, but the close relation between character '用' and divination seems to be proved by the oracle bone script. Please refer to Wu Haokun and Pan You, *The Chinese History of the OracleBone Script* (Shanghai: Shanghai People's Publishing House, 1985), 91–92.

[46] He Guanghu, *The Diversified Conception of God: An Overview of Western Religious Philosophy in the 20th Century* (Gui Yang: Guizhou People's Publishing House, 1991), 30.

[47] Xu Shen (许慎), 'Preface', *Origin of Chinese Characters*.

climbed to the sky. The character follows '匕', '目' and '𠃊', and '八' is something it carries'.⁴⁸

The communion between humanity and deity originated from the Warring States period and it has gained popularity in the Han Dynasty which was also the source of Taoism. The Pre-Qin philosopher Zhuangzi had given the promise to the later generation that people would become the immortals after they died:

> After living in the world for nearly a thousand years, they would hate the world and then go to the heaven. They drive the white clouds to the junction between the heaven and the earth. Disasters caused by the longevity and prosperity would never occur to me and I would not be suffering in my body.

The immortals in Zhuangzi's words are all the persons whose intelligence attained the high level and they are all deified persons. In Zhuangzi's opinion, Emperor Xi Wei, Fu Xi, Huang, Zhuan Xu, Peng Zu and Fu Shuo all became deities by their intelligence. By the Qin and Han Dynasties, being deities because of intelligence had become more secular. People could not pursue a high-level intelligence and they could achieve it only by a kind of medicine. So Emperor Shi of Qin and Emperor Wu of Han had tried their best to get the medicine and hope to become immortals through food. Emperor Wu of Han even said, 'If I could be like the Yellow Emperor (who became an immortal and rise to the heaven), I would believe that leaving my wife would be just like taking off my shoes'. The concept of being immortals through ascending to the heaven and transformation has attained the peak at that time. In Bao Pu Zi Dui Su (《抱朴子·对俗》), 'Those who became immortals in the ancient times will have their wings grow in their bodies and fly to the heaven'; in the stone figures of the Han Dynasty, there are a lot of immortals who have wings.⁴⁹

If Xu Shen provided an impeccable explanation to characters such as '僊', 'Xian' (仙) and 'Zhen' (真), then these three characters should

---

⁴⁸ Xu Shen, *Origin*, Chapter 8.

⁴⁹ Wang Jianzhong and Shan Xiushan, *Stone Figures of the Han Dynasty* (Beijing: Cultural Relics Press, 1990), 185, 198–99, 244, 248, 253–54, 262, 264.

have been produced after the concept transformation of religion in the Warring States period and they would not be at the same level with 'Wu' (巫), 'Xi' (覡), 'Zhan' (占) and 'Bu' (卜). If '僊', 'Xian' (仙) and 'Zhen' (真) are at the same level with 'Wu' (巫), 'Xi' (覡), 'Zhan' (占) and 'Bu' (卜), then Xu Shen's explanation of these characters are historically a misunderstanding. According to this, Xu Shen would not be inclined to divide the two groups of characters or to divide the two segments of history. Xu Shen obliterated both the historical level of Chinese characters and the historical level of Chinese culture.

The historical phases of Chinese characters and the historical relations between Chinese characters and Chinese culture can provide mutual proof and definition. The ignorance of the former makes the false friends between Chinese characters and Chinese culture; the ignorance of the latter also makes the discrete match between Chinese characters and the legends or history since the Three Kings period, Five Emperors period and even the Spring and Autumn and Warring States period.

There is no doubt that the research in Chinese characters should return to the historical connection between Chinese characters and Chinese culture. This is in fact an irresistible direction of the research in Chinese characters. But people will encounter many difficulties on their way.

Difficulty 1: The forms, meanings and sounds of Chinese characters (especially for the Chinese characters in the early period) need to be testified.

Over the past hundreds of years, people have made out more than four thousand Chinese characters, different in shapes, among which only one thousand could be recognized. What's more, they could not gain a good understanding even for these one thousand characters. For example, people know that characters 'Yi' (一) 'Er' (二) 'San' (三) and 'Si' (四) record the numbers according to the cumulative strokes, but they do not know why these four characters took this configuration pattern and they also do not know the earliest origin and background experience of these four concepts.

Difficulty 2: So far, the oracle bone script, the most-integral symbol system of Chinese characters, which were excavated very early, has presented a relatively mature pattern. Some of them have been incorporated into the corresponding system 'the oracle bone script, the bronze script, the small seal script, the clerical script'. However, people are still ignorant of the Chinese characters at the stage of the oracle bone script, so the corresponding relations between Chinese characters and the oracle bone script could not be rebuilt.

Difficulty 3: People could hardly present the inherent historical phases of Chinese characters themselves. In other words, people could not replace Chinese characters into the historical background in which they were produced and which had chronological significance.

From Xu Shen's the *Origin of Chinese Characters*, the main study of Chinese characters in traditional philology is synchronic, which lacks efforts in synchronic research. What synchronic study pays attention to is the established relations in the system of Chinese characters while diachronic study focuses on the evolution and development of Chinese characters system in its formation. Basically, the six-category script theory is the result of synchronic study; although, theories in the evolution of Chinese character configuration take diachronic study as the principal method, they are still a kind of incomplete descriptions rather than 'explanations'. From the scientific perspective, 'explanations' do not refer to the arguments on some relevant reasons. Instead, they are the elaboration of the rules.[50]

Difficulty 4: Traditional philology does not provide sufficient preparation and necessary foundation for the study of the generation of Chinese characters. The 'bird and beast footprint' theory of Chinese characters cannot stand the test of evidence, and 'homology of books and drawings' and 'books coming from the drawings' are actually avoiding or shelving the issue of the generation of Chinese characters.

However, the issue of Chinese character generation is the most fundamental one in the science of Chinese characters. Once the correct

---

[50] Bagby, *Culture: The Reflection*, 159.

answer to this question is obtained, all other important issues will be solved. No other kind of research can reveal the nature and value of Chinese characters more than their scientific revelation. Unfortunately, it is not certain that the future research on Chinese characters can be traced back to some undoubted 'etymology of Chinese characters' with the typical generation of meaning in the original historical phase.

Difficulty 5: Due to the breakage and loss of history and culture, there are many areas in chaos under the history–culture background accompanied by the emergence and development of Chinese characters; therefore, culture itself needs to be proved.

The culture after Yin-Shang period lacks materialized manifestations. Sima Qian had an extensive reading of ancient books and books of the 'Golden Sarcophyllum'. He set the culmination of several generations of culture and travelled all over the Yangtze River, Huaihe River, the Yellow River Basin and even the southwestern territories. But he sighed reluctantly, 'Books in the periods of the Five Emperors and Three Generations cannot be found. I cannot get the descriptions about dukes before Yin. And only the events since Zhou Dynasty can be written'.[51] 'There has been a long time for the lack of books'.[52]

Relentless history makes the most important things the scarcest one; The obscure culture of the Xia and Shang Dynasties is the most important source of the generation and development of Chinese characters.

Fortunately, 'books' and 'records' are only the external representation of culture. The essence of culture lies in its tenacious vitality obtained by marking the human existence. It is the ghost of history and the soul of society. It exists in the classics and also exists in people's lives. It has its materiality as well. What can be burned with fire is merely its material image while the spirit of culture cannot be eliminated in any violence.[53]

Under normal circumstances, culture is delivered from generation to generation. The socialization process of each individual member

---

[51] *Records of the Historian*.
[52] Ibid.
[53] Jian Bozan, *The History of Qin and Han Dynasties*, 81.

is a process in which the individual recognizes the group's cultural patterns to varying degrees:

> The history of the individual's life begins with the adaptation of the patterns and standards of life passed down from generation to generation. The custom in which he was born molds his experience and behavior. When he speaks, he becomes a small creation of his own culture and when he grows up, he is able to participate in this cultural activity. Its cultural habits are his habit; the culture of faith is his belief; the cultural impossibility is his impossibility.[54]

This characteristic of culture allows people the opportunity to cross the distant historical interval and to find their own 'root of life'.

In addition, facing similar social and natural problems, primitive people[55] often form similar thinking and behaviour modes and concepts. Thus, when we reflect on Chinese cultural traditions, we can learn from the cultural achievements of various countries in the world.

As the saying goes in the *Book of Poetry*, 'Another's good quality or suggestion whereby one can remedy one's own defects'. Theories in the Western culturology usually make us know the meaning of some cultural phenomenon in ancient times. The *Spring and Autumn Annals* gives a description,

> In ancient times, Tang conquered Xia and became the king of the whole world. Then there had been a long time for drought and it didn't crop for 5 years. So Tang prayed for the good harvest in the Sang forest. He got his hair and finger nail cut and took his body as a sacrifice to pray for the god. Then the rain fell.

The *Records of the Historian* recalls, 'At the beginning, Emperor Cheng often fell illness when he was young, then Duke of Zhou cut his fingernails and threw them into the river to pray for the god'. The

---

[54] Ruth Benedict, *The Mode of Culture*, trans. He Xizhang and Huang Huan (Beijing: Hua Xia Publishing House, 1987), 2.
[55] Primitive people in the perspective of culturology is not equivalent to people in the primitive society.

Book of History also recorded this story about the self-sacrifice of duke of Zhou. There is a very important question: Why ancient books and records regarded the trimming of hair and fingernails of Shang Tang and Duke of Zhou as sacrifice? Several achievements in primitive cultural study have told us that the trimming fingernails and hair has great impact on the soul of the ancients, which seems common to us in modern times.

One of the most famous cultural scientists in Britain, James G. Frazer, divided the witchcraft into two categories after an in-depth study: imitation witchcraft and infection witchcraft. Infection witchcraft (also known as touching witchcraft) is based on the principle of the primitive mind that everything that comes into contact can continue to function after disengagement: If one thing is influenced, it is bound to affect others.

When aboriginal tribes in Australia hold a maternity ceremony for young people, they often have to wipe out one or more of their front teeth. They think that the front teeth must be kept properly, or else their hosts will be in great danger, even ants lying on it would make toothache for him. Australian natives also believe that as long as glass, sharp stone, bone or charcoal are placed on the person's footprints, the person will be lame. New South Wales natives also firmly believe that as long as hot charcoal is spread on the animal footprints, the animal will be out of breath.

This cultural background shows the deep meaning of the haircut and breaking of hand of Shang Tang and Duke of Zhou, which explains why the ancients regarded this behaviour as 'sacrifice'. What makes the ancestors terrified is not the universe in eternal silence but the ultimate existence of eternal silence, omnipotent God. Sinking the broken hand into the river means granting their entire life into the god of river. This chapter will not discuss the psychology of witchcraft which has an extremely far-reaching influence on the generation of Chinese characters.

Thus, reflection on the traditional culture not only lies in the deep understanding to classical literatures and archaeological excavations but also the profound understanding, grasping and application of cultural achievements. In the final analysis, reflection on culture is a nation's reflection for itself. In this connection, the practice and theory of Chinese character research must be open to both the Chinese culture and the world culture.

Difficulty 6: The relationship between Chinese characters and Chinese culture must be proved. It is better to be silent than to express it; it is better not to explain it than to explain a character of which other different cognitive results could not be excluded.

Difficulty 7: Yet another difficulty is the historical strata of the relationship between Chinese characters and Chinese culture. Why does the characters 'Yi' (一), 'Er' (二), 'San' (三) and 'Si' (四) can be arranged by strokes in ancient characters? In Guo Moruo's view, characters 'Yi' (一), 'Er' (二), 'San' (三) and 'Si' (四) are the pictograms of fingers. This view is quite insightful.

The rich cultural material proves that primitive peoples do not depart from the abstract numeral concepts of concrete things. Characters 'Yi' (一), 'Er' (二), 'San' (三) and 'Si' (四) in the oracle bone script is like the shape of fingers, and counting is to establish the correspondence between things and one, two, three and four fingers.

The idea that numbers from 'one' to 'ten' occur simultaneously is not scientific. Among a very large number of primitive people, the independent names used for numbers are often only 'one' and 'two', or sometimes 'three'; people usually use '许多 Xu Duo' '很多 Hen Duo' and '太多 Tai Duo' (all of them mean 'many' or 'too many') when they need to express the numbers more than three; or they will divide 'three' into 'two and one' and 'four' into 'two and two', and so on.

When Australian natives do counting, it is to establish things with many parts of the body contact: starting from the little finger of the left hand, to the ring finger, middle finger, index finger, thumb and then even to the wrist, elbow, axilla, shoulder, supraclavicular fossa, thorax; in the opposite direction, from the upper right supraclavicular fossa to the little finger of right hand and then they can be counted to

21; another 10 can be counted if the toe is considered. British New Guineans also use a similar method of counting.⁵⁶

It is certain that what characters 'Yi' (一), 'Er' (二), 'San' (三) and 'Si' (四) reflect is the earliest cultural connotation and also the representations of the character shapes for fingers.⁵⁷

With the development of history, the character 'Yi' (一) is the beginning of pure numbers and this is the second relation between the character 'Yi' and traditional culture.

From the Spring and Autumn and the Warring States period to Qin and Han Dynasties, people had given more meaning to the character 'Yi' (一). Chapter 14 of *Laozi,* 'Chinese Legalism and Inner Enterprise' in *Guanzi,* 'Yang Quan' in *Han Feizi,* 'Lun Ren and Jun Shou' in *Lüshi Chunqiu,* 'Seminal Breath and Spirit, Searching out Dao and An Explanatory Discourse' in *Huainanzi,* they all refer 'Yi' (一) to 'the invincible and unparalleled'. It is the 'Dao' that is the source of life and also the vigour and spirit of all the things in which 'temperament is not divided'. These two aspects are closely linked, which shows the third relation between the character 'Yi' (一) and the traditional culture.

In Gao Xiu's (a Confucian scholar) annotation about the sentence 'One refers to heaven, two refers to the earth and three refers to humans' in 'Forms of Earth' in *Huainanzi,* 'one refers to Yang while two refers to Yin'. As the *Rites by Dadai* said, 'Heaven is one, the earth is two and humans are three. Three times three is nine and Nine times nine is eighty-one. One refers to the sun'. 'Yi' (means one) refers to Yang, heaven or the sun and it is the fourth relation with the traditional culture.

The relation between Chinese characters and Chinese culture is in this slow cumulative process. Sometimes this process is coincided

---

⁵⁶ If you need more rich material, please refer to Levy-Bruhi, *Primitive Mentality* (London: George Allen & Unwin Ltd, 1923) 175–87.

⁵⁷ From the child's cognitive psychology, various ideas during the childhood period could be inferred. It is still a ubiquitous fact of experience today that children do counting activities with their fingers.

with the natural extension of word meaning and sometimes it is the historical–cultural giving.[58] It is a typical example of the latter one that characters of the Heavenly Stems and Earthly Branches have transformed into the representation of the flow of Yin and Yang.

There is a fundamental direction in the cumulative process in the relation between Chinese characters and Chinese culture, that is, from the concrete to the abstract, from irrational or primitive, simple to rational or civilized and scientific. The first kind of direction can be proved by the cumulative relation between the character 'Yi' (一) and Chinese culture. The second can be proved by some processes in which Chinese characters representing animals and plants release the old things, embrace the new things and also increasingly obtain scientific connotation.

The same vegetation, the same birds and beasts in different cultural phases will be given a different meaning. This phenomenon is not caused by the amount of knowledge, but by different cultural phases of heterogeneous content. The *Origin of Chinese Characters* explains: 'Huan (雈) belongs to the category of Chi (鴟), which has haired horn. When it chirps, it means there will be disasters'. The explanation of the *Origin of Chinese Characters* is obviously unscientific. As far as one specific historical stage is concerned, it will be truer than any of the scientific cognition of Huan bird. Huan is smaller than an owl with horned feather on head in the strigidae of aves. It is a category of owls. The ancients regarded owls as the representation of bad luck. Jia Yi, the Confucian scholar in Han Dynasty, had the feeling that 'the coming of a wild bird means the master would leave us'.[59] 鵩 bird is commonly known as owls. There is a parable in *Garden of Stories* (《说苑》) that 'Xiao (枭) birds made people migrate to the east'. It says, 'All people hate my tweet, so they migrate to the east'. Xiao birds are also owls.

---

[58] This means that most of the configuration and literal meaning of Chinese characters expressing complex philosophical thought could not be extended to the whole picture of the philosophical thought. Du Weiming has almost touched the law in revealing the language barrier of Confucian studies. Du Weiming, 'On Several Difficulties of Confucian Studies', in *Modern Transformation of Confucian Tradition* (Beijing: China Radio and TV Press, 1992).

[59] Jia Yi, 'Ode to Fu Bird'. Refer to 'Biographies of Qu Yuan and Jia Sheng', in *Records of the Historian*.

In Zhang Hua's *Natural History* (《博物志》) of the Jin Dynasty, Xiu Liu (鵂鶹) is in the category of Otus that does not have a good sight at day but can see everything clearly at night; after people cut their fingernails and threw them onto the land, the bird will pick them up and judge good or bad luck from them. If there is something unlucky, the bird will scream that there will be disasters in the family.[60] Both Xiu Liu and Huan bird are in strigidae. The *Origin of Chinese Characters* reveals the special relations between Huan bird and the ancient customs. Compared with the scientific knowledge of Huan bird, this relation is undoubtedly produced in the earlier history–culture phase.

The interpretation of Chinese characters must clearly strip layers of the historical deposition to explore the original relations between Chinese characters and the traditional culture. Only this relation has the generative significance; only this relation can show the function and connotation of Chinese character configuration to present the value and essence of Chinese characters. This is the principle that the interpretation of Chinese characters should adhere to and is also the direction that it should identify.

The Determination of the Function of the Formation of Chinese Characters

When it comes to the structure of Chinese characters, it is considered that the ultimate goal of the interpretation of Chinese characters lies in figuring out their functions. This means it is necessary to clarify whether the combination of character patterns with their meanings and pronunciations is incidental or inevitable, to clarify whether the character patterns indicate meanings or signify pronunciations, and to indicate exactly what meaning is intended.

The clarification of functions of Chinese character formation can be the most attractive, most complicated and difficult issue in the research on Chinese characters.

---

[60] This refers to the uncollected articles of *Natural History*, compiled by Editorial Department of Xin Wenfeng Book Publishing Co. Ltd, *New Collection* (Taipei: Xin Wenfeng Book Publishing Co. Ltd, 1985), 74.

Chinese characters cannot express themselves. Therefore, the uncertainty and confusion of the identification of functions of Chinese characters is the biggest trouble for interpreters. For instance, in the *Origin of Chinese Characters*, Duan Yucai annotates for 'Xiang' (襄) in Volume VIII: 'Xiang's ideographic and phono-semantic origins cannot be traced'; and for 'fan (㧃), que (阕)' in Volume IX, he says that 'the meaning, ideogram and pronunciation is unknown'. Hence, as the ultimate goal to interpret Chinese characters, it is quite difficult to make a clear and reasonable identification of functions of dots and strokes of Chinese characters. When people see a character of the oracle bone script '单' (of which grapheme can be seen in Volume II, Fourteenth of *Compilation of Oracle Bone Scripts* 《甲骨文编》), the most easily perceived information, without any doubt, is branches or grass. But some people believe it to be a pictograph of the cave of a male alligator. As for the two characters of '丧, 噩' (of which the structure can be seen in Volume II, Fourteenth of A *Compilation of Oracle Bone Scripts* 《甲骨文编》), there could be more associations produced in people's mind in that only the main part can be imagined as various trees with twisted branches and twigs. But there are different views that the two characters could probably be nothing but the pictographs of a female alligator's nest because the part like '口' in the two characters is exactly the same as the circle in the upper part of the '单' character, which indicates the mouth of the cave.[61] Actually, another explanation which is quite different from the aforementioned and made by the paleographers has been widely accepted. '单' used to be a tool used by people for hunting. It was made by a limb of a tree tied to a stone. And the main part of '丧' is the pictogram of 'mulberry'. The '口' in '丧' are tools for harvesting leaves from the mulberry tree, which was exactly the original meaning of '丧'. Only later its meaning changed to be 'lose or die';[62] '噩' equals '咢' in the *Origin* which means 'dispute loudly'.[63] Only one in most of these explanations is comparatively correct. Nevertheless, wrong explanations here mean

---

[61] '单, 丧, 噩' and other characters in the oracle bone script are not be quoted because of the difficulty to be printed.

[62] Yu Xingwu, *Jiagu Wenzi Shi Lin*. A work interpreting the oracle bone script.

[63] *Hanyu Da Zidian* (*Comprehensive Chinese Character Dictionary*) with Xu Zhongxu as the chief editor; *A Compilation of the Bronze Script* by Rong Geng.

nothing. At least their existence can prove that the function of ancient Chinese character formation has multiple possibilities in terms of its representation.

The function of Chinese character formation is complicated. And there is no inner principle to be followed by the formation. Therefore, we borrow the traditional so-called pictographs, simple indicatives, associate compounds, pictophonetic characters, symbolic characters and other terms to give them a specific illustration respectively.

1. *Pictographs*: Explaining pictographs, Xu Shen writes, '乙, a mythical bird ... a pictogram'; '册, bamboo slips for writing with long ones and short ones tied alternately with two leather straps and used to suggest the emperor taking his responsibility'; '出, being up, a state as growing up of plants'.[64] According to him, '乙' can never be interpreted as a pictogram of an inchworm wriggling its way but a silhouette when the phoenix is flying; the structure of '册' does not represent the fence around the courtyard but bamboo slips tied together; and '出' is not in the shape of fire leaping but plants growing up. The interpretations in the *Origin of Chinese Characters* by Xu Shen not only exclude those possible misunderstandings[65] of '乙, 册, 出' but also indicate the speciality featured by the pictographs, which imitate the shapes of the objects. To some extent, the original senses of pictographs are implicated inside the structures of these characters. The connections between the structures and meanings are not always incidental but later become specific to be the conventional rule through a long process of reinforcement. Certainly, as visual images, pictographs cannot self-prove this connection. Therefore, the character interpretation is duty bound to reveal the connection.

---

[64] Xu Shen, *Origin*, vol. 2, 6, 12.

[65] The three characters written in the seal script can be found below the same character in the *Origin of Chinese Characters*. Actually, Xu Shen's interpretations of '乙, 出' are not accurate. But it is not discussed in this work in that it is a totally different issue.

It is worth noticing that there exist rather delicate differences among the formation functions of every part of pictographs. The three characters '页, 身, 闻' quoted hereafter can be taken undoubtedly as nothing but an indivisible whole, respectively in which their head, middle and aural parts are obviously in a more prominent position.

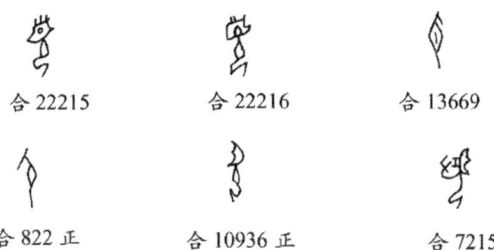

In this way, ancient Chinese people intend to show that each part of these characters does not convey equivalent sense loaded by the whole character but, as it were, the other parts are nothing but a preliminary definition and the parts which are highlighted tend to be those with more specific orientations.

There are many similar examples. If the parts delineating eyebrows, facial hairs and teeth of the characters in the next figure '眉, 须, 齿' are kept, people would definitely produce quite a few different associations; people who create Chinese characters adopt the images of relevant things to indicate, define and elucidate semantic information conveyed by '眉, 须, 齿' so as to have characters interpreted and pronounced as expected. Therefore, the images concerned with eyes, face and mouth do not participate in the semantic structure equally with the other parts; they are only the subordinate semantic components although they are indispensable. These subordinate semantic components possess a certain function similar to referential components such as the major semantic components of the characters '页, 身, 闻'. However, as visual images, these subordinate semantic components can never be taken as pure referential components for there exists, to some extent, an internal connection between them and the meanings.

合 3421　　　　　郑义伯盨　　　　　合 3523

2. *Simple indicatives*: In the *Origin of Chinese Characters*, Xu Shen writes, '本, root of a tree (木 mù) with the base indicated by an extra stroke'. '末, apex of the reverse of 本, a tree with the top highlighted by an extra stroke'. '朱, a type of tree belonging to pine and cypress genus, composed of a major part "木" with a horizontal stoke inside it'.[66] The semantic meaning of simple indicatives is also conveyed by the structure of characters such as pictographs, but their configurations can be separated into two parts: one is the pictographic component, and the other one is the referential component. The former, like '木' being the major part of '本, 末, 朱', is a general definition of the semantic meaning of the whole character while the latter, like '一' in the three characters '本, 末, 朱' refers to a specific meaning. The referential components in simple indicatives cannot be told their meanings according to their structures; on the contrary, these components can be replaced by the other components with different structures. If different colours represent certain particular semantic meanings just like ancient characters of some nations, a certain colour can be used to clarify the semantic meaning of the pictographic components of Chinese characters, which results in the total cancellation of referential components. For instance, Dongba characters of Naxi people can take advantage of blackening parts to differentiate between meaning and pronunciation. Therefore, the perceptual characteristics of referential components are incidental; in terms of the semantic meaning of a character, the position of the referential components and its relations with pictographic components are important.

3. *Associative compounds*: Xu Shen interprets '折' as 'an ax (斤) cutting off a piece of grass (扌)'; '秉' as 'a hand (又) holding

---

[66] Xu Shen, *Origin*, vol. 6.

a seedling (禾)'; and '伐' as 'a man (人) holding a dagger-axe (戈)'.⁶⁷ The similar Chinese characters like the above ones are mostly referred to as associative compounds. However, that view is evidently unscientific in that '折, 秉, 伐' and other similar characters concern and present two different images, although their semantic meanings and connotations are never simply equal to the one part plus the other one. In terms of the semantic meaning, each part of a character must be put together to be a visual whole. Therefore, the so-called problem of '会' (association) never exists. That feature is quite obvious in the oracle script (see the next figure).

合 7924   合 17444   合 888

Although these visual components are different from the pictographs for one part of them describing an event and the other indicating a thing, the functions of both of the characters are actually the same. Therefore, the traditional view that those visual components are associative compounds must be corrected. If the concept '会意' (association) intends to serve as a manner of the formation of Chinese characters, we should focus on the internal attributes of Chinese characters rather than consider whether Chinese characters can be separated into two or more associative visual parts. When the connection between the structures and meanings of characters takes some indivisible active or passive relations among the images rather than certain comparatively independent visual images as an intermediary, such Chinese characters should never be defined as 'associative compounds'.

Generally, associative compounds can be divided into the following three types:

a. The first one is simply made up of pictographs and each pictographic component presents a part meaning of the whole character as an independent visual image.

---

⁶⁷ Xu Shen, *Origin*, vol. 1, 3, 8.

According to Xu Shen, '吹 means "blow or puff" and is made up of a "口" (mouth) and "欠" (exhale)'.[68] The character '欠' itself in the oracle script is like a mouth blowing (of which the structure can be seen in the Volume II, Seventh of *Compilation of Oracle Bone Scripts*《甲骨文编》), but this image can be taken as an act of blowing of puffing or as a man blowing or puffing. Therefore, the part '口' is added to the original structure to make the connotation of this character more specific.

This type of associative compounds is quite similar to pictographs. Their fundamental difference lies in that some visual components contained in associative compounds cannot be referred to as an organic whole such as pictographs.

b. The second type of associative compounds is also made up of pictographs. But some (or a certain) pictographs contained in this type of characters do not present their meanings through their images while the borrowed or extended meaning of these components participate in the general meaning of the compound characters.

In the *Origin*, the character '驲' is interpreted as, 'a character made up of "马" (horse) and '八' (eight) means a horse in its eight years old'.[69] The part '马' presents some features of the object which the character '驲' refers to. However, the part '八' with two strokes written in opposite directions[70] displays certain connotations of the character '驲' with its borrowed meaning (namely, number eight). Here is another instance. Xu Shen interprets the character '雀' which is made up of '小' and '隹' as sparrows.[71] According to his interpretation, '隹', through its image, suggests some perceptual features of a short-tailed bird; '小' originally presents an image of scattered grits and then extends to indicate the smallness of the object. Apparently, it is not the features of the visual image or the original connotation of '小' but the extended meaning of

---

[68] Xu Shen, *Origin*, vol. 2.
[69] Xu Shen, *Origin*, vol. 10.
[70] Ibid., vol. 2.
[71] Ibid., vol. 6.

'小' that participates in the general meaning of the compound character '雀'.
c. The third type of associative compounds refers to those characters of which components have already transcended their original structures and connotations and participate in the general meaning of the compound character with their borrowed and extended meanings.

For example, the character '尖' is made up of '小' like scattered grits at the top and '大' like a man standing on his feet at the bottom. The semantic meaning of the whole character is composed of the extended meanings of the above parts. Another examples are '歪', which is made up of '不' which originally indicates the radicals growing underground when seeds sprout, and '正', which originally refers to an officer with one foot stepping ahead. The meaning of the whole character is composed of the borrowed meaning of '不' and extended meaning of '正'.

4. *Pictophonetic characters*: Pictophonetic characters are composed of two parts: one of a limited set of characters (the semantic component, often graphically simplified) which suggests the general meaning of the compound character, and the other part (the phonetic component) whose pronunciation suggests the pronunciation of the compound character. Certainly, the phonetic components, if investigated, are also pictographs, simple indicatives or associative compounds. But the structure and meaning of the phonetic components do not participate in the general meaning of pictophonetic characters.

According to Xu Shen, '"凤", a mythical bird, is mainly composed of "鸟" and is pronounced as "凡"'.[72] Actually, '鸟' is a semantic component to show the generic feature of '凤'. The character '凤' in the oracle bone script is a pictograph with the pronunciation of '凡'. Hereafter, the part '鸟' is used to indicate the generic feature of '凤' as a semantic component; the part '凡' is used to suggest the pronunciation of the whole character from the very beginning and its structure has nothing to do with the looking of '凤'. Here is another instance. In ancient times, fleshy dogs were used to be sacrificed for the worship of ancestors. Thus, '献'

---

[72] Ibid., vol. 4.

with the '犬' radical is pronounced as '臛'.[73] However, '祳' can never mean to sacrifice fleshy dogs for the worship of ancestors in that the part '示' serves as nothing but a phonetic component whose image and meaning have nothing to do with the character '祳'. Hereafter, we do not adopt the view of 'pictophonetic and associative compound characters', not just for the sake of interpreting clearly. Among the pictophonetic and associative compound characters, a certain part can serve as either a semantic or a phonetic component. In fact, we should first take these characters as associative compounds because Chinese characters do not possess a function of indicating pronunciations after all. The reason that the phonetic component is able to indicate the pronunciation of a character is no more than a fact that the connection between the structure and the pronunciation of a character has been reinforced repeatedly in the historical development.

5. *Symbolic characters*: The structure of Chinese symbolic characters is not only the outer manifestation of the meaning of the whole character but it also has nothing to do with its pronunciation. At the very beginning, the connection among the structure, meaning and pronunciation of the symbolic characters is incidental, so is the combination between the phonetic component and the pronunciation of pictophonetic characters. But that combination has gradually become fixed after practices for a long time to be reinforced repeatedly. Symbolic characters must be highlighted continually to combine the structure, meaning and pronunciation to be a firm whole. The numeral characters '五, 六, 七...' may well be typical symbolic characters.

These examples are undoubtedly far from enough, which, however, enable us to catch a glimpse of the complexity and instability of the functions of Chinese character formation. Therefore, when interpreting Chinese characters, we must 'identify, compare, exclude, confirm' various characters and make reasonable explanations of their structures, pronunciations and meanings, so as to clarify the functions of Chinese character formation. The accomplishment and results of these

---

[73] Ibid., vol. 10.

The Cultural Interpretation of Chinese Characters **283**

complicated processes also involve various factors relating to human efforts and times.

Specifically, how to clarify the functions of Chinese character formation? That can be a significant question that, however, has never been attached enough importance to and greatly involves theories and practices.

1. Generally, the fundamental method of clarifying the functions of Chinese character formation lies in building a connection between Chinese character formation and a certain experience or background. In other words, the profound connection between Chinese characters and its surrounding cultural systems must be paid attention to. Starting from the Chinese ancient folk customs, the *Origin* by Xu Shen interprets a series of Chinese characters. Although complex and even unfaithful, the arguments in the *Origin* are still inspiring.

   Xu Shen writes, '弃 means 捐, to abandon or throw away the baby with perverse labor. It is composed of 廾 and 㐬'.[74] The character '弃' in the seal script, large seal script and oracle bone script (see the next figure) can be interpreted as two hands holding a newborn with a dustpan. But that configuration possesses evident polysemy because it can be not only understood as 'to abandon or throw away' but interpreted as 'to arrange' or other meanings. Scholars have elucidated the function of its configuration from the perspective of the meaning of 'abandoning or throwing away', but the original meaning contained in the configuration of '弃' might not well be 'to abandon or throw away'.

   According to the records in 'Sheng Min' in *The Book of Poetry*, Hou Ji, the first ancestor of the Zhou Dynasty, has a unique experience of being abandoned on the street, in woods and in a frozen river, respectively, by his mother.

The character "弃" in seal scripts, large seal scripts and oracle bone scripts

---

[74] Ibid., vol. 4.

The Han people did not know well about that, which generated an old saying that 'the reason why Qi was given as a name was that parents wanted to abandon him at first'.[75] What the early configuration of '弃' reflects is an old folk custom—give the newborn a try. Human development has always been fraught with hardships and crimes. Numerous materials indicate huge pressure to survive, confronted with people, which could be traced back to early times of human history. Having analysed a few scars on skulls of Peking man, those anthropologists believe the scars were left by other humans. Through the research on 38 Peking men, people find that except for the 16 ones who died in adulthood without knowing their exact ages, there are 15 out of the 22 who died before 14 years of age.[76] That cruel fact enables us to know that surviving in the era of Hou Ji can never be easy. Newborns brought more worries than excitement. Therefore, it is reasonable and significant for the ancient people to put the newborn in a dustpan (or other things) to forecast its fate through various incidents. Although that folk custom has already faded away, some traditions in certain nations can still be taken as the evidence. In Volume II of *Bowuzhi* (*Natural History*), Zhang Hua, a Western Jin Dynasty (265–316) scholar, writes,

> People living in the very southwest region of Jingzhou and Shu are called Liaozi. A woman there gives birth to a child after pregnancy for seven months (which is believed to be ten months, a slip of pen, quoter's annotation) by a river. The child would be raised if it was floating on the water but abandoned if it sank into the water. The newborns of Kucong people would be wrapped in banana leaves and put right by a large pond.[77]

In the records of Yanshi Jiaxun (*The Family Instructions of Master Yan*), the custom of 'giving the newborn a try' in the regions south

---

[75] *Records of the Historian.*

[76] Deng Fuxing, *Art before Art*, 45.

[77] 'Research on Society and History of Lahu Ethnic Group', Part II, quoted from a secondary source: Workshop of Folk Literature of Ethnic Minorities, *Materials of Folk Customs of Ethnic Minorities*, vol. 1, 305.

of the Yangtze River, known as 'Shizui' and 'Zhuazhou' (an Asian ritual held at a child's first birthday party), may well be another form of evolution of the ancient folk custom of 'giving the newborn a try'. All these details are illuminating in our exploration of the contents of the folklore conveyed by the character '弃'.

There are rituals and customs finely connected with the custom of 'giving the newborn a try'. Xu Shen says, '葬, to bury, means the dead are buried in the grass with a straw mat covering them. According to the *Book of Change*, "In ancient times, the dead were buried with firewood covering them"'.[78]

> 弔, to condole, in ancient times relatives and friends who came for condolence would take bows and arrows to drive away wild animals in case the bodies were eaten by those animals because the dead at that time were buried only with firewood covering them.[79]

In terms of the formation of '葬', the part '艹' can be totally referred to as merely a phonetic indicator. But, as Xu Shen said, the formation of '葬' reflects the ancient custom of burying the dead with grass and firewood covering them. Therefore, the part '艹', with its image feature, undoubtedly presents a partial meaning of '葬'. The custom of being buried in the wild quoted by Xu Shen recorded in the second half of 'Xici' in the *Book of Change*: 'In ancient times, the dead were buried with firewood covering them in the wild without any graves or tombs as a mark... Later saints were buried in coffins'. However, it was inevitable to get rid of wild animals if a man was buried in the wild. 'Lie Yu Kou' in *Zhuangzi*: 'Body would be eaten by crows and eagles'. On this account, there was a custom of mourning for the death of a family and defending the body from wild birds in ancient times. In 'Stories of Goujian's Schemes' in *Spring and Autumn Annals of Wu and Yue*, a man named Chen Yin from the State of Chu told Goujian, the King of the State of Wu that

> ancient people endowed with honest and kindly nature lived on animals and dews. After their death, they would

---

[78] Xu Shen, *Origin*, vol. 1.
[79] Ibid., vol. 8.

be wrapped in pantropical weeds and thrown in the wild. The dutiful son could not bear seeing his parents eaten by animals. He made bullets and defended the dead from wild animals.

Therefore, mourners would help the son with their bows.[80] Xu Shen's explanations may not be completely correct. However, what the parts 人 and 弓 refer to would be unknown without the background of the above as a reference.

The character '婚' as well, similar to '葬', is composed of two parts. The meaning of '女' is obvious while the meaning of '昏' cannot be easily explained offhand. The part '昏' can be just understood as a pure phonetic indicator, which, however, is obviously quite different from the traditional view since Xu Shen's argument. Therefore, the specific functions of the part '昏' cannot be figured out if the character '婚' is not connected with its underlying folk customs in the ancient society. Xu Shen said, '婚, the family that bride is married to. Weddings are held at dusk (昏). Therefore, "婚" is composed of "女" (woman) and "昏" (dusk) which can also be taken as a phonetic indicator'.[81] Since the character '婚' reflects the ancient custom that weddings were held at dusk, it is understood that '昏' participates in the synthesis of the meaning of '婚'.

In addition to the aforementioned customs about birth, death and wedding that are considered as relevant backgrounds of Chinese characters by Xu Shen, some specific ways of thinking existing in the ancient folk customs are also taken as indispensable references for the *Origin*. Xu Shen explains, '腥, star-like parts in pork (星见食豕), which enable polyps (息肉) to grow in pork.[82] According to the annotation about that character, '息' means the parasitic part of the pork while '腥' refers to the polyp like rice in size of the pork. Xu Shen believed the production of '腥' is partly because '星见食豕' and '星' like '肉' present part of the meaning of '腥'.

---

[80] Duan Yucai (Qing Dynasty), *Annotations of the Origin*, 383.
[81] Xu Shen, *Origin*, vol. 12.
[82] Ibid., vol. 4.

Xu Shen's explanation on '腥' can never be far-fetched or obscure intentionally but indicates a thought-provoking tradition of folk psychology which is a concept of heterogeneous response quite similar to Frazer's so called 'imitate, infected sorcery'. Volume II of *Bowuzhi* (*Natural History*) by Zhang Hua writes,

> People do not want pregnant women to see ugly things or peculiar animals. And those women shall avoid unusual scents when eating.... So pregnant women in ancient times must be cautious about what they got in touch, for the baby's character could be influenced by what mothers saw. Pregnant women were not allowed to eat or see rabbits, which would cause babies' cleft lip and to eat fresh ginger, which would give babies more toes or fingers.

That is a typical embodiment of the concept of heterogeneous response, which can also be seen in 'white female waterfowls get conceived when taking a look at male ones'. The fundamental feature of the concept of heterogeneous response lies in taking incidental similarities as inevitable results caused by this kind of 'response'. The parasitic parts in rice size in the pork are similar to the shape of stars, which, therefore, were considered as a particular response of stars in pork. That makes the same sense as the aforementioned taboos for pregnant women.

In addition, as the formations of Chinese characters sometimes can be quite similar, it would be difficult to clarify small differences between their functions. Only through revealing the connections between characters and their particular backgrounds, the aforementioned differences can become specific and clear. For instance, for the two characters '集, 枭', why cannot the latter be understood as a long-tailed bird perching on a branch since the former can be interpreted as a short-tailed bird perching on a branch?

Xu Shen said, '枭, an evil bird, would be cut apart if caught, is in a formation of "鸟" (bird) perching on "木" (branch)'.[83] 枭, the

---

[83] Ibid., vol. 6. Originally, Da Xu believed '枭' is in a 'formation of the head part of "鸟" (bird) hanging on "木" (branch)'. Here the interpretation is revised according to Duan Yucai's annotation.

evil bird, would even eat its mother. According to *Annotations of the Origin of Chinese Characters* (《说文解字注》) by Duan Yucai, the Yellow Emperor would kill that evil bird so as to deracinate this species. Chinese emperors would grant officials the broth of '枭' on 5 May until the Han Dynasty.[84] Based on the above background to analyse the formation of '枭', the specific functions of its formation can be proved to be virtually different.

One of the distinctive features and profound significances of the *Origin* lies in the emphasis on the interpretations and studies about Chinese characters based on the actual experience and backgrounds, the instinctive senses and cognition of the formation of Chinese characters and the connections and correspondence between the formation and some backgrounds. The evidence can be easily available. It is unnecessary to present all examples.

2. In a deeper sense, the experience or background connected with the formation of Chinese characters must possess a certain universal meaning.

The formation of Chinese characters is incapable of presenting its functions through itself. This does not mean clarifying the functions of the formation of Chinese characters would rely on personal and purely subjective judgements. Actually, Chinese characters, as a symbolic system for recording language, must also possess undoubtedly social universality. As a product of the cultural mechanism enjoyed by a certain social group, the formation of Chinese characters cannot ignore a common approval of all members of that society. Therefore, in order to clarify the functions of the formation of Chinese characters, the cultural traditions featuring a universal significance and enjoyed by common members of a certain society must be first studied.

The *Origin of Chinese Characters* says, '秃 (bold) means hairless. It follows the character 人 (person) and its upper part looks like the shape of 禾粟 (millet)'. Wang Yu said, 'when Cang Jie came out and saw a bold person prostrate in the millet, he created the character 秃. However, the specific circumstance is unknown'. This 'experience background' provided by Wang Yu is only an

---

[84] Duan Yucai (Qing Dynasty), *Annotations of the Origin*, 271.

accidental and rare case. It does not have any features at any levels of the things or phenomena that form Chinese characters, and, therefore, it cannot influence the Chinese character formation. Duan Yucai hereby ridiculed, 'Just because of the accidental occurrence, the script was created and lasted for thousands of years. However, bold persons did not have to be prostrate in the millet, so this story cannot be true at all'. Then he added, 'like the shape of 禾粟 (millet)' should be 'like the shape of 禾秀 (millet ears)' to avoid a kind of taboo. 'It should be like millet ears because the tops of millet bend and droop. Their bending parts are smooth and round like hairpins, and the bold person is hairless with a bare and smooth head just like the shape of the millet ears'.[85] Although Mr Duan's explanation is highly imaginary, the experience background he provided is far more universal than what Wang Yu said, it has already implied huge possibilities approaching the truth.

In this aspect, Xu Shen's *Origin of Chinese Characters* also shows its particular profundity. More or less, Xu realized that it was not a certain sole and accidental phenomenon that influenced the formation and connotation of Chinese characters, but something with obvious common connotation. The ancient customs, totem legacy, religious faith, myths and legends, the theory of *yin* and *yang* and Five Elements (阴阳五行学说), Confucian traditions and daily experience, which were used by Xu Shen to interpret Chinese characters are all general features shared within some tribes or groups as well as permeating its thoughts and behaviours. As for Wang's explanation that the writing of the character was fixed according to the accidental encounter, Xu held apparent doubt.

3. It is worth noting that the connection between the formation of Chinese characters and certain experience should be also quite historic.

Chinese characters not only came into being under the background of a particular experience but also presented something in

---

[85] Duan Yucai (Qing Dynasty), *Exegesis on the Origin of Chinese Characters*, 407. In ancient writing, the character form of 'bald' is closely related to that of 'ears of grain'.

this background through its form. Thus, the combination of form and meaning usually has some impassable historical levels. The form of '监' (mirror) in the oracle bone script can be produced only in the specific historical period when 'water was taken as the mirror';[86] the form of '社' (society) recorded in the *Origin* can be produced only in the ancient times, a specific historical period, when 'each family in a society plants trees adjust to the local lands' (the character form can be seen in the *Origin*, Vol. 1A). It is obvious that Xu Shen was aware of this simple truth when interpreting Chinese characters. For example, Xu interpreted '表' (upper outer garment): 'The upper outer garment means clothes on the upper body. The character follows '衣' (clothes) and '毛' (fur), because the ancient garments are made of fur'.[87] For '姓' (surname), he interpreted, 'One's surname is born with him or her. In ancient times, the mother moves the god, thus giving birth to a baby. So it follows "女" (female) and "生" (birth), and birth is also the phonetic radical'.[88] The similar materials all declare that Xu Shen made great efforts to connect the formation of Chinese characters with folk customs that might exist in the same historical level with the formation.

However, these efforts work within certain limits. When interpreting the Ten Heavenly Stems (天干), the Twelve Earthly Branches (地支), as well as some other numbers and characters with the theory of *yin* and *yang* and Five Elements, which matured in the Spring and Autumn and the Warring States period and prevailed in the period of the Han Dynasties, Xu seemed to pay no attention to the connection between the formation of Chinese characters and the historical background with certain experience. Of course, what Xu scanned and scrutinized is mainly the small seal script, a writing system of Chinese characters that were intentionally edited and standardized by some people in the Qin Dynasty such as Li Si (李斯). It is entirely possible for the theory of *yin* and *yang* and Five Elements and other cultural thoughts

---

[86] See AICAS, *A Compilation of the Oracle Bone Script*, vol. 8: 9.
[87] Xu Shen, *Origin*, vol. 8A.
[88] Ibid., vol. 12B.

to guide that edition wrongly, but the historical mistake does not equal the truth. Moreover, the small seal script is just formed by the correspondent adjustment of character form that evolves from the oracle bone script and the bronze script in terms of the basic situation. Therefore, in the interpretation of Chinese characters, it must be noted that the Chinese character, since its coming into being, has been closely related to various cultural thoughts inevitably. Chinese characters such as '一, 二, 三, 四, 甲, 乙, 丙, 丁' (one, two, three, four, first, second, third, fourth), for instance, have close relation with *yin* and *yang* and Five Elements. But this relation is not an internal property of character forms; on the contrary, it is just an external repeated reinforcement of history. So the interpretation of Chinese characters should not be based on this relation.

We have mentioned earlier that sometimes Xu Shen 'seems to pay no attention to the connection between the formation of Chinese characters and the historical background with certain experience' because this tendency is only present within some field of the interpretation of Chinese characters. As for the rational level, it is entirely possible for him to regard 'historicity' as the basic premise of the interpretation of Chinese characters. However, the 'historicity' in his view sometimes is merely an illusion or a wrong identification after all.

4. I must make it clear that it is still quite hard to make sure that no mistakes in the interpretation of Chinese characters including even the three points mentioned here are committed because there is an indispensable prerequisite for correct interpretation—the connection between the formation of Chinese characters and the historical background with certain experience must be authentic.

Superficially, the formation of Chinese characters can sometimes be contacted with kinds of experience that is at the same historical level and has general significance. But only one connection is authentic in the sense of initial formation and meaning. Therefore, the scientific interpretation of Chinese characters must ensure its own authenticity.

The Chinese character structure that can reflect the initial meaning most often manifests its connection with historical experience more accurately, vividly and visually. Thus, the first thing to interpret Chinese characters must be to track the early formation of Chinese characters from various cultural relics as much as possible. For '美' (delicacy), Xu Shen interpreted, 'Delicacy, equivalent to sweetness, follows '羊' (goat) and '大' (big) in character form; as one of the six types of livestock, goat is mainly served as a meal'.[89] Then is the daily experience under 'delicacy', truly what Xu Shen and Xu Xuan (徐铉) said, 'The meat of big goats tastes delicious'. Does the form of 'delicacy' really reflect people's perception in the taste of lamb? What Xu Shen and Xu Xuan said is merely a subjective supposition until answers to those questions are positive.

Although the character forms of 'delicacy' in the oracle bone script and the bronze script[90] are similar to the writing in the small seal script in the *Origin*, they are more obvious to restore a complete visual image. This, to some degree, excludes the possibility that the character 'big' interferes with the initial connotation of 'delicacy' through its extended meaning. In fact, the Chinese character 'delicacy' originally looks like a standing man who wears a goat's head or horn; in the character form, the two stretching limbs and two legs are similar to the character 'big'; yet, accurately speaking, it presents the scene of singing and dancing. This analysis of the early formation of character 'delicacy' has doubtlessly shaken the explanation of Xu Shen and others.

Furthermore, the times that are inseparably related to Chinese characters, to some extents, can also prove whether the connection between the formation of Chinese characters and the historical experience is a misunderstanding or not. Still take the interpretation of 'delicacy' in the *Origin*, for example. If the connotation of 'delicacy' is exactly what Xu Shen said, that is, human's perception of taste, then why it comes from 'goat' instead of 'horse, cattle, pig, dog or chicken'? The *Origin* explains that 'as one of the six types of livestock, goat is mainly served as a meal', while 'the Chief Imperial Cook' in the *Rites of Zhou* (《周礼·膳夫》) says that 'six types of livestock are used for food'. Then why is goat used alone

---

[89] Ibid., 4A.
[90] See, AICAS, *A Compilation of the Oracle Bone Script*, vol. 4:14, 2:262.

here? In this sense, Xu Xuan's statements such as 'the meat of big goats tastes delicious' are just words of imagination. As for Duan Yucai, he claims in *Exegesis on the Origin of Chinese Characters* that 'goat stands for good luck, so "美" follows "羊"'.[91] It is clear that Duan's statement is closer to the truth. Then another question can be further raised: Why 'goat' can stand for 'good luck'?

The initial formation of 'delicacy' may show how our ancestors sing and dance, dressed as totems and deities. For them, totems and the images of deities can bless members of their tribes; and people are usually enchanted by, or even mad at, songs and dances of totem. In the former sense, goat is spontaneously regarded as the symbol of good luck; while, in the latter sense, it is natural that songs and dances of totem serve as the origin of aesthetic consciousness.[92] Yu Xingwu thinks that '美' follows '羊' because people disguise themselves to hunt by wearing goat's horn, which then is used as the common ornament for dress and gift.[93] There are many ancient tribes that take goat as their totem: Primitive Gui Fang Shi (鬼方氏) and the ancestor of Qiang ethnic minority (羌族) take goat as their indigenous totem; Gong Shi (共工氏) uses goat as its quasi-indigenous maternal totem; and clans of Yan Emperor (炎帝族) and Zhou (周族) take goat as their quasi-indigenous maternal totem as well.[94] All in all, the custom of taking goat as totem has a deep and wide influence on the life of ancient people. From this, it appears that the interpretation of '美' by Xu Shen and some others is merely a subjective supposition taken for granted.

Besides, the adoption of Chinese characters in cultural classics of the pre-Qin period (先秦) usually proves whether the interpretation

---

[91] Duan Yucai, *Exegesis on the Origin of Chinese Characters*, 146.
[92] Li Zehou (李泽厚) and Liu Gangji (刘纲纪), ed. *History of Chinese Esthetics* (《中国美学史》) vol. 1 (Beijing: China Social Sciences Press, 1984), 79–81.
[93] Yu Xingwu, 'The Interpretation of Qiang, Gou, Jing, Mei' (《释羌、苟、敬、美》), *Social Science Journal of Jilin University* (《吉林大学社会科学学报》) 1, (1963).
[94] Gong Weiying (龚维英), *Outline of Primitive Worship* (《原始崇拜纲要》) (Beijing: Chinese Folk Literature and Art Publishing House [中国民间文艺出版社], 1989), 6, 10, 28, 42.

is the truth or fallacy. But we cannot lay too much emphasis on prudence when verifying the initial formation or connotation of Chinese characters through cases of ancient prose: Some case cannot be rashly viewed as the outset of explicating the function of character form if it is not in many respects proved that it reflects the initial connotation of Chinese characters. Likewise, it can neither be rashly denied that character form does not work on the function of the formation when a case has not been in many respects proved to be entirely out of the early formation of Chinese characters.

In terms of verifying the authenticity of what Chinese characters have experienced, undoubtedly, there exist a variety of drawbacks in the *Origin* by Xu Shen. Xu can neither free himself from personal limitations nor transcend the historical and cultural rules shared by people at that time. He can only be himself, a man who has to be rooted in the given history, and, too, the *Origin* can only be itself, manifesting the meaning and function of Chinese characters on a particular individual–historical level.

The Deviation and Integration between the Meaning and Form of Chinese Characters[95]

Owning to the deep-rooted concept that 'the Chinese character is ideographic with its form', the traditional philology regards the unity of form and meaning as an inviolable principle in studying characters and ancient documentary language. On the one hand, it provides studies on Chinese philology and linguistics with solid foundation and unique features, but, on the other hand, it also restricts the theoretical thinking about the ancient philology because of which people cannot deeply ponder over and search for many important phenomena of language and character, thus misunderstanding some basic issues about philology—a situation that has witnessed no radical changes yet. The forms of Chinese characters, indeed, cannot specify the function. From the perspective of interpretation, people are often unable to conduct a correct conversion from the form to meaning of characters when just

---

[95] This article was written together with Chang Sen (常森), originally published in *Language Planning* (《语文建设》) 2 (1994).

scrutinizing those unfamiliar character forms. Besides, the formation and development of Chinese characters increasingly deviate from the principle of unity of form and meaning formed in early times.

According to the extant Chinese character system that is the earliest and most mature, the formation of Chinese characters has followed, consciously or unconsciously, the principle of conveying meaning with the form from the very beginning. But Chinese characters, since their appearance, are unable to shake off the trouble—they cannot overcome the polysemy of various visual images. For example, it is indeed reasonable to interpret '至' (reach) as 'an arrow shooting from afar and falling to the ground'.[96] While in terms of the pattern in the small seal script, there may be relevant experience and background when Xu Shen interprets it as 'a bird flying to the ground from high'.

The fundamental reason for this misinterpretation is not that the configuration of Chinese characters cannot convey the object and information more accurately and exquisitely. In fact, even the highly realistic image of an object cannot always eliminate misinterpretation of the researcher entirely, let alone Chinese characters.[97] Chinese characters are neither possible nor necessary to completely present what to be conveyed; instead, they can only and must generalize certain basic images or emotional characteristics of those objects, which assuredly sharpens the polysemy of Chinese character configuration as a kind of visual image.[98] As a component in the formation of Chinese characters, a square frame can be both viewed as an acre of city and as a piece of farmland, mat or a pigsty—as in characters such as '邑, 囲, 因, 囵'. The character form 孚 in the ancient script can be regarded as

---

[96] Xu Zhongshu (徐中舒), ed., *Oracle Dictionary* (《甲骨文字典》) (Chengdu: Sichuan Dictionary Press [四川辞书出版社], 1989), 1272.

[97] E. H. Gombrich once discussed human's probable misinterpretation of Konoha butterfly and moth, which can be referred to E. H. Gombrich, *The Image and the Eye: Further Studies in the Psychology of Pictorial Representation* (《图像与眼睛：图画再现心理学的再研究》), trans. Fan Jingzhong (范景中), et al. (Hangzhou: Zhejiang Photographic Press [浙江摄影出版社], 1981), 19–20.

[98] Randomness is quite obvious when humans experience the affection or opinion that may be contained in an image, which has been verified by a series of experiments. See Gombrich, *The Image and the Eye*, 195–96.

someone in a posture of holding something in his hand, like in '執', and it can also be viewed as someone in a posture of kneeling and praying, like in '祝'.[99] Related to this, '夙' in the oracle bone script and '扬' in the inscriptions of Ling Ding (Ling Cooking Vessel), on the one hand, can be interpreted as human toiling under the sun or the moon, and, on the other hand, it can be explained as a person worshiping and praying to the sun and the moon.[100] As for the latter, it can be learned from the past. For instance, *The Book of Rites*, vol. 20 (《礼记·祭法》) says that 'the sacrificial livestock is buried … The altar called "Wanggong (Palace)" is for sacrificing the sun and the altar named "Yeming (Bright Night)" is for sacrificing the moon'; *The Book of History*, vol. 1:1 (《尚书·尧典》) records 'greeting the morning sun politely' and 'seeing the setting sun respectfully'. The two cases exactly demonstrate that the ancient people often worship and pray to the sun and the moon.

Sometimes during the interpretation of Chinese characters, the polysemy of a character form even presents an opposite understanding of the same form. In terms of daily experience, 'the sun in the grass' (莫), 'the sun above the ground' (旦), 'the sun above the wood' (杲) and 'the sun under the wood' (杳) can be interpreted as the sign of a relevant vision before and after sunrise as well as vision before and after sunset. Generally, people believe that the character form of '朝' in the oracle bronze script resembles the sun and the moon in the grass, manifesting that the morning sun has risen while the waning moon still exists; as for the character '夙', it reflects a human gets up approaching dawn and toils under the moon, which means '早' (early). Obviously, these explanations can only manifest the definition of the formation function made by the known meanings of '朝' and '夙'. In fact, there is a huge gap between the form and the meaning of these two characters. If freed from the shackles of language background and established word meaning, the character form of '朝' in the oracle bone script can be assuredly interpreted that amidst brooding twilight the

---

[99] The two character forms can be seen in AICAS, *A Compilation of the Oracle Bone Script* (《甲骨文编》), vol. 3:11, vol. 1: 5.

[100] '夙' can be seen in AICAS *A Compilation of the Oracle Bone Script*, vol. 7:8; and '扬' in *A Compilation of the Bronze Script* (《金文编》), vol. 12.

setting sun, the crescent moon and the grass set each other off; as for the character form of '夙', it can be explained that under the sky with bright moon after the sun has already set, a man 'does not rest even when it is evening'.[101] According to this, it is the predetermination of meaning that has eliminated the original ambiguities of the character forms, not the character forms themselves. The theoretical study on Chinese characters, obviously, should not avoid the deviation between the meaning and form of Chinese characters, which is more prominent in the following aspects.

1. Phonogram is the main part in Chinese characters. As one of the two elements of character formation, the only effect of phonetic radicals is on phonetic notation, which breaks the principle of unity of form and meaning in the early character formation to a large extent. In the formation of phonogram, the phonetic radical is customary to abandon its original meaning, thus the characteristics in the form not influencing the meaning of the phonetic radical. As for the pictographic radical, the function is mainly on distinction and reference.[102] Therefore, the appearance and development of phonogram has shaken the principle of unity of form and meaning in the early character formation. Since phonetic radicals came into being relatively early, the form, pronunciation and meaning were combined together during the iterative process of reinforcement driven by history. Without the specific functions of Chinese character formation prescribed by those acquired knowledge and experience, an interpreter would have kind of perplexities when studying Chinese characters such as '棚', '㬢', '但': Does the saying that 'phoenix flies after preening' indicate partial meaning of the character '棚'? Do 'the sun in the grass' and 'the sun above the ground' manifest partial meaning of the characters '㬢' and '但'?[103] Likewise, without a wealth of knowledge and experience, people would be also unable to confirm that the connotations of

---

[101] Xu Shen, *Origin*, vol. 7A.
[102] See 'Phonetic Radicals in Phonetic Structure' (《形声结构的声符》) and 'Pictographic Radical in Phonetic Structure' (《形声结构的形符》) that are included in this book.
[103] See '棚', '㬢', '但' in the Xu Shen, *Origin*, vol. 6A, 7B, 8A.

'鴅', '聑' and '聚' are related to birds, ears and people standing together respectively.[104] In this sense, the massive production of phonograms can be viewed as the further deviation between the meaning and form of Chinese characters.

2. Sometimes it is difficult to make clear the reference of so-called traditional associative compounds. A certain component forming the associative compound may not only present partial connotation of the whole character with its own form, but it may also influence the compounding of all character meanings through its extended or borrowed meanings that have a little or no relation with the form. The *Origin* interprets that '"夹" (hold) follows "大" (big) and "侠" contains two "人" (human)', in which the character '大' integrates its own form and meaning into the meaning of 'hold'; the interpretation of '赤' (red) is that 'red is the colour of the South. The character "赤" follows "大" and "火"'.[105] Here, the character '大' integrates its extended meaning into 'the colour of the South'.[106] This situation, undoubtedly, can lead to misinterpretation of relevant characters. Take the character '美' for example, its exact original meaning is whether it is a human wearing a cap decorated with goat-like adornment[107] or a great goat that is delicious?[108] In terms of formation alone, the former explanation is rather reasonable, while the latter is by no means nonsense as well. To sum up, even for the associative compound formed by insisting on the principle of unity of form and meaning, when comprehending it, people obviously feel difficult to make decision only according to the character form, because the distance between form and meaning is various.

3. According to Xu Shen (许慎) and Duan Yucai et al., the connotations of some Chinese characters must be embodied through

---

[104] See Xu Shen, *Origin*, vol. 4A, 4B, 8A.

[105] Xu Shen, *Origin*, vol. 10B.

[106] Duan Yucai (段玉裁), *Exegesis on the Origin of Chinese Characters* (《说文解字注》), vol. 10B.

[107] Yu Xingwu (于省吾), 'The Interpretation of Qiang, Gou, Jing, Mei' (《释羌、苟、敬、美》); Li Zehou (李泽厚) and Liu Gangji (刘纲纪), *History of Chinese Esthetics* (《中国美学史》), 79–81.

[108] See the interpretation of '美' and exegeses of Xu Xuan (徐铉) et al. in the *Origin* (the version of Da Xu) (大徐本), vol. 4A.

particular stokes. Xu Shen interprets '丨' that 'the stroke of "丨" can be either upward or downward. If written from top to bottom, the character is pronounced as "xin (the fourth tone)"; and if the situation is inverse, the pronunciation is "tui (the fourth tone)"'.[109] Duan says, 'the vertical stroke can be written either from top to bottom or from bottom to top; for instance, "至" is written from bottom to top, while "不" from top to bottom and so do "才", "中", "木", "生"'.[110] The former refers to handling brush from top while the latter from bottom—Xu and Duan indicate that different directions when handling a brush can differentiate different meanings. Despite that this possibility may not be entirely excluded in the beginning of character formation, it clearly goes against the principle of unity of form and meaning. That is because that Chinese characters, as a semiotic system of recording language, can often be presented in a static integral form rather than some dynamic process.

4. During character formation, the deviation of the unity of form and meaning also lies in the fact that the same formation often contains different substances. In Chinese characters, the coexistence of two or three identical components always stands for 'polysemy', typically seen in the *Origin*, 'double "夕" (sunset) is "多" (excessive)'. On the basis of this principle invented by Xu Shen, '林' (woods) and '森' (trees) mean a multitude of trees or woods; '晶' (brilliant) indicates many bright stars; '品' (rank) means opinions of the public—instead of a simple addition of double or triple '木' (timber), triple '日' (sun) or triple '口' (mouth). Similarly, '噪' (noisy) indicates that a flock of birds twitter together; '聂' (whisper) means that many people whisper to each other; '羴' (mix) implies that a group of sheep live together... The connotations of the aforementioned characters all exceed the original ones. Nevertheless, Xu Shen explains '廿' (20) as two '十' (10) that are juxtaposed, '卅' (30) as three '十' juxtaposed, and '世' (generation) as three '十' that are juxtaposed and then extended. Similarly, '隻' (one) means holding a bird, '双' (double) means

---

[109] Xu Shen, *Origin*, vol. 1A.
[110] Duan Yucai, *Exegesis on the Origin of Chinese Characters*, 20.

holding two birds, '雔' means a couple of birds; '玨' is two pieces of jade; '秉' indicates taking a stalk of grain in one's hand and '兼' takes two—connotations of the characters mentioned above do not exceed the original ones. One manifestation of the deviation between the meaning and form is that the pattern of character formation is uniform yet the ideographic function different, an in coherence that is perplexing asssssnd incomprehensible. Without knowing the meaning of this kind of characters, we cannot confirm the accurate information conveyed by the coexistence of these components despite our awareness of the connotation of certain individual ones.

Moreover, during the development of Chinese characters in history, the form changes constantly, symbolization enhances and the specific application of characters gradually goes far from the original meaning, thus deepening the deviation between meaning and form. Only then should the interpretation of Chinese characters pursue the ancient form with coined meaning and seek the origin in order to bridge the gap between meaning and form.

That we point out the deviation of the unity principle in character formation does not mean that Chinese characters are in hot water entirely at the very beginning of implying meaning with the form. In some particular period of the occurrence and development of Chinese characters, the function of character formation does not have much uncertainty. But it is noteworthy that the certainty of the function (or connotation) clearly does not lie in the character form itself but the close connection between the signifier (i.e., the character form) and the signified (i.e., the initial meaning or pronunciation of the character). The meaning and pronunciation decide the indicative function of the form, while the form designates and reveals the meaning and pronunciation. The mutual effect between the signifier and signified can surely cover the deviation between the meaning and form of Chinese characters to some extent. From the perspective of the occurrence of characters, the mutual reference and prescription can be reflected only by specific members in society, whereas from the view of the interpretation of characters, the relation between the signifier and signified can be established only through the participation of those specific members. That is beyond the capability of the character form itself. In the first place, the signified that prescribes the function of character form is not self-evident. In the next place, the character form itself can only partially present the coined meaning. Or, the character form approaches the initial meaning rather finitely. Objectively speaking, such a quality of Chinese characters underlines the importance of the interpreter's intervention.

So how does the interpreter intervene with the interpretation of Chinese characters? In other words, by what means should the interpreter bridge the gap between the meaning and form of Chinese characters? Simply based on history, we can find that the interpreter almost 'goes back the starting point from the destination', who can only begin with visual perception of character forms.

It is no doubt that the searching for original meanings of Chinese characters cannot be separated from the perceptions of the visual perceptions associated with Chinese characters. However, people tend to ignore the close relationships between image associations and judgements in many cases. In fact, the information people perceive from character formation is simply what can be inferred and sometimes has no relation at all with the meanings of Chinese characters when they are created. For example, if people assert that the character '不' looks like 'calyx'.[111] Then they will confirm this judgement in every way intentionally, and if they assume that the character '不' resembles seed radicle growing downward to the earth, they also tend to verify and support the perception.[112] In other words, once people make judgements on one character formation, they tend to pay more attention to the formation characteristics which can prove their judgement and ignore the other characteristics that seem irrelevant with their judgement. Based on this, it is no surprise for us to notice that Xu Shen tries to explain the formation of Chinese characters by

---

[111] Guo Moruo (郭沫若), 'A Study of the Oracle Bone Script: Interpretation Comparison', *Complete Works of Guo Moruo: Archaeological Collection*, vol. 1 (Beijing: Science Press, 1982), 53.

[112] Lee Leyi (李乐毅), *Evolution of Chinese Characters: 500 Examples* (Beijing: Beijing Language University Press, 1992), 23.

analysing every human organization from head to toe as well as the rise and fall of *yin* and *yang*, the two opposite energies resided in human body. The reason is that we can extract our human senses as relevant characteristics in Chinese characters to prove our different perceptions about Chinese characters.

The judgement of perceptions on Chinese character formation is subject to both the language background when Chinese characters came into being (there has been great achievements in its critical interpretation of ancient texts and philology in this aspect) and the huge cultural system influencing interpreters. The common natural or social phenomena which people perceive from their experiences in daily life are the most obvious and specific ones. According to the interpretations of Chinese characters in the *Origin*, it can be seen clearly that Xu Shen's analysis of Chinese characters is inevitably influenced by his knowledge gained directly or indirectly from daily experience.

According to Xu Shen, '东 (east), means the movement of sun's rising through trees, and thus symbolizes the position';[113] '西 (west), means where birds' nests position and the sun falls, and thus is the opposite direction of "东"';[114] '南 (south), means where trees flourish'.[115] It is obvious that the daily experiences of the sunrise, sunset, birds nesting and the plants' luxuriant growth affected Xu Shen in his observation of the character formations of 东, 西, 南. When some Chinese characters are placed in several different contexts, deciding the relationship between the perception of character forms and the contexts is more complex. For example, the characters '寸、尺、咫、寻、仞、度', which are related to measurements, can be perceived in at least three different sets. First of all, *'Astronomical Terms'* in *Huainanzi* says that the meanings of characters like '尺、寸、寻' are determined by 'the Way of Heaven'. Second, *'The Classic of Areas Overseas: The East'* in *The Classic of Mountains and Rivers* records that 'the Songhei Mountain in the north stretches from the northeast to the southwest'. Absurd as it is, its experiential meaning is that people are the entities

---

[113] Xu Shen, *Origin*, Ch. 6, Session 1.
[114] Ibid., Ch. 12, Session 1.
[115] Ibid., Ch. 6, Session 1.

for measurements, which explains the relationship between '寸、度' and '又', and '尺', '仞' and '人'. Third, it is common to use human measurements to measure objects. For example, characters meaning measurements in the Zhou Dynasty are all 'based on human body'. Based on this experiential background, we can see that the fundamental reason why '寸, 尺, 咫, 寻, 仞' are similar to '又', '寸', '尸', or '人' is that measurement is originally based on human being's natural attributes. Under these three different backgrounds, drawing on his daily experiences, Xu Shen chooses the last one to explain the cultural sets behind Chinese character formation and points out that 'the measurements in the Zhou Dynasty, 寸, 尺, 咫, 寻, 常, 仞, are all based on the human body'. The form of '尺' 'follows 尸 and 乙'. 'The length of a middle-age female's hand is called one 咫, which is eight times of one 寸';[116] '寸' is 'the length of a hand, and the artery in hand is 寸口, which follows 又 and 一'. 'The length of one's two arms is 寻';[117] '仞, means one 寻 and eight 寸, pronounced as the combination of 人 and 刃'.[118] This choice is also in accordance with the unit and method of measuring length nowadays, such as, '指, 拃, 庹, 拱, 摟, 抱,' etc.

Realistically, 'misperceptions' are inevitable in perceiving Chinese character formations. The information that people extract from character formation and the clues people that gain from experiential knowledge are probably not complete, certain or specific. Therefore, the judgements concluded from the initial combination of the aforementioned cannot necessarily be proved by relevant facts and contexts in which Chinese characters appear. Chinese character formation conjures up multiple visual images, which sometimes connect the same Chinese character forms with multiple backgrounds. If the judgement made by the character forms is false, then fallacy will occur. This happens in the interpretations of the character '东' and '南'. '南' originally refers to a bell-shaped musical instrument made of tiles, and '东', a bag with the rope tied at both ends, which is unknown to Xu Shen. Due to his lack of experiences, Xu Shen thus has no related hints and is unable to make right judgements. In terms

---

[116] Ibid., Ch. 8, Session 2.
[117] Ibid., Ch. 3, Session 2.
[118] Ibid., Ch. 8, Session 1.

of ancient character forms, Xu Shen's explanation of '西' is wrong. However, we are still not certain of the background of the formation in '西' and cannot make further judgements even today. Because of the possibility of 'misconception', interpreters have to find evidence from time to time to correct their misjudgements. When Xu Shen interprets such characters as '寸' and '尺', he has probably been through the process of 'misconception' and 'correction'. The facts in Chinese character studies show that 'misconception and misconception' repeatedly occur even throughout the whole historical process of Chinese character interpretations.

In a word, when looking at Chinese character forms, interpreters can often associate them with different information, and they have to choose one as the interpretation of this word. Both the association and choice of interpreters are in relevance with their pre-knowledge about the possibilities of traditional cultural (including daily experiences) meanings. Without the pre-knowledge, people will not be able to reasonably perceive anything out of Chinese character forms. Certainly people's 'analysis of paragraphs and explanation of characters' do not necessarily start from observing character forms and end with the perceptions of character form references. For a large number of Chinese characters, the interpretation process actually initiates from the fixed character meaning and finishes by clarifying the function of character forms. However, even under this circumstance, interpreters still have to seek for the reasonability in naming and forming Chinese characters. For example, according to the *Origin*, '禾' is 'formed in February and mature in August, symbolizing the harmonious nature';[119] '乙 is similar to the form of 玄';[120] '狗 is called 叩 by Confucius'.[121] All these examples show how the pronunciations of Chinese characters are combined with their formations and meanings based on daily experiences. According to the *Origin*, the character '独' follows 犬 because '犬 likes to fight, and thus is always alone', while '名' follows 命, because 'by calling a name, one can tell the fate'.[122] Therefore, it is common that people tried to find evidence of Chinese character forms in daily life.

---

[119] Ibid., Ch. 7, Session 1.
[120] Ibid., Ch. 12, Session 1.
[121] Ibid., Ch. 10, Session 1.
[122] Ibid.

The discrepancies between Chinese character forms and meanings make Chinese character interpretations inseparable from interpreters' subjective judgements. As a result of its 'intentional violation', this judgement will never go beyond the specified regulations made by traditional cultures on the interpreters, which makes Chinese character interpretations rather complicated and intriguing. On one hand, the discrepancies between Chinese character forms and meaning must rely on interpreters to remove. On the other hand, as an agent between Chinese characters, traditional culture and real life, the interpreter has to involve in various cultural connotations while interpreting. It is this 'involvement' that becomes the key to removing the discrepancies in Chinese character forms and meanings. All of these are our initial conclusions on this issue. It suggests that we must objectively and properly estimate the function of Chinese characters in demonstrating meanings through forms, and make a more scientific and reasonable evaluation of the nature and the relationship between the forms and meanings of Chinese characters.

The Canonization of Confucianism and the Stability of the System of Chinese Characters[123]

The continuity of Chinese civilization is unique in the history of the world civilization development, and the stability of Chinese character system is the important basis to maintain the sustainability of Chinese civilization. The famous scholar Rao Zongyi (饶宗颐) believes that the stability of Chinese characters is 'the most remarkable and least understandable issue', and he calls it 'the "mystery" of the continual use of Chinese character graphs'.[124]

To reveal the reasons for the stability of Chinese character system is an important subject in the study of the history of Chinese civilization,

---

[123] This article was presented at the international symposium of 'Characters and Etiquettes in Asian American Ancient Civilization' (Shanghai, October 2005) held by the University of Bonn in Germany and other universities. Wang Xiaobing (王霄冰) and Dilmurat Omar, eds., *Character, Ceremony and Culture Memory* (Beijing: Nationalities Publishing House, 2007).

[124] Rao Zongyi (饶宗颐), *Symbol, Script and Letter—Chinese Character Tree* (Hong Kong: The Commercial Press, 1998), 174.

especially in Chinese philology, about which many scholars have stated their opinions. We believe that the study in this area can deepened in terms of two stages and three perspectives. The two stages refer to the formation and development of Chinese character system. Specifically, the formation stage of Chinese character system means the development from its emergence to forming a whole system. The selection and use as well as the features and tendencies in Chinese character system ultimately determine the basic status and features of its sophisticated stage. Chinese characters completed this stage at least in the late Yin-Shang period (before and after the 14th century BC). Since then, Chinese characters had stepped into the development stage, in which the Chinese character system continued to improve with no fundamental changes in nature despite a number of adjustments and renovations. This stage lasted from the late Yin-Shang period until now. The three perspectives include the formation and optimization of Chinese character signature system, the relationship between Chinese characters and the Chinese language and the cultural backgrounds in which Chinese characters came into being and developed. Previous research, intentionally or unintentionally, has all been conducted from the three perspectives. However, the focuses are usually different when studying the formation and development of Chinese character system in different stages. For example, in the early stage when Chinese characters came into being, the relationship between the confirmation of Chinese character types and the Chinese character features had always been the centre of research, and in-depth discussions had been made on this;[125] after the Chinese character system became mature, the research on the relationship between Chinese characters and cultural background was more important.[126] In the course of discussing the interaction between Chinese characters and Chinese culture, we have

---

[125] B. A. Easterlin, *The Emergence and Development of Words*, trans. Zuo Shaoxing (左少兴) (Beijing: Peking University Press, 1987), 155–56.

[126] The famous Swedish Sinologist Karlgren believes that Chinese character is the backbone of Chinese culture. China's not abolishing its special character system and maintaining the use of Pinyin is related to its cultural foundation and traditions. This view is endorsed by the British linguist L. R. Palmer. Cf. 'Chapter 6', in *Introduction to Linguistics*, trans. Li Rong (李荣) (Beijing: The Commercial Press, 1983).

realized that the influence of the canonization of Confucianism on the stability of Chinese characters is especially far-reaching.

Confucianism created by Confucius had already been the most influential school of thoughts in the Spring and Autumn period. Emperor Wu of Han Dynasty banned a hundred schools of thoughts, but only allowed the learning of Confucianism, and even set 'Five Classics Doctors', which laid the foundation of the legitimate status of Confucianism in the long history of China. The books written by Confucians, represented by Confucius, were 'canonized', and the comments made on these classics were 'the studies of Confucian classics'.[127] The canonization of Confucianism is not only of great significance in the history of Chinese ancient thoughts and academics but also has profound influence on Chinese characters for their long stability after the clerical and regular scripts.

The Canonization of Confucianism Established the Sacred Status of Chinese Characters

The canonization of Confucianism ensured the sacred status of 'Six Classics' established in the cultural contexts of the Western Zhou and Spring and Autumn periods[128] as well as the sacred status of Chinese characters. After Confucius's modification and teaching, 'Six Classics' gradually became Confucian classics. In the late Spring and Autumn

---

[127] Zhou Yutong (周予同), *Zhou Yutong's Selection of the History of Study of Confucian Classics* (Shanghai: Shanghai People's Publishing House, 1983), 649–61.

[128] The 'Six Classics' refer to the six books filed and spread by Qin Confucianists in the Qin Dynasty, including the *Book of Songs*, the *Book of History*, the *Book of Changes*, the *Book of Rites*, the *Spring and Autumn Annals* and the *Book of Music*. King Wu of the Han Dynasty set 'Doctors of Five Classics', excluding the *Book of Music*. In the late Han Dynasty, the 'Seven Classics' appeared by including the *Analects*; the Tang Dynasty then established 'Nine Classics', dividing the *Book of Rites* into the *Rites of Zhou*, *Etiquettes and Ceremonies*, the *Analects*, the *Book of Fidelity*, and including *Gongyang* and *Guliang*; the 'Thirteen Classics' in the Song Dynasty refers to the *Book of Songs*, the *Book of History*, the *Book of Changes* 'the three books of Rites', 'the three commentaries' and the added *Analects*, *Book of Fidelity*, *Mencius* and *Er Ya*.

period, Confucius inherited the cultural heritage of the Western Zhou Dynasty by taking the conservative attitude of 'teaching but not creating' the cultural heritage while reinterpreting and making proper improvements to make the cultural essence of the Western Zhou Dynasty 'lasting eternally'.[129] As the founder of Confucianism, Confucius

> on the one hand, considers his thoughts as Confucianism because of his loyalty towards the Western Zhou system, and on the other hand, criticizes the formalization of Confucianism. Therefore, taking problem setting and solving as the absolute standard, he also adopted systematical moral values without being confined to the Western Zhou ancient concepts.[130]

Confucianism was inherited and developed into Confucianism by Confucius's disciples and 'was divided into eight sections' in the late Spring and Autumn period, forming different branches.[131] However, during the Spring and Autumn era, with hundreds of schools emerging, Confucianism was on the same status of a noted school of thought as Mohism. The established Qin Dynasty had no respect for Confucianism, and advocated 'morality by law' and 'teaching by officials', which eventually led to the 'burning of books and burying of Confucian scholars'.[132] In the reigns of Wen and Jing of the Han Dynasty, the emperors adored the studies of Emperor Huang and Laozi, and paid no attention to Confucianism. Not until Emperor Wu of Han Dynasty abolished the hundred schools of thoughts did Confucianism obtain its exclusive status.

> Emperor Wu created the position of Doctors of Five Classics, recruited disciples, set branches and advocated related careers in the court. This lasted more than one hundred years, attracting an

---

[129] Feng Youlan (冯友兰), *A Short History of Chinese Philosophy* (Beijing: Peking University Press, 1996), 43.

[130] Hou Wailu (候外庐), *A General History of Chinese Thoughts*, vol. 1 (Beijing: The Joint Publishing Press, 1951), 125.

[131] 'Famous Doctrines' in *Han Feizi*.

[132] 'The First Emperor of the Qin Dynasty' in *Records of the Historian*.

increasing number of disciples and making Confucian classics studied by millions of students and taught by thousands of scholars. However, the only purpose of doing these is to achieve fame and fortune.[133]

In the Eastern Han period, there were more 30,000 students studying Confucianism. Meanwhile, the number of scholars teaching Confucianism was so large that some of them even had more than 10,000 disciples.[134] It was precisely after the emperor of Han Dynasty when Confucianism was defined as the national school of thoughts and studying Confucianism became the way of pursuing social status and wealth that the canonization of Confucianism was completed. Since the Han Dynasty, despite the huge changes in Chinese society and the adjustments in the concepts of Confucianism, its sacred status has never been shaken.

During the period when Confucian classics were established as the 'Six Classics', from the Western Zhou to Spring and Autumn period, Chinese characters rapidly developed and gradually improved. In the reign of Emperor Wu of the Han Dynasty, Chinese characters entered the mature stage of the clerical script. From then on, with the establishment of the sacred status of Confucian classics, the Chinese characters that recorded them also became stabilized and official. Although the studies of classics varied from age to age, Confucian scholars were all very cautious with the Confucian texts and dared not make any changes. To avoid mistakes which might happen in passing down the texts, the officials even took a series of measures. For example, Cai Yong (The Eastern Han Dynasty, 175 BC) engraved the classics on stones and put the stones outside for copying, known as, 'Xi Ping Stone Classic'. After that, the tradition of engraving texts on stones became a tradition. In the Zheng Shi period of the Kingdom of Wei (240–248), the King's Academy in Luoyang set up 'the stone classics in three forms' of the ancient script, the large seal script and the

---

[133] 'Biographies of Confucians' in the *History of the Han Dynasty*.
[134] 'Biographies of Mou Chang and Cai Xuan' in the *History of the Post-Han Dynasty*.

clerical script. In the second year of Kaicheng of the Tang Dynasty, the Imperial Academy corrected the classics and engraved the 'Tang stone classics'. In addition, the Post-Shu Kingdom engraved the 'Shu stone classics' (also called 'Guangzheng stone classics'). The Northern Song Dynasty made the 'imperial academy stone classics', and the Southern Song Dynasty completed 'Shaoxing imperial stone classics'. The trends and traditions of engraving classis on the stones by all the dynasties have ensured the accuracy of the texts, and have continuously guaranteed the stability of Chinese characters.

After the paper-making technology was invented in the Western Han Dynasty and improved by Cai Lunin the Eastern Han Dynasty, it gradually became popular, which promoted renovation in choosing Chinese character writing materials and contributed to the spread of classics. Furthermore, the printing, which was invented in the Shui Dynasty and flourished in Tang Dynasty, offered better conditions for the dissemination of classics.[135] In the period of the Five Dynasties and the Post-Tang Dynasty, the Imperial College was asked to engrave *Nine Classics*, which were widely spread to the public. During the Song Dynasties, the copies of classical works annotated by the Confucianists in the Han Dynasties, the Kingdom of Wei and the Six Dynasties were widely circulated, and the Imperial College also printed a large number of Confucian classics as textbooks. The invention of papermaking and printing not only provided technical supports for spreading the classics but also ensured no alterations of the texts in their copying and dissemination, and therefore strengthened the stability of Chinese character forms.

The Canonization of Confucianism Promoted the Establishment of 'Xiao Xue' (Chinese Philology) and the Standardization of Chinese Characters

The establishment of the traditional studies of the Chinese language and characters—'xiao xue' (Chinese philology)—is the result of the development in Confucian classics. After Confucianism reached its

---

[135] Pan Jixing (潘吉星), *The Four Great Inventions of Ancient China: Origin, Development and Impact on the world* (Hefei: University of Science and Technology of China Press, 2002).

'exclusive' status, the teaching of Confucian classics flourished in the period. In particular, Dong Zhongshu's 'study of the Gongyang version of the *Spring and Autumn Annals*' became a hit of the whole country. The classics thoughts at that time were written in the clerical script, namely, the modern script. In the late Western Han Dynasty, Emperor Cheng and Ai (32 BC–1 BC) were summoning the public to submit posthumous classics. Liu Xiang and his son Liu Xin took charge of proofreading the classics and they discovered the 'classics in ancient script'. Liu Xin compared classics written in the ancient script with that in the modern script 'to examine whether it is original or simplified, authentic or adapted', and he criticized the Confucian classics written in the modern script as 'simplified intentionally and deviated from the original meaning due to lack of thought and careful study'.[136] Scholars of Confucian classics in the modern script retorted upon the criticism, and they resulted in the debate on the modern and ancient scripts in Confucian classics, which had a far-reaching effect on both the study of Confucian classics and the development of Chinese philology. Modern writers refuted Liu Xin's criticism, and thus caused the debate on the studies of contemporary and ancient Confucian classics. This debate exerted profound influence on the development of the study of Confucian classics and Chinese philology.

The debate was mainly caused by textual differences. Scholars of the modern script disagreed to the texts in the ancient script in that 'they purposefully made the text impossible to understand as a way of showing off',[137] while the scholars of the ancient script refuted that their counterparts 'tried to avoid the complexity of the texts and interpreted them in a simple way without careful thinking', and 'they were confined in their own knowledge, and gave up the unseen, and eventually made a fool of themselves'.[138] The differences in the texts and language were the fundamental issue in the argument of the ancient and contemporary Confucian classics, and were commonly emphasized by emperors, Confucionists and scholars of Chinese philology. For

---

[136] 'Biography of Liu Xin' in the *History of the Han Dynasty*.
[137] Xu Shen (许慎), 'Preface', *Origin of Chinese Characters* (Beijing: Zhonghua Book Company, 1963).
[138] 'Literary Biographies' in the *History of the Han Dynasty*.

example, 'In the Yuanshi period (1–5 AD), hundreds of scholars, who were good at Chinese philology, were ordered to write in the court, and Yang Xiong chose those capable to compose *Xun Zhuan* as a sequel to *Changzhe*'.[139] 'In the Jianchu period (76–84 AD), scholars convened at Baihu Temple to discuss in detail the similarities and differences of the texts, which went on for consecutive months'.[140] These activities in large scale and influence contributed to the study of the language and characters and the emergence of Chinese philology whose main contents were the interpretations of Chinese characters in the ancient books. The classical scholars have made great contributions to Chinese philology, and most of such scholars in the two Han Dynasties were scholars of classics in the ancient script. As Wang Guowei said,

> It is well understood that most of the scholars of Chinese philology in the two Han dynasties are all in a family of studying the ancient script. The reason is that Confucian classics are mostly written in the ancient script and the interpretations must rely on Chinese philology. The character variants provide abundant resources for Chinese philology, and therefore have trained most of the Chinese philologists.[141]

The Chinese philology in the two Han Dynasties mainly serve for the study of Confucian classics. For instance, Xu Shen, known as 'the one and only master of Five Classics' completed the *Origin* which laid the foundation for Chinese philology, 'providing basis for the annotations and interpretations of the Six Classics',[142] with strong practicality and pertinence.

The traditional 'Chinese philology' that developed in the context of Confucian debate had long kept its traditions and were attachments

---

[139] Ibid.
[140] 'Biographies of Mou Chang and Cai Xuan' in the *History of the Post-Han Dynast*.
[141] Wang Guowei (王国维), *Collected Works of Guantang*, vol. 7 (Beijing: Zhonghua Book Company, 1959), 330.
[142] Xu Chong (许冲) (The Eastern Han Dynasty), 'Comment on the *Origin of Chinese Characters*', *The Origin of Chinese Characters* (Beijing: Zhonghua Book Company, 1963), 320.

of the Confucian classics. With revisions of Confucian classics, the roles of 'Chinese philology' in restricting and regulating language and characters have also been continuously strengthened. This regulation was especially clear in the Tang Dynasty. For example, in the early Zhenguan period of the Tang Dynasty, Yan Shigu was ordered to review the scripts in the Five Classics, who compiled the authorized *Five Classics for* the public, and then he compiled the *Yan's Scripts* as a model of written scripts. Yan Yuansun compiled *Ganlu Script Samples* to serve those who sought a career in the court. Zhang Can wrote the book *Scripts in Five Classics to avoid* 'the total disappearance of the basic scripts of the Five Classics'.[143] With the completion of 'Kaicheng stone classics', Tang Xuandu (唐玄度) was summoned to review the scripts of the Nine Classics again and compiled the *New Script Samples of Nine Classics*. Either in the interpretation and modification of classic scripts in the two Han Dynasties, or the learning of the 'script' resulting from the review of classics, or the revitalization of 'Chinese philology' in the Qing Dynasty, or the belief that 'Chinese philology promotes the studies of Confucian classics'.[144] The interdependent relationship between the studies of Confucian classics and 'Chinese philology' has become increasingly solid. The function of traditional 'Chinese philology' is constantly strengthening the stability and standardization of Chinese character system. Over the last two thousand years, there has been little space left for any official recognition for developing new elements in Chinese characters.

The Inclusion of Confucian Classics into the Imperial Examinations Strengthened the Stability of Chinese Character System

China's imperial examination system appeared in the Sui Dynasty and developed into a relatively complete official-selecting system. It lasted until the early 20th century. The Confucian classics have always

---

[143] Zhang Shen (张参) (Tang Dynasty), 'Preface', in *Characters in the Five Classics*.

[144] Wang Niansun (王念孙) (Qing Dynasty), 'Preface', *Annotations of the Origin of Chinese Characters*.

been a crucial part of the imperial examinations, making an education model for more than 1,300 years and revering Confucius as 'The Sage Master'. Although, since the Han Dynasty advocated Confucianism, a good command of Confucian classics became a means for scholars to seek for fame and fortune, the implementation of the imperial examinations made respecting Confucius and studying Confucianism the only choice for all scholars to pursue an official career. The subject of 'Mingjing' (understanding of the Confucian classics) was already set in the Southern Dynasty to open the door to people of ordinary families to take the official career. In the Tang Dynasty, not only did 'Mingjing' include the topics of Tiejing (贴经) and Moyi (墨义) but 'Jinshi' (进士) also included Tiejing. Zhu Xi in the Southern Song Dynasty developed neo-Confucianism into perfect academic system, and annotated the 'Four Books'—*Great Learning*, *Doctrine of the Mean*, *Analects* and *Menicius*). Neo-Confucianism then gradually became the basis for the imperial examinations. Since King Renzong of the Yuan Dynasty (1313) specified the 'Four Books' and the annotations made by Zhu Xias the standards, both Ming and Qing Dynasties had inherited this system and specified the use of the 'eight-part essay' (a literary composition prescribed for the imperial civil service examinations, known for its rigidity of form and poverty of ideas). As a result, scholars paid all of their attention to the 'Four Books' and Five Classics—*Book of Songs*, *Book of History*, *Book of Changes*, *Book of Rites*, and *Spring and Autumn Annals*)', limited themselves to the formality of the 'eight-part essay' and dared not to make any changes. As the problems existing in the imperial examination system became increasingly prominent, the system finally came to an end.

The long practice of the imperial examination system directly affected the development of education. The direct relationship between the study of Confucian classics and personal career ensured Confucian classics a supreme status. The respect for Confucian classics and requirement for standardizing the use of Chinese characters directly served for the imperial examination service, and indirectly had a great impact on the stability of the Chinese character system. *Ganlu Zishu* (《干禄字书》), compiled by Yan Yuansun in the Tang Dynasty, provided the official candidates with references for the standard use of Chinese characters. The study of the 'model of written characters' formed by collating Confucian classics which fully developed in the Qing Dynasty intensified the stability and standardization of characters written in Confucian classics. From the Sui and Tang Dynasties to the beginning of the 20th century (1905), the long practice of imperial examination system not only guaranteed the leading and stable role of Confucian classics in education but also ensured that 'Chinese philology', the traditional language and character study was inseparable from Confucianism. The combined influence of the two also kept the initial status of the canonization of Confucianism in the early stage without big changes.

As can be seen from the three aspects discussed, canonization of Confucianism and its long-standing central status in ancient China also made Chinese characters that record such classics privileged with the holy aura and long stability.

With the dissemination of Confucianism to the surrounding countries of China, Chinese characters were also adopted in Japan and Korea. Vietnam even named Chinese characters as 'Confucian Words'. All of these have also become a positive factor in maintaining the stability of Chinese character system. The closely interdependent relationship between Confucian classics and Chinese characters has even resulted in an extreme claim made by Qian Xuantong (钱玄同), the advocate of the 'New Cultural Movement', that 'to abolish Confucianism, Chinese characters must be abolished in the first place'.[145]

---

[145] Qian Xuantong, 'Future Problems of Chinese Characters', *New Youth 4, no. 2* (1918).

Part III

Norm and Research

CHAPTER 5

The Normalization of Chinese Characters and Philological Life

The Adjustment of Language Policies, Antiquity Worshipping and Philistinism[1]

These years have witnessed a phenomenon that people tend to use Chinese characters freely, which arises attentions of people from all the fields, including some people in the linguistic field who have expressed their opinions towards this. The irregular use of Chinese characters is mainly manifested in two aspects. The first aspect is the irregular use of the traditional Chinese characters that have already been simplified. The traditional Chinese characters used to be the regular characters in old times until the emergence of the simplified Chinese characters. Since the simplified Chinese characters have taken place to be the regular ones, the use of the traditional Chinese characters shows evidence that some people 'adore the ancient style'.[2] Dai Zhaoming (戴昭铭) made an analysis in his article 'On the Appreciation of Traditional

---
[1] See *Journal of Anhui University* (《安徽大学学报》).
[2] See Lu Shuxiang (吕叔湘), 'Within Forty Years' (《语文建设》), *Language Planning* 8 (1991).

Characters and the Legislation of Characters' (《繁体风、'识繁写简' 和语文立法问题》) about the 'adoration of the ancient style'.³ The second aspect of the inappropriate use of Chinese characters is to abuse irregular simplified Chinese characters. Those irregular simplified Chinese characters are called 'suti' (俗体), also called 'suzi' (俗字) or 'sutizi' (俗体字). The popular use of 'suzi' shows the tendency to 'seek philistinism' in the use of Chinese characters. We believe that the present 'adoration of the ancient style' and 'seeking philistinism' is a pair of complementary contradictions—a testimony to the rules of the development of the Chinese characters. We should analyse and study this pair of contradictions on the basis of the history of the development and use of the Chinese characters, and move forward to the issue of forming and adjusting policies about Chinese language.

It has been about 5,000 years since the Chinese characters have formed. Dating back to the systematic oracle bone script (inscriptions on bones or tortoise shells of the Shang Dynasty), the Chinese characters have enjoyed 3,300 years of development.⁴ Such a long history has always seen the contradictions between the regular characters, the traditional ones and the irregular ones. The conflict between the 'adoration of the ancient style' and 'seeking philistinism' brings up the issue of how to protect the position of regular characters.

The 'standardization of characters' (书同文), which took place in the late period of Western Zhou Dynasty and the time when Emperor Qin Shihuang reunified China, is the earliest record about this issue. The first 'standardization of characters' implemented in the late period of the Western Zhou Dynasty could only be traced in 'The Doctrine of the Mean' in the *Book of Rites* (《礼记·中庸》) and 'Ministers' in *Guanzi* (《管子·群臣》) by the general descriptions without details. However, it can be inferred undoubtedly that people had realized that the standardization and regularity of characters should be an important aspect of national 'rites and laws' (礼仪法度). We once inferred that the first

---

³ See Dai Zhaoming (戴昭铭), 'On the Appreciation of Traditional Characters and the Legislation of Characters' (《语言文字应用》), *Applied Linguistics* 1 (1992).

⁴ See Qiu Xigui (裘锡圭), *Essentials of Philology*, vol. 3 (《文字学概要·三》) (Beijing: The Commercial Press, 1988).

'standardization of characters' was influenced by the quick development of Chinese characters at that time. *Shizhoupian* (史籀篇) might be the model for the use of characters due to that event.[5] The second 'standardization of characters' enforced in the period of the Emperor Shihuang's rule could be attributed to both the well-known political factors and social factors, which seemed to be an essential measure at that time. During the Warring States period, it was said that 'the feudal lords governed separately and were not governed by the emperor'. The political cleavages led to the phenomena of increasingly 'different sounds in speech and various forms in characters'.[6] From the aspect of inheritance, the characters in the Qin Dynasty were the models from the Zhou Dynasty and the seal script in the Qin Dynasty was a fruit of the natural development of characters from the period of the Zhou Dynasty to the period of Warring States. The seal script in the Qin Dynasty did not change much in terms of the long existing construction methods and features of the forms of characters. *Cangjiepian*, written by Li Si, was just a work of combing the characters formulated from the period of the Warring Sates to the period of the Qin Dynasty. Although the characters in the six states inherited the ones in the Zhou Dynasty, they developed new elements respectively. Not only did they form distinct styles in different areas but also developed some simplified characters for convenience, some traditional characters with radicals, some variant characters with a transformed structure and radicals and some new forms of characters made by special marks.[7] This gave birth to a large number of irregular characters which were of different forms from those in the Zhou Dynasty. As Qin Shihuang unified China and respected the inherited characters from the Zhou Dynasty, characters at that time became more contradicted with the ones in the six states. Then Qin Shihuang adopted the suggestion of Li Si who proposed 'abolishing the characters different from those of the Qin dynasty'.[8] What Li Si advocated to abolish was the irregular

---

[5] See Huang Dekuan, 'Chapter 1', in *A History of Chinese Philology* (Hefei: Anhui Education Press, 1990).

[6] See Xu Shen, 'Preface to the *Origin of Chinese Characters*'.

[7] See He Linyi (何琳仪), *General Introduction to the Characters in the Warring States Period* (《战国文字通论》) (Beijing: Zhonghua Book Company, 1989).

[8] See Xu Shen, 'Preface to the *Origin of Chinese Characters*'.

characters. The 'standardization of characters' in the Qin Dynasty was to officially use the seal script inherited and then developed from the Zhou Dynasty to set the standards for the characters of the six states.

Characters in the six states were unified and the seal script took the official place and was widely used in stonecutting, eliminating the confrontation of the official characters in the Qin Dynasty and irregular characters in the six states. However, another kinds of characters which had already been born and developed, the clerical script, also a kind of irregular characters, were commonly used in a large area. Unlike official characters, the seal script did not constrain the development of such irregular characters. In the Han Dynasty, the clerical script gained the absolute advantage and took the place of the seal script to become the official characters, whereas the seal script became the traditional ones. During the process when the clerical characters took the place, there was a long existing confrontation between the irregular ones and the traditional ones. The laws said that people who did not write the claim with the official characters would be punished and those who were going to become officials should know both of the traditional and current characters.[9] However, there was a serious phenomenon that people used characters freely.[10] It was recorded that 'even the officials of the same county would use different characters'.[11] There were two events that the emperors asked those experts who were good at the use of characters to comb and classify the characters from the first year of the Emperor Ping Di's rule of the Han Dynasty to the first year of the Emperor An Di's rule of the Han Dynasty.[12] By studying the characters carved on bamboos and the stonecutting in the Han Dynasty, we can clearly know the situation of the irregular characters. After the late period of the Western Han Dynasty, there was a dispute between two groups of people who respectively upheld the traditional characters

---

[9] 'Literary Biographies', in *History of the Han Dynasty* (《汉书·艺文志》).

[10] See Xu Shen, 'Preface to the *Origin of Chinese Characters*'.

[11] 'Biography of Ma Yuan', in *History of the Post-Han Dynasty* (《后汉书·马援传》).

[12] 'Literary Biographies' in *History of the Han Dynasty* (《汉书·艺文志》); 'Biography of Emperor Xiao An', in *History of the Post-Han Dynasty* (《后汉书·孝安帝纪》).

and the simplified characters, showing the confrontation of the clerical script and the traditional characters. The *Origin of Chinese Characters* (The *Origin*) written by Xu Shen explicitly said that the characters were what the ancient people left for the descendants who could also know the ancient things by those characters. It also demanded the respect for the traditional characters.[13] The *Origin* was written with the seal script, the large seal scripts were the irregular ones. It pursued the original forms and meanings of the characters, which was also the typical view of appreciation of the traditional ones held by scholars who studied the classics.

During the periods of the Wei, Jin and Southern and Northern dynasties, Chinese characters experienced a transformation from the clerical ones to the regular script. With some particular political factors, the use of characters had no rules and new irregular characters became popular. *Shang GuJin Wen Zi Biao* (《上<古今文字>表》) by Jiang Shi (江式) of the Northern Wei Dynasty said, 'The characters change as the time changes. There are mistakes in the use of the seal script and the clerical script. Secular studies and shabby research were conducted. Eloquent people could not tell the correct and wrong forms of characters apart'. Yan Zhitui (颜之推) of the Northern Qi Dynasty also said:

> During the late period of the Liang dynasty, there were many variant characters. Xiao Ziyun changed the forms of the characters and Prince Shao Ling pushed forward the non-official characters. People who modeled the characters could not gain benefit but only found that their characters seemed to be weirder…During the wartime of the Northern Qi dynasty, the characters were shabby in forms, coupled with the inventions of new characters by some people in the Yangze River area.[14]

Those records are consistent with the situation of the use of characters reflected in the existing literature. Books of characters at that time, such as *Gujin zigu* (《古今字诂》) by Zhang Yi of the Wei Dynasty,

---

[13] See Xu Shen, 'Preface to the *Origin of Chinese Characters*'.
[14] 'Miscellany', in *Teachings of the Yan Family* (《颜氏家训·杂艺》).

Zi Lin (《字》林) by Lu Chen of the Western Jin Dynasty, *Yu Pian* (《玉篇》) of Prince Gu Ye of the Liang Dynasty, took the *Origin* as the standard, thereby demonstrating an obvious appreciation of the traditional characters. In the fourth year rule of Emperor Dao Wu Di of the Northern Wei Dynasty (401 AD), Confucian disciples were required to comb the characters used in classics. In the second year rule of Emperor Tai Wu Di (425 AD), over 1,000 new characters were released by the emperor and the popular irregular characters were recognized for the first time.[15] However, it did not tackle the problems in terms of using characters for the public at that time.

After the establishment of the Tang Dynasty, there was a series of policies about the characters. Emperor Tai Zong of the Tang Dynasty asked Yan Shigu to correct the wrong characters in classic books and differentiate and analyse the exotic characters, and then issued the characters for enforcement all over the country, thereby marking the beginning of the study of 'Zi Yang' (字样 the forms of characters). Then books with a purpose to tell the variant characters from the official ones came out. The study of 'Zi Yang' contributed to the official place of the regular script and had profound significance for relieving the chaos of using characters after the Wei and Jin dynasties. However, the guiding principle of those events in the Tang Dynasty still appreciated the traditional characters. Many books, such as *Kai Yuan Wen Zi Yin Yi* (《开元文字音义》), *Wu Jing Wen Zi* (《五经文字》) and *Xin Jia Jiu Jing Wen Zi* (《新加九经字样》), *all took* the *Origin, Zi Lin* (《字林》) and *Shi Jing* (《石经》) as the standards to correct the mistakes. This was consistent with the policy made at that time. In the Tang Dynasty, the imperial examinations included the contents of the *Origin* and *Shi Jing*. The officials in the Imperial Academy, the highest educational administration in feudal China, also advocated the contents of the *Origin, Zi Lin* and *Shi Jing*.[16] Such appreciation of traditional characters in the field of correcting the characters in the Tang Dynasty also influenced the books of the Song, Yuan, Ming and Qing dynasties. *Fu GuBian* (《复古编》), by Zhang You (张有), thought that only the

---

[15] 'Biographies of Tai Zu and Shi Zu', in *History of the Wei Dynasty* (《魏书·太祖纪、世祖纪》).

[16] *Datangliudian Libu Kaogongyuanwailang* (《大唐六典·吏部·考功员外郎》); *Xintangshu Baiguanzhi* (《新唐书·百官志》).

characters in the *Origin* were correct and other new characters were the variant ones. He advocated to reserve the traditional characters in the *Origin* and even said, 'One can break his hand but not change his characters'.[17] After Zhang You, there emerged *XuFu GuBian* (《续复古编》), *Zeng Xiu Fu GuBian* (《增修复古编》), *Hou Fu GuBian* (《后复古编》) and *Fu Gu Jiu MiuBian* (《复古纠谬编》), resulting in a wave of using the traditional characters. Its influence remained until the Yuan and Ming dynasties and even the modern times.

Yan Zhitui of the Northern Qi Dynasty felt that it was not practical to 'rely on the seal script and neglect the traditional ones'.[18] Yan Yuansun (颜元孙) of the Tang Dynasty said, 'If we only obey what the *Origin* says, it's difficult to write'. In his book, *Gan Lu Zi Shu* (《干禄字书》), he adopted another measure of correcting the characters. He said, 'Characters should be used with the irregular ones, the commonly used ones and the official ones', showing the range of each set of characters and the attitude of correction respectively.[19] Yan Yuansun's method was very remarkable because it recognized the official place of the standard characters, accepted the position of the commonly used character as a kind of social characters and allowed the irregular characters being used within a certain range. This method did much help to the development of the system of Chinese characters. *Long KanShou Jing* (《龙龛手镜》), *Su Shu Kan Wu* (《俗书刊误》), *Zi Hui* (《字汇》) and *Kang Xi Zi Dian* (《康熙字典》) were all influenced by this method.

After the Tang and Song dynasties, the guiding principle of correcting characters centring on the appreciations of the traditional characters did contribute to the stability of characters in feudal society. However, this stability was just a relative one. The system of characters had some changes over thousands of years. On the one hand, some popular irregular characters came to be the official ones, while some traditional and sophisticated characters were replaced by them. On the other hand, the emerging irregular characters still prevailed

---

[17] Chen Zhensun (陈振孙), *Shuluqijie* (《书录题解》).
[18] Yan Zhitui (颜之推), 'Shuzheng', in *Teachings of the Yan Family* (《颜氏家训·书证》).
[19] Yan Yuansun (颜元孙), 'Preface to Ganluzishu' (《干禄字书·序》).

among the grassroots, such as the folk novels, operas and poems after the Song and Yuan dynasties in which the wide use of irregular characters had been common.[20]

In the early period of the 20th century, with the end of the feudalism, some people with foresight suggested 'adopting the irregular characters' and 'cutting the number of strokes of Chinese characters'.[21] After a long period of discussion, the *Plan of Simplification of Chinese Characters* was released in the 1950s and the *Standard Model for Xingshu Script* was published in the 1970s in Taiwan. Through this, the prevailing irregular characters since the Song and Yuan dynasties were absorbed. Besides, mainland China took the simplified characters as the official ones, while Taiwan recognized the legal place of written simplified characters. After the 20th century, the confrontation between the appreciation of the traditional characters and the tendency to irregularity remained prominent during the discussions on the reform of characters. Nowadays, some issues about the use of characters and some discussions on characters are the reflections of this confrontation in a new period.

It is easy to find that this confrontation exists in the whole period of the development and use of Chinese characters. The focus of the appreciation of the traditional characters and the tendency of irregularity is different in different periods.

The long existence of this confrontation can be attributed to the following factors. It is a long process with slow pace of changes for the formation and development of Chinese characters. As an ancient set of characters, the development of Chinese characters was confined to the inner adjustment and amelioration rather than substantial changes. The inner adjustment of the system of Chinese characters was embodied in two aspects. One is that the shapes of characters tend to be clear and

---

[20] See Li Jiarui and Liufu (李家瑞 and 刘复), eds., *Songyuanyilaisuzipu* (《宋元以来俗字谱》) (Beiping: Institute of Historical Linguistics, National Central Academy, 1930).

[21] See Lu Feikui (陆费逵), *Putong Jiaoyu Ying Caiyong Sutizi* (《普通教育应采用俗体字》), *Journal of Education* (《教育杂志》) (1909); Qian Xuantong (钱玄同), 'Jiansheng Hanzi Bihua Di Tiyi' (《减省汉字笔画底提议》), *New Youth* (《新青年》) 7, no. 3 (1920).

easy to write and remember. The other is that the kinds of structures tend to be unified and easy to be combined to form new ones. From the ancient characters through the clerical script to the regular script, the shapes of Chinese characters also changed from the combination of curling lines to straight strokes. With such changes, the early and ancient shapes of Chinese characters disappeared, while the shapes tended to use more marks. The basic unit, strokes, came out, and there was also the adjustment of the combination of the shapes and strokes. Chinese characters became easier to write after the system of strokes came out and the distinct features of shapes also emerged. However, those changes were just minor adjustments in terms of the shapes rather than the changes that could alter the essential part of Chinese characters. The method of forming shapes of Chinese characters also experienced a process of selection, like the process of the strokes. In the ancient times, the methods were pictographs, simple indicatives, associative compounds, while after the Shang Dynasty, pictophonetic characters became the main method of formation after development. After the clerical script and regular script, pictographs and simple indicatives lost the basic functions of formation. As for the associative compounds, they also changed from the early method centring on shapes such as '步', '保' and '伐' to the abstract method centring on meanings such as '岩', '尖', '歪' and '凭'. After that, the associative compounds only remained with the little function of formation and the pictophonetic characters came to be the only method of the formation of Chinese characters. This shows that the kinds of structures of Chinese characters tend to be plain and unified. With the premise of the stable formation of the structure of characters, the records of phonetics met the needs of the development of a society and the use of the language, contributing to the relative stability of Chinese characters. So, generally, the range of the system of Chinese characters was not expanded.

The long-time stable system of Chinese characters directly influenced the research and studies on Chinese characters in different periods. After the *Origin*, research on characters focused on the origins of the characters and pursued the original meanings of characters. Furthermore, it also became the ultimate goal of the study of characters in China. The traditional approach of studying characters preferred to the exploration of the historic shapes of characters and paid less attention to the current system and situations of characters. This was obviously caused by the long stability of the system of characters. This fact and the basic understanding of the characters by this approach had naturally influenced the teaching of characters. The traditional teaching of characters always tends to give students the inherited experience and knowledge and ask them to accept and follow the existing standard. So it is easy to understand that people have the habits of following the traditional rules while using Chinese characters.

However, the system of Chinese characters was also in development and adjustment. Wang Guowei said, 'If we say the system changes, there seems no big changes; if we say the system has not changed, there seems to be minor and slow paces of changes'.[22] The changes from the seal script through the clerical script and to the regular script show the trails of the development of Chinese characters. Every periodical change was a leapfrog of the shapes of these kinds of characters. The shapes of Chinese characters also changed as the users, culture and regions changed. These kinds of changes would give birth to the irregular characters. The birth and population of those irregular characters broke the traditional rules of characters and proved to be the new elements in the relatively stable system of Chinese characters. During the process of the development of Chinese characters, the irregular ones always confronted with the official ones and then tool placed the official ones. If we analyse the irregular characters recorded in the *Origin*, *Gan Lu Zi Shu* and *Long Kan Shou Jing*, we can find that many of those characters jumped to be the official ones. Considering the history of the development of Chinese characters, this kind of process is the main way through which the irregular ones change their positions. It is common in the development of Chinese characters that those characters pursue the stability within rules and develop by breaking the rules.

There is a pair of basic confrontations between the stability and development of Chinese characters. The confrontations between the

---

[22] Wang Guowei, 'Preface to *Shizhoupian Shuzheng*' (《史籀篇疏证 · 序》); See *Guan Tang Ji Lin*, vol. 5 (《观堂集林》, 卷 5) (Beijing: Zhonghua Book Company, 1959).

official characters and the irregular ones as well as the appreciation of the traditional characters and the tendency of irregularity are reflections of these basic confrontations. Because of the existing rules and traditions, Chinese characters are able to develop without stagnancy, contributing much to the transmission and development of the Han culture. Chinese characters keep meeting the needs of the development of society and the language due to the emerging elements which are born in the existing rules and also make breakouts. The mutual influence of this pair of basic confrontations keeps Chinese characters stable in a volatile situation and enjoys long time vitality.

The confrontations between the appreciation of traditional characters and the tendency to the irregularity can also be attributed to the basic functions of Chinese characters. The functions of Chinese characters mainly include two aspects: the tool of communications and one of the important carriers of history and culture. However, the first aspect is not so much performed as the second one if we study the history. From their inception, Chinese characters were monopolized by the privileged people who remained as the ruling class. Thus, Chinese characters became the tool of recording and transmitting the ideas and values of the ruling class. For example, Confucianism was regarded as the official study after the Han Dynasty and nearly all the intellectuals followed the path of 'reading classics and being officials', which was encouraged by this philosophy of life. The goal of teaching characters was to make students to read the classics and have a good command of the study named 'xiao xue' (小学, Chinese philology), a study of characters. Chinese characters, which record the classics appreciated by Confucianism, were respected as 'the basis of classics and the beginning of governing'.[23] The study of 'xiao xue' was listed as part of the study of Confucian classics. Meanwhile, 'learning the classics by studying the characters and studying the characters by learning the classics' became the basic method of the traditional study of characters.[24] Even the development of the traditional study of characters had a close tie with the development of the study of classics.

---

[23] See Xu Shen, 'Preface to the *Origin of Chinese Characters*'.
[24] See Chen Huan, 'Postscript of *Annotations of the Origin of Chinese Characters*' (《说文解字注 • 跋》).

People's respect towards the classics of Confucianism was expanded to the aspect of Chinese characters that enjoyed a divine place in the intellectuals' mind. So it is natural that people develop an appreciation of the traditions and are confined to the old rules. The essential function of characters should be a tool for communication. The range of the use of Chinese characters was limited in daily communications in history, particularly for the people with poor education and of lower class, who did not have the access to communications with characters. However, once Chinese characters were used in communications by people with some educational background, it would follow the principle of communications and gain progress. Once characters were used by common people rather than only by those people of higher hierarchies, they would unveil their mask and appear to be more practical, and, thus, Chinese characters had the chances to make breakouts. In fact, there were irregular characters in different periods of the development of Chinese characters. Those irregular characters came out as the 'non-elegant' characters among common people in the initial stage, used in the daily communications and cultural exchanges. Because of the social factors and the practical needs of the users, those irregular characters had much space to use and many people welcomed them. Then, the tendency to irregularity naturally came to people's mind during the process of using Chinese characters, and the obsolete and existing rules were abandoned. In this aspect, the confrontation between the appreciation of the traditional characters and the tendency to irregularity should be the inevitable reflection born in the process of communications with Chinese characters. That is to say, this confrontation also embodied the confrontation between people of different cultural backgrounds. In recent years, although the function as a tool of communications has been fully performed, the long existing stereotypes and ideas towards the Chinese characters still have some potential influence on the use and development of Chinese characters.

Although there are some inevitabilities of the existence of this pair of confrontations, there are also some factors related to history, society and cultural background. Every time when a society develops fast and the cultural background changes rapidly, this pair of confrontations would be prominent. The descriptions above have testified this argument. Over the past 30 years, the confrontation has been the reflection of the reform and opening up. Dai Zhaoming has shed some light onto this problem through his analysis of the appreciation of the traditional characters.[25] We believe that this confrontation in this new era is the reflection of the conflicts in the inner system of Chinese characters. Traditional characters are protected by the appreciation of the traditions and they have their own historical and practical bases. As far as the misuse of the traditional characters among people is concerned, it is because the people have no cultural intentions and the misuse is just caused by the group psychology. The combination use of the traditional and simplified characters shows the lack of education among people. Nowadays, the prevailing irregular characters are new to the simplified characters which have the official place. They also form a new pair of confrontations and are the reflection of the long existing ones in the system of Chinese characters.

As for the solution to this long existing confrontation, Dai Zhaoming proposes the idea of 'legislation for the use of characters'.[26] The development of the language and characters is quite complicated and it is not easy to tackle this problem by legislation. We may encounter with many theoretical and practical problems if doing so. On the basis of the analysis and practical use of characters, we believe that we should give priority to adjusting and improving the existing policies of characters and helping those policies to perform the function of guiding the use of the language and characters. The adjustment and improvement of those policies include many parts, especially the following three points.

First, we should make the national standard of Chinese characters more clear. Only with a standard can we use characters properly. The history of the use and development of Chinese characters has shown that the standard of characters is the fruit of development of characters themselves and the influence of people. Although the essence of the standards in different periods is different, it always has a model to follow, the official characters. It is those standards

---

[25] See Dai Zhaoming, 'On the Appreciation of Traditional Characters and the Legislation of Characters' (《繁体风、'识繁写简' 和语文立法问题》).
[26] Ibid.

that have kept the inner order of the use of Chinese characters and the long stability of characters. Now, we should make the national standard of characters more clear by taking the current practice into consideration. The modern simplified characters, as the official ones, have been used for 36 years. However, as a national standard, the *General List of Simplified Chinese Characters* alone is not enough. The national standard should include more contents and should at least make restrictions on the following aspects: (a) The essence and expansion of the conception of 'standard characters'. (b) The detailed standard of the 'standard characters'. (c) The range of the use of the 'standard characters'. (d) The measures of observing the use of the 'standard characters'. (e) To acknowledge and adjust the departments in charge of characters. Now, we have not formed a clear and perfect national standard. First, the conception of the 'standard characters' is not clear. The modern simplified characters are the national 'standard characters', but there is no authoritative and scientific conclusion which clarifies the essence and expansion of this conception. Are the 'standard characters' equal to the 'modern simplified characters'? If the answer is positive, then are the traditional characters not standard characters? In China, traditional characters are allowed to use in a certain range. Are the traditional characters the standard character in this case? We have no clear instructions on those issues. If we say the traditional characters belong to the standard characters in some case but not in other, we cannot convince others. In fact, the modern simplified characters are one kind of the official characters, and the standard characters should contain the official characters. Traditional characters should be classified as the standard characters. Second, the standards of the 'standard characters' should be improved. The *General List of Simplified Chinese Characters*, the *List of Commonly Used Chinese Characters for Publications*, the *List of Modern Commonly Used Chinese Characters* and the *Character Set of Chinese Characters for Information Exchange* are all the national standards. However, those lists have not included all the standard characters and what are the rules for those not included in those lists? Those lists did not answer this question when they were published. The *Rules of the Uses of Pinyin and Chinese Characters for Radios, Films and Television Programs* and the *Rules of the Uses of Pinyin and Chinese Characters in Enterprises, Packs, Brands and Ads* did not give the answer, either. Only the *Rules of Uses of Chinese Characters in Publications* and the *Third Draft of the Consultations* said that the 'standard characters' are the simplified characters included in the *General List of Simplified Chinese Characters* released in October 1986 and the new characters in the *List of Commonly Used Chinese Characters for Publications* in 1965. It also added that those 'having not been simplified characters' in the *Chinese Dictionary* are also 'standard characters'. It seems to be an answer, but it is too ambiguous and difficult to observe the uses of characters in various fields, even in the field of publications. Now, many people misuse and abuse the traditional characters, so where are the standards for the traditional characters? Those documents above did not give the answer. Third, there is no specific range of the uses of 'standard characters'. The existing documents only vaguely draw some lines of the range of some of the characters. The misuses of the traditional characters have a close tie with the vague range of the uses. Chinese characters are used in various fields and we should make a unified and national standard to tackle the urgent problem.

Second, we should make the policies of characters more scientific. By scientifically understanding the rules of the language and characters, we can make the policies more scientific. A scientific and complete police of characters will take more effects in terms of the work of standardization. The formulation of those policies should fully consider the rules of the development of Chinese characters. The future of development, essence, the relationship among the shapes, pronunciations and meanings and the advantages and disadvantages of Chinese characters as well as the position of them in Chinese cultures should all be considered. Our views towards those issues will impact the formulations of the policy. There are some inappropriate parts in the past policies and some extreme opinions. They are caused by the inappropriate views towards those issues. To build a real national standard of characters, we must respect the rules of the development of Chinese characters. For example, when formulating the standards of characters, generally, we should take into consideration the stability of Chinese characters in the long-time development and the outstanding functions of the system of Chinese characters in transmitting Chinese culture. Besides, we should also notice the relations between the irregular characters and the official ones. In the process of standardization, we should also respect the classification of Chinese characters. While keeping the official position of the modern simplified characters, we should carry out some standards for the use of traditional characters, making the standards of Chinese characters consistent with the classifications and the uses of characters. Apart from the official characters, we should also allow the traditional characters performing their functions in some aspects in order to preserve the systems of Chinese characters and cultural traditions. We are supposed to tolerate the situations that the irregular characters could develop within limited ranges for the future development of the Chinese characters. As for the details, while formulating the standards, we should notice the constant adjustment in the inner system of Chinese characters. By doing so, we can provide the standards with enough evidence and also make them to be elastic to adjust the characters for a better development. To make the policies of characters more scientific, we should, on the one hand, strengthen the theoretical research on the basic issues of Chinese characters to unveil the rules of the development of Chinese characters. On the other hand, we should make clear guiding principles of the policies of characters without the interference of one's partial ideas. We should always respect the rules of Chinese characters and the practice of Chinese characters to allow the scientific policies for the direct use of characters. Meanwhile, we should avoid the situations in which those policies may become stiff and obsolete framework and items.

Third, we should improve the ability of self-adjustment of the policies of characters. Language and characters are a dynamic equivalence. So the policies of characters should also be dynamic and equivalent. While adjusting the use of characters, the policies should do self-adjustment according to the development and the changes of the use of characters. This can keep the system of characters staying in the best condition. If the policies lack the ability of self-adjustment, they can hardly keep the pace with the changes in the system of characters and the practical use of the language and characters, and thus cannot perform their functions. Although some people and departments have voiced their ideas and taken some measures to fight against the chaos of the use of characters, the results are not satisfying. It implies that the current policies cannot yet perform their functions. The social and cultural backgrounds of the policies that we made in the 1950s and 1960s are different from those of today. After the cultural revolution and the reform and opening up, in particular, things have changed greatly. In order to keep up with the changes, we held the National Language and Characters Convention in 1986 which released the guidelines and missions of the work of language and characters in a new period and adjusted the previous policies. However, some detailed policies did not come out in time, and the problem of the standards of characters was one of the results of the convention. As for the use of the traditional characters, we should, on the one hand, concede that it is inevitable to use them in some cases. On the other hand, we should axe the advantages of the traditional characters caused by some historical reasons with the methods of making scientific policies, drawing the lines of the ranges of the use and limiting the range and sphere where the traditional characters are used. It will help consolidate the official position of the modern simplified characters. We have no policies on these issues. The related policies in time to face the increasing chaos of the use of traditional characters have not come out, while the released policies cannot perform their functions. It unveils the fact that the ability of self-adjustment of the policies is poor and unable to adjust themselves according to the practical use of the characters. Now, it is urgent to improve the policies and build a set of rules with sufficient scientific and practical bases. While formulating the relevant rules, we should take the ability of self-adjustment into consideration to enable them to provide practical and specific measures, as well as the open and timely adjustments.

The Philological Life Moving Towards Normalization and Vitality

The philological life refers to various applications of words and language by people in a certain society. It depends on not only the levels of application of language and characters of a society and the stage of development of language and civilization but also the political, economic and cultural development. It is thus no easy matter to scientifically estimate the use of characters in a society.

Before we move to the current situation of the philological life in China, we should be specific about the following issues.

First, the normalization of a language is the basis for the assessment of the use of language. Although the use of language could be assessed by various aspects and different criteria, the most typical one is the level of the normalization concerning the use of language. Generally, a complete standard of the use of language would help expand the scale of langue use, enhance the level of regularity and is conducive to the use of language of a society.

Second, assessing the use of language of a society should focus on the main factors. In any society, the use of language covers various and sophisticated aspects. Although the use of language observes the basic laws of a society, there are still some discrepancies between the use of language and the social life because of some factors concerning geography, hierarchy and professions and so on. So it is significant to choose the appropriate aspects to assess. The uses of language concerning official activities of a government, education in schools, radio and television programmes, published books, transmissions of information and public sites can best represent the levels of language use in a society and thus should be given the priority to be assessed.

Third, we should adopt a dynamic view when assessing the social and philological life. Language and characters are a dynamic system, the development of which is influenced by the use and reflected in people's life. The standards and regularity of the use of language are carved with factors of certain times and stability, which means that those standards could only take effect in certain period. Then, it dawns on us that we should probe into the historical and current causes, rather than just adopt the existing principles or make a simple conclusion when assessing the use of language.

Based on that, we believe that the general situation of the use of language in our country is satisfactory and we have made real historical achievements in the language field. Since the establishment of New China, we have formed and released a series of standards and policies concerning the use of language, especially after 1986 when

To speak putonghua, use simplified characters, and *pinyin* has become the mainstream in the language use in China. The various policies and standards of language use made by us have proved to be quite influential in changing the situations of language use in China. This kind of change met with the development of Chinese characters themselves and also met the needs of building modern society, reform and opening up.

The normalization of a language signifies the unity and prosperity of a country and also echoes the development of modernization and political, economic and cultural affairs. So many enthusiastic people have devoted themselves to the reform activities in language field out of their love of China over the past hundreds of years. Yet only in New China could their dream come true and such great achievements in the language field be made.

As we appreciate the situations of language use now, we should also make analysis on the unsatisfying phenomena based on facts. Such analysis does not only have a close tie with the responding measures we are going to carry out but also proves to be an inevitable part in assessing the current situations of language use. In our view, although the irregular use of characters is still serious in the public, it does not affect our basic assessment of the present philological life.

Some phenomena are determined by the cultural diversity and reflect the complexity of language use. For example, speaking putonghua and writing official simplified characters are the mainstream in language use but there still remains the situation where various dialects exist and play their respective roles and the traditional characters are still in use in some regions such as Hong Kong, Taiwan and Macao. This reflects the diverse situation of language use to some extent. Thus, there are some historical and current reasons of using traditional characters and dialects in inappropriate ways.

Some phenomena show the influence that the fast development of culture and economy has imposed on the system of language and characters. The current language use is closely bonded with the development of the society. A society of steady development embraces a relatively slow the National Language Convention was held. Those standards have played a profound role in the current society.

We have expanded the coverage of putonghua or mandarin step by step with a focus. Schools at all levels have enjoyed impressive progress, especially the achievements that elementary schools and middle schools have made during this process. The programmes on air broadcast in putonghua have been a significant push. The National Language Committee adjusted the plans of pushing forward putonghua in 1992 and coordinated with concerning departments to carry out the *Decision on Tests of Putonghua* in order to uplift the work to a new period. The status of putonghua, the legal official language, has thus been elevated. The number of people who can understand and speak putonghua has gained a constant increase. For China, a developing country of a huge population and a large territory, there is a strong divide between areas with different dialects. Against that background, we should be proud of our great achievements.

The release of plans of simplifying characters and corresponding standards has ensured the official status of current Chinese characters. Since 1986, we have conducted work actively in making Chinese characters regular and official. The *List of Common Chinese Characters* and the *List of Chinese Characters in Common Use* and other standards have met the needs of teaching Chinese, publishing and printing and information management. Those standards help move the work of making characters regular forward; besides, the administrative work of the public use of characters have been strengthened. The National Language Committee, with other departments, has issued a series of directions to give the right use of characters, making positive effects in the work of normalization. The current Chinese characters now have been commonly recognized by the international community and become one of the important language characters in the field of international political, economic and academic activities.

The Standards of Pinyin, as the guidebook of *pinyin* which means the symbols of the pronunciations of Chinese, has played an indispensable role in Chinese teaching, pushing forward putonghua, Chinese information processing, news and publishing, literature search and international communications and other fields.

development of language and characters, while a society in transformation or not in order (wartime, for example) or with a fast development of economy and culture imposes huge forces on the language use. This has been proved by the history of the development of Chinese characters. Now, a great number of emerging new words and the introduction of foreign words are apparently the reflection of the reform and opening up and the quick development in the fields of economy and culture. We must admit that during this period, there are not only new elements which can push forward the development of language and characters but also negative factors which will do harm to the sound use of language and characters. There are many negative factors in current language practices, such as fabricating phrases freely, adopting poorly translated foreign words and using foreign words unnecessarily. All of those have weakened the purity and effects of the Chinese language.

Some phenomena emerged due to the relatively low levels of people's basic education. Since China is a large populated country with imbalanced levels of social economy and culture, people's educational backgrounds vary greatly. So it is common that we can easily see some poor language use cases, such as using wrong pronunciations, writing with wrong characters and using words and characters in inappropriate ways. These cases can be attributed to people's lack of basic language knowledge. Some people use traditional characters freely, fabricate words freely and use wrong simplified characters due to their lack of awareness of the importance of language normalization. As for the vulgar use of language and too much use of foreign words, they are caused by people's lower levels of intellectual consciousness and linguistic civility.

In a word, some phenomena in the current language use are inevitable to some extent. As for those phenomena, we should, on the one hand, pay enough attention to the facts of the present philological life, improve people's education and strengthen the application of the standards of language use in order to foster a sound development of language and characters; on the other hand, we should keep improving various standards concerning language and take even greater efforts to prevent the spread of negative factors.

A Few Points of Suggestion on the Normalization of Chinese Characters[27]

When dealing with the issue of the normalization of Chinese characters, we should take the construction and development of Chinese characters into consideration and work in a practical way. The application of Chinese characters has been seen in various fields and people can voice their suggestions and ideas about the plans of simplifying Chinese characters. Thus, those ideas that we would receive may differ greatly. For example, the opinions are quite different centring on the following issues: whether the characters of the same pronunciations in the *Scheme of Simplified Chinese Characters* could be exchanged and restored to their original state, and whether the simplification of Chinese characters can still be continued according to analogy and those existing simplified characters by that analogy should be recognized. It is easy for us to understand such differences.

In my view, we should adapt to the demand of the information age, lay a solid foundation for the future work and avoid any chaos caused by mistakes. First, we should keep the current system of Chinese characters stable. When dealing with the existing simplified characters and characters which could be exchanged between those with the same pronunciations, we should be careful and only make some changes after much thought. Some scholars believe that the first plan of simplifying characters has some deficiencies. For example, some simplified characters and characters which could be exchanged between those with the same pronunciations contradict with the rules of the constructions of Chinese characters and those characters should retain their traditional forms. This kind of opinion makes sense if we just focus on certain characters in terms of their meanings. However, the meanings of the characters were volatile through the history of the development of Chinese characters. The breakouts happened in Chinese characters. The system of Chinese characters can only gain improvement when it makes breakouts in terms of meanings. The phenomena of some simplified characters and characters which

---

[27] See Li Yuming and Fei Jinchan, eds. (李宇明, 费锦昌), *Hanzi Guifan Baijiatan* (《汉字规范百家谈》) (Beijing: The Commercial Press, 2004).

could be exchanged between those with the same pronunciations are not rare in the history of the development of Chinese characters. The transformation into the clerical script is a kind of simplification through breaking out the meanings of characters, while the variation of forms and pronunciations of characters, a unique case, are made through leaving the mistakes alone and making the best use of them. Without those variations and transformations, we could not imagine the existence of the current characters full of vitality through constant improvement. So we should not simply concentrate on the meanings of characters while neglecting the other phenomena in the development of Chinese characters. In this aspect, we should keep stable the existing plans of simplification without making adjustment and changes. The practice and application of Chinese characters also call for us to keep the system of Chinese characters stable. After the spread of the movement of simplifying the Chinese characters, the current simplified characters have been recognized both internationally and domestically. In that case, even a minor change or adjustment will affect the fields of education, journalism and publication, information processing and the use of characters, influencing hundreds of millions of people, and bring unnecessary problems and imbalance of people's mind. Once a rule or standard is established and accepted by the society, it will also frame our work of normalization. We cannot change the existing rules freely. Considering the use of characters in Hong Kong, Macao and Taiwan, I think we should better stop the future work of simplifying the characters. If we simplify some characters which have little values of use, we would enlarge the gap between the levels of using characters, add new problems to the information processing of characters and exchanges and even release a wrong signal that the current characters belong to a system that we can constantly change. These will impose unnecessary negative influence on the work of regularity and normalization.

Second, we should strengthen the research and collection of characters and make new rules and standards which can be applied to different characters. Since Chinese characters are used by people from different fields and in various situations, we should make new standards of characters through research and analysis on characters in order to meet different needs. Generally, the *List of Modern Chinese*

Characters published by the National Language Committee in 1988 can meet the general needs of a society. However, some names of people and regions have very rare characters. Some people's names may contain those characters that are not often seen, and some regions still use their traditional names which may cover some characters out of this list. Some dialects also involve certain characters which are not included in this list. To handle such problems, we should examine those characters and make a list for the use of names of people and regions and characters of dialects particularly. We can also make some restrictions on the names of newly born children in order to decrease the rate of using rare characters as names. Traditional characters still play an important role in publishing the ancient classics and exchanges with the foreign countries. It urges us to publicize a list for traditional characters in order to meet the needs of international coding work of characters as well as make the use of traditional characters with fewer chaos and mistakes. We should try our best to collect traditional characters when combing the systems of them. Besides, we are also supposed to take the use of characters overseas into consideration while respecting the history and reality of the application of Chinese characters. We should seek for common ground while putting aside difference and avoid new chaos. We should make three lists to cover all the characters, one for common characters, one for special characters and one for traditional characters. This can help us to establish the rules for different kinds of characters. We believe that it is a proper choice both in a current stance and a future view to keep the system of Chinese characters stable and also meet the needs for the use of characters.

Last but not least, we should follow the trends of the information age and achieve the 'standardization of characters' (书同文) regarding the use of Chinese characters around the world. With the speed-up of the globalization of information and economy, the return of Hong Kong and Macao and the increase of economic and cultural exchanges between mainland China and Taiwan as well as the situation that China plays a more and more important role in international affairs, Chinese characters have become one of the most important characters in the areas of global politics, economy, science and education, and so on. This also brings changes to the work of normalization of Chinese characters. Against that background, people in the field of language and characters in China will shoulder more responsibilities and take a glorious mission. We should take this opportunity to speed up our work of research on different kinds of characters, carry out the rules of the use of characters and devote ourselves to the overall work. Meanwhile, we should conduct coordinated research with Hong Kong, Macao, Taiwan and other nations in which Chinese characters are used in order to achieve an agreement which all the parties involved can accept, and realize the 'standardization of characters'. To achieve this goal, we should especially keep the current simplified characters stable.

The Present Foundations of and Approaches to the Normalization of Chinese Characters[28]

After initiating the work of formulating the *List of Standard Chinese Characters*, our work has drawn much attention from all fields.[29] I have participated in many panel work and committees and thus have access to many kinds of suggestions and ideas from all parties and groups. I have deepened my understanding about the work. We have a very clear principle regarding the work of formulating this list.[30] People involved in this work are discreet and have done it very carefully. The department of language and characters of the Ministry of Education and other departments have convened four national seminars in order to ensure this list could absorb the professors' opinions and suggestions. Many scholars have published their research papers on this issue,[31] and some

---

[28] See *Applied Linguistics* 4 (2007) (《语言文字应用》).

[29] The *List of Standard Chinese Characters* was started in April 2001 and the panel of this work was established in October 2004. In April 2006, the *List of Standard Chinese Characters* was sent for the permission of publication. Then, panels were asked to revise the edition. Now the *List of Standard Chinese Characters* is about to be finished.

[30] Wang Tiekun (王铁琨), 'Guanyu Guifan Hanzibiao De Yanzhi' (《关于规范汉字表的研制》), *Applied Linguistics* 2 (2004) (《语言文字应用》).

[31] Wang Ning (王宁), 'Lun Hanzi Guifan De Shehuixing He Kexuexing' (《论汉字规范的社会性和科学性》), *China Social Sciences* 3 (2004) (《中国社会科学》); Wang Ning. 'Zailun Hanzi Guifan De Shehuixing He Kexuexing' (《再论汉字规范的社会性和科学性》), *Applied Linguistics* 4 (2006) (《语言文字应用》); Su Peicheng (苏培成), 'Guifan Hanzibiao De Yanzhi' (《规范汉字表的研制》), *Applied Linguistics* 2 (2004) (《语言文字应用》).

of the journals in the field of linguistics have opened special columns to spark discussions.[32]

The work of standardization of Chinese characters is to meet the needs of using characters in a society, featured by making standards and classifying the characters in a certain period. Because of the difference of using characters in different periods, the goals and missions of the standards are also different. On the one hand, the standards of Chinese characters should suit the needs of using characters in a society; on the other hand, we should respect the features of language and characters and the rules of its development in order to avoid discrepancies which are beyond the goals. If we cannot handle this properly, we may go against the rules of the development of language and characters, cause unnecessary chaos and disputes, and bring difficulties to the realization of our goals. We have some successful experience as well as some mistakes in this aspect. After over 30 years' reform and opening up, the social, political, economic and cultural situation have enjoyed impressive changes. Meanwhile, the wide application of information technology has changed the use of characters greatly. Against this backdrop, the new *List of Standard Chinese Characters* has profound and significant meanings. So our work will attract much attention and expectations from the society and international community.

The first issue we encounter when formulating this list is to make clear the conception of 'standard characters'. The second item of *Law of the People's Republic of China on the Standard Spoken and Written Chinese Language* says, 'The standard Chinese spoken and written language refers to putonghua (mandarin) and standard Chinese characters'. The third item says, 'China will push forward the use of putonghua and standard Chinese characters'. The conception of 'standard Chinese characters' is closely tied with the formulation of the *List of Standard Chinese Characters*. There is no such a clear conception to give the extent and expansion of standard Chinese characters which can be accepted widely. Wang Tiekun (王铁琨) once said that the research on 'standard Chinese characters' should pay attention to

---

[32] See *Yuwen Jianshe Tongxun* 12 (2006) (《语文建设通讯》).

four issues, the most important one of which is the 'classifications of Chinese characters'. He said, 'The standard Chinese characters we talk about refer to the modern Chinese characters which are commonly used in mainland China in the occasions of social communications'. 'Modern', 'mainland China' and 'commonly used' are the three important factors which restrict the application of countries (regions), time, fields and occasions, in accord with the current situations of the application of Chinese characters.[33] We think that the new *List of Standard Chinese Characters* should not only consider and be based on the three factors but also take an overall view. It demands that we should take a scientific view in terms of the standardization and development of Chinese characters on a foundation of analysing the history of the application of Chinese characters and the basis of the current situations in a systematic way. Through this, we can make the *List of Standard Chinese Characters* 'coordinate science with social application' and finally become an 'ideal standard of Chinese characters'.[34]

In fact, it is not easy to formulate an 'ideal standard of Chinese characters'. The development and practical application of Chinese characters are complicated, coupled with the large population of the users and the variety of people who are in need of using Chinese characters. An ideal standard can hardly exist because it has to pass the tests and assessment from all groups in different kinds of stances. So we should obey the rules of the construction, application and development of Chinese characters and assess the practical foundation of using Chinese characters.

People with different views will express different ideas. Although we should assess the practical use of Chinese characters within the range of *Law of the People's Republic of China on the Standard Spoken and Written Chinese Language*, we cannot neglect the fact that there is a coexistence of simplified characters and traditional characters if we adopt an overall view. As one of the six working languages, Chinese characters have become the commonly used characters in

---

[33] Wang Tiekun (王铁琨), 'Guanyu Guifan Hanzibiao De Yanzhi' (《关于规范汉字表的研制》).

[34] Wang Ning (王宁), 'Zailun Hanzi Guifan De Shehuixing He Kexuexing'.

Hong Kong, Macao, Taiwan and the world, rather than just in mainland China. Chinese characters are not only used for the 'occasions of modern communications' but also used in the historical texts that we have inherited. So we should not constrain Chinese characters in the range of 'standard Chinese characters' or 'three factors' but take all the parts into consideration and lay a solid foundation. Only by this can we take a discreet view in our work of standardization. Besides, it will also help us to meet the needs of 'pushing forward standard Chinese characters' in mainland China and embody the substantial features of the standard of Chinese characters to the maximum.

The 'coexistence' refers to the phenomena that both traditional characters and simplified characters are used in mainland China and other regions in various fields. This 'coexistence' does not mean that the two kinds of characters are just used without interactions. In fact, in some cases, one kind of characters takes the main place, while the other complements it. In addition, the two kinds of characters may also be used in combination, and when one part is used more often, the other less is used less.

In mainland China, simplified characters, as the legal, official and commonly used characters, are used not only in the fields of education, journalism and publication, public service, information processing and public affairs but also around the world after having been pushed forward by the international communications and Chinese teaching. According to the statistics of *Report on the Uses of Chinese in China* (2005), 95.25 per cent of the people in mainland China write simplified characters and 3.84 per cent of people write both traditional and simplified characters. The most satisfactory fields go to education, journalism and publication which enjoy the highest rate of using simplified characters, higher than the average level across the country. There remain differences in other fields in terms of the rate of using simplified characters. In the field of government, 90.76 per cent of public servants draft with simplified characters, while 0.29 per cent with traditional characters and 6.51 per cent with both. Of the public servants' name cards, 88.35 per cent are written with simplified characters, 7.09 per cent with traditional characters and 4.56 per cent with both. In the field of judiciary, 93.1 per cent of people draft with simplified characters, 0.3 per cent with traditional characters and 5.1 per cent with both. Of the judiciary staff's name cards, 94.6 per cent are written with simplified characters, 2.7 per cent with traditional characters and 2.7 per cent with both.[35] On the Internet, 93.1 per cent of the coding and using of characters are simplified ones, while 3.7 per cent are traditional ones. As for the language and characters in various websites, 96.3 per cent of the contents are written with simplified characters and 3.5 per cent with traditional ones.[36] These statistics show that simplified characters have been commonly used in mainland China and traditional ones are still used due to some people's personal habits. A survey of 2005 covering the newspapers, radio programmes and the Internet shows that among all the 8,218 characters involved, only 361 are traditional ones and 193 are variant characters, accounting for 4.93 per cent and 2.35 per cent, respectively.[37] This indicates that the simplified characters not only have gained the official place but also are used as a habit by most people, holding the absolute advantage in the use of characters.

Traditional characters are still used in some circumstances. According to the seventeenth item of the *Law of the People's Republic of China on the Standard Spoken and Written Chinese Language*, traditional characters and variant characters are used in six circumstances. There is a large number of ancient classics in China, and thus traditional characters still have some opportunities for use in terms of reading, studying and publishing those classics. When editing some important dictionaries, editors tend to include some traditional characters and variant ones. Those dictionaries are also used for reference works, so it is necessary to do so. The mutual transformation between traditional ones and simplified ones are inevitable in information processing considering the increasing exchanges between mainland China with Hong Kong, Macao and Taiwan. Those who are accustomed to simplified characters should also be familiar with traditional ones in

---

[35] See Li Yuming (李宇明), *Zhongguo Yuyan Shenghuo Diaocha Baogao 2005*, vol. 1 (《中国语言生活调查报告2005》) (Beijing: The Commercial Press, 2006), 14, 15, 17.

[36] Ibid.

[37] Ibid.

order to communicate with others. Some typewriting software includes traditional characters which are not included in the *List of Simplified Characters* and the *List of Modern Common Chinese Characters*, resulting in the coexistence of two kinds of characters. In order to meet the needs of the exchange of international Chinese character information, the International Organization for Standardization officially publicized a character set named ISO 10646.1 (GB 13000.1) which includes both traditional characters and simplified characters. Besides, it also contains Japanese and Korean characters, amounting to 20,902 characters. Then we have expanded this set to a larger one with 27,874 characters (GB 18030). The wide application of this set has embodied the contradiction between the 'coexistence' and the standard characters while ensuring effective communications.[38]

Traditional Chinese characters are officially used in Hong Kong, Macao and Taiwan. Taiwan has released the *List of Commonly Used Chinese Characters* and the *List of Less Commonly Used Chinese Characters*, including 15,548 characters in total. With the increasing exchanges of trade and commerce between mainland China and Taiwan as well as the return of Hong Kong and Macao, the mutual influence between the official characters in those areas keep enhancing. On the one hand, mainland China uses more traditional Chinese characters due to the influence of Hong Kong, Macao and Taiwan; on the other hand, more exchanges with mainland China make simplified characters more often used in Hong Kong, Macao and Taiwan.[39] After the prevalence of simplified characters, there has been a coexistence of traditional characters and simplified ones in Hong Kong, Macao and Taiwan.

This 'coexistence' is more frequently seen in a world range in terms of using Chinese characters. With China's status improving and more exchanges between China and other countries, there has been a craze of learning Chinese. Chinese teaching worldwide has been conducted

---

[38] See GuXiaofeng (郭小凤), 'Jisuanji Yingyong Zhong De Hanzi Guifan Wenti' (《计算机应用中的汉字规范问题》); Li Yuming and Fei Jinchan, eds. (李宇明, 费锦昌), *Hanzi Guifan Baijiatan* (《汉字规范百家谈》).

[39] See Li Yuming (李宇明), *Zhongguo Yuyan Shenghuo Diaocha Baogao 2005*, 337.

with both traditional characters and simplified ones. Besides, the use of simplified characters will prevail over the traditional ones.[40] The number of Chinese people who use Chinese characters around the world is huge, and there are 50 million people overseas according to the statistics in 2004.[41] Chinese people who live abroad are accustomed to using characters. However, with the reform and opening up as well as the prosperity of China, coupled with the closer exchanges between overseas Chinese and mainland China and the high birth rate of Chinese or the increasing number of those who have received education in China, their habits of character use are changing. The 'coexistence' shows that not only overseas Chinese tend to use both simplified characters and traditional ones but the status of simplified Chinese characters is also being elevated.

So, generally, this 'coexistence' is undeniably a fact in Chinese character use. It does not only add some difficulties to the exchange of information, the study and the use of Chinese but also contradicts the current status and long history of Chinese and Chinese characters around the world. We should set it an ultimate goal to realize the 'standardization of characters' around the world in Chinese character use. However, due to some social factors and other issues, it is hard to eliminate the 'coexistence' in a short period, which means we have to work more vigorously to achieve our goal.

Any work of standardization of certain characters should be based on a practical foundation in some period, and thus it has some historic features of its time. Such work should follow the rules of the development of languages and characters and meet the needs of social communications. So does the work of standardization of Chinese characters. Emperor Qin Shihuang unified the characters of the six states with the small seal script, while the clerical script was most commonly used at that time among people, resulting in the coexistence of the small seal script and the clerical script. In the Tang Dynasty, Yan Yuansun wrote a book named *Ganluzishu* (《干禄字书》) which adopted the coexistence of three kinds of characters: the

---

[40] Ibid., 243–56.
[41] Ibid., 398–400.

secular ones, the commonly used ones and the official ones, showing a proper attitude of respecting characters and practice. Whether the coexistence of the small seal script and the clerical script or the coexistence of the secular ones, the commonly used ones and the official ones, they all show the differences and discrepancies in the development of Chinese characters. Besides, the inner ties in the coexistence are more than their differences. The differences existing for a certain period of time, did not result in internal chaos/disorder of the Chinese character system. No other than allowing those differences made the Chinese character system reserve some space for the development of new elements. This has helped Chinese characters to remain stable and vital in constant development. However, with the changes of the methods of transmitting information and communications, the standardization of language and characters has been distinct from that of any period in history. So we should pay enough attention to the coexistence of traditional characters and the simplified ones. While formulating the *List of Standard Chinese Characters*, we cannot neglect this problem and its practical foundation and should work carefully to decrease the problem it may bring us to the minimum. If we take a grand and overall view, we should realize that though the standardization of Chinese characterless is applied to the modern and commonly used Chinese characters in mainland China, it also has a close tie with the uses of Chinese characters by people in Hong Kong, Macao, Taiwan and other places around the world. It will also influence the global interaction, international Chinese teaching, the inheritance and development of the long and profound history of China. We should make the guiding principle of our work clear and deal with the problems discreetly.

Not long ago, people's opinions on this issue were various and most of them were about the following issues.

The first one was how to deal with the switch of traditional characters and simplified ones. Some standards, for example, the *List of General Commonly Used Simplified Characters*, have resulted in the problem that one simplified character could be switched to several traditional ones due to the method of transformation between those characters with the same pronunciations. This has always been what the critics frowned on. This problem has become more prominent because of the frequent errors in the process of the switch between the traditional ones and simplified ones. So some people believed that we should take this opportunity of formulating this list to adjust the existing standards and restore some traditional characters, while some held the stance that since the simplified characters had been widely used, there was no such necessity of restoring a small number of characters and might even bring new chaos. The latter part of people insisted that we should keep the current situation stable and tackle the errors during switch process through technological methods.

The second is how to deal with the variant characters. The *First List of Variant Characters* covered some characters which were not strictly variant ones. If we recognized them as variant ones, it would block our understanding and uses of characters. Some characters reserved as official were rare secular characters, while some variant characters regarded obsolete were still used in names of people and regions. Based on that, some people believed that we should analyse the relationships of variant characters again and only eliminate those absolute variant characters. Besides, they suggested that we should restore some seeming variant characters born due to the misuse of their meanings which might have some relationships of inclusion and intersection or because of the misuse of characters with the same pronunciations. Some variant characters used in the names of people and places should also be reserved.

The third one is how to deal with the analogized simplification. The second edition of the *List of General Commonly Used Simplified Characters* includes 132 simplified characters which can be used as radicals and 14 simplified radicals. The list says,

> What the third edition includes contains the simplified characters which are made by the simplified characters and radicals in the second edition. However, the total number of the characters remains the same.... As for the characters not included in the third edition and the simplified characters used as radicals and simplified radicals, they should also be simplified.

This is where the 'analogized simplification' comes from. Such simplification without strict restrictions has brought many problems and chaos.[42] Since the new *List of Standard Chinese Characters* increases the number of characters, it will definitely surpass the number of characters in the *List of Modern Chinese Characters*. As for the characters not included in the *List of Modern Chinese Characters*, some thought we should simplify them all with the analogy method in order to keep the system of Chinese characters stable. While some people said that we should not release those words which did not exist before and were not used in practice based on the premise that those characters were not commonly used, some others were in favour of a compromise and suggested that we should analogize simplified characters discreetly.

Those problems have emerged with the standardization of Chinese characters and can be thought as the reflection of the coexistence of traditional characters and the simplified ones in our work. People's opinions over those issues are quite different. Some people, in a more scientific view, uphold that we should take the opportunity to tackle those problems while formulating new standards, while some scholars focusing on the social factors of the use of characters believe that Chinese characters are just relatively scientific. In their views, we should realize that after their wide application, the simplified characters have formed a new system which can only sustain its stability through further work of simplification. Some scholars raise the assumption of 'classification of Chinese characters' after analysing the fact of the use of characters and the classification of characters in China.[43] The majority think that it is more important to keep the standards of Chinese characters stable and avoid the new disputes

---

[42] Zhang Jing (章琼), 'Hanzi Leitui Jianhua De Kaocha Yu Fenxi' (《汉字类推简化的考察与分析》); Li Guoying (李国英), 'Jianlun Leitui Jianhua' (《简论类推简化》); Li Guanggeng (李先耕), 'Jianhuazi Leitui De Fanwei Wenti' (《简化字类推的范围问题》); see Shi Dingguo, ed. (史定国), *Jianhuazi Yanjiu* (《简化字研究》) (Beijing: The Commercial Press, 2004).

[43] Fei Jinchnag and Xu Lili (费锦昌, 徐莉莉), 'Hanzi Guifan De Huanwei Sikao' (《汉字规范的换位思考》), in *Collected Works for Mr. Zhou Youguan's Anniversary of 100 Years Old*, ed. Wang Tiekun (王铁琨) (Beijing: Yuwen Press, 2007).

and discrepancies due to inappropriate measures. They believe that it would cost much to make some partial and unnecessary changes which might also have negative effects on the standardization of Chinese characters. Those opinions have shown that the solution to the coexistence of traditional characters and the simplified ones is in a dilemma.

Based on that, we believe that the only way that our work of standardization can take is to face the reality, take a foresight, decrease disputes and keep the stability. We should develop an overall view and keep the existing standards of characters stable on the basis of the current practice. Meanwhile, we should try our best not to enlarge the gap between different countries and regions in Chinese character use. Besides, we are supposed to discreetly hear and accept opinions from all walks of life. If we can take an overall view and follow this way, we will have much assurance in handling those disputes while formulating the *List of Standard Chinese Characters*. So we prefer not to change the existing standards of Chinese characters and meanwhile come out with some measures to tackle the aforementioned problems. First, we should resort to technological measures over the issue of 'one simplified character switched to several traditional characters', rather than restore some traditional characters. Second, we should cooperate with scholars and professors in Hong Kong, Macao and Taiwan to formulate the *List of Traditional Characters–Simplified Characters*, and strengthen the coordination with countries where Chinese characters are also used, such as Japan and Korea, on the basis of the practice and the history of characters in order to lay a better foundation for the Chinese character information processing. Third, we should conduct deepened and systematic research over the problems when handling with the variant characters. We are supposed to formulate a *List of Variant Characters* to adjust and decide on the relationships of those variant characters in order to provide evidence for the work of Chinese teaching and handling with those characters. Fourth, while reserving some variant characters which have been used in the names of people and regions, we should draw a clear line to define the range. Fifth, we should define the range of simplification strictly. As for the newly included characters in the *List of Standard Chinese Characters*, we should list the requirement which restrains the analogized simplification. This can help us to analogize some radicals while ensuring that we do not change the original structure of characters and the relations between them. We believe that facing the coexistence of traditional characters and simplified ones, to keep the existing standards of Chinese characters stable, not to widen the differences of using characters and to tackle the problems which are brought by the coexistence are not only practical in but also beneficial for the ultimate solution to the coexistent problem.

CHAPTER 6

The Research of Chinese Characters
Past and Future

The Theory Exploration and System Construction[1]

The traditional study of Chinese philology has always been under the shadow of Xu Shen's *Origin of Chinese Characters*. Chinese philology, despite its long history, still fails to be established as a scientific theoretical system due to the research methods which regard individual characters as objects of analysis and lay particular stress on archaeology, and the research purposes which use philology as the appendages to interpret Confucian classics for practice use. After the late Qing Dynasty, the discovery of the oracle bone script promoted the comprehensive development of the studies of ancient Chinese characters. Influenced by the Western academic culture, a large-scale Chinese character reform movement was germinated. At the same time, the construction of the system of philology and the studies of Chinese characters' basic theory started and scored important results.

---

[1] Originally published in Huang Dekuan, *A History of Chinese Philology* (Hefei: Anhui Education Press, 1990).

The End of Traditional Philology—The Theories of Zhang and Huang

There are two well-known scholars studying ancient philology in modern times, Zhang Binglin (章炳麟), the master of Chinese traditional classics, and his disciple Huang Kan (黄侃). Their studies are related to every aspect of traditional Chinese philology. They not only inherited the fine tradition from textology of the Qing Dynasty, but also acquired great development and achievements. The traditional 'xiao xue' (ancient Chinese philology) was at the peak of its development in the Qing Dynasty. Zhang and Huang, recognized as the top scholars in this field, marked its finality. The development and achievements they made also brought about the rise of modern Chinese philology. When it comes to the theoretical studies of Chinese philology, the theories of Zhang and Huang can never be ignored.

Zhang Binglin (1869–1936 AD), whose alternative name is Jiang (绛), was born in Yuhang, Zhejiang Province. His courtesy name is Meishu, and his pseudonym is Taiyan. His main works on language include *Essentials of Chinese Characters* (《文始》), *New Dialects* (《新方言》), *Questions and Answers on Ancient Chinese Philology* (《小学答问》), related articles in *Assessments of Chinese Cultural Heritage* (《国故论衡》) and so on. Zhang Taiyan once said,

> With little talent, in the time of decline, I am grieved to see the disappearance of ancient meanings of characters and sympathetic with the fact that the common speech is not properly studied. Thus, I wrote *Essentials of Chinese Characters* to explicate the derivations of language and *Questions and Answers on Ancient Chinese Philology* to show the original characters. The book *New Dialects* was written to briefly define the meanings of the local dialects.[2]

While studying philology, Zhang Taiyan equally emphasized the significance of graphemes, phonology and exegesis. He thought,

> Ever since the large seal script, there have been lots of changes and alterations in Chinese characters. Though the six classics

---

[2] Zhang Binglin (章炳麟), 'Brief Introduction of Ancient Chinese Philology', in *Assessments of Chinese Cultural Heritage*, vol. 1 (Chinese Ancient Literature Assembly, 1910).

are remote from now, they can still be understood. Some ancient characters continue to be used by borrowing from their homonyms. Nowadays, errors have been increasing in philology. So to study philology and phonology is like to distinguish color by the eye and turn tuned to the sound by the ear, both of which enhance each other. The study of character forms started with the *Origin of Chinese Characters*. The study of exegesis started with *Er Ya* (《尔雅》). The study of phonology started with *Classified Chinese Rhymes* (《声类》). Any imbalance of the three would lead to failure of ancient Chinese philology.

He then added,

> Those who are in favor of pinyin (phonetic symbols) would suggest eliminating characters; however, if so, the path between writing and speech would be obstructed and the southern Chinese would sound like a foreign tongue. Those who are in favor of characters would suggest abolishing phonology; however, if so, characters would be void of contents and writing and speech would be separated.[3]

Zhang Taiyan had extended the methods of studying Chinese philology in the Qing Dynasty by means of combining form, sound and meaning together. His methods place emphasis on the relations between language and characters, which forms a distinctive feature.

Essentials of Chinese Characters was written to explore the derivation of language. Its 'Preface' says,

> In terms of the origins and sources, dozens of forms may be derived from one form, which, however, cannot reveal the shades of their differences. Despite my ignorance, I have gained some basic knowledge. I pity the predecessors' lack of completeness and grieve for the successors' arrogance. I intend to trace the origins and study their ins and outs. Therefore, I take the independent characters from the Origin of Chinese Characters and call them 'primary characters' (初文); I call their variants, ideographs, simple indicatives, phonetic components with partial pictographic components and homonyms 'sub-primary characters'. Altogether, I include 510 characters with 430 entries. I discuss their categories and compare

---

[3] Ibid.

their pronunciations. When the pronunciation contradicts the meaning, it is called 'transformation'; when the meaning comes from the pronunciation, it is called 'derivation.' After all these, there are altogether 5000 to 6000 characters.

Essentials of Chinese Characters has determined 510 primary characters (including sub-primary characters), and applied 23 categories of ancient vowels that Zhang Taiyan determined and 21 groups of ancient initial consonants to seek meanings by pronunciations and sort out the 'transformation' and 'derivation' of Chinese characters. It has thus established the 'word family' system of the Chinese language. This is the first theoretical and systematic work of etymology in the history of Chinese linguistics. This system is based on the original characters in the *Origin of Chinese Characters* and the classical phonology system built by Zhang Taiyan. Therefore, a large part of this book is about the variation and derivation of Chinese characters, with some research on word origin and word family involved. There are obvious defects in this book, because the 'original characters' were defined only according to the small seal script in the *Origin of Chinese Characters*, the words and characters were mixed, the boundary of transformation and mutual transformation was blurred, and there are still loopholes in Zhang's system of the original pronunciations. However, this study has broken new ground and has established a large system which deserves a good appraisal.

His opinions and theories on philology were well elaborated in *Questions and Answers on Ancient Chinese Philology* and *Brief Introduction to Ancient Chinese Philology* (《小学略说》). Although Zhang Taiyan has few large-volume works in the theoretical study of philology, he refined and developed his ideas from traditional philology. He once stated that the study of Chinese characters should include the studies of forms, sounds and meanings. It is forms that enable characters to be passed down. Speaking of the origin, meanings came first and sounds and forms emerged after them. People who know well about not only forms but also sounds and meanings can be regarded as good at philology.[4] When it comes to the *Six Categories*

---

[4] Zhang Binglin (章炳麟), *Speeches about Chinese Ancient Literature*, Stereotype Edition (Department of Chinese, Nanjing University), 1–4.

of *Chinese Characters* (《六书》), Zhang Taiyan agreed to the idea 'simple indicatives come first' in the *Origin of Chinese Characters*. He also pointed out that simple indicatives were not only characters signifying directions and numbers but also characters revealing their meanings according to additions and deletions of strokes. Simple indicatives can be divided into single (locatives and numerals) and combined ones (characters not related with each other). In his book, *Theory of Synonymous and Borrowing Characters* (《转注假借说》), he also put forward new ideas about synonyms. As erudite as Zhang is, philology is only one subject in his research area. Due to his distrust of inscriptions on the ancient bronze inscriptions and oracle bone script, most of his references were in the small seal script and a few were related to the stone inscriptions, which limits the development of his research. It is a real pity in the history of philology compared with his other research fields.

In 1906, Zhang Taiyan had his article 'On Language and Philology' published, and it indicated that since Xu Shen's *Origin of Chinese Characters*, research had been mainly focused on the forms of characters while phonology and exegesis became subordinate. There were former studies such as *Er Ya, Xiao Er Ya* and *Dialects* (《小尔雅》,《方言》). And further studies which gave priority to exegesis such as *Notes to Nominations* (《释名》) and *Guang Ya* (《广雅》) had no relations to forms. *Notes to Nominations* is specialized in its sound-exegesis. In Li Deng's (李登) *Classified Rhymes,* Wei Zhao's (韦昭) and Sun Yan's (孙炎) fanqie (反切), and Lu Fayan's (陆法言) *Qie Yun* (《切韵》), there are 260 rhymes in total. Today's *Guang Yun* (《广韵》) which is based on *Qie Yun* takes sounds as the primary research object. Exegesis study follows. And there's no specific explanation of forms. The combination of the three kinds of studies can be regarded as the studies of philology. Although this subject called xiao xue (it literally means primary school) surely does not aim at children, it keeps its name from ancient times for convenience. In fact, the accurate name of the subject should be philology.[5]

---

[5] Zhang Jiang (章绛, 章炳麟), 'On Language Philology', *Chinese Quintessence Journal* 2, no. 5 (1906).

Zhang Taiyan was the first person who suggested using the name 'philology' instead of the traditional name of 'xiao xue'. His practices and the suggestion of this name indicate the awareness that philology should be taken as an independent academic subject and that the traditional xiao xue which used to be courses for kids and reference for Confucian classics reached its end. According to this, Zhang Taiyan is not only a pioneer of traditional xiao xue but also the founder of modern Chinese philology.

Huang Kan (1886–1935), whose courtesy name is Jigang and who styled himself as Liangshou Jushi, was born in Qichun, Hubei Province. As a disciple of Zhang Binglin, he specialized in the study of graphemes, phonology and exegesis. Huang Kan became a master by widely absorbing former achievements made in the Qing Dynasty, and inheriting and further developing theories of Zhang Binglin, his mentor. Research done by Zhang Binglin and Huang Kan were highly respected by academia and were known as 'theories of Zhang and Huang'.

Huang Kan's method in researching philology was taught by Zhang Taiyan. He said,

> To explore the development of characters from the perspective of phonology and exegesis, we should start from studying my mentor's work. What was called as sounds by the ancients are in fact composed of vowels and consonants. Neither of them can be studied alone for the reason that vowels and consonants cannot be separated from each other. Exegesis symbolizes the meanings of characters. We cannot read and understand a character without knowing its sound and meaning, and that is why Wang Niansun combined phonology and exegesis together. Form is the shape of a character. The variants of forms are like differences in sounds caused by regions, customs and times, and diverse interpretations of meanings. Combining these three elements together, philology was completed. Hence, from the Ming [D]ynasty to the present, research methods in studying philology started with the unilateral study of sounds. Then it changed into the study of exegesis through sounds and study of philological development through sounds and exegesis. The study of sounds, meanings and forms started from separated analysis and ended up with comprehensive ones.

Thus, the invention of philology and its studying approaches were popularized.⁶

It is the comprehensive approaches to studying forms, sounds and meanings which Huang Kan used to establish his own academic system. He was well versed in the aspect of grapheme, phonology and exegesis. Especially in phonology, he set up a system of ancient sounds, on the basis of former achievements, which made him 'the successor of the ancient phonology of the three hundred years'. In his opinion, philology consists of forms, sounds and meanings. Among them, sounds come first, then meanings, and forms are the last. Because of this, his research started with phonology, and then he studied exegesis and grapheme. Huang Kan had few works published in his life. Those came out after his death include 17 kinds of *Huang Kan's Notes on Study* (《论学杂著》).⁷ In recent years, his nephew Huang Chao (黄焯) helped with the publication of *Notes on Characters, Phonology and Exegesis* (《文字声韵训诂笔记》), *Four Kinds of Notes on the Origin of Chinese Characters* (《说文笺识四种》), *Sound-Exegesis in Er Ya* (《尔雅音训》) *and Notes on Books of Liang Shoulu* (《量守庐群书笺识》).⁸ These works which represent parts of his achievements can help us to know his philological research.

Huang Kan had a lot of innovations in the origin, formation, derivation and variation of Chinese characters and the relations between sounds and meanings. 'On the Times When Characters Rose' (《论文字初起之时代》) records: 'As characters were generated, they must be acknowledged by the public after gradual generalization and

---

⁶ Huang Kan (黄侃), *Notes on Grapheme, Phonology and Exegesis* (Shanghai: Shanghai Classics Publishing House, 1983), 4.

⁷ The original *Special Issue of Mr. Huang Jigang's Posthumous Works* compiled by Literature Series in National Central University. In total, 19 kinds of notes are included. The 'Notes on the *Literature Mind and the Carving of Dragons*' was selected out for single print in the version compiled in 1964, in which the 'Bibliography of Feng Guifen's Explanation of *Origin of Chinese Characters*' was deleted.

⁸ Huang Kan (黄侃), 'Notes on Characters, Phonology and Exegesis', in *Four Kinds of Notes on the Origin of Chinese Characters. Sound-Exegesis in Er Ya* (Shanghai: Shanghai Classics Publishing House, 1983); Huang Kan, *Notes on Books of Liang Shoulu* (Wuhan: Wuhan University Press, 1985).

establishment by usage, which made them used without any obstacles'. In my speculation, characters came into being since remote ancient times and had changed a lot. It is hard for characters to be unified for the areas for their use are different. Since the beginning of the Xia Dynasty after Huangdi replaced Yandi, it was the official historians, such as Shi Zhou (史籀) in the Zhou Dynasty and Li Si (李斯) in the Qin Dynasty, who started to set a standard for characters. In 'On the Orders of Character Creating' (《论文字制造之先后》), there are statements such as: 'there must be half-words existing between language and characters' and 'the order of character creating is language, half-word, character and miscellaneous form'. Articles such as 'On Origin and Order of the Six Categories' (《论六书起源及次第》) and 'On the General Usage of the Regulations in Six Categories among Chinese Characters' besides the *Origin of Chinese Characters* (《论六书条例为中国一切字所循, 不仅施于说文》) elaborate on the six categories' origin, order and their relation with character forms. In 'On Variants and Derivations' (A & B) (《论变易、孳乳二大例》(上下)), which reveals the developing rules of variants and derivations, he wrote:

> There are three categories of variants, including variants with small change in forms, variants with big change in forms but keep their meanings, and those changed in forms which keep their sounds alike but their meanings different. It is difficult to recognize the relation between the third category and their original characters. Compared with this, derivations can also be divided into three categories. The first one is derivations with the same sounds or rise from their original forms. The second one is derivations with different sounds and forms, which can be understood through exegesis. The third one is other various derivations, of which the roots are hard to find.

In brief, 'variants' signify characters with the same sounds and meanings, but in other forms. 'Derivations' signify characters with the same root, but different in both forms and meanings.[9] Works such as *The Relation among Phonology, Philology and Exegesis* (《音韵与

---

[9] The listed papers are in reference to Huang Kan, 'The Brief Introduction of *Origin of Chinese Characters*', in *Huang Kan's Notes on Study*.

文字训诂之关系》), 'Most Similar Chinese Characters Share Same Sounds, Opposite Characters also Rooted in Same Sounds' (《中国文字凡相类者多同音, 其相反相对之字, 亦往往同一音根》), 'Form, Sound and Meaning Are Inseparable' (《形音义三者不可分离》), 'Brief Discussion about Methods of Searching for Original Character Forms' (《略论推寻本字之法》), 'Brief Discussion about Methods of Searching for Language Roots' (《略论推寻语根之法》) and 'Searching for Original Characters' Synonyms with the Same Sounds; (《就初文同声求其同类》), all reflect Huang Kan's understanding of the relations between Chinese characters' forms, sounds and meanings. He inherited and carried forward Zhang Taiyan's appeal of combining characters, phonology and exegesis in the study of philology.[10] Huang Kan also had some original views on the strokes, fonts and handwriting of Chinese characters.[11]

The aforementioned treaties generally reflect Huang Kan's research on philology. We can see the outline of Huang Kan's fundamental system, which combines forms, sounds and meanings together, based on the six categories, and studies characters' changes throughout variants and derivations. Nonetheless, it is a pity that there are no completed treaties of Huang Kan to spread his theories.

One feature of Huang Kan's system of philology is that it is based on the *Origin of Chinese Characters,* in which he had profound research. Most of his views about philology were generated from the *Origin of Chinese Characters.* There are a few of his treaties of research on the *Origin of Chinese Characters.* His article 'On the Origin of Chinese Characters' Basis' (A, B & C) (《论说文所依据》(上、中、下)) indicates: 'You can find proof of every word in the *Origin of Chinese Characters.* Hence, it must go against the

---

[10] The listed papers are in reference to Huang Kan's *Notes on Grapheme, Phonology and Exegesis.*

[11] *The Brief Introduction of Origin of Chinese Characters* includes 'On Classification of Character Forms' and 'On Changes in the Formation of Character Writing'. *Notes on Grapheme, Phonology and Exegesis* includes 'Four Categories of Character Writing', 'Discussion about Formation of Character Writing', 'Three Great Men of Zhang Cao Calligraphy', 'Inscriptions on Ancient Bronze Objects and Bones', 'Changes of Handwriting', etc.

views in other books for a reason'. The article 'On the Philological Scholars from the Han Dynasty to the Song Dynasty' (《论自汉迄宋为说文之学者》) was written to provide an analysis of the *Origin of Chinese Characters*, in order to make clear the source of the current version of the *Origin of Chinese Characters*. 'Common Characters in the Explanation of the *Origin of Chinese Characters*' (《说文说解常用字》) serves as a reference for books of this kind by collecting and organizing common characters in the explanation of the *Origin of Chinese Characters* according to their strokes. The article 'Records of Stresses of Initial Words in the Origin of Chinese Characters' (《说文声母字重音钞》) collects stresses of the phonograms in the *Origin of Chinese Characters* in order and marks characters indicated by other characters in preparation for studies of sound changes.[12] 'Common Characters in Origin of Chinese Characters' (《说文同文》) collects and compares characters with common or similar sounds and meanings in order to reveal the variations and derivations of characters. The *Dictionary of Phonetic Loan Characters* (《字通》) clarifies the interchangeability, origins, variants, vernacular forms and formal forms of characters. It covers the exploration of characters' roots, differentiations of formal and informal forms, and differences in graphemes. 'Duan's Notes of Origin of Chinese Characters' (《说文段注小笺》) discusses and corrects over a thousand of Duan's notes. 'Research on New Appendix' in the *Origin of Chinese Characters*' (《说文新附考》) collects and indicates new appendix Xu Xuan added after proofreading.[13] Articles such as 'Notes on Proofread of Origin of Chinese Characters' (《说文解字斠诠笺识》), 'Supplementary Notes on Origin of Chinese Characters' (《说文外编笺识》) and 'Notes on the Illustration of the *Origin of Chinese Characters*' (《说文释例笺识》) collect notes on the proofreading of the works by Qian Dian (钱坫), Lei Jun (雷浚) and Wang Yun (王筠).[14] *Notes on Grapheme, Phonology and Exegesis* (《文字声韵训诂笔记》) also includes many

---

[12] The listed papers are in reference to Huang Kan's *Other Works of Huang Kan*.

[13] The listed papers are in reference to Huang Kan's *Four Kinds of Notes on Origin of Chinese Characters*.

[14] The listed papers are in reference to Huang Kan's *Notes on Books of Liang Shoulu*.

treaties related to the *Origin of Chinese Characters* such as 'Principles in the *Origin of Chinese Characters*' (《说文纲领》). Huang Kan had studied the *Origin of Chinese Characters* in a systematic way by means of studying the academic source and further research on this book. He devoted himself to his research.[15] The comprehensive and in-depth study of the *Origin of Chinese Characters* is the basis of Huang Kan's research on philology. As for the comment of Zhang and Huang's research on the *Origin of Chinese Characters,* Xu Jialu (许嘉璐) once said: 'There had never been scientific and systematic theoretical elaboration on the *Origin of Chinese Characters* on its value, function and methods from the reigns of Emperor Qianlong and Emperor Jiaqing to the end of the Qing Dynasty. Zhang Binglin (Taiyan) and Huang Kan (Jigang) marked the beginning. They unbounded the research on the *Origin of Chinese Characters* from being the appendages of Confucian classics. Extending from the *Origin of Chinese Characters* to the study of language, they provided a systematic discussion about changes in language, which broke new and broader ground for the research.'

Zhang and Huang are both significant revolutionaries in the history of Chinese linguistics. On the one hand, they inherited, developed and completed traditional philology, and absorbed advantages from it. On the other hand, they made a breakthrough which changed Chinese philology into an independent subject. The contributions they made in the aspects of theory, method and practice laid the foundations for modern Chinese philology. In addition, they also made a huge contribution to education, which has brought up a multitude of academic heirs. Their scholarship is honoured as Zhang Huang School by academia, which shows their status and influence on the study of Chinese philology. Although the theories of Zhang and Huang did not just focus on the study of philology, they were a pioneering work in the theoretical system construction of Chinese philology.[16]

---

[15] Huang Kan, 'Introductory Notes' in *Four Kinds of Notes on Origin of Chinese Characters.*

[16] Xu Jialu (许嘉璐), *The Preface of General Introduction of the Origin of Chinese Characters*, in reference to Lu Zongda (陆宗达), *The General Introduction of Origin of Chinese Characters* (Beijing: Beijing Press, 1981).

Construction of Theoretical System

Since modern times, theoretical research on Chinese philology has stepped up to a new stage of constructing a scientific system. There has been dozens of theoretical treaties on philology published in the last hundred years, most of which focus on establishing theories systematically and scientifically. This phenomenon reflects the development of philological theory. From the perspective of content and framework, these treaties fall into three types: the Comprehensive School, studying forms, sounds and meanings comprehensively from all perspectives; the Form-Meaning School, establishing a system from perspectives of forms and meanings; and the Structure School, focusing on the study of characters' structures. These three schools symbolize the construction and development of Chinese philology's in modern times.

Comprehensive School

Studying Chinese philology from the perspective of forms, sounds and meanings started from the Qing Dynasty, and was spread by Zhang Taiyan. The first philological treatise of this school is the first book in *Textbooks of Chinese Literature* (《中国文学教科书》) written by Liu Shipei (刘师培; 1884–1919). There are 10 books to be compiled in the series *Textbooks of Chinese Literature*. Contents such as philology, character types, syntax, art of composition, text composition, and ancient and modern literary styles and selections are covered in it. There are 36 lessons in the first book, which aims at explaining philology. Liu once said: 'There are three types of philology, which are grapheme, phonology and exegesis. Without philology, forms and sounds of characters cannot be distinguished and exegesis will lack evidence. Then there will be a lot of barriers in writing articles'.[17] The first lesson in this book is 'Philology is the Basis of Writing'. From the second lesson to the fourth lesson, the origins of phonology, exegesis and grapheme are discussed. The

---

[17] Liu Shipei (刘师培), *Textbook of Chinese Literature*, Book 1: *Sequence*, in reference to *Posthumous of Mr. Liu Shenshu*.

fifth lesson is about the analysis of ancient character types (parts of speech). There are illustrations of the six categories from the 6th lesson to the 14th one. The 15th lesson to the 18th lesson discuss changes of fonts, while the 19th lesson to the 30th lesson are related to the study of phonology, including topics such as the overview of phonology, illustrations about alliteration and assonance, illustrations about pronunciations of Confucian classics, the four tones, and a brief introduction to rhymes, letters and equal rhymes. It also includes a discussion about phonetic alphabets and characters with several sounds. The 32nd to 35th lesson studies meanings, which includes illustrations of exegesis in the Zhou, Han and Song Dynasties and examples of exegesis books. The 36th lesson is a brief introduction of the analytical method of character types. In general, this book elaborates on the knowledge in philology, phonology and exegesis from the perspective of forms, sounds and meanings. Parts of grammar knowledge are involved too (for example, in the 5th and 36th lesson). As the first book in the series of *Textbooks of Chinese Literature,* this book is the basic preparation for the study of Chinese literature. That is why the first lesson is 'Philology is the Basis of Writing'. Although not named as 'philology', it provides a brief and comprehensive introduction to traditional philology which makes it undoubtedly the first systematic philology work composed of forms, sounds and meanings. Completed in 1905, this book has obvious transitional features showing that traditional philology was transforming into a modern one.

In 1922, He Zhongying (何仲英) published *New Outline of Chinese Philology* (《新著中国文字学大纲》) (including *Reference Book* (《参考书》)), which is a philology textbook for secondary schools. With accurate and meaningful materials written in the vernacular language, this book not only takes the time but also forms, sounds and meanings into account. There are five parts of this book. The first part is the 'introduction'. The second part is about 'phonology' and is composed of six chapters, including the origin and changes of phonology, theories of vowels and consonants, and fanqie (phonetic indication by way of the pronunciations of two other words). The third part is composed of four chapters about exegesis, including its origin, changes, division and combination, exegesis and overview of exegesis in each dynasty. The fifth part is the epilogue. In the introduction part, the author said:

> Form, sound and meaning is to characters, what vigor, qi and spirit to people. None of them can be ignored. In terms of the structure of characters, meanings come first, sounds come second, followed by forms. In terms of the existence of characters, sounds are inherent in forms while meanings are inherent in sounds, which makes them closely related to each other. All the academic research on the interrelations among the three elements are called philology. Those who studies philology need to give consideration to all of them without any bias.

He also said:

> The comprehensive study of forms, sounds and meanings starts from Dai Zhen (戴震) in the Qing [D]ynasty, and then continued by Qian Daxin (钱大昕), Duan Yucai (段玉裁), Wang Niansun (王念孙), Hao Yixing (郝懿行), Zhu Junsheng (朱骏声) and Zhang Binglin of the present times, who carried forward this quintessence of Chinese culture. Thanks to this, Chinese philology started to become a systematic subject.

In pursuit of systematic approaches and intelligible language in writing this outline, the book was written according to Zhang Taiyan's theories, which are more complete compared with Liu Shipei's.

In 1931, He Kai (贺凯) compiled a philology textbook *Essentials of Chinese Philology* (《中国文字学概要》) for liberal arts students and normal university students. This book consists of five chapters. The first chapter is the 'general introduction', which generally introduces Chinese characters and Chinese philology. The second chapter is 'grapheme', which includes its origin, changes, meanings in the six categories and interchangeability among characters. The third chapter is 'phonology', which consists of the generation, changes, knots, rhymes, fanqie and phonetic alphabets. The fourth chapter, 'exegesis,' is composed of the changes of meaning, reasons and examples. The fifth chapter is the conclusion of this book. The author stated in the first chapter: 'Philology is a subject which focuses on the origin, structure and changes of Chinese characters by taking forms, sounds and meanings as its research objects'. This definition put emphasis on 'origin', 'structure' and 'changes', which is also reflected in the arrangement of contents. Half of the contents are related to this topic. The author also put up the idea of 'the new construction of philology'. He said:

> The philology created by Zhang (Taiyan) is based on the comprehensive study of forms, sounds and meanings. Relations between languages and characters are created by taking phonology as characters' basis. The research objectives of scholars in the Qing [D]ynasty lie in 'understanding the classics,' regarding philology as a tool of reading ancient books. In this way, philology is regarded as 'appendages of Confucian classics.' The new construction of philology we call for now, is the exploration of the contribution of characters' origin, structures and changes made to history, customs and social culture by taking the forms, sounds and meanings of characters as research objects. The research on philology is for the study of characters, rather than understanding ancient books only. Only in this way can we foster and enhance the development of philology!

The author also pointed out in the 'conclusion' that '[t]he study of philology requires historical vision'. All the characters or inscriptions on bones, bronze objects or stones should be involved. Hence, to create new things outside the context of the *Origin of Chinese Characters* and to find its explanations in history are the conditions for being a philology scholar. He also added an appendix about 'oracle bone script' after the chapter of characters' changes. He clarified, 'the discovery of the oracle bone script opened a new era in philology study'. The author is quite insightful in his awareness of the importance of discoveries to the construction of philological system.

Ma Zonghuo's (马宗霍) *Introduction to Philology* (《文字学发凡》) (1935) is a treatise with informative materials, which consists of four volumes. The first volume, the 'introduction,' includes the signification and status of philology, the ups and downs of philology, the order of its study and the research methods. The topic of the second volume is 'grapheme', which includes research on 'the origin of characters', 'the changes of characters' and 'the usage of characters' (the six categories). Introduction to 'ancient sounds', 'modern sounds' and 'equal rhymes' are included in the third volume, 'phonology'. Contents such as 'the origin of meanings', 'analysis of word types' and 'the gist of exegesis' are included in the last volume, 'exegesis'. From Ma's point view, '[p]hilology is the study of forms, sounds and meanings'. He said,

> There are three aspects in philology study. The grapheme shows the differences in strokes and forms. The exegesis indicates differences in meanings. The phonology is used to reveal the differences in sounds. (*Yu Hai* (《玉海》)). Briefly speaking, the three elements are forms, sounds and meanings.[18]

These are the three aspects used in this book for the establishment of systems in 'forms,' 'sounds' and 'meanings.'

The works on philology listed earlier inherited research methods in the Qing Dynasty; put emphasis on the interdependence of forms, sounds and meanings; and created a theoretical system for philology. Although there are differences in depth, scope and emphasis among these works, the fundamental structures of them are similar. It is a great improvement that the links between forms, sounds and meanings were realized instead of being separated studies. However, the system constructed by these works is only a simple mixture of contents from traditional theories of grapheme changes, regulations in the six categories, and phonology and exegesis. They do not reflect the essential connotations of such comprehensive studies of forms, sounds and meanings. If we assume that 'xiao xue' can still represent grapheme, phonology and exegesis, on the contrary, it is hard for the other name, 'philology,' to cover phonology and exegesis. It is not quite precise to equate 'sounds' and 'meanings' with 'phonology' and 'exegesis'. Thus, treaties of the early Comprehensive School did not rid themselves of the restraint of traditional philology and the philological standard in the Qing Dynasty.

The *Brief Introduction of Chinese Philology*[19] written by Zhang Shilu (张世禄) is a book full of creativity which claims comprehensive

---

[18] Ma Zonghuo (马宗霍), introduction to *Introduction to Philology* (Shanghai: The Commercial Press, 1935).

[19] Zhang Shilu (张世禄), *Brief Introduction of Chinese Philology* Guiyang: Wentong Press, 1941).

research on forms, sounds and meanings. This book can be divided into two parts and four chapters. The first part, 'general introduction of Chinese philology' includes two chapters, which are 'explanations of philology' and 'materials and methods for research on Chinese philology'. There are also two chapters in the second part 'fundamental theories of Chinese characters', which are the 'origin of Chinese characters' and the 'structure of Chinese characters'. In regards to the 'range' of philology, Zhang Shilu wrote:

> Why should we combine grapheme, phonology and exegesis together when studying Chinese philology? As mentioned above, characters have two kinds of meanings, which are the forms in written language and sounds in spoken language. The meanings of language is manifested by means of sounds. Since characters can represent for language, sounds and meanings of language are manifested in characters. The tool used to record sounds and meanings is the written form. Hence, the essence of language is always sound and meaning. The forms of characters are different fonts. All characters contains the aspects of forms, sounds and meaning....
> At first, we can infer the original meanings of the characters from the analysis of character forms and investigate whether there are any signs of similarity in sound. Next, the reason why character forms changed can be found out referring to similar relations of their sounds. Then, similarities and differences of forms can be verified according to changes in their meanings or forms. In this way, the mutual exploration between forms, sounds and meanings combines the study of components, exegesis and phonology of Chinese characters together, which forms the complete philology so as to find the secret of Chinese characters.

According to this, Zhang had an advanced view on the comprehensive study of forms, sounds and meanings. Not only did he point out the necessity of connection between forms, sounds and meanings but he also explicated the steps and methods of the mutual exploration according to features of Chinese philology. This book has overcome early Comprehensive School's disadvantages in the simple combination of grapheme, phonology and exegesis, and has established a brand new philological system.

In 'explanations of philology', the first chapter of 'introduction', the author provided a scientific introduction to the 'name', 'range', 'scientific construction', 'aims and methods', and 'functions' of philology. He also claimed that in order to 'establish the science of Chinese philology', apart from the comprehensive research by means of combining forms, sounds and meanings together, there are also several kinds of knowledge needed. For example, knowledge about ancient myths and legends, folklore and psychology, ancient culture, systems and facts, linguistics and dialects, paintings and history of arts, literature, research on calligraphy and its tools, and some supplementary knowledge about archaeology. With the aid of such knowledge, it is possible for Chinese philology to become a real science. The author's consideration is rigorous and insightful.[20] Speaking of 'materials and methods for research on Chinese philology' in chapter two, the author regards the *Origin of Chinese Characters* as one of the primary materials. He also stressed on the value of philology research on the oracle bone script and the inscriptions on the ancient bronze objects and stones. He wrote: 'The discovery of the oracle bone script is significant to the cognition of Chinese character forms in ancient times and the evolution of Chinese characters'. For the discussion about characters' structures, the author pointed out his opinion despite the traditional six categories, 'Chinese characters are idiographic writings in the middle between hieroglyphics and alphabetic writings. But none of the forms, sounds and meanings can be ignored. So the coinage of characters consists of realistic "writing," "symbolization" and "alphabet notation"'. 'Realistic writing' represents for coined signs by using the realistic images of specific objects, such as '日, 月, 山, 水, 雨, 胃, 金 and 齿'. 'Symbolization' represents for the coinage of abstract meanings and method symbols or realistic images, such as '上, 下, 中, 旦 and 甘'. Using realistic images to represent abstract concepts and combinations of realistic images to represent abstract meanings is also a kind of 'symbolization', such as '凶, 大, 高, 鲜, 思 and 妇'. As for 'alphabet notation', it refers to using a part of compound characters composed of some ideographical and some phonetic elements, such

---

[20] The author's original note, 'The Construction of Philology', is in reference to a Japanese writer's book *Studies on Characters*, Part 1, Chapter 1.

as '政, 征, 整, 钩 and 筍', which is one kind of this method. Using the form of one character to represent another character with the same sound is the simple 'alphabet notation' method, for example, using the character '来' as an action and the character '万' as an expression of large quantity. 'Phonetic compound characters' (pictophonetic ones) are composed of realistic images developed from the first two kinds and a phonetic alphabet, such as characters like '江河'. Zhang described the structural system by way of 'realistic writing', 'symbolization' and 'alphabet notation', which is original in research on characters' structures.

Although in Zhang Shilu's *Brief Introduction of Chinese Philology* characters are also studied comprehensively from the aspect of forms, sounds and meanings, it has broken the traditional mode compared with the other Comprehensive School works. This book abandons the method of adding grapheme, phonology and exegesis together, but focuses on the inner relations between forms, sounds and meanings in order to build up a new system. Because of the proficiency of the author in linguistic theories and his clear understanding of characters' properties, features, functions and relations with language, his system has exceeded his predecessors' in the value and scientificity of theory. This book signifies that Comprehensive School finally become independent from traditional philology and has stepped into the constructive stage of scientific philology.

Form-Meaning School

In 1917, philology classes in Peking University were divided into two parts. Qian Xuantong (钱玄同) was the teacher of *Sounds in Philology* (《文字学音篇》), which is equal to the phonology part in the philology system of the early Comprehensive School. He made phonology independent from philology. Zhu Zonglai (朱宗莱) taught *Forms and Meanings in Philology* (《文字学形义篇》), introducing the form, structure and exegesis of characters. This kind of separation generates the system of Form-Meaning School. At the beginning of the 1920s, Shen Jianshi (沈兼士) worked as a teacher at Peking University. His class was a philology course called 'The Study on Form-Meaning of Characters' (《文字形义学》). In the introduction of this course,

Xu Jianshi defined the form-meaning of characters as a subject studying the origins, functions and changes of Chinese characters and clarifying the related common rules. He published 'Research Methods on Forms and Meanings in Philology' (《研究文字学'形'和'义'的几个方法》) in August 1920.[21]

Shen's *Form-Meaning of Characters* are uncompleted teaching materials. His general conception can be seen in its table of contents. The whole teaching materials are divided into Part A and Part B. The 'definition', 'characters' origins, forms and functions' and the four period of form-meaning of characters are included in Part A; Part B includes 'coinage', 'coinage theory focusing on "ancient bronze objects script" and "oracle bone script"', 'exegesis', 'study of national language and dialects', 'evolutional viewpoint of Chinese ancient society on form-meaning of characters' and 'discussion about character forms'. The main content of Part A is the history of exegesis,[22] while the main content of Part B is about structures, forms and exegesis. It can be seen from the 'coinage theory focusing on "ancient bronze objects script" and "oracle bone script"' that Shen had studied character structures by using materials in the ancient characters. His form-meaning of character system includes the historical and theoretical aspects, which focus on grapheme and exegesis. He once said:

> When editing teaching materials, I divided this course into two parts. The first part is the description of historical system. The other part is discussions about theories. With this method, the readers are able to have concepts about the study of the form-meaning of characters before their research on various theories. It seems more systematic and well-founded to study in this way.[23]

The theoretical part of the teaching materials can never be known to us now, for what Shen left to us is an uncompleted system. Shen

---

[21] Shen Jianshi (沈兼士), 'Research Methods on Froms and Meanings in Philology', *Peking University Monthly* 1, no. 8 (2006). This article is included in Shen Jianshi, *Academic Papers of Shen Jianshi* (Beijing: Zhonghua Book Company, 1986).

[22] In fact, it had only been written till the Song Dynasty, 'Part Two of The Revolution: Establishing Period'.

[23] Shen Jianshi (沈兼士), 'Introduction', in *Form-Meaning of Characters*.

Jianshi had done remarkable works on exegesis in philology, and also published significant treaties such as the 'Development, Study and Explanation on the Theory of Phonetic Component on the Right Side in Exegesis' (《右文说在训诂学上之沿革及其推阐》) in which his theories on form-meaning characters are manifested. Yu Xingwu (于省吾) commented, 'Predecessors named discussions about form-meaning characters as philology'. Since Mr. Zhang Binglin changed the name into philology, studies in this field has no longer been an appendage of Confucian classics. It inherited Gu Jiang (顾江) and Dai Duanwang (戴段王)'s theories and sorted out their works. Mr. Shen himself wrote the introduction part. The exploration and explanation in this book became the foundation of language roots and word family study, which made the book orthodox in this area. Mr. Shen explained,

> There are two purposes of my philology study: the study of ideographic characters and phonograms. There are three topics in ideographic characters study, which are character drawing, the unfixed forms, sounds and meanings in the initial stage, and synonyms with different sounds. There are also three topics in phonogram study, which are the study and explanation of the theory of phonetic components on the right side, sound explanations and polyphones. Both of them are basis of the study on Chinese word family. According to himself, that is the synopsis of his works.[24]

The Study of the Form-Meaning of Characters (《文字形义学》) written by Zhou Zhaoyuan (周兆沅) is also divided into two parts.[25] One part of this book is 'chirography' and the other part is 'the theory of form'. This book differs from Shen Jianshi's version in its contents. The author listed and discussed various chirographies in the first part: introduction of the source, its features, and especially the values of the bronze objects and the oracle bone script on the study of seal script origin. He divided the chirography of inscriptions on the bronze objects into the 'pictographic without any united standards', 'maintaining

---

[24] Yu Xingwu (于省吾), *Preface of Essays Wrote in Duan Yan House,* in reference to Shen Jianshi's *Academic Papers of Shen Jianshi.*

[25] Zhou Zhaoyuan (周兆沅), *The Study on Form-Meaning of Characters* (Shanghai: The Commercial Press, 1935).

sounds despite of its forms', 'shifting based on context' and 'borrowing from its synonyms regardless of the differences'. He also classified the chirography of the oracle bone script into 'uncommon characters', 'variants', 'compound characters' and 'phonetic loan characters', and gave illustrations about the four examples. In 'the theory of forms', he elaborated on 'the six categories' and analyzed character structures by illustrations. There is no related introduction of 'meanings' in *The Study on Form-Meaning of Characters*. The inclination that philology is the study of the form-meaning of characters, that is, the study of forms, is shown in the book.

Yang Shuda (杨树达) also wrote a book named *The Study of the Form-Meaning of Characters*,[26] which is divided into 'form' and 'meaning'. 'Form' includes the analysis of characters' structures based on 'the six categories'. It makes 'associative compounds and phonograms', and 'quasi associative compounds' paralleled with 'pictograms, simple indicatives, associative compounds and phonograms'. It collects examples based on further analysis, citing Xu Shen's theory and using inscriptions on bones and bronze objects as a proof, which includes his achievements on ancient characters' study. 'Meaning' is written on the basis of the author's books *Exegesis Syllabus* (《训诂学大纲》) and *History of Exegesis* (《训诂学小史》) in which 'mutually explanatory characters' and 'phonetic loan characters' are included. The length of chapter 'meaning' takes up a small proportion of this book. This book has been revised many times in his teaching and was finalized in the early 1950s. The finalized version was scattered and lost before publication. Yang Shuda was extraordinary in the study of ancient characters. He was also proficient at subjects such as exegesis, grammar and phonology. Thus, his *Study on the Form-Meaning of Characters* not only includes research achievements made by predecessors and excellent scholars at that time but also represent the fruit of the author's hard work on philology, ancient characters, exegesis and phonology. It is recognized as a Form-Meaning School masterpiece with a fine system and great value. The author once commented, 'I spent over ten years doing painstaking work for this book.

---

[26] Yang Shuda (杨树达), *The Study on the Form-Meaning of Characters*. Lithographed Edition (Changsha: Hunan University Press, 1943).

I have confidence that based on this book Chinese philology might become a science.[27]

Gao Heng's *Introduction of Study on the Form-Meaning of Characters* (《文字形义学概论》),[28] published in 1963, is regarded as the closer of the Form-Meaning School. It used to be teaching materials of Gao Heng's course, and was completed after multiple revisions. The whole book is limited within 'discussion about character's forms and meanings, without any involvement in phonology'. The first chapter is a general introduction to concepts in 'philology'. The second chapter is 'legends about the origin of characters', which contains different statements on the origin of Chinese characters in the history of Chinese philology. The third chapter is 'changes of characters' including sources of changes of various fonts. The fourth chapter is 'general study on the six categories', which introduces the name, order and gist of the six categories generally. The fifth chapter is 'character structures', which is based on 'pictograms, indicative characters, associative compound and phonograms'. By means of classification, enumeration, citing from Xu Shen's theory and proof of inscriptions on the bronze objects and bones, this book takes the complex 'compound characters' coined from the four kinds of characters into the same chapter. 'Figures and time recording characters' are listed in one chapter due to their similar properties. All the five chapters stress the study of 'character forms'. The sixth chapter is 'character meaning regulations', which includes 'mutually explanatory characters', 'phonetic loan characters', 'extended meanings', 'stretch characters' and a 'brief introduction to exegesis'. The seventh chapter is the 'other discussion', which discusses 'characters generated from interrelation between forms, sounds and meanings' and 'characters generated from the connection between sound and meaning'. The last two chapters

---

[27] Quoted from Yang Deyu (杨德豫), *Introduction of Study on the Form-Meaning of Characters,* in reference to 'Festschrift of Yang Shuda's One Hundred Year's of Birth,' *Hunan Normal University Journal* (Changsha: Hunan Education Press, 1985).

[28] Gao Heng (高亨), *The Study on the Form-Meaning of Characters* (1963; repr., Jinan: Shandong People's Publishing House; Jinan: Shandong Qilu Press Co. Ltd, 1980).

stress the study of 'character meanings' and relations between characters' sounds and meanings, which takes up a small portion in this book and cannot be completely equal to 'exegesis'.

Compared with the Comprehensive School, the Form-Meaning School seems to have obvious defects in its theory, which is only focused on 'form-meaning' and excludes the 'pronunciation', so it is theoretically vulnerable. However, the emergence of the Form-Meaning School marks the transformation from traditional philology to a scientific philological system. From the perspective of modern linguistics, the phonetic-ideographic aspects of Chinese characters are within the linguistic field, and phonology as well as exegesis are branches of linguistics. Therefore, that philology covers phonology, exegesis and forms is not convincible. The secession of phonology is a progress for a theoretical system of philology. The Form-Meaning School authors put more of their focus on forms (e.g., structure, evolution of forms, etc.), much less on exegesis. They then have consciously avoided the practice of simply replacing the ideograph with the exegesis to investigate the inner relations of 'form, phonology and ideograph' as well as 'phonology and ideograph', which means that this school attempts to efface any trace of traditional philology to make the ideographic research become an organic part of the theoretical system of philology rather than a simple patchwork of forms and exegesis. *The Form-Meaning Study of Characters* by Zhou Zhaoyuan (周兆沅) is by no means about 'ideographs', but should belong to the Structural School in consideration of its contents.

The Structural School

The Structural School constitutes its system by entirely regarding the structural forms of Chinese characters as the objects of its study which excludes not only 'phonology' (about phonetic study) but also 'exegesis' (about ideograph). Representing the mainstream of modern philology, the development of this school can be roughly divided into two periods.

Some works are concentrated on the evolution and structure of Chinese characters' forms such as *On the Vicissitudes of Chinese*

Characters by Lu Simian, *Chinese Philology* by Gu Shi, *Philology ABC* by Hu Puan, *The Origin and Structure of Chinese Characters* by Jiang Shanguo, *Chinese Philology: Forms* by Rong Geng and so forth.[29] These works describe the evolution of Chinese characters by threading together calligraphies such as the oracle bone script, the bronze script, the ancient script, the large seal script, the small seal script, the clerical script, the running script and the cursive script. To analyze the structure, they are methodical and punctilious by following the 'six categories'. For instance, in Gu Shi's book, 'associative compounds' is explained by 'supporting examples' (正例) and 'flexible examples' (变例. The former can be divided into 2 families, 8 genera and 22 species, and the latter consists of 3 families and 6 genera. The works mentioned earlier generally represent the first period of the Structural School that intends to remove 'exegesis' from philology and takes the 'evolution of forms' and the traditional 'six categories' as the basic framework or the origin of Chinese characters. In 1949, *Chinese Philology* by Tang Lan came out, which represented the vital shift of the Structural School and marked the formation of the scientific system of philological theory.

The research of philological theory has fared continuously after the founding of New China owing to works such as *The Structure and Evolution of Chinese Characters* (1959) by Liang Donghan,[30] *Form Study of Chinese Characters* (1959), *Composition and Nature of Chinese Characters* (1960) and *Studies of Chinese Characters* (1987) by Jiang Shanguo. The *Essentials of Philology* by Qiu Xigui published in 1988 represents a newer level of research on philology. A brief introduction to the research of Tang Lan, Jiang Shanguo and Qiu Xigui will be listed further.

---

[29] Lu Simian (吕思勉), *On the Vicissitudes of Chinese characters* (Shanghai: Commercial Press, 1926); Gu shi (顾实), *Chinese Philology* (Shanghai: The Commercial Press, 1926); Hu Puan (胡朴安), *Philology ABC* (Shanghai: World Journal Book Store, 1929); Jiang Shanguo (蒋善国), *The Origin and Structure of Chinese Characters*. (Shanghai: The Commercial Press, 1930); Rong Geng (容庚), *Chinese Philology: Forms*. Lithographic Edition (Beijing: Yenching Institute, 1931).

[30] Liang Donghan (梁东汉), *The Structure and Evolution of Chinese Characters* (Shanghai: Shanghai Education Press, 1965).

By 1934, when Tang worked as a teacher at Peking University, he had finished *An Introduction of Ancient Philology*. This book consists of two parts. The first part is to study philology from the standpoint of ancient philology and the second part is to clarify the methods and rules of studying it.[31] In this book, the author makes a beneficial exploration of the theoretical system of the ancient philology by means of regarding the ancient philology as the most essential part and putting forward the famous 'three categories', that is, 'pictographs, ideographs and pictophonetic characters' (象形、象意和形声文字). The author himself once said:

> The introduction of ancient Chinese characters begins to bridge the gap between philological theory and the study of ancient characters by adding to the vapid philology the characters from Yin-Xu [P]eriod and the ancient scriptures which are a thousand years earlier than *Shi Zhou Pian*, and the number of characters from the Western and Eastern Zhou [D]ynasties, the Six States and the Qin-Han [P]eriod is much more than from *Cang Jie Pian*. Having acquired facts from so many precious materials, I change the traditional theory into a new formation mode of Chinese characters, laying the foundation for new philology.[32]

Then he further developed his philological view in *Chinese Philology* published in 1949 when he completed constructing the theoretical system of scientific philology. The book consists of 'Preface', 'the Creation of Chinese Characters', 'Formation', 'Evolution' and 'Revolution'. Afterwards, Tang summarized the research on modern theory of philology, and pointed out: 'Since the Republic of China, philology, seemingly consisting of form, phonology and ideograph, has only been focused on the form'.

> Philology should not include exegesis and phonology. Although the pronunciation and meaning of a character is relative to the form, in essence, they belong to linguistics. Strictly speaking, the

---

[31] Tang Lan (唐兰), preface to *An Introduction of Ancient Philology*.
[32] Tang Lan (唐兰), *Chinese Philology*, (Shanghai: Shanghai Classics Press, 1979).

meaning of characters is a part of ideograph, and the pronunciation is a part of phonology. Then both ideograph and phonology belong to linguistics.

In this way, philology has turned into the 'philology exclusively about form'. With form as a core, the 'collection of new materials, study of the formation theory and the evolutionary rules of form from ancient times till now in a new method are tasks to be shouldered by future scholars'.[33] *Chinese Philology* is a systematic and innovative book. The 'Preface' generalizes the history, scope and characteristics of Chinese philology. In the second chapter, Tang for the first time criticizes the traditional 'six categories' which has obvious loopholes but is regarded as a guideline throughout many dynasties. 'Hence the boundaries are even more practically unclear'. Then he proposes a new system—'three categories' based on materials about ancient characters to illustrate the construction of characters, which is a breakthrough in the formation mode. In this part, the 'six technologies' (differentiation, extension, loan, derivation, explanation, amplification (縺益) and issues such as 'pictorial writing', 'sign' and 'pinyin (拼音)', which are relative to the theory, are discussed. For the fourth part, he emphasizes the vital influence of subtle variations on form in a dynamic way. Caused by changes of the calligraph in technology, form, habituation, psychology and so forth, the 'evolution' of the forms of characters is given full attention. After the author's consideration of the dynamism of characters, 'evolution' is introduced, making contributions to theory construction. It is valuable in revealing various complex phenomena in Chinese character system. 'Revolution', relative to 'evolution', refers to the dramatic changes in the character system. Tang said, '"evolution" is gradual, and it could cause abrupt and dramatic changes due to certain conditions. That will be explained in the following chapter'.[34] From these aspects, it is possible to understand the important achievements made by *Chinese Philology*, and that this is the most significant book of philological theory. Because of the author's profound theoretical cultivation and solid knowledge

---

[33] Ibid., 6, 9, 25.
[34] Ibid., 116.

of ancient philology, the foundation of his philological system theory is theoretically solid and the system he established has a far-reaching impact on research of philology.

Four influential philological works written by Jiang Shanguo are listed further. *The Origin and Structure of Chinese Characters* is divided into two parts. The first part, 'The Exploration of Primitive Chinese Characters' has four episodes: 'Language, Characters and Faith of Primitive Man in characters', 'Channels of Written Language before the Creation of Characters', 'The Original Pictograph' and 'Changes of Chinese Characters and Ways of Research'. The second part, 'Composition of Chinese Characters,' is centred on 'six categories' to probe into the structure of characters. The author believed,

> [T]he study of Chinese philology never ceases since the Han [D]ynasty but all are deeply affected by Xu Shen; Till now no exploration of the procedure of the creation and reasons for the transformation has been made... Learning from the traces of the European primitive men, we try to investigate the period before the creation of the characters in China and the structure of characters through extensive range of antiquities.[35]

Comparing original materials found by European scholars, he sought for the make-up of characters by the oracle bone script and bronze script, which is a prominent feature.

The Composition and the Nature of Chinese Characters analyzes the composition, evolution and nature of structure on the basis of the traditional 'six categories' to establish a scientific system of philology. The book is divided into two parts: 'Pictographs' (象形文字) and 'Phonetic Characters' (标音文字). In 'Pictographs', he discusses the types, differences, origin, creation methods, evolution, advantages and disadvantages. Moreover, pictographs, simple indicatives and associative compounds in the 'six categories' are involved for a deep analysis. In 'Phonetic Characters' (标音文字), he is focused on the study of phonetic loan characters, explanatory characters and pictophonetic

---

[35] Jiang Shanguo (蒋善国), preface to *The Origin and Structure of Chinese Characters* (Shanghai: The Commercial Press, 1930).

characters. The author clarifies the naming and the definition, the nature and the affects, causes of occurrence, relations between their referred objects and traces of development, and components of the pictophonetic characters. He also makes an in-depth analysis of phonetic and ideographic components. On the nature of Chinese characters, the author ponders, 'After the rise of the clerical script, the pictographs, indicatives and associative compounds lost their vitality gradually, while phonetic loan characters, mutually explanatory characters and pictophonetic characters increasingly developed. So characters became ideographic-cum-phonetic rather than pictographic-cum-ideographic'. After pointing out the defects of the semantic and phonetic, and the components of pictophonetic characters, the author advocates 'the abolition of pictophonetic characters and popularization of pure pinyin'.[36]

Chinese Character Morphology follows the evolution of Chinese characters as its clue. The author defines the period from the Yin-Zhou Dynasty to the Qin Dynasty as the 'ancient character era', and from the Han dynasty till now as the 'modern era'. Ancient characters are pictographic-cum-ideographic, while the modern ones are ideographic-cum-phonetic. The late period of the Qin Dynasty is a turning point when the clerical script functions as a transitional form. The 'ancient characters era' is divided into 'the large seal script times' (including the oracle bone script, bronze script, lithoglyphic script 石鼓文 and cursed script (诅楚文), the large seal script and the ancient script) and 'the small seal script times'; the 'transitional times' is focused on the ancient clerical script and its rise; the 'modern era' tells the origin and characteristics of the clerical script, the Han script (真书), cursive script, running script and simplified Chinese characters and so forth. In this book, the rise of clerical script is deeply investigated, and many new ideas are included, such as the transformation from the seal script to the small clerical script by erroneous transformation (讹变), abrupt transforming (突变), omitting transformation (省变) and simplifying (简变). During the rise of the seal script, 61 types of Glyph Differentiations and 89 types of Mixed Components were concluded. The influence of the rise of the seal script on the ideographic

---

[36] Jiang Shanguo (蒋善国), *The Composition and the Nature of Chinese Characters* (Beijing: Character Reform Press, 1960), 33, 296.

Chinese characters and the great role played by it on the change of Chinese ideograph were revealed as never before. Through systematic investigation, he generally draws eight conclusions of the evolution of Chinese characters: (a) the Chinese characters are gradually created by the mass, not by a person or an era alone; (b) the calligraphy develops gradually and not abruptly in any period of history; (c) the obsolete and the innovative characters overlap or are parallel during different periods; (d) Chinese characters vary from the realistic pictographs into signs or strokes, that is, ideographic characters become indirect rather than direct; (e) the change of form and the rule of writing gain the upper hand; (f) the evolution of Chinese characters functions as simplification; (g) the tendency of the developmental Chinese characters is from solitude to unification; and (h) innovative characters appear and spread among the people, and later gradually get legal status by replacing the obsolete ones.[37]

Jiang's new *Philology*, a summing-up, is based upon his decades of research on the structure of Chinese characters and rules of developing to explore the scientific system of philology. The book consists of 'Introduction', 'Origin of Chinese Characters', 'Characteristics of Chinese Characters', 'Creative Types of Chinese Characters' and 'Development of Chinese Characters'. In 'Origin of Chinese Characters', Jiang brings 'rope knotting' (结绳), 'carved contact' (刻契), 'pictorial writing' and 'formation of pictographs' into the overall historical process so as to analyze and absorb the latest archaeological discoveries of the origin of Chinese characters. 'Characteristics of Chinese Characters' gives a detailed introduction to the characteristics of calligraph, the form, phonology, ideograph and other aspects. He analyzes four types of structure (i.e., pictograph, indicatives, associative compounds and especially pictophonetic characters) in 'Creative Types of Chinese Characters'. In 'Characteristics of Chinese Characters', after the argument of 'the rule of the evolution of the general philology,' he connects '"phonetic loan', 'explanation', 'the creation of pictophonetic characters', 'loan', 'replacement of the same pronunciation' (同音替代) and 'supplementary phonetic expression' (辅助表

---

[37] Jiang Shanguo (蒋善国), *Chinese Character Morphology* (Beijing: Character Reform Press, 1959).

音法) together with 'pronouncing' (音化), and combines the large seal script (including the oracle bone script and bronze script), the small seal script, the clerical script, cursive script, the Han script (真书), running script and simplified Chinese characters with 'simplifying'. In this way, two major systems of the development of philology are established.[38] Qiu Xigui's *Essentials of Philology* published recently is a crucial book on the basis of his teaching materials. It has 13 chapters. Chapters 1, 2 and 3 are about the nature, formation and development of Chinese characters. Chapters 4 and 5 explain the evolution of Chinese characters. Chapters 6 and 9 discuss the structural theory of Chinese characters by the analysis of the 'ideographic characters' and 'picto-phonetic characters', and 'phonetic loan characters'. From Chapters 10 to 12, he introduces the differential and intricate relations among form, phonology and ideograph. In Chapter 13, he outlines the collation and simplification of Chinese characters throughout dynasties. The author draws on a large amount of information from preserved and excavated documents, and many achievements of the predecessors to further improve the theory of philology. Much important progress has been made in the theory of Chinese characters. His achievements in the mode of Chinese characters, evolution of forms and basic structures greatly exceed his predecessors. Inventive points are pervasive in this book such as the conceptions of 'marking characters', 'semi-marking characters', 'ideographic characters', 'variant characters', 'isomorphic characters', 'exchange of synonymous characters with distinct pronunciations' (同义换读), 'polyseme' and so on.[39] This book has two salient features: First, his profound knowledge in ancient philology lays a solid foundation for the collation, investigation and appropriate use of ancient characters; theoretical explanation during his analysis of the formation of characters; and the evolution of form and type of structure. In his book, materials are abundant, the argument sufficient and the conclusions reliable. Second, Qiu is thoughtful and elaborate, so his book is strongly scientific and theoretically deep. We can consider

---

[38] Jiang Shanguo (蒋善国), *Philology* (Shanghai: Shanghai Education Press, 1987).

[39] Qiu Xigui (裘锡圭), *Essentials of Philology* (Beijing: The Commercial Press, 1988).

that this book is most successful in the study of philological theory and systematic construction after Tang Lan's *Chinese Philology,* and it represents the level of contemporary research on philological theory.

The objects of 'philological system' based on forms are direct and explicit. It is a big progress compared with the Comprehensive School and Form-Meaning School. Since the 1930s, it has gradually become the mainstream of philological theory. This book put emphasis on the study of the occurrence, evolution, structural type and intricate relations of form, phonology and ideograph. This period has witnessed the preliminary establishment of a distinctive theoretical system of Chinese philology.

By the classification of the three schools, we mean to make clear the names of the three basic types of books and systems. Historically, the transformation from the comprehensive study of form, phonology and ideograph to the study of form and ideograph and then to the research on form reflects the progressive modern theory of Chinese philology and is an enhancement from traditional philology to scientific linguistics and philology.

The Main Progress of Philological Theories

In modern times, important progress has been made in the study of the basic theories of Chinese characters. The traditional Chinese philology begins transforming to modern philology, and a large number of theoretical books and essays on philology are published. This phenomenon is attributed to two factors: first, people are influenced by Western scholars in investigating theories and establishing a scientific system; and second, the extensive discoveries of materials and the prosperity of the philology of ancient philology create a favourable condition for the research of basic theories. Although a number of theoretical studies have been listed earlier, a brief summary is given.

On the Origin of Chinese Characters

The origin of Chinese characters is the first issue in the field of its research. The legends and speculations in the embryonic period of philology reflect the ideas of the ancient people. However, no substantial progress had been made upto to the pre-modern times in the study of this problem. Therefore, it was quite a breakthrough when Zheng Qiao pointed out: 'Calligraphy and painting have the same source'. Since the 20th century, the view of 'characters stemming from drawing' has been generally accepted by people, such as Shen Shi, Tang Lan and Jiang Shan who explicitly pointed out that pictographs and paintings were initially relatives.[40] After the 1950s, the findings of primitive symbolic characters in relic sites, such as the Yangshao Ancient Cultural Relic Site at Ban Po in Xi'an and Dawenkou Ancient Cultural Relic Site in Shangdong, have provided us with precious information for the study of the origin of Chinese characters. Guo Moruo published 'Dialectical Development of Ancient Characters' in 1972, and he proposed: 'We can determine the time of the origin by calculating the length of time from the Banpo civilization till today'. He pondered: 'Banpo relic site has a history of six thousand years…and this is the history of Chinese characters'. Moreover 'the marks on painted pottery are the beginning of Chinese characters or the remains of them' and 'this is the initial stage of Chinese characters'. The article also says: 'The origin of Chinese characters should be from the two systems of simple indicatives and pictographs, and the simple indicatives precede the other'.[41] Guo put forward these ideas according to the archaeological materials and made breakthroughs on the origin of Chinese characters. He published many essays to discuss the origin and formation of Chinese characters after Yu Shengwu, Tang Lan and the like who all studied the signs from Banpo and Dawenkou cultural relic sites.[42] 'The Initial

---

[40] Cf. Sheng Jianshi (沈兼士), Form of Characters: Part 1: 2; Tang Lan (唐兰): *An Introduction of Ancient Philology:* Part 1: chap. 2; Jiang Shanguo (蒋善国), *The Origin and Structure of Chinese Characters,* Part 1.

[41] Guo Moruo, 'Dialectical Development of Ancient Characters', *Journal of Archaeology* 1(1972). This passage is collected in his *Slavery Era* (Beijing: Renmin Press, 1972).

[42] Essays are: Yu Shengwu, 'About Research of Ancient Characters.' *Cultural Relics* 2 (1973); Tang Lan (唐兰), 'A Preliminary Exploration of the Cultural Relic Site at Wucheng, Jiangxi Province and Chinese Characters *Cultural Relics* 7 (1975); Tang Lan (唐兰). An Review of Our Earliest Culture form Lottery Characters of Dawenkou Culture,' *Guang Ming Daily,* 14 August 1975; Chen Weizhan (陈炜湛), 'A Tentative Study on the Origin of Chinese Characters,' *Journal of Sun Yat-Sen University* 1 (1978); Wang Ningsheng (汪宁生), 'From Primitive Recording to the Convention of Characters,' *Journal of Archaeology* 1 (1981) and so on.

Exploration of the Formation of Chinese Characters' by Qiu Shigui is a paper comprehensively analyzing cultural signs from Yangshao, Majiayao, Longshan and Liangzhu as well as pictographic signs from the Dawenkou relic site. He puts forward his primary view[43] on the formation of Chinese characters and discusses it again in *Essentials of Philology*. Qiu considers that what Banpo signs represent is by no means an intact system, and there is a very low possibility for them to be the primitive characters. Except for a small number of signs absorbed by modern characters (mainly counting numbers), the majority are not directly related to the formation of Chinese characters. It is possible for Dawenkou signs to be used as primitive characters. The formation of the Chinese characters date no later than the middle of the third millennium BC, while an entire system is probably in the Xia-Shang period (about the 17th century BC).[44] Due to the limited information of the original Chinese characters, the study of the origin is still in its initial stages. However, the use of archaeological discoveries to explore its origin and to presume its development as well as formation and get a preliminary idea is our progress in recent years.

On the Evolution and Development of the Forms of Chinese Characters

This has also been one of the important issues since the establishment of philology. Based on materials, the 'Preface to the *Origin of Chinese Characters*' by Xu Shen outlines the evolution of the form: the Ancient Script—the Small Seal Script (史籀)—the Small Seal Script—the Clerical Script. As far as the form preserved in his time is concerned, this process is probably correct. Later descriptions of the evolution of character forms basically followed suit, except that they added the regular script, the running script and the cursive script after the clerical script. The discovery of the oracle bone script helps people unveil the real shape of characters used in the Shang Dynasty and research on the bronze script deepens our understanding of the

---

[43] Qiu Xigui (裘锡圭), 'A Preliminary Exploration of the Formation of Chinese Characters,' *Chinese* 3 (1978).

[44] Qiu Xigui (裘锡圭), *Essentials of Philology*.

changing forms. Especially since the founding of New China, more materials of the bronze script of the Zhou Dynasty, and characters of the Warring States period, the Qin Dynasty and the early Han Dynasty have supported the research of the evolution and development of forms. Jiang's *Form of Characters* introduced earlier as a powerful work was written in New China. Here we only summarize the major achievements from two aspects of the studies of character forms since the founding of New China and especially since 1970s.

The first is the description of the evolution of forms on the basis of excavated relics. Most works published before the founding of New China give a brief introduction to the oracle bone script and bronze script listed in the evolutionary process. In recent years, the analyses of the evolution tend to be detailed. Scholars also take into account the differences of the fauna (区系) in the pursuit of vertical developmental process. Zhang Zhenlin also probes into the external changes of inscriptions a thousand years ago in 'A Tentative Study of the Timing Brands of the Bronze Inscriptions'.[45] In the *Essentials of Philology*, Qiu divides 'the evolution of form' into the 'ancient scripts' and 'the clerical-regular script'. In the first stage, in view of Tang's division, he divides this period into 'the Shang Dynasty', the 'Western Zhou-Spring-Autumn period', 'the Six States in the Warring States period', the 'Qin Dynasty' and 'the formation of the clerical script'. In 'the clerical-regular script', he illustrates the development of the clerical script in the Han Dynasty, the influence of the clerical script on the seal script, the cursive script in the Han Dynasty, new clerical script, early running script, formation and development of regular script, evolution of running script and so forth. Qiu's analysis of the evolution is based on the extant documents or excavated materials, so he can give elaborate commentary of various phenomena, characteristics and time limits of the revolution, and objectively depict the historical features and the process of evolution.

The second are the summaries and explorations of the developmental rules of forms. The research on these is mainly conducted after New

---

[45] Zhang Zhenlin (梁东汉), 'An Tentative Study of the Timing Brands of the Bronze Inscriptions', in *Research on Ancient Characters*, 5th ed. (Beijing: Zhonghua Book Company, 1981).

China, such as *The Structure and the Evolution of Chinese Characters* by Liang Donghan which shows the tendency of simplification and complication, and reveals the inevitable 'metabolism' of the Chinese characters. Then he claims that the rules are 'simplification' and 'phonetic expression' (表音), and 'the change of squared characters is actually a history of the two'.[46] Jiang Shanguo generalizes the rule as 'pronouncing' (音化) and 'simplification'[47] in light of character system and form evolution. Lin Yun suggests 'simplification', 'differentiation' and 'standardization'[48] for the evolution, according to the study of the materials of ancient characters. Then Gao Ming supports 'simplification' and 'standardization'.[49] To sum up, we can obtain four rules—simplification, pronouncing, differentiation and standardization, which need to be further studied.

On the Structure of Chinese Characters and Their Types of Research

The study of the structure of Chinese characters and the history of philology start at the same time. As the classical theory about the structure of Chinese characters, the 'six categories' had always been admired by scholars. However since the 1930s, with the deeper analysis of the individual structures of characters based on the excavated materials, scholars have corrected many mistakes in the *Origin of Chinese Characters*, and they have been able to understand many early forms of characters. These are paving the way for certain breakthroughs in the studies of the character forms. By his 'three categories', Tang Lan challenged the traditional 'six categories' for the first time and proposed a new theory of the structure of Chinese characters, which was a pioneering work in the history of philology.[50]

---

[46] Liang Donghan (梁东汉), *The Structure and Evolution of Chinese Characters*, 189.

[47] Jiang Shanguo (蒋善国), *Philology*: Part 4.

[48] Lin Yun (林沄), *A Brief Commentary of Ancient Characters* (Changchun: Jilin University Press, 1986), chap. 3.

[49] Gao Ming (高明), *A Well-Round Argument on Ancient Chinese Characters* (Beijing: Relics Press, 1987), chap. 3.

[50] Tang Lan (唐兰), *An Introduction of Ancient Philology,* Part 1: chap. 2; Tang Lan (唐兰), 'The Composition of Characters', *Chinese Philology*.

Tang respects excavated materials, but does not stick to tradition. This is of innovative significance to future research. Zhang Shilu employs 'realism', 'symbolic approach' and 'transcription' (标音法) to summarize the structure of Chinese characters.[51] Chen Mengjia criticizes the 'three categories' in his *Summary of Oracle Inscriptions in the Shang Dynasty* and believes that 'pictographs, phonetic loan characters and pictophonetic characters are the three basic types that gradually came into being under the pictographic construction principle'.[52] From the way of recording Chinese characters, Lin Yun pays much attention to the essence of various opinions in the extant discussions of the 'six categories', and is not limited to its framework. After the scientific conclusion and specific analysis, Lin puts forward three basic structural methods, that is, the 'explanation of meaning through form', 'to record sound by form' and the 'combination of ideograph and phonology'.[53] Then Qiu gives an even more penetrating critique that the 'three categories' has four defects: (a) the attachment of the three categories to 'form, ideograph and phonology'; (b) the exclusion of non-pictorialideographic characters; (c) the worthless differentiation of the 'pictograph and pictographic characters'; and (d) the exclusion of phonetic loan characters from basic types of characters. Qiu has no opinion of the 'three categories' but appreciates Chen's new one and changes Chen's 'pictographic' to 'ideographic'. He once said,

> Divide the Chinese characters into ideographic characters, phonetic loan characters and phonetic characters. Ideographic characters use ideographic components, so they can also be called the symbolic characters; phonetic loan characters use phonetic components, so we can call them phonetic characters. Such classification is clearer and more logical than the "six categories".

Qiu carries out a detailed classification and in-depth study of the 'three categories', but he also notices other special types that cannot

---

[51] Zhang Shilu (张世禄). *Outline of Chinese Philology*, chap. 4.
[52] Chen Mengjia (陈梦家), *Oracle Inscriptions of the Shang Dynasty* (Beijing: Zhonghua Book Company, 1988), chap. 2.
[53] Lin Yun (林沄), *A Brief Commentary of Ancient Characters*, chap. 1.

be incorporated into the 'three categories', such as 'marking characters, semi-marking characters, variant phonetic characters and polyphone'.[54] In addition, Qiu's research on the structure of Chinese characters are comprehensive, accurate, reliable and abundantly exemplified, which indicates that the study of character structures has entered a new stage.

On the Nature of Chinese Characters

The nature of Chinese characters was not raised until the introduction of Western linguistics. Western scholars, according to the function of writing symbols, divide the human writing system into two types—'ideographic writing' and 'phonetic writing'—and Chinese characters are regarded as typical ideographic characters. This influential view has been generally accepted by Chinese scholars. When Shen Jianshi taught 'Form of Characters', he said: 'Current types of language in the world are numerous, but they are either ideographic or phonetic'.[55] Since the 1950s, Chinese scholars have expressed their new ideas on the nature of Chinese characters. Zhou Youguang ponders that the evolution of the character system includes the 'pictographic-ideographic', 'ideographic-phonetic' and 'phonetic' while Chinese characters are ideographic-phonetic.[56] Cao Bohan holds a division of the ideographic-phonetic and the phonetic, and he also advocates that Chinese characters are ideographic-phonetic.[57] Qiu thinks,

> In the early stages of the higher degree of pictographism (roughly the period before the Western Zhou Dynasty), Chinese characters are basically a system of words that use ideographic components and phonetic components (strictly phonetic loan components); with the changes of form, phonology, ideograph and so on, it gradually became a system by employing ideographic components, phonetic components and signs (the formation of the clerical script can be seen

---

[54] Qiu Xigui (裘锡圭), *Essentials of Philology*, chaps. 6, 7, 8, 9.
[55] Shen Jiansh (沈兼士). *Collected Papers of Shen Jianshi*386.
[56] Zhou Youguang (周有光), 'General Rules of Character Evolution', *Chinese* 7 (1957).
[57] Cao Bohan (周有光), 'Characters and Philology', *Chinese* 6, no. 7(1958).

as a completion of this evolution). If we must name the two stages, the former can be called ideographic-phonetic component character or ideophonographic character and the latter ideographic-phonetic-component sign character. On account that all Chinese characters were derived from ideographic components and phonetic components, and the majority are still constituted by them, we can call them post-ideographic-phonetic components, post-phonetic components or post-ideophonographic characters.[58]

Considering the connection between characters and language, foreign scholars named Chinese character 'word writing'[59] (表词文字), 'word-syllabic characters'[60] (词—音节文字) and 'morpheme characters'.[61] Different views and arguments on the nature of Chinese characters are caused by distinct perspectives. Qiu lays stress on the nature of the signs used in the analysis of Chinese characters and ponders: 'The nature of a character is determined by the nature of the signs used in such writing. Its naming is only secondary'.[62] We believe that this view has some guiding significance for further discussion of the nature of Chinese characters.

From the brief introduction earlier, we can see that in modern times, brilliant achievements have been made in the basic theories of the origin, development, structure and nature of Chinese characters. However, from the perspective of the construction of the philological theory, the research in this field is still relatively weak, the research fields narrow and the subjects monotonous, so it cannot adapt to the establishment of the scientific system of Chinese philological theory, and meet the required depth and breadth to establish a scientific system of the theory. Many questions are to be further studied and discussed.

---

[58] Qiu Xigui (裘锡圭). 'The Nature of Characters', *Chinese* 1 (1985).

[59] Bloomfield. *Language,* Translated Version, trans. Yuan Jiahua, etc. (Beijing: The Commercial Press, 1980), 360.

[60] I. J. Gelb, *A Study of Writing* (Chicago, IL: University of Chicago Press, 1963), chap. 3.

[61] Zhao Yuanren (赵元任), *On Language* (Beijing: The Commercial Press, 1980), 144.

[62] Qiu Xigui (裘锡圭), 'The Nature of Characters'.

New Discoveries of Ancient Chinese Characters and the Research of Chinese Developmental History[63]

Introduction

Chinese characters are the only writing system with the ancient origin and continuous use, which are the main objects of research in Chinese philology that has a long history of nearly 2,000 years. However, until now, there are still no comprehensive and systematic works describing the developmental history of Chinese characters or summarizing its developmental rules.

The reason is that scholars cannot have an in-depth research on philology without reference to the *Origin of Chinese Characters* before the 20th century, including written materials, theories and research methods. Even the description of Chinese characters' developmental history cannot be separated from the *Origin of Chinese Characters*. They know little about the materials before the publication of the *Origin of Chinese Characters* and care less about the materials (such as clerical script and regular script) after its publication. By the end of the 19th century to the 20th century, ancient characters had been found; in addition, it was a booming time when the research on philology and ancient philology had been developed. However, after one hundred years, a comprehensive and systematic research work still has not appeared, though we have achieved a lot in the study of Chinese characters' developmental history. The reason for this phenomenon is that the findings and amounts in this research field are too abundant for scholars to study. Besides, it is very complicated and difficult for scholars to make textual criticisms and explanations of new materials. These scholars are mainly focused on compiling the materials of ancient characters, checking and interpreting the single character, or making monographic research. Therefore, they did not have a comprehensive and systematic study. Meanwhile, the previous research

---

[63] The text was based on my lecture at Ancient Classics Research Institution in Zhejiang University on 9 September 2003. See Dekhuan Huang, *Collected Papers on the Theory of Chinese Characters* (Beijing: The Commercial Press, 2006).

did not lay much stress on the clerical script and regular script, which also influenced the study in Chinese characters' developmental history. Therefore, it is understandable that a comprehensive and systematic research work did not appear in the 20th century.

In the 21st century, it is not only of great possibility but also of necessity to make further research on Chinese characters' developmental history. This requires a high proficiency in the ancient and modern characters. As Zhang Yongquan (张涌泉) said, 'The research on ancient and modern Chinese characters is like two wheels of a cart or two wings of a bird, complementing each other indispensably'.[64] Here we will only discuss the new discoveries about ancient characters and research on Chinese characters' developmental history.

The New Discoveries of Ancient Characters Providing Possibilities of Research on Chinese Characters' Developmental History

The nearer the time to the characters, the more historical materials of Chinese characters will be reserved. The materials of recent Chinese characters since the clerical script are much abundant. Except for the engraved materials (刻版图书) and manuscripts, we still have bamboo slips in the Han and Jin Dynasties (西陲汉晋简牍), posthumous scripts in Dunhuang and bamboo slips in the state of Wu (Changsha, Hunan province) as well as amounts of other character materials such as engraved scripts on engraved monuments and non-governmental memorandum in writings.[65] As for the research on character developmental history, the conditions in this period were of great advantage; however, they did not receive enough attention. Many materials of ancient characters have been lost because of the long history. Therefore, how the Chinese characters developed has become a mystery from the past to now. Before the 20th century, people only had a general understanding about characters in the pre-Qin period,

---

[64] Zhang Yongquan (张涌泉), 'Strengthening the Research of Chinese Characters in Recent Years'. *Zhejiang Educational Institute Journal* 6 (2003).

[65] Over 300,000 pieces of memorandum in Huizhou, which were written by hand in the Ming Qing Periods.

which they learned from copying some episodes of ancient characters, the large seal script (籀文) in the *Origin of Chinese Characters* or the inscriptions. In general, they still felt puzzled about ancient characters in the pre-Qin period. Xu Shenin of the Eastern Han Dynasty felt pitiful and said 'Ancient characters have disappeared since the change in the clerical script'.

We have found a series of important discoveries of ancient characters since the 20th century, which presented us the historical features of Chinese characters in different periods between the late Yin-Shang Period and the clerical script period. Such phenomenon has fundamentally changed the situation lacking materials in the pre-Qin period. Comprehensive and systematic research on Chinese characters' development history is not only possible but also of great opportunities. The materials are as the following.

First, Yin-Shang characters. The main oracle bone script and bronze script represent the Yin-Shang materials. Now we have discovered more than 100,000 oracle bone script pieces from Wu Ding to Di Xin Times (武丁时代帝辛时代) when the structure, development and usage of characters were all complete. Although the oracle bone script has unique usage, we can make the aforementioned judgment compared with the bronze script in the same period. From the pottery script in Xiao Shuangqiao, Zhengzhou, in the mid of the Shang Dynasty, we can predict that the oracle bone script in Yin-Shang has been the mature script which developed sustainably in a long history, so that we can use it as the sample of research on Chinese character developmental history in the late Yin-Shang period.[66]

Second, the Western Zhou characters. The discovery of the Western Zhou oracle bone script opens the features of characters in the early Zhou Dynasty, which proves that the Western Zhou Dynasty characters inherited the Yin-Shang characters. This is of great significance to the research on the Chinese characters' developmental history. The representatives of the Western Zhou characters are the bronze script, which were discovered in the past century especially after the establishment of the People's Republic of China. For example, there

---

[66] Song Guoding (宋国定), 'A Ceramic Vase with Red Chinese Characters Unearthed in Relics of Xiaoshuang Bridge, Zhenzhou', *Cultural Relics* 5 (2003).

are Li Gui (利簋) recording King Wu defeating Yin and He Zun (何尊) recording King Cheng moving to Chengzhou. We have found a lot of materials, which can be used for identifying the times from the Western Zhou tomb in Zhangjiapo, Changan, the Yan dynasty tomb in Liuli River, Beijing, the tomb of the Jin dynasty in Quwo Zhao village, Shaanxi, and the bronze ware groups which were unearthed from Shanxi Fufengzhuang village, Qijia village, Zhaochen village, Qiangjia village, Dongjia village and Yangjia village. The *Collection of Yin-Zhou Bronze Script* (《殷周金文集成》) published in 1994 has collected 11,983 pieces of the bronze script, of which the latest collection year was 1988. Then, the new bronze script has reached more than 1,500 pieces, among which the Western Zhou bronze script was the first reliable material of research on the Chinese characters' developmental history in this period.

Third, the Spring and Autumn characters. The main materials of the Spring and Autumn characters are also the bronze script. In this period, the bronze script is mainly the casting moulds of the vassal states that were different from the long pieces of the Western Zhou characters. Other scripts such as stone-drum inscriptions and the covenant inscriptions of the Jin Dynasty (晋盟书) can make up for this shortage in this aspect.[67]

Fourth, Warring States characters. The character materials in this period are not only carved in the bronzeware but also in other places. A large number of characters are carved in the seals, coins and potteries. Especially the discovery of Chu characters has made the status of Warring States characters much elevated. Although Warring States characters are simply structured, which always change a lot in different areas, we can compare them with the Pre-Qin characters or Warring States ancient characters. These materials illustrate that Chinese characters developed rapidly and were used complicatedly in this period.

Fifth, the Qin-Han characters. These Qin-Han characters are the materials of characters written/appeared on unearthed cultural relics between the Qin Dynasty and the early Western Han Dynasty. After

---

[67] There still exits disagreement on the time of stone-drum inscriptions and covenant inscriptions of the Jin Dynasty (晋盟书), but we think they are in the Spring and Autumn periods.

the state of Qin united the other six feudal states in the Warring States period, Qin characters became the official characters of Chinese characters while small seal script became the standard structure. Actually, Chinese characters had changed based on the Qin characters since the late Warring States period. Before the early Western Han Dynasty, the clerical script was always in the process of improvement. The formation of the clerical script has transformed the frame of Chinese characters from the past to the present, which is the most important research topic of study in Chinese characters' developmental history. Qin-Han characters include many bamboo slip materials such as Shuihudi, Liye bamboo slips, and Mawangdui and Yinque Mountain bamboo slips (睡虎地, 里耶秦简和马王堆, 银雀山简牍) in addition to the bronze script, the small seal script, etc. These important discoveries provided complete and systematic materials used for research on the historical framework and development rules of Chinese characters.

Above all, from Yin-Shang characters to the clerical script in the Han Dynasty, new discoveries of ancient characters have provided complete and systematic materials for us, which make it possible to have a thorough and systematic research on Chinese characters' developmental history. As for the materials before the Yin-Shang characters, some important symbols of cultural relics have also been found in the late Neolithic Age. This provides precious materials and important clues for discussing the origin and formation of Chinese characters. However, if we only have the recent accumulation of materials, we are still unable to find out the complete developmental stage of Chinese characters—the primordial stage of Chinese characters—which we do not include in our discussion for the time being.

Some Basic Works of Research on Chinese Characters' Developmental History

The development of Chinese characters has a long history, and the situations are complicated. Only by taking up some basic research work can we create a fundamental basis of the research on Chinese characters' history.

First, establish the basic theoretical framework of the research. Faced with so many sophisticated developmental situations, what aspects can we take to accurately understand the essential development of Chinese character system? This is the primary question that we should consider. In other words, what standard should we set in assessing the essential development of Chinese character system? Looking into the recent works related to Chinese characters development, we do not seem to have reached a definite agreement. Many works and theories have been only conducted in the development of Chinese character forms, which is far from enough. We hold the view that to establish the basic theoretical framework of the research, we need to consider Chinese character system in different aspects from the macro and micro, surface and deep, partial and whole, and still and dynamic levels.

The first thing is to describe and analyze the development of Chinese character forms. Decades of changes of Chinese character forms are forthright and clear, which are the basis of the development of Chinese characters. If we want to describe the development of Chinese character forms, we should not only divide them into different stages but also analyze many phenomena occurring during the development, such as additions, deletions, aberrant misunderstandings and so on. From these aspects, we will reveal the rules of its development.

The second thing is to investigate the development of Chinese character forms. The structure of Chinese characters includes the construction method and structural types, both of which are correlated but not completely the same. The former refers to the way of the formation and construction of the character signs. The latter refers to the categorical generalization of Chinese characters that have the same features in structure. The construction way of Chinese characters is a system following the time, which presents to us the change of distribution in characters with different structures. Therefore, we need to find out the deep changes of Chinese character construction methods while describing the change of Chinese characters forms.[68] The preliminary study reveals that the development of Chinese character construction methods is influenced by the development of Chinese character forms, but they do not develop in step with each other.

---

[68] Cf. 'The Formation Methods of Chinese Characters: A Systematic Transformation' and 'The Dynamic Analysis of Chinese Characters' in this book.

The third thing is to compare the usage of Chinese characters dynamically. Chinese characters have been used for thousands of years, resulting in the adaption to the constant requirements. The usage of Chinese characters in different periods directly reflects the change and development of Chinese characters. Compared with the last century, the new factor appearing in the usage of Chinese characters is an important spot in assessing the development of Chinese character system. For example, the adjustment of usage function of Chinese characters or the fort and structure changes all deserve enough attention. In the whole development of Chinese character system, some characters disappeared while some new ones appeared. These new characters are of great research value. These new ones intensively reflect the new developmental trend in construction methods, representative words and usage. Therefore, analyzing the obsolescent characters and additions are important in the research on Chinese characters' developmental history. We should pay much attention to the changes of the overall usage based on the dynamic comparative analysis, and put the actual situations, usage frequency and function changes of the inherited characters, additions, and obsolescent characters as the basic concepts of research.

The fourth thing is to study the related background of Chinese character development. The formation and development of Chinese characters have their distinctive features. We should emphasize the background factors that have influenced the development of Chinese characters directly or indirectly. The relations between Chinese characters and the historical culture of the Chinese nation are very complicated. Such a culture is extensive and profound as well as long-standing. The formation, development and transformation of Chinese characters were all the way influenced by the development of historical culture. This influence is both physical and mental, which needs deep discussion and revelation.

Second, take the studies of characters in the separate age as the basis. The basic and preceding work of research on Chinese character development is to sort out character situations in every stage. Diverse materials unearthed about ancient characters have been studied and sorted out by many scholars, such as the publications of original materials, recognition and interpretation of characters as well as the compilation of character tables. They have made outstanding achievements in all these fields, which created beneficial conditions for the research on the characters in the separate age in philology. In fact, what we have done in this research is not enough from the complete philology. There is a shortage of comprehensive description about the basic framework in every stage. The cohort study of philology in a real sense has not been yet carried out. It is of urgency to carry out the research on the cohort characters based on an appropriate theoretical framework.

Third, carry out the monographic study combined with the cohort research. The deep monographic study of the key factors during the process of Chinese characters development is beneficial to grasp the whole development of Chinese character system. For example, in the research on Chinese character patterns, we can study the transformation history of a single character, the formation of ancient characters and the reasons of these phenomena such as additions and character deletions during the transformation process; in the research on structure development, we can study the changes of different Chinese character structures, the adjustment of formation functions and the relations between patterns, sounds and meanings inside the structure; in the research on the relations of characters, we can study the differentiation of Chinese characters, and the substitution, universal use and mutual borrowing in the application process of Chinese characters; in the research on the related background, we can study the relations between Chinese characters and Chinese language, between Chinese characters and Chinese culture, and so on. To carry out these monographic studies, it is much beneficial for us to learn about Chinese character development deeply and comprehensively.

In that we pay much attention to the above three basic aspects of the basic research, it is probable to describe and reveal the real history in the process of Chinese character development from the macro and micro perspectives.

The Significance of Research on Chinese Character Developmental History

The primary significance of carrying out the research on Chinese characters' developmental history is to learn better about the historical rules of Chinese characters development and promote the theoretical construction of Chinese philology, which are useful to provide references for the policy-making of the Chinese discipline.

First, the continuous use and gradual change of Chinese character development. In the past thousands of years, the development and evolution of both Chinese character system and single Chinese character have undergone a process from the gradual micro accumulation to the macro whole system. Every minor change of Chinese characters and adjustment of components including the new characters can be traced. The continuous use and gradual change have made Chinese characters come down in a continuous succession, which illustrates a state of steady development. Nothing like the fierce revolution of characters has happened in the history. This warns us that we should not disobey the rules of continuous use and gradual change in the evolution and adjustment of Chinese characters, and should not take actions subjectively.

Second, different features of Chinese characters in different historical stages. From the materials that we have, we can see that the Chinese character patterns from Yin-Shang to Western Zhou period were improved mainly in structures, along with the development of regular lines. For instance, pictophonetic characters have become the main structure of character additions. But from the Warring States period to the Han Dynasty, the radical evolution of character patterns was the main aspect, along with differentiation and gradual derivation.

Third, the gradability of Chinese character system. One of the main weaknesses of Chinese characters is the large quantities. Actually, the number of its usage in different stages is limited. The number of commonly used characters in different periods is only 5,000 to 6,000. Such large quantities resulted from the gradual accumulation in the long history. As for the characters used in one period, they include the inherited words, added characters and those which had been used before but actually were already obsolete in their practical use. The accumulation of characters in different times has made up the total number in one period. Therefore, the gradability of Chinese characters has not only made its number large but also presented complicated meanings. In the long run, the philology research has ignored this feature, but put Chinese characters in different stages into one area so that it cannot make a scientific analysis of many phenomena. Taking full use of a great deal of research methods in archaeology and ancient character materials, we can learn better about the gradability of Chinese characters based on the cohort study. Therefore, we can more accurately reveal the rules and features of Chinese character evolution.

Next, carrying out the research on Chinese character developmental history can deeply and completely promote the study of Chinese language. The relation between Chinese characters and Chinese language is one of the most important objects of philology and Chinese language history. As the written symbols of Chinese language, on one hand, Chinese characters are restricted and influenced by Chinese language. On the other hand, the development of Chinese language is correlated with the features and development of Chinese characters. To some extent, the research on Chinese language developmental history is not complete without the research on Chinese character development. Therefore, it is inevitable to learn about the history of Chinese character development if we want to carry out the in-depth research on the history of Chinese language development.

Last but not least, to carry out the research on Chinese character developmental history is an important task to study Chinese culture. The formation of Chinese characters symbolizes the formation of Chinese culture. It is difficult to measure the impact that Chinese characters have on Chinese culture. To carry out the in-depth research on Chinese character developmental history is helpful to know more about the formation and development of Chinese culture. Therefore, there is no denying that the research on Chinese character developmental history should be the important object of research on Chinese culture.[69]

---

[69] Li Xueqin (李学勤), 'The Research on the Source of Chinese Characters is an Important Object in Science', *Chinese Calligraphy* 2 (2001).

The Promising Prospect of the Research of Chinese Philology[70]

Tremendous achievements of Chinese philology have been made in the 20th century, which contributes to the transformation of the traditional philology of a long history to a modern academic discipline.

We hold the opinion that the development of Chinese philology in the 20th century is mainly shown in the following aspects:

First, the large number of discoveries of new unearthed materials has contributed to the establishment of Chinese palaeography and a series of achievements. From the discovery of the oracle bone inscriptions in the 19th century to the scientific exploration and study of the oracle bone inscriptions in the 20th century, the study of the oracle bone inscriptions, which is a distinct sub-discipline, was established. The collation and study of the bronze inscriptions in large quantities have brought about changes to traditional epigraph, making the study of bronze inscriptions whose main research subjects are inscriptions on the bronzes a sub-discipline of palaeography; the constant excavations of written materials of the Warring States period, especially those of the state of Chu, made the study of characters of the Warring States period the most active field in the latter 30 years of the 20th century, and a sub-discipline was formed rapidly whose main research subjects are characters of the Warring States period; at the same time, the large number of unearthed written materials including bamboo slips and silk manuscripts of the Qin Dynasty and Han Dynasty makes the study in this field have the trend of being formed into a sub-discipline. The great achievements of palaeography are reflected in numerous aspects such as the collation of excavated materials of ancient characters, the textual criticisms and explanations of characters, and the comprehensive research which is carried out by the use of these materials. The formation and development of palaeography, which is an integrated subject that combines multi-disciplines, are parts of the important signals showing that great progress has been made in philology in the 20th century.

---

[70] Originally published in *Chinese Philology in the 21st Century* (Beijing: The Commercial Press, 2003).

Second, progress has been made in the study of several important basic theoretical issues of Chinese characters. The discoveries and the study results of large number of the materials of ancient characters provide the reliable first-hand information to the study of several important basic theoretical issues of Chinese characters, which contributes to the breakthroughs in this research field. For example, the study of the origins, the development and evolution of the form, and of the structure and functions of Chinese characters has gained a series of remarkable achievements, and the understanding of the configuration, the formation and the development history of Chinese characters is closer to the historical reality. The rise of a number of important theoretical issues and its research progress have fundamentally changed traditional Chinese philology.

Third, prominent progress has been made in the applied research of Chinese characters. The research in this area has changed the traditional way of study of Chinese philology to a large extent. The issues centring around the reformation of Chinese characters have brought about the movement of Chinese over a century, and the intensity and the huge influence of the debate are rare in the academic history of China. With the prominent achievements of the collation, simplification and standardization of Chinese characters, the present Chinese character system has been established; the information processing of Chinese characters has become an important area where philology is combined with information science, and its application level is being improved continuously; more attention is paid to the teaching and acquisition research of Chinese characters, of which the spread and the wide application are unprecedented.

Fourth, great success has been achieved in the discipline construction of Chinese philology. The Chinese philology in the 20th century was changed from the dependent status as a traditional 'small discipline' (xiao xue '小学') to scientific philology, and the discipline system of philology was gradually established, which has won Chinese philology the status it deserves in the system of modern disciplines. A series of outstanding theoretical monographs were published and a number of Chinese philology researchers with modern consciousness were fostered, some of whom have exerted great world influence by their achievements of the study of Chinese philology and of its discipline construction.

If it is thought that Chinese philology completed the transformation from a traditional academic discipline to a modern academic discipline in a better way in the 20th century, then the 21st century will be a promising era of the exploration and innovation of Chinese philology. We suppose that major breakthroughs and great progress of the whole discipline will be made if the following aspects of the study of Chinese philology can be strengthened and innovated.

First, the study of information processing of Chinese characters should be strengthened, and the study and application of Chinese characters should be promoted by means of taking full advantage of the achievements of information science and technology. The arrival of informationization times of human society, which will have influence on philology, makes the improvement of the level of information processing of Chinese characters necessary and urgent, and also makes it possible. The information processing of modern Chinese characters gained outstanding achievements in the 20th century, but China's accession into the World Trade Organization and the accelerating development of the economic globalization set forth higher requirements. As a result, the major tasks faced by philology are to solve the difficulties in information processing of Chinese characters as soon as possible and to bring the features and advantages of Chinese characters and the Chinese language into full play for the better service of modern Chinese characters to economic and social development in the background of science and technology. It is believed that the joint efforts of philologists and researchers of science and technology will make this study field full of vitality and opportunities in the 21st century. For another example, the construction of databases of Chinese characters is also a basic project of great importance. The richness of the materials of Chinese characters is unique in the world. The written materials which include the oracle bone inscriptions, bronze inscriptions, characters of the Warring States period, and those since the Qin and Han Dynasties provide both endless resources and huge pressure on researchers. How to use the achievements of information science and technology to collate and study these materials scientifically and to make them easier to use is a common task for both philologists and researchers of information science and technology. Quite a few institutions and scholars are trying to establish databases, and they have achieved preliminary achievements and accumulated some experience. However, the lack of the communication of their work has caused the noticeable repeated work and the lack of application. A better organization of work in these aspects is probable in the 21st century due to the good foundation of the collation of the various materials of Chinese characters in the 20th century. The completion of databases of all Chinese characters, which will be brought about by the unified planning and design and coordinated work, will provide conditions for the use of modern methods in the study of Chinese characters. The benefits this cause will bring to the future will be certainly beyond measures.

Second, the study of modern Chinese characters should be strengthened. The collation, simplification and standardization of modern Chinese characters have gained relatively great achievements while the study of modern Chinese characters is relatively weak in the 20th century. The study of theory and application of modern Chinese characters must be given priority status in the 21st century, for there are increasingly close connection and communication between China and the international community with the advancement of informationization. The study of modern Chinese characters which appeared in the 20th century will continue to be developed and improved with the fields of its research application which includes information processing, standardization and teaching of Chinese characters, which have become more active and require a higher demand of the theoretical study of modern Chinese characters.

Third, great attention should be attached to the study of the development history of Chinese characters which is the basis of the study of Chinese characters. The materials of Chinese characters through the ages have been coherent since the formation of Chinese characters, and modern Chinese characters are the inevitable results of the development of historical Chinese characters. The understanding has been insufficient of the formation, development and evolution of Chinese characters. As a written language of a long history in the world, Chinese characters are unique, which provides favourable conditions for the valuable study of the development history of Chinese characters. It is foreseeable that the study of Chinese characters in the pre-Qin period will still be an important research field. The collation and study of discovered materials of ancient characters, together with the further exploration of new materials, bring vitality to palaeography. The study of Chinese characters in the stage of official and regular script is a key field to be expanded in the study of the developmental history of Chinese characters in the 21st century. From the formation and development of the official script in the Qin and Han Dynasties to the regular script in the Wei, Jin, and Southern and Northern Dynasties, and later the written materials of various bamboo slips, inscriptions, block-printed books and private copies of books are the precious resources of this stage. However, this stage is the weakest part of the study of the historical development of Chinese characters. We should pay more attention to the collation and research work of this stage; otherwise, we would not be able to reveal the panorama of the history well nor would we better understand and study modern Chinese characters. It is believed that a number of high-level works studying the development of Chinese characters in terms of their dynastic history, general history or special subject history will emerge in the 21st century.

Fourth, the research on the relationship between Chinese characters and Chinese traditional culture should be done scientifically. The close relation between Chinese characters and Chinese culture has drawn wide attention from scholars at home and abroad. Many works on Chinese characters and Chinese culture emerged in the last decade of the 20th century, but the overall level is not high. The most common problem is that the deep relations of Chinese characters and Chinese culture are only analogized and explained to a superficial extent, which has to do with the authors' level of scientific understanding of Chinese characters and Chinese culture. The study of relations between Chinese characters and Chinese culture has drawn attention—which is a very a natural phenomenon—because of the historical facts that Chinese characters contain a large amount of culture information, and their formation and development are rooted in Chinese culture. It is foreseeable that this will still be an appealing field which will be attached great importance to in the 21st century. We believe that the key is to guide this kind of study with right methods, strict truth-seeking spirit and scientific theory. Only in this way can the study of the relations between Chinese characters and Chinese culture provide new materials for the study of Chinese history, culture and philology, and make new discoveries. Otherwise, the research would be easy to go astray.

Fifth, the innovation in the research on the basic theoretical issues should be stressed. The objects in Chinese philological research and the richness of its research materials make Chinese philology unique in the academic field, and they also provide Chinese philologists with the possibility of making contributions to world philology. Chinese philologists in the 20th century made prominent achievements because they both complied with the historical traditions and were influenced by Western philology, and the progress of new discoveries and study of materials of ancient characters contributed to their achievements. Overall, however, the innovation and breakthroughs of the basic theoretical research of Chinese characters are far from being enough, compared with the possibilities offered by the times. The 21st century should be the time for the innovation of the theories of Chinese philology. We should, on the basis of what has been accumulated in the past, try hard to build scientific theoretical system which corresponds with the Chinese language and the actual situations of Chinese characters by opening up new areas of research and more deeply exploring some basic theoretical issues of Chinese characters. We should also use the achievements of the theoretical innovation of the study of Chinese characters to enrich and improve the theories of world philology and eventually contribute our Chinese scholars' wisdom to the progress of the world philology.

About the Author

Dekuan Huang is Professor, School of Humanities, Tsinghua University. He is a former president of Anhui University and the Chairman of the Chinese Writing Society. He completed his PhD in Chinese paleography from Jilin University, China, and has been engaged in the study of Chinese language and characters for around three decades. He is also Deputy Director of Unearthed Research and Protection Centre, Tsinghua University. By unearthing and explicating many important documents, he has made a major contribution to the study of the Chinese civilization.

He has many publications to his credit, for example, *A History of Chinese Philology, Annotated Genealogy of Ancient Chinese Characters, Collected Papers on the Theory of Chinese Characters, Chinese Characters Interpretation and Cultural Tradition, Development of Ancient Chinese characters*, and so on. Professor Huang has been a member of the Committee of Chinese Education and the Committee of Social Science of the Ministry of Education of the People's Republic of China.